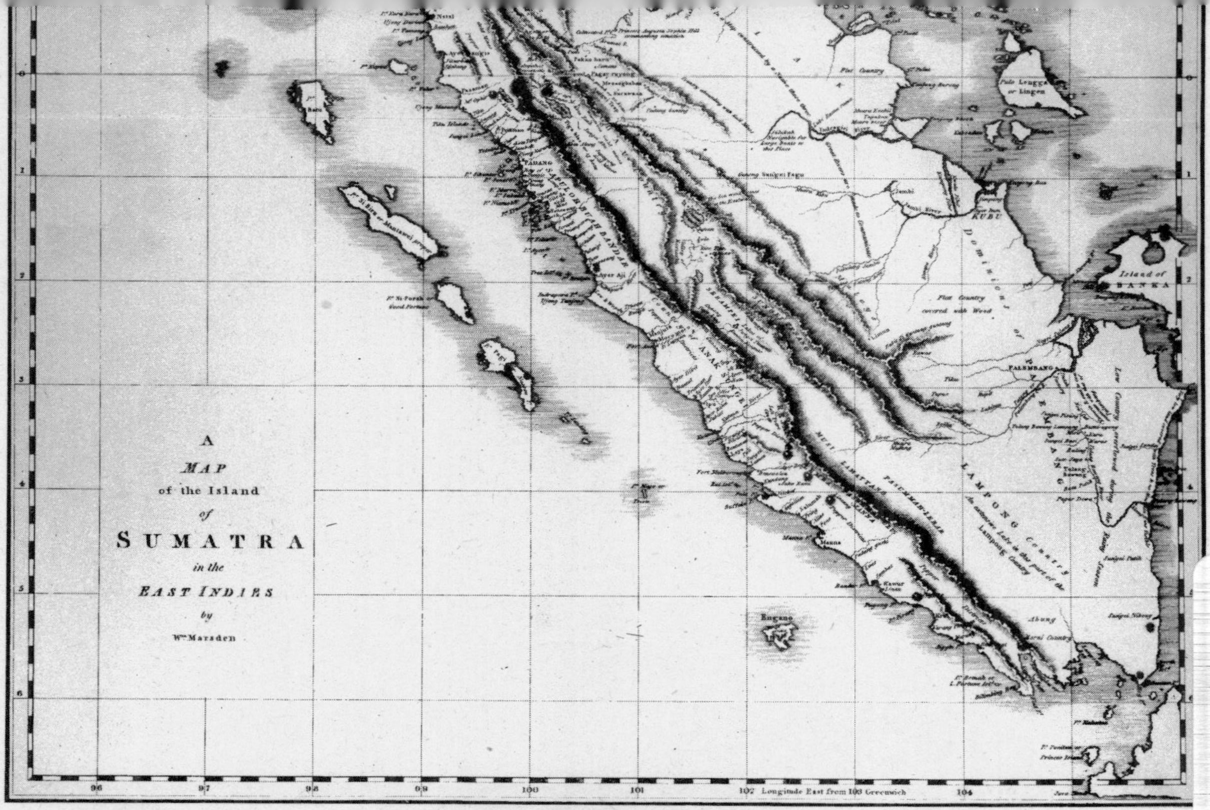

A
MAP
of the Island
of
SUMATRA
in the
EAST INDIES
by
Wᵐ Marsden

TAMING THE COOLIE BEAST

Oxford University Press, Walton Street, Oxford OX2 6DP

NEW YORK TORONTO
DELHI BOMBAY CALCUTTA MADRAS KARACHI
PETALING JAYA SINGAPORE HONGKONG TOKYO
NAIROBI DAR ES SALAAM
MELBOURNE AUCKLAND
and associates in
BERLIN IBADAN

SBN 19 562365 7

Typeset by Goyal Printofast Pvt. Ltd. New Delhi-110 001.
Printed by Rekha Printers Pvt Ltd., New Delhi 110 020
and Published by S. K. Mookerjee, Oxford University Press
YMCA Library Building, Jai Singh Road, New Delhi 110 001

CONTENTS

CONTENTS

LIST OF TABLES

PREFACE
TO THE ENGLISH EDITION

The discovery, a few years ago of a report, which until then had lain hidden in the state archives, was the immediate motivation for the writing of this book. The report related to 'coolie scandals' on the plantations of Sumatra's East Coast. I gave up my initial plan to content myself with writing a short introduction to the publication of a shocking historical document, when it proved that a proper understanding of its contents required a greater knowledge of the broader setting of plantation economy and society. This more ambitious goal made it necessary for me to comment on the state of affairs on the plantation regime itself as well as to the way in which the life and work of the coolies was conditioned by outside forces. In addition to contributing to the history of industrial labour in Asia, this study is intended to provide an analysis of colonial policies in promoting the interests of agrarian capitalism.

I have elaborately dealt with the question of why and how the authorities at home and in the colony successfully managed to prevent the disclosure of the sensational results of the investigation made by the Public Prosecutor, J.L.T. Rhemrev. However, the refusal to make these results public can in no way explain the surprising lack of curiosity that has since been shown by colonial historiographers about this document which records the misery suffered by Asian workers on large-scale estates under western management. I can think of no other reason for that neglect than a reluctance to learn too much about the shadow side of economic growth under colonial rule. The negative effects could hardly be brought to light without detracting from the success story of white entrepreneurship in a tropical environment. The image that has been laid down in the conventional writings on colonial history is imbued with homage to the Dutch and other European planter-pioneers who, with inconceivable energy and perseverance, transformed sparsely populated jungle areas into prosperous agricultural lands.

Against such a background, it is understandable that the monograph which I published together with the Rhemrev Report in 1987 attracted wide public attention. It quite obviously did not fit into the wave of nostalgic literature on *tempo dulu*, the good old times, which still lingers on in the minds of colonial officials and their nostalgic successors. Radio, newspapers and weeklies in the Netherlands all gave extensive coverage to my book; the comments made are typified by the opinion voiced by a prominent columnist to the effect that the re-discovered official document represented for the Dutch public the most horrific revelation of this century. But even in 1987, attempts were made to tone down the scandal, reactions which were not so different from those made more than eighty years ago. At the end of the public lecture that I gave at the invitation of the Royal Institute of Linguistics and Anthropology on the occasion of the public presentation of the book, a few members of the audience asked a number of leading questions. Although they acknowledged that 'coolie scandals' had occurred, it was their opinion that these had been restricted to remote plantations and had not taken place on estates that were under Dutch management; or that a system of labour control such as I had described had perhaps been practiced in Sumatra before the end of the nineteenth century, but that it would have been inconceivable on the sugar plantations on Java, for example. In effect, these were the same type of objections that I had found in the colonial sources, and I am unable to escape the impression that they were raised from a need to exonerate rather than from a desire to promote objectivity by introducing shades of opinion. The tendency to reduce systematic maltreatment that could not bear the light of day to the status of deplorable mishaps resulting from an exceptional coincidence of circumstances, still obstinately persists. Seen from this point of view, it is only natural that those who consider that the outrages were in fact inherent to the labour regime that pertained on colonial plantations, should be accused of bad faith and calumny. In such a climate there was little interest, for example, in pointing out that the founder of the famous Deli Company—which had developed into a state within a state—was compelled to leave Sumatra's East Coast like a thief in the night so as to avoid being charged with the murder of seven coolies by flogging.

In 1904 the Minister for the Colonies accompanied his refusal to submit the Rhemrev Report to the Netherlands Parliament with promises that a number of reforms would be introduced immediately, including the setting-up of a Labour Inspectorate to ensure that the Asian workforce on the East Coast of Sumatra would in future be given better treatment. Although the publication after more than eighty years of what was then kept secret has aroused wide interest in this 'black page' out of colonial historiography, I also noticed that almost none of the press reviews have compared the ministerial promises made at the time with subsequent policies. This omission is all the more surprising because, in the concluding chapter, I expressed my doubts not only regarding the fulfilment of the many good intentions, but also regarding the sincerity with which they were expressed and pursued. My scepticism was based on official papers and other documents that I had found together with the Rhemrev Report. The voluminous dossier provided a fascinating insight into the workings of colonial policy-making and, in particular, enabled me to examine how the responsible politicians and bureaucrats had reacted to the scandal. I would contend that the lessons to be drawn are of more than mere historical significance. My conviction has been strengthened even further by the coincidence that, while working on the book, I was able to follow on television lengthy debates on the ways in which a Cabinet Minister and his officials had attempted to suppress a scandal over the financial debâcle of a major Dutch shipbuilding industry. While watching the hearings to which high-ranking policy-makers were subjected by a parliamentary investigatory committee, and listening to the half-truths and even downright lies that they permitted themselves, it was only too easy to visualize how, at the beginning of this century, the curtain was rung down over 'the coolie question'.

I have further been struck by the fact that the renewed interest in the past state of affairs seems to have been confined to this one episode. This is regrettable, because it entails under-exposure of the continuity in the inhuman treatment that has been the lot of plantation workers also in later years. At any rate, it is quite incorrect to assume, as some do, that although the scandals mentioned in the Rhemrev Report were concealed from the public eye at the time, their re-occurrence was prevented by the resolute stand taken by the colonial authorities. There are numerous examples which show that the abuses continued and, as before, whenever any of them became publicly known, ingenious excuses were found. This is the first major reason why it would be highly misleading to dispose of what became for a short while a major issue as being nothing more than 'a black page' which terminated the pioneering era on Sumatra's East Coast.

A second correction, of at least equal importance, is to remove the idea that the Rhemrev Report fell like a thunderbolt on a suddenly awakened public conscience. It needs to be emphasized that the Public Prosecutor did no more than verify facts that, although bewildering, were already since long common knowledge. The indictment brought by the lawyer Van den Brand, whose accusations in *De Millioenen uit Deli* (The Millions from Deli) had formed the motive for the official investigation, was the first instance in which systematic attention was given to abuses that had long been the subject of incidental reports in the colonial press. In the racist milieu which characterized the social climate at the top of colonial society, however, it seemed that only eccentrics such as Van den Brand took any exception to such news. It is true that the contents of the Rhemrev Report caused considerable shock, but that was restricted primarily to the mother country and even there compelled attention for a short time only. There was no question of any lasting reversal of public opinion, or of any halt to the misery suffered by the coolies. It is not the natural tendency of authorities towards secrecy that should be emphasized, but rather their disinclination to acknowledge that abuses did exist on a wide scale. Such denial of reality enabled them to adopt, and later to persist in, a formalistic attitude of 'we knew nothing about it'.

Rhemrev made it quite clear in his report that the use of physical coercion and of other forms of force against the workers was linked indissolubly to the plantation economy. This was no aberration typical only of the regime as it had come into existence on Sumatra's East Coast under Dutch rule. In the British and French territories in the wider region of Asia the colonial state also introduced penal sanctions against any breach of labour contract into which, according to the official mind, coolies entered out of their own free will. In addition to the use of legalized force, blows and kicks and even worse were meted out by the white bosses as they saw fit in their efforts to instill 'discipline' in the Asian workforce. There is an intriguing similarity in the methods of torture with which planters and also the owners or managers of mining enterprises throughout Asia indulged themselves. The manner by which recalcitrant contract workers were beaten, sometimes until death followed, the way in which female coolies were tethered to a post of the planter's bungalow, and the practice of rubbing finely-ground pepper into their sexual organs, did not only occur in Deli. Descriptions of such practices may be found in almost identical wording in English and French sources concerning the tea estates of Assam and the rubber plantations in Indo-China. A study of the terrorization techniques used in the management of labour would undoubtedly show that close contacts existed between enclaves of capitalist production throughout various colonial domains within Asia. However, the systematic use of intimidation and terror was not confined to this region of the world. A textbook currently in use for secondary school students in the Netherlands shows a photograph taken in the Belgian Congo at the beginning of the twentieth century. While two white men stand watchfully by, a few African workers hold up the chopped-off hands of some of their fellows, who have been punished in this way for not delivering their full rubber quota. With such horrific examples before us, it seems useless to enter into any discussion as to which particular colonial regime distinguished itself by using the cruellest methods of control. Research into the origins and social background of such practices would seem to be of greater benefit.

But did the colonial authorities do nothing to check these atrocities, especially when they became public knowledge? It is impossible to give an unqualified affirmative to this question. No doubt, the worst excesses decreased in frequency and intensity in the later colonial period, a moderation which, in my view, had less to do with official concern than with changes in production relations—in particular systems of wage payment—on the plantations. Planters gradually came to understand that, from the economic viewpoint, the injury or even destruction of labour was counterproductive while, on the other hand, the workforce showed some signs of internalizing the principles on which capitalist industrial relations were based.

Behind the facade of a so-called 'Ethical Policy', which implied little more than lip-service to the idea that the economic and social advancement of the native population was the prime task of the colonial government after the turn of the century, was hidden the conviction that the Asian worker could be brought to improve himself only with a strong hand. On Sumatra, the plantation system continued to be based on forced labour. 'A miserable history of suffering and injustice', wrote the Minister for Colonies in 1904 on the original Rhemrev Report before having it hastily filed away in the archives. But a few years later, while playing a new star role as Governor-General of the Netherlands Indies, this same Christian-Democrat politician who, even now, is well known for being a strong proponent of ethical policies, sanctioned measures that facilitated more severe punishment for contract workers who showed themselves to be disobedient or recalcitrant. It is hardly surprising, in view of such continuity, that the Labour Inspectorate on Sumatra's East Coast, set up with the intention of providing protection to the workers, actually became an instrument with which the coolies were conditioned in accordance with the wishes and needs of their employers. The maintenance of penal sanctions in the labour contract almost until the end of colonial rule, had the complete agreement of officials of that inspectorate.

In the first decade of the twentieth century, the economist J.H. Boeke, who became a major policy adviser to the Netherlands Indies government, formulated his well-known thesis on dualism as being the foundation of colonial society (Boeke 1953 & 1966). In his own works and in subsequent debates which arose, emphasis is placed on the traditional mentality of the Asian peasant, marked by the instinct towards immediate gratification of a limited number of material needs. In Boeke's opinion, the social behaviour to which this gave rise conflicted with the principle of profit maximation on which the work ethos of the western man, *homo economicus* par excellence, was based. The tenor of his dualism theory, tainted by racial prejudice, was that Javanese peasants were incapable of operating in a commercialized economy subject to the rules of capitalism. They had no alternative but to withdraw from market transactions as much as possible and to concentrate on subsistence agriculture in a way which would enable them to remain close to their own cultural heritage. Boeke seized on the unbridgeable gap which, in his opinion, existed between different tenets of rationality in East and West, to refer the great mass of Asian peasants back to a social sphere of their own in which there was, and would always be, latitude for everyone according to the principle that all had a right to a share in the scarce means of existence.

His analysis ignored the fact, however, that employers in the capitalist enclaves were not prepared to leave the native domain unimpaired, in that the greater proportion of the workforce needed for their industries derived from the rural hinterland. A study of colonial literature shows that native society was far less homogeneous than the dualism theory would have us believe. It is clear from these sources that the peasant society included a subaltern class which due to their sheer number was becoming increasingly redundant in the village economy. This land-poor or landless mass formed the reservoir from which plantations, mines and other large-scale capitalist enterprises throughout Asia recruited their workers. The endless repetition of statements which said that the workforce belonged to the scum of the villages, not only backed up the Colonial stigma of economic inferiority that was applied to all natives, but also served to justify a ruthless work regime. Only rigid discipline, it was argued, would make it possible for the coolies to break loose from their animal state of existence and remold them into proper and reliable workmen.

'The Taming of the Beast' was the title that I gave to a recent article written in reply to reviews of the Dutch edition of my plantation monograph (Breman 1988). In that essay I have tried to demonstrate that the occurrence of coolie scandals on Sumatra's East Coast cannot be explained by reference to the relative isolation of the region or to a weak regional government that was no match for the planters' hegemony. It is impossible to understand what happened on the East Coast at the beginning of this century without considering the colonial order in its entirety. Contrary to the tendency to stress the exceptional circumstances that occurred only in an outlying corner of the Netherlands Indies during the pioneering era, I would posit that the relationship between the planter and the coolie, which was so imbued with the use of public and private violence, represented an extreme form of the lack of freedom of colonized labour under Dutch rule. On the capitalist plantations in the Outer Provinces this subjugation acquired the character of an adapted, modern form of slavery. Elsewhere in the archipelago, however, the native workforce was also exposed to physical compulsion. To give a fairly arbitrary example: during an investigation held in 1926 among factory workers in the industrial city of Surabaya (Eastern Java) it was found that blows and kicks were part of the normal management style. The inferior quality of the workers was also in this instance cited as an excuse for such behaviour (Metal Industry Report 1926:15–16).

Labour relations continued to be imbued with elements of force, legalized or not, even when they were structured along capitalist lines. Scarcity or any other factor of a predominantly economic nature were certainly of importance but their role was not a conclusive one. The relationship of superior boss and inferior coolie was based on the racist ideology which permeated colonial society. That racism was pushed into the background as the process of decolonization became completed, but it did not disappear. International development co-operation became the slogan in the post-colonial world but the relationship of partnership between states and ethnicities on the basis of equality continues to be a fiction, and still hides feelings of fear and contempt among a small section of mankind against the greater majority of their fellow beings. A study of the colonial past is, therefore, not only of historical interest but also highly relevant in any attempt to expose and to combat such expressions of false social consciousness at the global level.

The Hague,
October 1988

ACKNOWLEDGEMENTS

The publication which I wrote in the Dutch language on the life and work of plantation coolies in colonial Sumatra around the turn of the century, *Koelies, Planters en Koloniale Politiek* (Coolies, Planters and Colonial Policies) appeared in 1987 under the auspices of the Koninklijk Instituut voor Taal-, Land- en Volkenkunde (Royal Institute of Linguistics and Anthropology) in Leiden. That work consisted of three parts: (1) my own monograph, based on published and unpublished sources; (2) the Rhemrev Report, which I had retraced in the General State Archive in The Hague; and (3) a reprint of the *Millioenen uit Deli* (The Millions from Deli), written by J. Van den Brand in 1902 in an effort to arouse public opinion. Van den Brand's booklet gave rise to the official investigation for which J.L.T. Rhemrev was sent to the East Coast of Sumatra as Public Prosecutor by the Governor-General of the Netherlands Indies.

The English translation had to be restricted to Part 1, but in this edition I have referred extensively to, and quoted from, the Rhemrev Report. Considerable reference is also made to the documents and archives that formerly belonged to the collection of the East Coast of Sumatra Institute and which are now kept in the library of the Koninklijk Instituut voor de Tropen (Royal Tropical Institute) in Amsterdam. Mrs A. Winkel kindly helped me to gain access to this material which has only partially been catalogued. Without subsidies provided by the Erasmus University Fund in Rotterdam, the Indo-Dutch Programme on Alternatives in Development, and the Faculty of Social Sciences of Amsterdam University. This translation into English, ably made by Mrs Jean Sanders, could not have been completed. Mrs Ineke Rijkschroeff-Kwa bravely coped with the burdensome task of producing a legible typescript from my partly handwritten pages. Ilse Burke provided a strong dose of both moral and critical support. Wim Hendrix has once again been a good companion in the search for historical documents and a ruthless commentator on early drafts of several chapters. Wim Wertheim drew my attention to some colonial reports that otherwise I would have overlooked. I am grateful to all these I have named, and to many more.

Many of the photographs reproduced here belong to memorial volumes or albums, the publication of which was often sponsored by major plantation corporations. Apart from the private collection built up by the author, these visual sources can be found at the *Koninklijk Instituut voor Taal-, Land- en Volkenkunde (Leiden) and the Koninklijk Instituut voor de Tropen* (Amsterdam). The photograph on the jacket is from the collection on the N.I. colonial army, located at the *Sectie Militaire Geschiedenis van de Landmachtstaf (The Hague).*

I

THE MAKING OF A SCANDAL

The study of plantation systems is concentrated primarily on those of the Americas and the Caribbean region. It is my profound conviction that the rapid rise of modern plantations in the exploited colonies of South and Southeast Asia since the second half of the nineteenth century has not been given the attention it deserves. In countries such as British India, Ceylon, French Indo-China, Malaya, the Netherlands East Indies and the Philippines, relatively empty regions that were initially poorly accessible, were opened-up on the initiative of western entrepreneurs, for the large-scale cultivation of cash crops for the world market. Land was plentiful but there was an enormous shortage of labour. Both the coolies and the managerial staff for these land clearances had to be brought in from elsewhere and normally stayed only a couple of years in these new enclaves of capitalist production. In the colonization of the new land, which began in the second half of the nineteenth century, forced labour and state intervention played crucial roles. There is a fairly extensive literature on plantation life and labour in each of the countries mentioned above, but a more comparative regional study on the emergence of large scale agri-business under colonial domination is conspicuous by its absence. This is all the more surprising because, during the first half of the twentieth century, this new Asian agri-business came to surpass the much older American industry in terms of land use, labour, yield, profit and accumulated capital.

This monograph is a case study confined to the plantation milieu on Sumatra's East Coast in its formative period. The main focus is on the labour system, regulated according to the Coolie Ordinance which came into effect in 1880. The shift in relations between land and labour, which were the two major factors of production, had significant consequences for the organization of the colonial economy. In Java, in the first half of the nineteenth century, sugar-cane plantations had been located in the midst of the peasant population living in the plains (Breman 1983). Subsequently, however, the colony's economic base gravitated increasingly towards the land that was abundantly available in the Outer Provinces of the Netherlands East Indies. Labour proved to be as mobile as capital due largely to the growing social control of the colonial state. Suitable legislation was introduced which provided the conditions necessary for an unbridled development of capitalist enterprise.

Public discussion about the advantages and disadvantages of forced labour on the plantations must have been very uncommon in Medan, the heart of the plantation country on Sumatra's East Coast, at the beginning of this century. On 29 March 1902 in the Oranje Hotel, the local branch of the Indian Alliance (*Indische Bond*) held a public meeting in order to allow the Dutch parliamentarian, H. van Kol, MP for the Social Democratic Labour Party (SDAP) who was on a study tour, to form an opinion of the conditions prevailing in the region. Non-controversial subjects were discussed during the first part of the meeting, but after the interval attention was focused on the labour question of Deli. Approximately a hundred thousand indentured coolies were employed in the region, who found it impossible to extricate themselves from their labour contracts. Agreements stipulated that the advance payments handed over to the coolies on recruitment marked the beginning of their employment by one of the plantations in Sumatra. Their indenture implied that they would be subjected to penal sanctions if they tried to break away. The first speaker was the local correspondent of one of the dailies published from Java whose articles, until then had been anonymous. On this occasion he stood up as a fierce opponent of the Coolie Ordinance characterizing this system of labour regulation as a modern form of slavery. Then came the turn of the owner of a recruitment office who, naturally enough, ignored the grim side and light-heartedly stressed the need to maintain the prevailing system. The last speaker was Johannes van den Brand, a practising lawyer in the capital city of the Residency, who condemned the Coolie Ordinance on moral grounds, illustrating his views with examples taken from the local press and from his own professional experience.

Reports on the meeting carried in the local newspapers for Medan and its surrounding areas brought a stream of indignant reactions from the planters. Van den Brand, far from being deterred was made more militant by the criticisms, and addressed himself to a wider audience, putting the future of his legal practice at stake. The pamphlet he published immediately afterwards, *The Millions from Deli* (*De millioe nen uit Deli*), caused a sensation, particularly in the Netherlands. It sent a new chill of horror through the country half-a-century after Multatuli (Eduard Douwes Dekker) had published *Max Havelaar*, a devastating critique of the Dutch colonial order in the East Indies.

Why was there such a strong reaction? In the light of whatever little that was written about 'the coolie affair' at the beginning of the twentieth century, Van den Brand's allegations seemed to be completely unexpected. However, this idea of a first stone being cast into unruffled waters was patently incorrect. In the Netherlands Indies towards the end of the last century the press reported regularly and extensively on all manner of abuses that were a common practice on the plantations, and mining enterprises throughout the archipelago. At the time, the maltreatment of labour formed a regular item in the Dutch Parliament's annual discussions on the budget of the Netherlands Indies. Considerable attention was also given to conditions in Deli, particularly when ex-planter J.T. Cremer became the Minister of Colonies (1897–1901). This mouthpiece of colonial capitalism found fierce adversaries among members of the Socialist Opposition, including Van Kol and Pieter Troelstra. The fact that Van den Brand's pamphlet caused such an enormous shock thus requires further explanation.

A prime reason was undoubtedly the shift in colonial ideology. At the beginning of the nineteenth century it was still taken for granted that '... every colony does or ought to exist for the benefit of the Mother-country', as H.W. Muntinghe wrote in an advice to Lieutenant-Governor Raffles in 1813 (Raffles 1814:280). The system of forced deliveries from the 1830s onwards was a logical result of this point of view. By the end of that century, however, all this had been replaced with the conviction that the Netherlands ought to recognize its responsibility for the growing impoverishment of its colonies—in this case that of the archipelago. To be sure, profits made in the colonies were no longer flowing into the Dutch

Treasury as had been the case under state exploitation. Since the last quarter of the nineteenth century, private enterprise had replaced the cultivation system based on forced labour. The obligation to acknowledge a debt of honour, i.e. to restitute the surplus that had been extracted from the Netherlands East Indies during the early colonial period led to the adoption of a welfare policy for the archipelago. In a book published in 1901 in which he launched the term 'Ethical Politics', Brooshooft specifically referred to the wretched life led by the coolie-labourer on the Sumatran plantations and urged (to my knowledge the first to do so) that an independent Labour Inspectorate be set up (Brooshooft 1901:100–6). Van den Brand's indictment was thus apposite for the critical reappraisal of colonial policies that was then in progress.

The nature of the pamphlet itself was an additional reason for the kind of reaction it evoked. It was the first instance in which an author had not contented himself with merely describing some isolated incidents but had traced the source of oppression of the coolies to the actual operation of the contract labour system itself. Under a number of subtitles such as 'Mistreatment and cruelty', 'Insensitivity and thirst for money', 'Arbitrariness and deceit', 'How does a Javanese woman have to earn her sarong?', Van den Brand elaborated at length the terror and exploitation suffered by the coolies, in a style that was reminiscent of Multatuli's sincerity and indignation rather than his literary brilliance. Van den Brand also differed from the colonial commentator-essayist in the religious tone of his work. It was this in particular which made him a troublesome opponent of the planters' lobby. The onslaught this time came not from a familiar corner, to be shrugged-off as that coming from a socialist scandal mongerer, but from someone who appealed to the Christian conscience of the Dutch people. The author, moreover, illustrated his pamphlet very effectively, with advertisements taken from local newspapers. One such advertisement asked for the detention of a run-away Javanese (blind in one eye); another offered to supply robust, young and healthy workers (insured against the risk of desertion during transport) together with prime cattle for slaughter or for draught work, all in one package! To the reader, the association with *Uncle Tom's Cabin* was unmistakable.

Finally, Van den Brand impressed his audience by the fact that he attacked not only the employers but also the colonial government which he accused of making common cause with the planters. The coolies came from China and from Java and pledged to work for three years in return for periodic advances of money. The contract into which they entered included a number of binding clauses stipulating the nature, duration and other details of the work to be performed. Any infringement of the clauses was subject to disciplinary action imposed by the government officials who also acted as magistrates. The employer on his side, undertook to provide the contract coolie with a livelihood and to give him or her a decent treatment. Van den Brand alleged that while the mere bringing of a charge against a coolie was sufficient cause for the latter to be given a disproportionately severe punishment, the planters who indulged in cruel and horrifying treatment of their workers went scot-free, unlikely to be prosecuted. The lawyer was strident in his censure regarding the effects of the Coolie Ordinance with its penal sanctions and of the way in which it was wielded by the colonial authorities.

It was inevitable for the affair to become a political issue in the mother country. The right-wing Kuyper Cabinet was in power (1901-5) and the Anti-Revolutionary A.W.F. Idenburg had just become the new Minister for Colonial Affairs. As a career officer in the Netherlands East Indies colonial army, he had established links with the Christian Party leadership while on leave in the Netherlands, and had been an MP for hardly a year, when he was given ministerial responsibility. He was undeniably a protege of Prime Minister Kuypers and for that reason his appointment was criticized by the colonial press. When the Netherlands Indies' budget was discussed in the Parliament later that year, the new Minister could not avoid the coolie question but said non-committally that he would bring the pamphlet to the notice of Governor-General W. Rooseboom. However, the diatribes on the coolie issue in the press continued to hold the attention of the public. Initial responses by those who considered themselves pre-eminently qualified to give an opinion were extremely negative. Planters upbraided Van den Brand for wanting to ruin the prosperous plantation belt on Sumatra's East Coast, the most beautiful emerald in the crown of the East Indies. Former government officials also joined the fray. Ex-Resident P.J. Kooreman of Sumatra's East Coast argued that the Coolie Ordinance was intended not to keep coolies in bondage but to prevent them from breaching their contract. Had not the eminent professor of law G.A. van Hamel said in 1892 that the system was so successful because it suited the interests of both the parties in such an excellent and balanced fashion? (Van Hamel 1892). This scholar had even recommended the introduction of the Coolie Ordinance into Java. Kooreman denied that the authorities had been negligent and said he knew nothing about the abuses. He considered Van den Brand's tales to be grossly exaggerated and incorrect. On the basis of his own five-year experience, Kooreman gave the assurance that the coolies were usually well treated. Moreover, they were always allowed to lodge complaints, which were subjected to thorough examination by the local authorities.

An editorial in the *Nieuwe Rotterdamsche Courant* on 26 January 1903 noted with satisfaction that 'the scandalous affair' had turned out to be a non-issue. Van den Brand persisted, probably encouraged by private support and by the fresh information that reached him through informal channels. He published a second pamphlet: *Again: The Millions from Deli (Nog eens: De millioenen uit Deli)*, in which he described the slander and opposition to which he had been subjected in Medan since the publication of his pamphlet. He repeated his charges with the addition of new facts, revealed how and why he had been unable to get a hearing from the colonial government, denounced Kooreman's so-called ignorance of the situation, and urged the Minister of Colonies, with whom he shared membership of the same political party, to order a thorough investigation.

Discussions both in the bourgeois and opposition press made it clear that many people were not to be fobbed-off with exclamations of colonial grandiloquence and the standard assurances that, apart from occasional lapses, nothing was wrong in Deli. Public opinion seemed to be giving the angry lawyer, who appeared to many as being a trifle self-righteous, nevertheless, the benefit of a doubt. An official investigation could no longer be avoided. The Minister made it clear that he awaited the end result with complete confidence.

Contrary to the majority of his predecessors and successors, Governor-General Rooseboom (1899–1904) was not a specialist on the Netherlands East Indies. A former general whose military career had been entirely within the mother country, his task was to pacify the colony once and for all, from Merauke (New Guinea) where a military post was established in the east, to North Sumatra, in the west of the archipelago. As the highest representative of colonial authority he tended to avoid all policies that were non-military in nature. The Atjeh War was still in progress, and Rooseboom depended on his official apparatus in civilian affairs. By government decree of 24 May 1903, Public Prosecutor J.L.T. Rhemrev, a staff member of the Council of Justice in Batavia, was ordered to carry out an administrative investigation into 'the maltreatment alleged by Mr J. Van den Brand in his pamphlet entitled *The Millions from Deli* and the illegal imprisonment of coolies and other persons employed by the industrial enterprises in the said Residency, as well as the alleged irregularities by the judiciary of the region'. The Attorney General gave Rhemrev the additional order to investigate penal offences and to institute criminal proceedings against their perpetrators. Rhemrev went to Medan in the summer of 1903 and finished his inquiries by the end of the year.

The Governor-General received Rhemrev's report early in 1904 and almost immediately sent it on to the Netherlands. It was accompanied by various memoranda written by top-ranking colonial bureaucrats, in particular the Directors of the Civil Service and of Justice, and a recommendation from the Council of the Netherlands East Indies. All of these had been written prior to Rhemrev being given his task. It was *not* accompanied, however, by a thick bundle of supplementary material which Rhemrev had appended to his report, including reports of visits to individual plantations and transcripts of his official hearings. When the East Indies' budget was discussed in the Netherlands Parliament in the autumn of 1904, it became abundantly clear that the Minister of Colonies would go to any lengths to prevent the disclosure of the contents of Rhemrev's report. His official reason for refusing to allow MPs to see the document even in confidence was that those who had been accused of misdeeds or other reprehensible actions had not been given the opportunity to defend themselves against the charges. Moreover, publication would not serve any useful purpose. Rather than dwell on what had happened in the past, he thought it better to concentrate on improvements for the future. It was only after considerable pressure and that too from members of friendly parties which formed the ruling coalition, that the

Minister reluctantly agreed to outline the principal conclusions of the Report.

It transpired that Van den Brand had not exaggerated the grim description of the conditions on Deli's plantations. What Rhemrev had brought to light was in some ways worse than what had been previously established or even conjectured. The successful concealment of malpractices, which had occurred on such a large scale, from the outside world, was found to be even more reprehensible than the revelation of the systematic use of violence. The social climate that had made this possible will be discussed extensively in the following pages. The report's conclusions, read aloud by Idenburg to the Chamber, were nothing more than the tip of the iceberg, but even the political opposition reconciled itself eventually to a motion submitted by members of the government parties. This motion thanked the Minister for the information he had provided and noted with approval his promise to take measures that would put an end to the maltreatment of Deli's coolie workers.

At that time it was by no means exceptional for government reports to be kept secret, particularly where conditions in the Netherlands East Indies were concerned, and there was to be no change in this matter in the years to come. What made the disclosure of the scandalous state of affairs on Sumatra's East Coast particularly shocking, however, was that it was *not* one of the minor incidents which regularly occurred somewhere or other in the archipelago. What was concerned in this case was a concentration of modern, large-scale, agri-industries which had to be fed by an enormous army of workers from outside the region. Even after the initial shock, the on-going expansion of the plantation economy continued to attract public interest. Looking back, it seems justified to conclude that the disclosure of the coolie scandals of the early 1900s marked the end of the pioneering era. Since then, drastic changes have taken place in labour relations, but the events of the past were to remain concealed in enigmatic silence. The glossy commemorative volumes produced by the great plantation companies make no mention of the dark side of life on the plantations. Even authors who, later in the colonial period, set out to write the history of the region with the express intention of obliterating the image of coolie scandals and of Deli 'millions', were not permitted to examine the findings of Rhemrev's investigations (Broersma 1919:277, n.1).

Later, this official report was lost in oblivion. In one of the few recent books on the plantation society of Sumatra's East Coast, Pelzer mentions the assignment given to Rhemrev. The fact that his report had successfully been kept beyond the reach of all researchers caused Pelzer to deduce, quite correctly as it has now been proven, that the facts reported therein must have been even more shocking than those recorded by Van den Brand (Pelzer 1978:138). I came across this remark while working on a study of labour migration in colonial times in South and Southeast Asia (Breman 1985). In fact, the report had not been destroyed, as we fear it most certainly would have been, if such a scandal had taken place today. It had been securely stacked away in the General State Archives (GSA) until such a time when the coolie scandal would have been forgotten by the general public.

The outcome of the Rhemrev Report was what caused me to write this book, but to place that source in the right context I needed to read extensively about the plantation system as it had developed on Sumatra's East Coast in the early 1900s. In reconstructing the past in this way, I had to consult writings that were strongly suggestive of a planters' epic, a glorification of all that the western entrepreneurial spirit had brought about in tropical Asia. Many authors were themselves ex-planters or held positions that made them extremely biased observers, such as the Secretary of the Deli Planters Association (DPV), or the Director of the East Sumatra Institute or of the Tobacco Bureau. Such bias is even more pronounced in the commemorative volumes published by the big corporations, in which coolies figure principally as mere objects against the background of the crops that they grew.

When the DPV was set up, its board of directors had immediately pointed out that publicity was not in the best interests of its members. Until the publication of Van den Brand's pamphlet and even for many years after that, those directly interested, i.e. primarily the planters, were able to restrict the flow of undesirable information about labour conditions on the plantations. The rare authors who expressed criticisms, often scathing, of labour conditions on the plantations, did not venture to describe the life and work of those who worked on them at close quarters. The source material lacks many particulars that are necessary to give colour and shape to the story of the coolies. Only during the last few years has interest grown in this chapter of colonial history. The geographer Karl Pelzer (1978, 1982) places great emphasis on the ways in which autochthonous peoples were ejected from their land. The economist and historian Thee Kian-Wie (1977) concentrates mostly on the rise of the plantation economy on Sumatra's East Coast and its significance for the export trade under Dutch rule. Another Indonesian author, Mohammad Said (1977), has written an economic-historical treatise on the same subject in which he gives particular attention to wage levels and living standards. The excellent book by Ann Stoler (1985) undoubtedly provides the most extensive and complete account of the labour regime on Sumatran plantations. The scope of my own work is similar to her study from which I have derived much inspiration. But while Stoler concentrates on the late-colonial era from where she extrapolates until after the Independence of Indonesia, my own story stops at the beginning of the twentieth century. The body of literature and archival material referred to in this monograph deal with the first decade of that period. With a few exceptions, I shall mention publications of later date only insofar as they are relevant for the earlier history of the Sumatran plantation.

The next chapter of this book sketches the opening-up of the region from the arrival of the original planters to the consolidation of the large estates at the end of the nineteenth century, with a total labour force of almost a hundred thousand coolies. Chapter III discusses labour hierarchy, the organization of production, and the conditions of employment prevalent on the plantations around the turn of the century. The fourth chapter goes into the disciplining of the coolies: the diverse ways in which they tried to escape the plantation regime; and the punishments that were then meted out. Chapter V describes Sumatra's East Coast as a frontier society, the nature of the plantocracy and the violence used against the coolies as a structural feature of plantation life during the pioneering period. For long the tendency has been to deny the existence of abuses, to minimize their occurrence and even to find excuses for them. The official inquiry, once this could no longer be avoided, made it clear that it was no over-statement to speak of a colonial labour scandal. The sixth chapter starts with a brief review of reactions to Rhemrev's report in the Dutch and colonial press, and then concentrates on ways in which bureaucrats and politicians handled it in the East Indies as well as in the Netherlands. The measures taken to preclude the continuation of such abuses are also examined. In evaluating such measures I have made use of official memoranda, letters and other papers which I was singularly fortunate to find in the archives together with Rhemrev's report. This background material has made it possible for me to find out, firstly, how the Minister of Colonies and top civil servants in the Netherlands Indies and in The Hague reacted to the coolie scandal and, secondly, the narrow parameters within which colonial policy-makers looked for a solution.

The concluding chapter makes it clear that, even after the disclosures, the planters' hold over the coolies remained unchanged in which they continued to be assured of co-operation, actively and passively, by the colonial authorities. In the course of time, excesses such as those reported by Rhemrev decreased in number and intensity. This, in my opinion, was only partly due to state protection. The planters gradually came to prefer the presence of a permanent and stable proletariat. Naked force made way for more restrained methods of labour control in subsequent decades; physical violence did not disappear, but was used in less extreme ways than before. Life on the plantations continued to be ruthlessly hard and cruel for the coolies. The fact that available sources give so little information on these features should not merely be explained by purposeful distortion or falsification of the facts, a conscious attempt to cover up something that was dishonourable. The attitude of the planters was in fact characterized by complete indifference to the fate of their coolies. They refused to acknowledge them as human beings. Coolies existed as a mass, not as a collection of individuals, and were collectively anathematized for characteristics that were almost entirely negative. To get any idea of the work regime 'from the bottom up' we have to read carefully between the lines, sometimes take remarks out of their context, and even to read fortuitously, in ways other than those intended. Only then can the history of the plantation workers and of subaltern classes in general be laboriously reconstructed. Photographs can be a great help in clarifying social relations, but they can also distort reality. What is needed is a special photo album that will depict the structure and culture of work and labour control on the colonial plantation. In this present study I have been able to include a series of photographs on different subjects, mostly poses taken by professional photographers. These frozen tableaus record the grim facts, even if they do not allow one to get any closer to the horrors that they conceal.

I do not know of contemporary documents that describe the life and work of the coolies from the inside such as told by Tran Tu Binh, a Vietnamese coolie on a rubber plantation in French Indo-China at the end of the twenties. His memoirs *The Red Earth* were written down much later. The counterpoint perspective that his story provides could never have come out of the colonial setting of Sumatra's East Coast, where labour had no human value. Everything revolved around the product, the famous Deli tobacco. The yield and the price it fetched in the world market were all-important, as the *Sumatra Post* reported in proud retrospective.

... the planters of those days kept no account of all the facts and figures on the East Coast except for the paramount, all-important record, the tobacco record, the list of the number of parcels produced and the prices negotiated for them (Jubilee issue on 50 years of Deli, published on 5 May 1913).

Multatuli's famous novel on the coffee auctions held by the Netherlands Trading Company in the mid-nineteenth century, gave a graphic description of the manifestation of Dutch mercantile capitalism in the East Indies; half-a-century later this story had lost none of its topicality.

II

THE EMERGENCE OF PLANTATION SOCIETY

The Opening-up of the Land

The colonial policy that had been followed in the Netherlands East-Indies changed soon after the middle of the last century. The government started withdrawing from direct involvement in economic production and increasingly concentrated on creating incentives that would stimulate private initiative: The 1870 Agrarian Act, which officially put an end to the forced cultivation system in Java and started the transition to an era of unbridled liberalism, indicated the orientation of the new policy: the archipelago's natural resources were henceforth to be made accessible to capitalist interests in the mother country. In Java this brought a gradual expansion of estate agriculture that had first been established under the forced cultivation system and which now began to appropriate more and more of the available land, at the expense of peasant production. By comparison, the exploitation of natural resources in the sparsely-populated Outer Provinces was still in its initial phase. Concessions for mineral exploitation were to be granted during the next few decades, but however important the mining industry was to become in the long term, the rise of a plantation society on the East Coast of Sumatra was of more immediate significance for the colonial economy.

According to planters' folklore, the first man to settle in Deli with the declared intention of starting an estate in what was almost unknown territory to the Dutch, was Jacobus Nienhuys, who arrived there in 1863. Nienhuys came to be seen as the founder of the tobacco industry for which the East Coast was to become famous all over the world. The company that he founded (the Deli Company) became one of the largest colonial enterprises. Legend has it that this pioneer ended up in an almost uninhabited region

and, almost single-handedly, converted the surrounding jungle
into neatly laid–out tobacco fields. A never-ending stream of
commemorative volumes have recorded this event, which however do not stand up to closer scrutiny. In earlier centuries a
number of small Malayan coastal states had been established on
both sides of the Strait of Malacca. Led by local rajas, these states
lived in continual mutual rivalry, making every effort to extend
their influence into the Batak-inhabited hinterland of Sumatra's
East Coast. This eventually brought about a political hierarchy in
which the rulers of the most prominent of these early state forma-
tions attached into vassalage the heads of the lesser units. Van
Langenberg has characterized the social landscape, which was
structured along familial rather than territorial lines, as follows:

At the top of a well delineated pyramidical hierarchy was the sultan, the
premier chieftain, whose position was based upon his personification of
the political and socio-cultural identity of the kingdom. Below him was a
hierarchy of aristocracy—members of the sultan's immediate family, court
officials and local chieftains—all bearing hereditary titles such as *raja,
tengku, datuk* or *orangkaya.* Next came a class of wealthy and powerful
commoners—usually traders and senior Islamic officials such as ulama,
kiyai or imam. At the base of this 'feudal' structure were the peasant-farm-
ing and fishing communities who made up the overwhelming bulk of the
population (Van Langenberg 1977:82).

In this connection, the 'overwhelming bulk' is a relative term
since there were seldom more than a few tens of thousands of
people living within the ill-defined borders of these small-scale
political entities with their strong trading orientation. Most of these
loosely-structured Malayan mini-states were extremely vulnerable
due to changing loyalties and the re-grouping of coalitions. Traffic
and trade along the Strait of Malacca and with the hinterland
formed the economic basis of these coastal states, which were
mostly situated on the river mouths. Nevertheless, reports dating
back to the early nineteenth century show that there were already
signs of sedentary agriculture and even of cash crop production for
wider markets.

In 1823 John Anderson journeyed to the other side of the Strait
of Malacca on the orders of the British authorities in Penang. The
following quotations (published in Schadee 1918:29–37) are taken

from his report of the expedition. Of the ruler of Serdang, Anderson wrote that 'trade and agriculture flourish under his mild and benevolent rule'. Serdang's population was made up of 3000 Malays and 8000 Bataks, and the pepper crop that was grown in the higher regions was brought down to the coast by river. Langkat had a population of approximately 7000 Malays and 13,000 Bataks.

The pepper crop was continually being expanded and the quality was exceptionally good. Other export articles included rattan, wax, pulses, gambir [a plant extract used in tanning], gold (from Bohorok), tobacco and rice. They imported salt, opium, linens (European and Indian), iron and steel goods, tools, etc.

The biggest harbour had at least 10,000 inhabitants, whose headman 'lived in a house built in European style and furnished with chairs, tables and a bed. This *sjahbandar* came from Deli. He had travelled far and had even visited Batavia, and was well acquainted with the customs and habits of the Europeans.' Asahan's main crop was rice, 'of which the production was so abundant that Asahan could supply its neighbouring states with this foodstuff. Pepper was also grown.' Finally, the region of Deli, which in common usage would later come to refer to the whole of the East Coast,

gave an impression of prosperity, especially because of the pepper crop, which was cultivated on a large scale. In 1822 more than 26,000 *picul* [1 picul = 133.33 pounds] of pepper were exported. Tobacco was also grown for export. Rice, sugarcane, maize, various kinds of groundnuts, cotton, etc., were planted only for subsistence needs. Sugar palms and nutmeg trees were found in great numbers.

The *kampongs* contained spacious and well-built houses and were surrounded by bamboo thickets and fruit trees. There were many chickens, goats, etc. The Bataks were numerous in the hills.

Anderson was undoubtedly describing the conditions in a number of relatively well-developed enclaves, some of which had fallen into decay before the middle of the nineteenth century. By the time Nienhuys came to the region, the Sultan of Deli's annual income was certainly not more than 1,000 dollars (*Sumatra Post*, 5 May 1913). Yet the cherished image promoted in Dutch colonial history of a deserted corner of the archipelago, a jungle region being opened-up for the first time by Dutch pioneers, needs to be revised in the light of the information provided by English travellers such as Anderson at the beginning of the nineteenth century.

The story that hailed Nienhuys as the first planter on Sumatra's East Coast was later contradicted by one of the earliest Dutch civil servants in the region. According to this official, the founder of the Deli Company had been preceded by another Dutchman who initially shipped the native tobacco grown on Sumatra to Singapore and subsequently settled in Deli to grow nutmeg (Ibid., 14 May 1913). Far from drifting to Deli more or less by accident, Nienhuys went there by invitation. The Malayan ruler of this area had in fact sent an Arab envoy called Said Abdullah to Java in an attempt to interest trading houses in the commercial possibilities of the region. Abdullah, a mercantile agent, sought purchasers for the 30,000 picul of prime quality tobacco which were produced annually, so he claimed, by the inhabitants of the region. This trail-blazer met with an unfortunate end, which also fitted colonial imagery. He was taken a prisoner and accused of theft. He has now taken his place in history as a swindler (Broersma 1919:28-9). Nienhuys's achievements, on the other hand, gained even greater lustre through the emphasis placed on the poverty of the milieu in which he started his plantation. In the middle of a marshy and unhealthy region was the filthy *kampong* Labuan, at that time the most important locality in Deli.

The *kampong* had only a few wooden houses, the majority being of bamboo and *nibung* leaves, in a decrepit state, built three feet above the ground on piles, and with rubbish heaped-up under the huts. The people were shabbily dressed. At the end of the *kampong* stood the sultan's ... palace, a large wooden dwelling on piles standing eight feet above the ground (Ibid.:30).

This biased source does not mention that two thousand people lived in this *kampong*, including twenty Chinese and a hundred Indians (Pelzer 1978:33). Other reports point to the presence of these trading minorities and to the political influence that was exercised from continental Asia which dated back to many centuries (Sinar 1978:178-9).

The first Europeans to establish themselves as planters had to do so without any protection provided by a colonial administration. In the middle of the nineteenth century, the headmen of those regions on Sumatra's East Coast who earlier had loosely owed tribute to Atjeh now fell within the sphere of influence of the Sultanate of Siak, situated more to the south. Siak had originally formed part of the princedom of Johore in the Malay peninsula which, in 1745, ceded its rights to the Dutch East Indies Company (VOC), which opened a trading post on an island in the Siak estuary. Trade soon proved insufficient to warrant the maintenance of the settlement, and it was not until the mid-nineteenth century that the Netherlands again took steps to enforce her rights in this part of the archipelago. Before the Outer Provinces could be opened-up, they first had to be occupied. The Dutch extended their rule over Sumatra very gradually and cautiously, edging-in from the south and west of the island, aware that the British authorities in Malacca continued to show keen interest in the East Coast. Siak, which in 1858 again formally recognized the sovereignty of the Netherlands and which was in alliance with Minangkabau, was in a state of decline. One indication of this was that the rulers of coastal mini-states to the north were no longer so punctilious about acknowledging their subordination. Formerly, they used to send some of their subjects periodically to Siak to perform corvee labour (Broersma 1919:25). On the other hand, the sultan seemed to have no idea who his representatives were in the regions that owed him tribute. Moreover, he could not enforce his claim with any documentary evidence because all 'state papers' had been lost (Schadee 1918:90; Sinar 1978:181). Atjeh, in North Sumatra, had made use of the power vacuum that thus came about to extend its sphere of influence along the East Coast (Reid 1969:16). Deli had been submissive to Atjeh in the seventeenth century, and this occurred again in 1854. Serdang was yet another disputed region.

The Malayan settlements along the coast could not achieve prosperity because they were restricted to a narrow coastal strip. They were continually at loggerheads with one another. Each raja tried to expand his territory at the expense of his neighbours or by enticing trade from neighbouring ports to his own. Independent small states had only a few thousand inhabitants, and sometimes only a few hundred. Their rajas had too little power and could not put up a proper defence against the raids

that Siak and Atjeh alternately made along the East Coast and which had
no other purpose than to plunder and to vassalize the tiny states. Permanent occupation was not the objective and power was only exercized
for the exaction of levies or for the extortion of some other benefits (Schadee
1918:98).

It was only to be expected that the local headmen would try to
use the situation in such a way as to increase their own power and
status, thus causing even greater confusion in the region's political
system. The ruler of Deli in particular wanted to extend his
authority over the surrounding areas, which fell under Serdang
and Langkat. The Malayan element, initially restricted to the coastal area, gradually penetrated further into the Batak hinterland.
The presence of foreign powers served the local rulers well in this
expansion and also helped them to shake off their subordination
to their more dominant neighbours to the north and south. In 1862,
as a result of the treaty that had been signed in 1858, the newly-
designated Assistant Resident of Siak went on a tour of inspection.
He sailed along the East Coast, with one or two naval vessels, to
dependencies claimed by Siak, with the aim of establishing Dutch
hegemony. The expedition did not always meet with a warm
reception. Some harbours flew the British flag, which was hoisted
again as soon as the party had left. This was indicative of strong
commercial ties between the region and Penang, in which the
Chinese traders played a pivotal role. They could easily become
instruments of British penetration, and the anxiety that this created
became a strong motive in the Dutch decision to occupy the whole
of Sumatra's East Coast. The rulers of some of the coastal mini-
states immediately and voluntarily concluded political treaties,
acknowledging Dutch sovereignty. Others only agreed to do so
after a repeated show of military power, and then on conditions
that were naturally less favourable. The Sultan of Deli, aware of his
own insignificance, adopted a less defiant attitude towards the
demand that he submit to Dutch authority. He thus succeeded in
obtaining equal rather than subordinate status in relation to Siak,
and also the recognition of his extremely vague claims to several
bordering 'dependencies' in 1862. His ascendancy was at the cost
of the rulers of Serdang and Asahan who showed an attitude of
greater independence. At first, they continued to cast their lot with
Atjeh and were only persuaded to change their minds in 1865 after

repeated visits by the Dutch accompanied by military intimidation. The Sultan of Atjeh, who had tried in vain to prevent the incorporation of the small East Coast states into the greater colonial realm, was the main loser. Later on, the Dutch came to regret that no allowance was made at the time for Atjeh's supremacy in the region. This was to become one of the causes of the protracted war with this northern-Sumatran state towards the end of the century, which broke out for the first time in 1873 (Ibid.:148–51).

The establishment of an orderly administration meant that the English presence on the East Coast came to an end, notwithstanding the resistance by the traders of Penang (Reid 1969:49–69). Shortly after the Assistant Resident's tour of inspection in 1862, the first government officers (*controleurs*) were appointed to the principal districts (1864). As a part of the so-called Sumatra Treaty concluded between Great Britain and the Netherlands in 1871, the Government of the Straits Settlements waived all further interference in the affairs of the opposite coast in reconfirmation of an agreement already reached in 1824. In recompense, the economic penetration of British capital interests in the East Coast would remain unimpeded.

From Britain's point of view the East Coast of Sumatra was a model foreign colony. Though administration was a charge on the Dutch, no restrictions were placed on British trade or investment. By 1929 British capital in the plantations of this district had reached 124 million guilders, almost as much as in the whole of Java. Although not bound to do by the letter of the 1871 Treaty, Holland in fact accepted the area covered by that treaty as one where it should do nothing to limit the complete freedom of commerce existing before the Dutch annexation. Whereas in every other Residency of the Netherlands India only one or two ports were open to foreign trade, customs posts were installed at all the twenty-one tiny ports of the East Coast of Sumatra to cater for merchants from the Straits. Until 1886 British ships monopolized the busy traffic across the Straits. With the exception of some Deli tobacco taken to Batavia after 1891, all the imports and exports of this district passed through Penang or Singapore until the 1920s, when Belawan was developed as an international port (Ibid.:184–5).

I am well aware that this brief account of the way in which the East Coast was incorporated into the territory of the Netherlands Indies bears traces of colonial historiography. This gives pride of place to concepts such as 'territoriality' and 'hierarchy' which do not agree

with the fluid political structure, determined by kinship, ethnicity
and trade, which was found on both sides of the Strait of Malacca
in the mid-nineteenth century. The interests of a later period have
to a large extent modelled the interpretation of the situation as it
existed earlier.

The Seizure of Land

The colonial government bought the loyalty of the indigenous
rulers by acknowledging the dignity of their position, sometimes
even enhancing that of the minor rajas by permitting them to use
the title of 'sultan'. That this 'elevation' was made with 'tongue in
cheek' can be derived from opinions expressed by the early
planters that the local headmen were simple folk who had little to
differentiate them from their subjects (Nienhuys 1888:223). Nevertheless, it was important to uphold the jurisdiction of the Malay
rajas. In fact, their control over smaller notables and the population
at large became even greater than before. For instance, by giving
Europeans long-term land leases, which was one of the few
transactions requiring permission from the colonial authorities, the
rulers usurped ownership rights that had previously not been
theirs and were legitimized by protection from above in doing so
(Pelzer 1978:69-71; De Iongh 1982:542). Initially, land concessions
were easily made. The Resident of Riouw, under whom the East
Coast provisionally fell, had openly recommended Deli for private
agricultural development. In 1864 the Sultan gave Nienhuys permission to grow as much tobacco as he wanted, without asking any
rent for the land taken into cultivation (Broersma 1919:32). Two
years later, together with a German and two Swiss planters who
meanwhile had also settled in Deli, Nienhuys signed a 99-year
agreement. He managed to take possession of approximately
12,000 bahu (1 bahu=0.7 ha) of land, in a manner which later
commentaries praised as advantageous and resourceful (Ibid.:35).
On the basis of Nienhuys's own blatant statement, it would seem
more appropriate to speak of fraud and deception, both of the
population and of the colonial authorities:
The condition that was laid down therein [i.e. the agreement] to the effect
that I might take as much land as could be cultivated within 5 years, I
enforced, by taking over a great expanse of land which I planted with
plantain trees set far apart. Although they were not visible above the tall
grass, the plantain trees still provided sufficient evidence that this area was

being cultivated by me. Although the Resident, on his next visit, asserted that this had not been his intention and that a request should first be submitted to the authorities, we would not surrender the contracts that had been executed and enforced our property rights (Nienhuys 1888).

In the initial period labour was far more scarce than land. In 1874, a decade after the first estates had gone into operation, the population of Deli and its dependencies consisted of approximately 20,000 Bataks spread among 272 villages in the interior, and 12,000 Malays living in seventy-eight *kampongs* in the coastal belt. At that time, only 3,979 Chinese coolies had been imported into the region (*Colonial Report* 1874:16; Halewijn 1876:148-52).

Nienhuys at first continued with the existing mode of production, advancing cash to the Bataks to persuade them to grow more tobacco and to do so exclusively for him. The results were disappointing, however, and when this became clear, Nienhuys decided to lay out his own tobacco gardens and to engage labourers for the necessary work (Memoirs Arendsburg 1927:28, 31). The Malays in the coastal area refused to perform wage labour, and the Bataks in the hinterland were just as 'unwilling' and 'unsuitable' (Broersma 1919:32). Nienhuys himself used a rather more straightforward language, stating that the local inhabitants were undisciplined and lazy, and therefore absolutely unfit to become plantation workers. The Bataks were described by him as 'a stupid race' (Nienhuys 1888). An experiment with ten Hadjis, brought over from Penang by Nienhuys in 1864, was equally unsuccessful; some of them deserted before even reaching Deli, and others were more interested in giving religious instruction than in carrying-out waged labour. The first planter on the East Coast then made a virtue of necessity and handed over the management of the newly-created tobacco fields to the remaining Hadjis who then set their disciples to work. They were to produce a certain amount of tobacco in return for being freed from the obligation to repay the money advanced to them. This principle of farming-out was to become an essential feature of the later coolie contract system. Instead of paying a daily wage, Nienhuys switched in 1865 to a system under which remuneration depended on the quantity and quality of the tobacco harvested (Schadee 1918:178). A larger workforce was urgently needed, and Nienhuys again visited Penang where he succeeded in engaging 120 Chinese coolies. Since there was no accommodation for them, he was forced to take them into his own house. The first District Officer, appointed in Deli in 1864, also lodged with Nienhuys, and for a short while the planter, coolies and the colonial administrator all lived together under one roof. In view of the relations that would come about in later years, this was a truly remarkable fact.

The work remuneration system introduced by Nienhuys was to remain the basis of the industrial organization of tobacco cultivation. Instead of a daily wage the coolie received an advance on the payment made at the end of the crop season. Production was thus organized on the principle of contract work (Ibid.:178). At first, the head of a gang of Chinese coolies (*kongsi*) acted as a contractor. He was allotted a plot of land and he distributed seedlings among the members of his gang. These were then sold back to his employer at the end of the cycle as fullgrown plants. Around 1870, however, the planters switched to a system under which they dealt with each worker individually. The heads of the coolie gangs no longer worked for their own account and at their own risk, but were reduced to the position of overseer (Reid 1970:293). This direct involvement of the planters with the organization of production marked the transition to full- fledged industrial capitalism.

In the early years experiments were made with various other crops (Memorandum Tobacco Cultivation in Deli 1883:205–6). A number of planters took over nutmeg or coconut palm plantations from indigenous growers, or planted these crops on newly-cleared land. Following the example of a few small native establishments which processed their own coconut oil, plans were made to open a modern factory (Broersma 1919:36). In addition to the European planters, a few local notables were also involved in the production of these and other market crops: indigo, sugarcane, coffee, quinine, cacao. Nienhuys originally intended to open-up plantations with a number of crops, in co-operation with the Sultan of Deli. During the initial years, this pioneer was not solely occupied with the growth or even the buying-up of tobacco. Much to the displeasure of his financial backers in Rotterdam, he also traded in black pepper, nutmeg, rice, opium and textiles (Memorial Arendsburg 1927:29). In other words, in these pioneering years he was a trader rather than an industrial capitalist. In the hinterland the Bataks had laid out pepper gardens as long ago as the beginning of the nineteenth century. They also cultivated tobacco. Commercialized agriculture was on a small-scale, however, since their social organization, revolving around the household, did not permit the mobilization of labour power in a more aggregate mode of production.

... no Karo Batak family had the manpower to convert each new swidden, year after year, into a pepper garden. Once two or three swiddens had been transformed into pepper gardens, the family had more than enough work with their upkeep and harvesting, since it was still necessary to cut a new swidden every year for upland rice. Yet the enterprising character of the Karo Batak was manifest. Some of their leaders, with commendable acuity, found ways and means to organise a new industry, systematising both production and marketing and operating their own boats between East Sumatra and Penang (Pelzer 1978:57).

Soon it turned out that tobacco was the most profitable crop for the European market. Nienhuys's new European partner lent him 30,000 guilders to cover the cost of harvesting. When the crop was sold a year later in Amsterdam it brought in more than double that amount, which was 67,000 guilders (*Sumatra Post*, 5 May 1913). The Deli region became world famous for growing the wrapper leaf for the cigar industry, and the production of most other crops was subsequently dropped. To grow tobacco on a large scale required more capital than the planters themselves could raise. In 1869, therefore, together with a few partners and with the aid of the Nederlandsche Handelmaatschappij (NHM), Nienhuys set up the Deli Company (Deli Maatschappij, DM), the first limited liability company to operate in the Netherlands East Indies. His input consisted of a number of nutmeg gardens, coconut groves, an oil mill and land contracts.

Plantations now increased rapidly in number, requiring the import in 1869 of 800 to 900 coolies. It is indicative of the staggering mortality rate that, within a year, 213 of them had died (Schadee 1918:183). In addition to the Chinese coolies, the plantations employed a few hundred Klings (from the Indian Coromandel coast), Siamese and Javanese. It was not only the workers who showed such a mixed composition. In 1872 there were about seventy-five Europeans in Deli, most of whom were planters, representing many nationalities. The names given to the first plantations illustrate the heterogeneity of their owners: Riverside,

Karlsruhe, Helvetia, Perseverance, Polonia. Cremer retrospectively gave a clear example of the widespread origins of the pioneering community: 'Until 20 years ago it was common for seven people to dine together who represented eight nations: a Dutchman, a Prussian, a Bavarian, a Dane, an Englishman, a Pole, a naturalized Swiss, and a Norwegian' (Cremer 1890:676).

Plantations increased in number from thirteen in 1873 to twenty-three in 1874. By 1876 forty plantations were in business, and applications for another fifteen had just been granted or were pending permission (Gramberg 1881). According to that same source, 7,600 coolies were employed in 1876, averaging less than 200 per plantation.

The Deli Company maintained its position as a front runner. In 1873 its land covered an area of 26,000 bahu, divided among three plantations. It had a permanent labour force of 1525 coolies, 1,400 of whom were Chinese, and approximately 358 casual labourers (Bataks and Malays) (Veth 1877: 146–7). In 1870 the head office was moved to Medan and in the following year Nienhuys returned to the Netherlands. He appointed as his successor a man of twenty-four years whom he had met as a junior executive in the office of the Netherlands Trading Company in Singapore and who had made an excellent impression on him. Herbert Cremer indeed proved to be a true captain of industry and the Deli Company flourished greatly under his leadership. Cremer's talents were managerial rather than agricultural. He financed the annual operations of numerous private tobacco growers, who in return committed themselves to marketing their harvest through the company. This was the first step towards industrial concentration and the formation of cartels which was to determine the East Coast plantation economy towards the end of the nineteenth century. Under Cremer's management, production increased from 1315 bales of tobacco (1 bale = 158 kg) in 1870 to 22,000 in 1883; capital investment increased from 300,000 to two million guilders, and annual profits averaged 73 per cent (Fasseur 1979:122–5).

Tobacco is notorious for rapidly exhausting the soil, and to ensure the quality, for which Deli became world famous, the fields had to be left fallow for long periods. After the harvest, the land was given back to the local peasantry for one season to grow rice, and was then left untilled for eight to ten years. Each plantation thus needed a very large acreage, of which only a small portion would be used in any one year. This seems to have caused few problems as long as the rapidly growing demand could be met by grants of waste land. The lease stipulated that the fields cultivated by the indigenous population and communal property belonging to the *kampongs* were not included in the concessions (Veth 1877:160). As a result of the extensive cropping system, almost all land suitable for cultivation in the regions of Deli, Serdang and Langkat had been taken over by tobacco plantations only a few decades after the first settlement. This was largely due to the very easy conditions on which concessions were granted. At first these were for varying periods of up to ninety-nine years, free of any land rent. The Sultan of Deli was satisfied with the payment of import and export duties, sometimes supplemented with a levy on each coolie employed (Pelzer 1978:67; De Iongh 1982:544). Starting in 1878, on the insistence of the colonial authorities, a land rent (*hasil tanah*) was levied at a nominal rate of one guilder per bahu; at the same time leases were standardized at a seventy-five-year term, but without affecting any rights that had earlier been obtained. Subsequent concessions were based on the fiction that local rulers could dispose of the land of their subjects as they thought fit. The reactions of the Batak chiefs in the hinterland clearly showed that those rulers had over-played their hand. The Bataks were prepared to take up arms in protest against the continuous expansion of plantations in their region, for which they had neither given permission nor received compensation (Sinar 1978:186–7). Military expeditions were despatched to put an end to such 'native impertinence'. 'In later years it became clear . . . that the Sultan of Deli, relying on government support, wanted to exercise power in the Batak part of his state as he did in the Malayan part, but this was contrary to tradition and usage' (Schadee 1919:99).

In the 1870s and early in the following decade, the local peasants gave vent to their resentment of the new plantations by firing the sheds in which the tobacco leaves were hung up to dry, as an act of resistance to which they drew attention in advance by so-called fire letters (*moesimbringin*). The planters insisted that such rebelliousness was due to personal grievances and rapaciousness, and refused to believe that it could be caused by any political motivation. Finally, in 1881, it was found more effective to give the Batak chiefs a share of the lease money received each year by the sultans, than to send out military patrols again and again (Bool 1903b:94).

Yet this arrangement did not alter the principle that only a very few people were paid for the use of capital that was withdrawn from so many. Not until the beginning of the twentieth century did a very modest share of the land rent find its way into the regional treasury. Furthermore, by not only giving the lesser headmen a share of the compensation but by also making them responsible for any shed fires that occurred in their immediate neighbourhood, i.e. by recovering the cost of policing from them if the perpetrators were not caught, the destruction of plantation property could at last be brought to an end (Broersma 1919:159–60; Memorial DPV 1929:72–3). The attempt to convert the Bataks to Christianity was also a part of the policy to pacify the hinterland. It was with this in mind that in 1889 Cremer created a fund to enable the missionaries to open a number of schools, outside the plantations of course, through which to propagate the religion of the 'civilized' world— with little success at first.

Only European planters could apply for land grants. Even in the early years, Chinese traders were prepared to participate in the cultivation of market crops. One of the first colonial administrators reported:

Little by little, more Chinese are settling here. Businessmen are taking the risk of starting new enterprises. At only one or two hours distance from Deli there are now three planters, one of whom is engaged in growing tobacco and has already planted about 20,000 coconut palms while thousands more await planting. Another has leased a nutmeg garden in which there are two thousand trees bearing a heavy crop; this same entrepreneur has a plantation of 20,000 coconut palmtrees and also a nursery with 10,000 nutmeg plants waiting to be transplanted when they are the right size. A third businessman has also leased a nutmeg garden which, previously in a deplorable condition, is now beginning to yield plenty of fruit (Van Cats de Raet 1876:31).

The western planters, however, did not want competition from this quarter. The pressure they brought to bear on the authorities soon resulted in a prohibition on the cultivation of commercial crops by the Chinese. Henceforth, they could establish themselves only as greengrocers or as pig breeders (Bool 1903b:24).

The monopoly of land by plantations continued. As we have seen, rights to open new estates were granted on condition that the existing peasant swiddens and other customary rights of the local population were not affected. The Model Contract of 1878 obliged each planter to give four bahu to each inhabitant living within the boundaries of his estate for shifting cultivation (*ladang*). In daily usage an 'inhabitant' was taken to mean head of a household. As a government official was to state some years later, this amount of land was quite insufficient to meet the needs of a peasant family (Ibid.:12). The problem was never discussed, because it soon became the custom to hand over the harvested tobacco fields to those living in the area for one season in order to grow rice or corn. In return for this favour the peasants were frequently obliged to give the planter a tenth of their harvested crop or a fixed amount from each field, and sometimes even to sell the entire yield at a price fixed in advance by the planter (*Colonial Report* 1883:204; 1884:197). Increasingly, however, the planters grew less inclined to continue what had become standard practice, arguing that the planting of rice, even for only one season, retarded the recovery of the soil. During the early years of the plantation, they preferred to give the land to their own workers to grow food crops (Broersma 1919:116).

This was partly due to the planters' exasperation with the peasants, whom they 'considered a redundant and troublesome element, too lazy to work' (Bool 1903b:119). In 1884, to ensure that land should be accessible to the original claimants, the Resident decreed that, after harvesting, the plantations should put 1 to 1.5 bahu of tobacco land at the disposal of each local head of household for growing rice or corn. The peasants were only allowed to produce food grains, however, and were not given the chance to cultivate other than subsistence crops:

... the harvested tobacco land (*jaluran*) was used only for the growing of a single rice or corn crop. No second planting was permitted, above all no planting of such crops as cassava, bananas, or pepper. This meant that the agricultural system of the Karo Batak and of other inhabitants of agricultural concessions in East Sumatra was severely curtailed and the people deprived of any flexibility in the development of new crops, such as rubber or other export crops, in response to new market demands or other stimuli (Pelzer 1978:74).

No allowance at all was made for the fact that the people needed land for purposes other than agriculture. The right to gather the products of the forest and to cut wood, for example, was severely restricted in the course of time until it ultimately became a punishable offence (Memorial DPV 1929:88-9). I deduce from the above that the installation of new sultans was an important tool in creating the plantation system. Explicit recognition of the rights of the local rulers, rights that they had never before enjoyed to such a far-reaching degree, meant that a legitimate basis was found on which to curtail and ultimately to negate the rights of the people.

Labour Bondage

The legal fiction which assumed the transfer of powers from the local rulers to the planters was not concerned with natural resources only but also extended to alleged control over labour. As we have already seen, labour was a far more scarce commodity than land. The workers who came from elsewhere had to be bound to the work place by coercive means. To start with, this was done by paying them some earnest money at the time of recruitment. In exchange for the cash that the coolies received when they left their homes, and which was needed to pay off existing debts or to meet the needs of family members who were left behind, they committed themselves to continue to work on the plantations until their debt was discharged. As the Model Contract reproduced here shows, the term of employment was initially for one year. However, its extension was automatic if the employer still had a claim on his labourer after the harvest (Broersma 1919:72). Such servitude on the basis of debt, it was argued, far from creating a breach of existing practice, actually harmonized with customary law. 'Malay adat gives the planter the opportunity to ensure that his coolie meets his obligations; because he can punish them if they try to evade them' (Veth 1877:168).

Thus, a coolie who broke his service contract was in default. The planters' view was that, under the 1862 Treaty, all legal and police powers·remained under the purview of the Sultan of Deli, an interpretation that was tacitly endorsed by the colonial authorities. But instead of exercising his own judicial powers, which only applied in the event of serious offence and even then naturally only when committed by a non-European, the sultan implicitly transferred his authority to the planters. By means of this legal construct, the latter thus obtained complete control over the workforce. The planters arrogated to themselves the right to ensure that strict work discipline was complied with and to administer punishment to the coolies who did not meet their obligations. This was the contract into which, after all, they had entered voluntarily.

One argument used was that the low quality of the workers, commonly said to belong largely to 'the dregs of the Chinese nation' (Ibid.:161) and among whom discord was rife, resulting in frequent quarrels (Broersma 1919:78), made it necessary to enforce a rigid regime. Desertion to the hinterland or overseas to Malaya was a considerable threat to the industry from the very beginning, and had to be dealt with in a decisive manner. Desertion was said to be due, not to wretched treatment, but to the wasteful and wayward behaviour of the coolies.

The reasons for desertion are numerous: laziness, minor quarrels with fellow workers or foremen, gaming debts, the losing of small sums entrusted to a coolie to buy something for himself and his mates in one of the gambling dens along his route; the longing to evade his financial commitments and to seek work elsewhere, etc., etc. (Cremer 1876:17).

It was suggested that the planters, partly out of self-interest, punished more justly than did the sultan and that they did so in accordance with the customs and preferences of the Chinese themselves (Broersma 1919:80). According to this view, paternalistic authority governed relations on the estates, to the benefit of all parties.

The colonial authorities apparently held a different opinion and tried to halt the unbridled autonomy of the planters by expanding the government apparatus. In 1873 Deli, falling provisionally under the Siak Residency, was given an Assistant Resident, who was posted first to Labuan and in 1879 to Medan. Among other things he was charged with the administration of justice over aliens—mainly the Chinese coolies—whom the government now defined explicitly as its subjects. At the same time, the local rulers transferred their right to collect taxes, to the Dutch authorities, in return for an annual allowance. The amounts involved were quite considerable. The Sultan of Deli alone received 85,000 guilders per annum and his vassals together received almost half that sum. The native rulers of the other states in the region had to make do with less, but even their compensation was princely compared to the salaries paid to the Assistant Resident and the District Officers in the region (Cremer 1881:36). Complaints made by the British authorities in 1870 to the Governor-General in Batavia regarding the unjust treatment of plantation workers shipped from Malaya, and the severe sentences meted out by the Sultan of Deli in 1871 after the murderous attacks on two planters, compelled greater official intervention. Legislation dealing with indigenous labour had already been introduced much earlier in Java. Under a bye-law passed in 1829, house servants in Surabaya could be prosecuted if they left their master without his permission. This regulation gradually came to apply to all workers who were contracted to European employers, but it is not clear whether it was implemented on any large scale. The cultivation system which, from 1830 onwards, marshalled the rural population of Java, through their village headmen, to perform corvee labour on a collective basis, meant that it was not necessary to force them to work individually. Once the heyday of the cultivation system was over, however, the need for such a regulation apparently came to be felt because in 1851 the order that had previously applied only to Surabaya was declared applicable to all of Java. Protests against this measure were voiced by the spokesmen of the new liberal doctrine who were of the opinion that government should desist from intervening in the economy and from any involvement in relations between employers and employees. Such a drastic reform was more than what the industrialists in Java were willing to accept. In 1872 a new bye-law was enacted for the archipelago as a whole under which workers could be penalized if they broke their contract without giving proper notice or if they refused to work (Coolie 1918:361). However vaguely worded and arbitrary, the introduction into the East Coast of this regulation and the sanctions that applied to any breach of its provisions, was not found sufficiently drastic by the planters who worked there. What they wanted above all was a clause to the effect that a transgressor would be obliged to return to his employer after punishment in order to work out his period of contract. The government dismissed the petition in which the planters spelt out their objections. Local relations between the authorities and the planters can be judged by the fact that the Assistant Resident said that he shared the planters' views and unofficially supported their recommendations (Veth 1877:168-9). In actual practice little changed, since the increase in personnel necessary to put the new instruction into effect was not forthcoming. The government apparatus on the East Coast, an area roughly thrice that of the Netherlands or, perhaps more significantly, five-sevenths that of Java, was then extremely small, consisting merely of an Assistant Resident and a few junior officers (*controleurs*). Deli's entire police force included one *mandur* and twelve constables; the neighbouring regions of Langkat and Serdang, still in the early stages of clearance, had no police at all. According to the planters, the safety and discipline which had been assured under the sultan's rule, had deteriorated into growing lawlessness. Desertion among the workers was large scale, signifying not only a financial loss, i.e. the loss of a labourer and of the money that he owed, but also a threat to law and order on the plantations.

At that time, coolies who could not legally be held against their will formed gangs of twenty to forty men which prowled through the region, where roads were almost non-existent (Memorial DBM 1925:70-1; Memorandum Tobacco Cultivation 1883:196). Runaway labourers occasionally teamed up with dissatisfied elements among the Bataks in order to raid the plantations, and the coolies who worked there were then likely to join in, out of revenge for the cruelty to which they were exposed. Military action was needed to put an end to the looting, arson and murders committed by the coolie gangs (*Colonial Report* 1877:19; *Historical Survey* 1897:14). Naturally enough, the planters had a different explanation of such outrages:

When a Chinese workman who 'is taken on on piece-work', as we call it, has not earned as much as he thinks suitable, perhaps as a result of unfavourable weather which naturally affects the plantation itself to a much more serious degree, then he does not complain to Buddha or to the dragons but to the company's manager who contracted him (the workman). Knowing quite well that he has nothing more to claim than is paid to him, he nevertheless grumbles and sulks because he is not getting more. In such cases, in fact, a voluntary compensation is frequently given, but if the amount is less than what he had hoped for, then the sheds and other buildings and everything inflammable are sometimes in danger (Memorial DBM 1925:24).

The rising middle class of Chinese traders, plantation shop-keepers, proprietors of gaming houses and opium dens, also fell victim to the looting coolies who had deserted or had been sacked. Attempts to check such activities by prohibitions on 'vagrancy', by erecting guardhouses and by patrolling the area, had little success. According to the planters, the lack of effective official protection left them with no choice but to take things into their own hands. A means for doing so was found in the regulation that any resident might detain and arrest anyone guilty of a misdemeanour or crime, if he was caught in the act. What 'caught in the act' actually meant, and on what terms the miscreant was to be brought before the magistrate in the nearest town, were left undefined. The latitude thus left to the planters made it possible for them to exercise their own authority with impunity.

Is it any wonder that the planters more and more often decided not to ask the authorities for punishment of the offences or crimes, and gave preference to punishing the coolies themselves? Many found this the only possible way in which to keep order on their plantation and to pursue their business. It became so common and was thought so natural that it was no longer found objectionable. The officials knew what was going on, but they were too few in number and so overloaded with other work that they had no time to visit the estates in person to check the conditions prevailing there (Schadee 1919:15).

Scandals occurred that were impossible to cover up. According to a press report in 1913 Nienhuys, reputedly the first planter and founding father of the famous Deli Company, had to leave the East Coast with undue haste. He was forced to do so not for reasons of health, which was the story told to outsiders, but in order to escape prosecution because of a crime he had committed; which was the flogging of seven coolies to death. This remarkable story does not, of course, appear in the company's historiography! The Deli Company asked for a fresh investigation into this affair in 1875 in a clear attempt to erase the stain on its entrepreneurial record, but the official to whom this delicate task was entrusted did not succeed in repudiating the accusation. He concluded that no evidence had been found to contradict the story as it had been told (*Sumatra Post*, 14 May 1913). Needless to say, this damaging statement is also missing from the colonial literature on the plantations of Sumatra. In 1876 a member of the judiciary in Batavia, accompanied by a Chinese interpreter, was sent to Deli to investigate the complaints about the maltreatment of coolies by a number of planters (cf. *Colonial Report* 1877). Deli then had the reputation of being a sort of 'Wild West' (Volker 1928:21). It was said in defence that these were unavoidable excesses, incidents that were bound to happen because the government was not properly equipped for maintaining order in this frontier society. And if the planters took the law into their own hands, was not that in the interest of the coolies themselves? According to one source, the lack of even the most elementary care at the time ensured that at least one-third of those who were imprisoned for longer than three months never came out alive (Memorial DBM 1925:69). Instead of locking them up in prison, where they died like rats, chastisement on the plantation itself meant that a pack of disorderly and low-grade coolies could be disciplined into honest and skilled workers.

Planter Hegemony

The planters' origins remained diverse. In 1884 the European population on the East Coast included 390 Dutchmen, 88 Britons, 123 Germans, 40 Swiss, 12 French, 11 Austrians, and 24 people representing seven other nationalities. Perhaps it was this heterogeneity which contributed to the promotion of common interests. The submission of a joint petition in 1873 in connection with the transfer of judicial powers to the colonial government was the beginning of a more orchestrated action in later years. The planters refused to resign themselves to losing the total control that they had exercised over their workers under the sultan's rule. As a labour immigration region the East Coast deserved special treatment; so said Cremer at a meeting of planters held in Medan in 1875, on his initiative. Specific demands were made for more severe punishment of coolies who refused to work or who ran away. Fines were to be imposed on planters who enticed coolies away from other plantations. During the meeting 10,000 guilders were collected, paid proportionately by the largest plantations, as remuneration for a lawyer who would lobby on their behalf in Batavia and if necessary in the Netherlands also (Memorial DPV 1929:5–6). This amount enabled them to obtain the services and influence of L.W.C. Keuchenius and they could not have wished for anyone better. Keuchenius had been the Vice-Chairman of the Supreme Council of the Netherlands Indies and a judge at the Supreme Court. Of equal importance were his political links in the mother country where, in 1866, he had been a member of the Anti-Revolutionary Party (ARP) in the Lower House. At that moment a well-oiled lobby was most opportune since the Parliament was considering a motion to repeal the Workmen's Breach of Contract Act (Algemeen Politiestrafreglement voor Inlanders). This was due to the fact that employers in Java had made such 'ignoble use' of this instruction, which had been introduced there in 1872 (but which the Deli planters had considered quite inadequate for effective control over their coolies!) that its abolition was thought necessary in order that justice might be done to the principle of free labour (Bartelds 1894:8). The adjournment of this proposal in the Lower House, allowing the colonial authorities to react to questions raised, enabled the planters to draw up a new petition. Cremer himself presented this to the Governor-General and explained its contents, adding a copy of the Coolie Ordinance that was operative in the Straits Settlement. Attention was also drawn to similar measures that had been taken earlier in British India (*De Indische Gids* 1879,I:515–16). Deli's Assistant Resident joined in the chorus, writing a memorandum in which he advocated special penal sanctions against deserting coolies. Articles of similar tenor appeared in the colonial press, and public opinion was also worked upon in the mother country. In 1876 Cremer addressed the Dutch Members of Parliament in a pamphlet, 'A Word from Deli to the Lower House of the States General', in which he warned that the enactment of the motion would ruin the flourishing plantation industry on Sumatra's East Coast. In 1879 the Parliament scrapped the clause which had forced the native worker to continue his employment unreservedly. In Java, it was argued, the employers had other and more effective means than penalization at their disposal, such as the compulsory mobilization of labour through the village headmen, to assure themselves of an adequate workforce. However, the very efficient and modern method of lobbying by the planters, who demanded special provisions for the East Coast estates, was not without effect. The government made it known that the legal relationship between employers and workers who were imported from other countries would be framed in a special statute. The example provided by the British colonial administration in neighbouring Malaya was to be followed.

The common front presented by the planters was not intended only to bring pressure on the government. United action also enabled them to safeguard tobacco cultivation and marketing against undesirable competition by non-Europeans. The planters agreed not to buy tobacco from the Chinese or from native growers, a decision that they rationalized with the argument that it would be impossible to check whether the Asians had really grown the crop themselves or whether it had been stolen (Broersma 1919:125). Moreover, the reputation of Deli tobacco would suffer if an inferior product was marketed (Memorial DPV 1929:9). In 1877, what had originally been merely an informal agreement was laid down in an accord that was binding for all planters. In other words, it was attempted to turn the growing of tobacco, originally a peasant crop, into the exclusive monopoly of the European plantation industry. In 1872 there were fifteen plantations operating in Sumatra; by the end of 1875 these had increased to twenty, providing employment for 4476 Chinese, 459 Klings and 316 Javanese (*Sumatra Post*, 5 May 1913). By 1880 all land on the East Coast that was considered suitable for growing good quality tobacco was in the hands of the European planters (Broersma 1919:98). Efforts by prominent Chinese to gain a share in this profitable agri-business were resolutely blocked, and applications for land grants made by non-Europeans were not even eligible for administrative consideration.

An agreement under which the *pangeran* of Langkat had granted land for development to the Lieutenant-Chinese there, was not ratified by the Resident because the Government of the Netherlands Indies did not consider it advisable for the time being to admit Chinese as agricultural entrepreneurs to the East Coast of Sumatra where there were no means by which to exercise proper supervision over their activities (*Colonial Report* 1879:203,n.1).

Even more important was the regulation of labour relations by the planters. While trying to bring in workers from Malaya they encountered opposition by the owners of tin-mines and planta- tions, who disapproved of their Chinese coolies leaving for Suma tra. In addition, Deli had always been notorious for poor working conditions, partly because of the payment of piece-work rates rather than a daily wage, as was the custom in Malaya. The only way by which East Coast planters could hope to keep up a constant flow of workers was to act collectively and to disprove the basis of objections made by the British.

A minimum of co-operation among the planters was also necessary to prevent the recruiting agents in Penang and Singapore from demanding an ever-increasing commission on each coolie supplied. The opening-up of new plantations and the increased capacity of the older ones caused an acute labour shortage, from which the coolie brokers naturally profited. It had also become clear that the desertion by coolies could only be stopped by concerted action. An important step in this direction was the prohibition on employing a coolie who was already under contract in another plantation. Employers avoided asking too many questions about the origins of a coolie who came to a plantation voluntarily or through the mediation of a foreman. Although the sources have little to say on this matter, the pilfering of coolies from other planters was a frequent occurrence, and it was on this point in particular that 'self-regulation' left a lot to be desired. Combatting the *shanghai-ing* of coolies was of vital importance for the further expansion of plantation agriculture. As a result the government had already been asked in the 1873 petition to impose a penalty on such practices. 'Crimps scoured the country, inciting workers to desert, and then earned a large commission by offering them to other planters as contract coolies' (Report DM 1894:12).

The planters entered into agreements which aimed at checking competition by enforcing uniformity in the working conditions on the plantations. For example, the cash advance paid on renewal of a contract was now not to exceed a certain maximum; piece-work rates were reduced (back even to the level established by Nienhuys); the planters committed themselves to registering their coolies by name; the labour contract could now only be terminated if a standard letter of dismissal was issued; and finally, short shrift was given to the growing practice of employing non-contracted (i.e. free) coolies.

The formation of the DPV in 1879 was a logical step in view of the necessity to regulate and implement these measures. The direct reason, and the most important, for establishing this employers' union was the labour issue. It was illustrative of the international character of the East Coast milieu that the minutes of the DPV's first meeting had to be recorded both in English and in Dutch. The owners or managers of twenty-two companies, including the largest ones, authorized, with their signatures, the decisions taken at the meeting. The outcome was immediately endorsed by the representatives of twenty-four plantations who had not been present, and a short while later another twenty-three, mostly smaller estates, also joined the Association (Memorial DPV 1929:21-2). Management was entrusted to a triumvirate, the Planters Committee, chaired for a number of years by Cremer.

It is interesting to note the stand taken in the inaugural meeting. It was agreed that publicity was prejudicial to the industry, and that members would be well advised to seek the opinion of the Planters Committee before publishing anything they wrote in newspapers or magazines (Ibid.:18). The anxiety that negative publicity could give outsiders an unfavourable opinion of plantation society was probably caused by the recurrent outbursts of labour protest on the East Coast. In 1878 the coolies working on one or two plantations had rebelled against their wretched working conditions. A case of maltreatment on a plantation in 1879 had also caused a stir:

A coolie was tied to a tree and left there for a few days with nothing to eat or drink, as a result of which he fell ill and died. The manager and one of the assistants were prosecuted: the former was acquitted because of lack of evidence, the assistant was sentenced to two years imprisonment, but he absconded (Broersma 1919:95).

In the official version at least, such cases were very exceptional. In the Parliament, the Minister of Colonies stated reassuringly that conditions on the plantations left very little to be desired. Nevertheless, police action was necessary, and repeatedly so, in order to put an end to labour agitation. Official pacification sometimes resulted in the killing of coolies (*Colonial Report* 1890:12).

The Colonial State and the Labour System

The DPV kept a close watch on the planters and fined any member caught infringing the decisions taken by the Association. A major objective of this was to prevent the desertion of coolies. Cash advances were reduced towards this end. The idea of entering another contract was no longer attractive. Pressure was brought to bear on the authorities for the strict application of penalties on 'vagabondage'. Finally, the Planters Committee concluded an agreement with the Chinese headmen for the employment of *mataglaps*, a body of guards, who would inspect incoming and outgoing migrants on the ships in harbours along the East Coast. The Committee's principal concern, however, was to pressurize the government to regulate the coolie question, in a manner that accorded with the wishes of the planters.

An eminent lawyer summoned to Deli by the planters in 1876 had, with the help of Cremer, drawn up a draft ordinance. This was based on the principle that a stable labour force could only be ensured by punishing any coolie who unilaterally breached his contract. Its design was modelled on a similar regulation that had already been in force for some time in Malaya. The Netherlands Parliament proved susceptible to Cremer's very simple reasoning: 'The only thing a worker owns is his labour power; on his side it represents his collateral. If that is lost then nothing is left, and Government therefore has no alternative but to confiscate it if the worker's proper fulfilment of the contract is to be guaranteed to some extent' (Cremer 1876:11–12).

The call for state intervention in the labour system, in other words to legalize the coercive methods already in use, actually conflicted with current colonial ideology which postulated maximum economic liberty. In 1864 Van Rees, later to become the Governor-General, had suggested that the provisions of the Civil Code should be declared applicable to labour contracts. Similarly, Fransen van de Putte, Minister of Colonies from 1872 to 1874, repeatedly showed himself to be averse to any administrative, let alone police interference in the matter. Even the lawyer Keuchenius, whom the planters had called upon in 1875 to advance their interests, had earlier argued, as member of the Council of the Netherlands East Indies, for complete freedom of private contracts (Coolie 1918:361). When Keuchenius left for the Netherlands in 1875 he undertook to continue to promote the interests of the planters in the Lower House, as a member of the Anti-Revolutionary Party in 1879 (Memorial DPV 1929:25). His appointment as the Minister of Colonies (1888-90) provided him with an even better opportunity to try to further the case of agri-business.

The government proved susceptible to the argument that the situation on the East Coast was exceptional. In view of the great interests that were at stake, i.e. the continued existence of the plantations, it did not seem unreasonable to deviate from the generally accepted principles, and protect the employer by threatening the defaulting workers with severe punishment. This was presented in a manner which placed the emphasis on reciprocity: 'to protect workers against bad masters and the employers against wrongdoing by the workers' (Bool 1904:9). The first had to be given some semblance of genuineness in order to convince the British administration in Malaya that the Netherlands Indies authorities stood guarantee for proper treatment of workers, the greater majority of whom came from the Straits Settlements. It was also hoped that the British would allow the import of labour from India. Moreover, the Netherlands Parliament was inclined to be far more critical than were the colonial authorities in Batavia: the coolie scandals had damaged Deli's reputation. The government's draft, prepared in 1877, was submitted to the planters for their advice, which they gave early in 1878. It was a matter of urgency because a regulation was to come into force, the same year, according to which a worker could be punished only if he refused to work after taking a cash advance: a form of fraud which was almost impossible to prove (Van Hamel 1881). There was some delay because the authorities of the Netherlands Indies, on the instigation of the Deli lobby, continued to insist that penal sanctions were essential. Had not the recent riots provided convincing proof that, in the interest of law and order, the coolies had to be placed under severe discipline? Minister Van Rees objected in vain that penal sanctions were unduly biased in favour of the employers. A majority in Parliament, however, succumbed to the pressure that was brought to bear and the Coolie Ordinance was promulgated in 1880. The main clauses were:

that no labourer-employer relationship could exist without a written contract;

that the contract, specifying the name, nature of the work and method of payment based on a ten-hour working day and for a maximum period of three years, should be registered immediately after the coolie's arrival by the local administration. The official in charge had to verify whether the contract was entered into voluntarily;

that the coolie must faithfully carry out the work assigned to him and might not leave the plantation without written permission; conversely, the employer must issue a leave-pass if the coolie intended to complain to the authorities about maltreatment, but only if he did so as an individual;

that the worker was entitled to decent treatment (a regular wage, accommodation, washing and drinking water, and medical care);

that, after termination of the contract, the coolie was to be returned to the place of recruitment, if he so wished.

The coolie was subject to penalization if he ran away or refused to work diligently. However, rebelliousness; insults or threats to his employer or foreman, disturbance of peace, inciting others to desertion or disobedience, fights, drunkenness and similar misdemeanours all counted as violations even though they were not really a breach of contract.

The government considered that order on the plantations could only be maintained by stern measures. It consequently yielded to the wishes of Cremer who spoke on behalf of the planters, that the penal sanctions should be more stringently worded (*Historical Survey* 1897:56-7). The Ordinance only touched indirectly on possible infringements by the employer. To incite a coolie to terminate his contract was punishable, and this was taken to be the case if a deserter was given shelter. But even this 'anti-kidnapping' clause seemed to be oriented more against the agents of other plantations, e.g. a foreman or another worker, than against the employer. In practice, therefore, only the coolies had to run the gauntlet of the penal sanctions. The administration of justice, i.e. the investigation of complaints and passing appropriate sentences, was initially entrusted to the Resident and subsequently to the *controleurs* based in the district towns. Sentences included forced labour on public works (*krakal*) for periods of twelve days, three months or a year, depending on the severity of the misdemeanour. As in the case of illness lasting more than a month, and unlawful absence, the time taken to serve out the sentence was added to the contracted period still to be worked out. In other words, the time that was thus lost had to be made good after the termination date. These conditions were broadly similar to those suggested by the planters in their 1876 petition. The only request that was not granted was the right of the planters to punish minor offences themselves. At first, the provision that coolies should be returned to the plantation by the police if they were captured after desertion or on release from prison, was omitted. In practice, however, and in close co-operation with the regional authorities, it was possible to fill this lacuna.

In the event of desertion it could always be maintained that the coolie had been caught in the act, in which case he might legally be arrested by the plantation's staff. Coolies who had served a prison sentence were escorted back to the plantations by orderlies who were taken on especially for guard and security duties (Schadee 1919:40–1).

Finally, a contract period of three years was in excess of what had been customary before the Ordinance came into force. In the early years, coolies who came to Sumatra from Malaya were indentured for one year only, and no explanation was given as to why a much longer period was now found to be reasonable or necessary. It was only much later that planters argued that a coolie cost more than he produced until long after the first year. It was not before the third year, when he had become a skilled worker, that he was able to repay his debt and, according to this deceptive line of reasoning, gave his employer a useful return on his outlay.

To be able both to recoup the advances and recruitment costs from the contracted labourer and to obtain the profit yielded to an estate by the initially unskilled workman after he had been trained, it was necessary that the work contract should cover a long enough period. The performance of a Chinese coolie—and he was the first to come to the planter's mind—only became of real value for employment in the second year after he came to Deli, and his capabilities reached their full scope in the third year of his stay (Hoetink 1902:24–5, in GSA Vb, 29 April 1903, no. 39).

The Coolie Ordinance was designed especially for the East Coast but was gradually introduced into various other parts of the colony outside Java (Endt 1919:99–100). It was argued that the development of mining and estate agriculture depended on the availability of an abundant workforce. According to this line of thinking, the lack of a local supply of voluntary workers necessitated the importation of indentured labour from outside. There was thus a very clear relationship between further development of the capitalist mode of production and labour coercion that was exercised in capitalist enclaves (Breman 1985). The Coolie Ordinance was initially designed to be an intermediate device. The government guaranteed that the regulation would be repealed as soon as possible to make way for what ranked as the normal situation: free labour. Later, however, the colonial authorities were to back away from this stated objective. In 1896 a general Coolie Ordinance was in preparation, intended for implementation in all the Outer Provinces of the Netherlands East Indies. It was now argued that, regardless of the nature of the industry, a penal sanction could not be avoided wherever imported labour was used (Bool 1904:14). Having been accepted under extraordinary conditions, this work regime had become an indispensable element with which to secure labour in a situation of scarcity, even when the state itself was the employer. Even in Java, the authorities started to rely on penalty clauses in order to control the workforce brought together for the new irrigation works in the Solo Valley and the construction of the harbour of Tanjung Priok. This was done on the pretext of public interest (Bartelds 1894:12). In West Sumatra, the Coolie Ordinance was applied in the laying of railways and in the working of the state coal-mines.

State intervention in industrial relations won the emphatic approval of Van Hamel who had earlier recommended the introduction of the Coolie Ordinance into Sumatra's East Coast (Van Hamel 1881). This eminent jurist was a staunch advocate of the effects of the Ordinance, and the planters were grateful for his support. In a lecture given to the Netherlands Indies Association in 1892 in The Hague, Van Hamel stated that the Coolie Ordinance had been a complete success, both in theory and in practice. He extolled the measure as a model of labour legislation in that the rights and duties of the parties involved complemented each other outstandingly and kept one another in equilibrium. Why, he wondered, had not the Coolie Ordinance become a leading principle of labour relations in Java as well? (Van Hamel 1892:82). Impressed by this recommendation, the Minister of Colonies asked the authorities of the Indies to consider the suggestion. In 1894, however, the idea was rejected, notwithstanding the support given to it by the sugar manufacturers in regions which suffered from a shortage of labour. The majority of planters in Java, however, did not think it would be of any practical benefit. Some had more fundamental objections which accorded with the spirit of the times: 'Each intervention by the state is a step down a slippery slope which will end with complete government regulation of labour, and will take us back to the conditions pertaining at the beginning of the Cultivation System' (Bartelds 1894:24).

It is important to note that doubts were voiced immediately after the Ordinance was introduced about the need for coercion in compelling the fulfilment of labour contracts. In the opinion of the Assistant Resident of Billiton, it was not really necessary to subject the Chinese coolies, working in the tin-mines on this island off Sumatra's East Coast, to such penal sanctions (Proceedings Lower House 1876–7, App.B:4.47). Similar reservations were uttered when it was introduced in other Outer Provinces (Bartelds 1894:14). To my knowledge, the expediency of the Coolie Ordinance as regards the East Coast was never discussed during its early years. The colonial literature always connects the Ordinance with this region as a special case. Among the reasons for its introduction, mention is invariably made of the need to guarantee industrial stability and to ensure that coolies repaid the cash advances given to them with their labour, as well as the need to maintain a tight discipline in a frontier region. Lastly, an added reason for the introduction of the Ordinance was the lack of any other means for breaking-in Asian workers to steady labour (Hoetink 1902:24). At the end of 1882 it was noted with satisfaction that the introduction of the Ordinance had proved to be very effective: 'No-one wants any change worthy of the name to be made; industry in Deli is progressing with great strides, and the treatment and quality of the workers are improving daily' (*Historical Survey* 1897:71).

When its implementation nevertheless showed a number of lacunae, amendments had to be made. The terms of the regulation also needed to be adapted continually to changing circumstances. A fundamental modification, introduced at the first revision in 1889, was the clause permitting migrants from other islands in the archipelago to be employed as free labour. After that, the Coolie Ordinance applied only to labourers imported from abroad, i.e. the Chinese. The planters refused to use this opportunity to introduce a free labour system, however, and continued to employ almost solely, coolies who were indentured by means of a contract with penal sanctions. Remarkably enough, the tea planters of India reacted in exactly the same way when the colonial authorities there made similar efforts to relax the coercion that was brought to bear on the workers (Guha 1977:17).

A number of other amendments introduced in 1889 were intended to ensure better treatment of the workers: the numerous

extra chores that were assigned to them were not to exceed beyond
ten hours; the employer was obligated to pay wages regularly; if a
coolie was accompanied by his family, he was not to be parted from
it against his will; the employer was not to charge for housing and
medication, or to make any other wage deductions than had been
agreed in writing; on his days off the coolie no longer needed a
leave pass, but he had to carry an identity card at all times. Finally,
the worker was allowed to leave the plantation to lodge a complaint about maltreatment with the authorities, without first
having to ask his employer for explicit permission to do so and,
more importantly, receive that permission. In fact, however, such
a protest could only be made if it concerned a personal grievance
and even that was really going too far for the employers:

The stipulation that the worker has the right to leave the estate when going
to bring a charge of maltreatment against his employer or against the
latter's staff, renders the plantation vulnerable to a sudden strike. Just one
troublemaker needs to delude his comrades into thinking that they are
badly treated or are in some way deprived of their rights, and the whole
pack of coolies will strike half-way through the season or in the middle of
the harvest, in order to go traipsing off to the government official who lives
some days' march away (Bartelds 1894:19).

In 1886, meanwhile, Resident Scherer of the East Coast had
drawn the attention of the authorities to abuses that were common
during recruitment in Java. Investigation made it clear that, in
addition to the men, women were increasingly being indentured
on the basis of promises that they would have only light work to
do, such as they were accustomed to in Java. Other supplements
to the rules made in 1889 under Minister Keuchenius, who continued to serve the interests of the planters, were that 'excessive
laziness' and 'wilful disobedience' on the part of the worker were
punishable offences. In 1891 an additional obligation was imposed
on the contract labourer to serve extra time if he had not worked
his full quota due to desertion and imprisonment. The employer
was also empowered to recoup from a coolie's wage all expenses
incurred in apprehending him or her, after desertion. In 1897,
finally, came an article covering the compulsory return of the coolie
to the plantation after serving a prison sentence. Plantation
production continued to be based on indentured labour, and

employers continued to reject any other form of employment that conflicted with it. They could count on the support of the colonial state in this matter and, in fact, authorities at higher levels declared themselves to be in agreement with the proposal made by the Resident in 1890 that the Coolie Ordinance should be declared at least partially applicable to non-contract workers (Bool 1904:13). This implied the legitimization of measures that local officials had earlier enacted against ex-contract coolies who hired themselves as free labourers for temporary work on the estates without cash advances. In countering new developments in this way, the colonial state made it clear that, under pressure from the planters, it was operating the Coolie Ordinance not in any passive sense while awaiting transition to a system of free labour relations, but in an active sense by blocking any tendency in that direction.

Expansion

Retrospectively, it is easy to think that when a number of pioneers took the initiative to cultivate what was almost virgin territory, success was inevitable. Accordingly, planters seemed to be captains of industry who could go ahead and set to work with energy and dash, knew what they were about, and continually improved and expanded their estates with the aid of modern production techniques and accurate planning. But this would be a gross over-simplification of conditions which prevailed without taking into account the uncertainty and the consequent speculative nature of western enterprise. that characterized the initial phase of the development of the East Coast. During the first few years, tobacco growing was nothing more than a form of predatory cultivation. Due to the exhaustive effect that the crop was said to have, the planters assumed that it would never be possible to plant twice on the same land. At that stage, and partly because experiments with perennial crops proved unsatisfactory, they could do nothing other than abandon the land after harvest. With this in mind, it was only natural that roads and other facilities were restricted to the bare minimum. Vegetation was slow in returning to the spent fields and Deli's landscape gradually changed into an enormous area of *alang alang* (a tall plumed grass) with occasional oases of tobacco fields (Van Sandick 1892:91). This changed in the mid-1880s when a solution to the cropping problem was found. The use of fertilizers, combined with letting the land to lie fallow for long periods, put tobacco cultivation on a firm footing (De Waard 1934:218). The plantations also increasingly took up reforestation as a means of improving the fertility of the soil. They were encouraged to do so by none other than Cremer: 'If care is given to forestation, I would dare to say that Deli could almost continually produce good tobacco; but not otherwise. Only woodland can give the soil the *loessial humus* that is necessary for fine tobacco' (Cremer 1888:537).

This could only be done by denying the peasants access to land after harvest. Although the plantations were unable to keep their acreage entirely free of 'that stupid messing-about with paddy by the natives' (Haarsma 1889:63-4), the importance of reforestation ultimately became the deciding factor (*De Indische Mercuur* 1889,12:24,26,31; Bool 1903b:128). This necessitated such an extensive use of land that plantation production took on the character of shifting cultivation, a technique which the indigenous peasants used in growing their food crops. Only a small proportion of a plantation's acreage was actually used each year. In spite of the low population density, Deli's natural resources became very scarce in the early 1890s as a result of the enormous demands on land made by the plantations at the expense of the local peasantry. It was many years before it was realized that this extensive use of land might not be in the best interest of soil fertility and that continuous cultivation might be preferable (Van Bijlert 1913:554–5).

The consolidation of estate agriculture gave an important stimulus to the infrastructural development of the region, and communications with the outside world gradually improved. Trading had at first been oriented solely towards the other coast of the Malacca Strait. In Nienhuys's time freight was carried by small *dhows*, the trip lasted about two weeks, and accommodation allotted to the passenger was 'a man's length in the round' (Broersma 1919:31). In 1873 the first Dutch shipping line started on the East Coast, but tobacco destined for the European market continued to be shipped via Penang. Roads were scarce at first, and the earliest plantations were laid out along the rivers so that their produce might be transported by boat. The authorities continued to pay scant attention to road building, and the planters had no choice but to bear a great deal of the expense themselves. To their unqualified delight, Governor-General Van Rees's carriage became bogged-down in heavy rain on the road from Medan to the harbour of Labuan in 1884. This newly-appointed highest representative of

colonial authority, who visited Deli on his way from the Netherlands to Batavia, was forced to wade through mud that came up to
his knees! Cremer then took the initiative for setting-up the Deli
Railway Company, of which he became the director, one of his
many assignments, after being repatriated in 1883. It did not take
much time to build a regional network once the opening of the first
line in 1886 was accomplished. Telegraph and telephone services
were established at about the same time.

The standard of public facilities in the region also improved.
Medan acquired its own post-office in 1883. In that same year Siak
renounced its claims to former dependencies along the East Coast
and the sultanate sank into oblivion. In 1887 Medan was made the
capital of the new East Coast Residency, which covered an area of
90,000 square kilometers. When the Sultan of Deli moved to Medan
and had a spacious palace built to underline his new dignity and
wealth, the town also became the seat of indigenous administration. The Deli region, which included Serdang and Langkat, was
divided into a number of districts, each headed by a *controleur*, to
whom a magistrate's power was also delegated in 1887. In the early
1880s there were at least sixty shops in Medan, most of which were
owned by the Chinese (Memorandum Tobacco Cultivation
1883:202). The first Deli newspaper rolled from the presses in 1885.
Some of the larger plantations opened their own hospitals: in fact,
the Deli Company had brought out a Dutch doctor as early as 1871.
The Chartered Bank opened a branch in Medan in 1888, to be
followed rather tardily in 1892 by the Nederlandsche Handelmaatschappij (Netherlands Trading Company, NHM). Penang lost
some of its significance as a financial centre, but as yet there was
no question of re-routing money transactions made to the Straits
Settlements. The main currency was the Spanish *mat*, then the
Mexican dollar, and finally the Straits dollar, despite import and
export duties being levied in Dutch currency. It was not until 1908
that the East Indies guilder replaced the dollar (Volker 1928:91;
Memorial DBM 1925:47–50).

The expansion of the government machinery had difficulty in
keeping up with the economic development of the region. Notwithstanding the gradually increasing numbers of officials and
police, the regional authorities were insufficiently equipped to
cope with the quantity and variety of the tasks assigned to them.
The imbalance was not merely a matter of numbers, a dispropor-

tion between private managers and public officials. It was of far greater significance that the latter had not preceded the former to Deli, as had been the case in Java, but had been obliged to establish their authority, as it were, in the shadow of the planters. From the beginning this gave rise to an entirely different social relationship than that which had traditionally existed in large areas of Java. What such a plantocracy signified can be illustrated with the help of a few examples. Some time in the 1870s, when heavy rainfall hindered the departure of the General Manager of a major company because the muddy road was impassable for carriages, the Assistant Resident gave him the use of fifty coolies undergoing hard labour who, working in shifts, carried the manager's wife to the harbour in a litter (*Sumatra Post*, 5 May 1913). It would be an exaggeration to posit that civil servants behaved as though they were servants of the planters; nevertheless, the hegemony of the former over the latter, which characterized the situation in Java, the oldest and most important area of Dutch colonial power, was entirely lacking in Sumatra's East Coast.

To guarantee effective control over compliance with the Coolie Ordinance, the authorities initially suggested that officials should pay weekly visits to the plantations in order to enable the coolies, who could not leave the estates without a written permission from their employers, to submit complaints to the government. Indeed, the Resident assigned this task to his junior officers, but shortly afterwards was forced to admit that nothing had come of the weekly inspection tours and that supervision over the plantations left a great deal to be desired (Bool 1904:11). Chinese immigrant workers had the reputation of being troublesome and in 1880 an interpreter in the Chinese language was posted in Medan in order to obtain more information on what was happening among them. This was B. Hoetink, whom we shall meet frequently in subsequent chapters. However, he had neither the brief nor the qualifications of the Protector of Chinese appointed in 1877 in Penang and Singapore after a British investigatory committee in the Straits Settlements had ascertained that gross abuses occurred in coolie recruitment for Sumatra (Cremer 1882:13; Reid 1970:296-7). The planters on the East Coast continued to hold the upper hand, and even more than that: the administration gratefully accepted their help in the collection of taxes, for instance. The employers paid one guilder for the official registration of each contract coolie, which they recovered from the coolie's wage. Initially, it was proposed that this money should be given to the officials in recognition of their extra work (*Historical Survey* 1897:49). Acceptance of this proposal would have been an excellent demonstration of the close alliance between the government and the industry. But that was not all. The establishment tax which had to be paid by Alien Orientals, and which an iron colonial logic also caused to be levied on the coolies, was advanced by the plantations and subsequently also deducted from their wages.

Small wonder that the planters behaved as though the local administration existed to enable them to run their estates without hindrance. They readily assumed that officials would not meddle with the work regime apart from interpreting the rules in such a way that the planter, in acting high-handedly, could be assured of support and protection. The young and often inexperienced District Officers were no match for the pressure exerted by the planters. The latitude that they had as magistrates in applying the regulations was consistently used against the plantation coolies. The civil servants received the reward for services rendered on their transfer to another post. The custom of auctioning possessions that could not be taken with them provided planters with an opportunity to show their gratitude to 'decent' officials by bidding against one another and thus driving up the prices. When the Resident left Medan in 1902, such an auction brought in no less than 43,250 guilders! (*De Amsterdammer* 22 March 1903.)

The constant state of insecurity provided a welcome reason for continuing to enforce a stringent labour regime.

... in Deli in particular there are many bad people roaming around, usually run-away Chinese coolies who collect together in gangs and are a danger to the plantations. In August 1883, in an attempt to check these vagabonds, the army co-operated with the police by sending out patrols. Many suspects were taken into custody (*Colonial Report* 1884:17).

... great effort is continually needed to keep the rebellious Chinese people under restraint (Ibid. 1885:15).

Under circumstances such as these, it was easy to argue that planters really acted in the public interest by taking the law into their own hands.

Efforts to put an end to coolie desertion continued with zest. It proved quite frequently that it was provoked by other plantations which had an acute shortage of workers and were only too willing to pay the cost involved in a new labour contract, i.e. payment of a new advance on wages. To prevent coolies succumbing to such temptations, the planters collectively decided to reduce the amount of the advance (Ibid.1877:204).

During the first ten years the archives of the Planters Association were largely made up of a chain of correspondence and mutual charges about taking on deserters, whereupon the suspect planters denied any guilt in noble indignation. The stories of raids made on plantations which had bad reputations and the triumphant turning-out of the absconders are indeed amusing (Bool 1904:89).

Malayans who sheltered deserted coolies were also guilty of breaking the law and were punished by the Native Authorities. In their inspection efforts, government officials and police were given assistance by the Chinese headmen, who employed their own mercenaries. The workforce represented a considerable amount of capital, which formed the stake of fierce contention among those who arrogated the rights to it. Early in the 1880s this caused bitter fighting, sometimes resulting in murder, among members of secret Chinese societies that operated from Penang (Reid 1970:310). The colonial societies in the Netherlands Indies prohibited such societies, though without much understanding of their background and operations.

The Search for Labour

The coercion which was inherent in the labour system on the plantations was caused largely by the desperate shortage of workers required for the very labour-intensive cultivation of the wrapper leaf. The supply of coolies from Malaya was not enough to meet the ever-increasing demand for field-hands (see Table 1).

As early as 1875 Cremer had gone to China to examine the possibility of recruiting directly from the source. The results were meagre, partly due to the opposition of the Chinese authorities. Nevertheless, the opening-up of a new reservoir was urgently needed. The supply in Malaya showed signs of drying-up. Moreover, in 1881 the Protector of Chinese in Singapore had made known his displeasure with the bad working conditions in Deli. At a time when Chinese coolies were being shipped to all parts of the

Table 1.
COOLIE CONTRACTS REGISTERED IN PENANG AND SINGAPORE

Year	Penang	Singapore	Total
1879	3,529	500 *	4,000*
1880	6,600*	1,381	8,000*
1881	7,426	2,378	9,804
1882	5,990	1,498	7,488
1883	6,740	1,977	8,717
1884	8,540	2,464	11,004
1885	11,434	3,617	15,051
1886	12,391	4,317	16,708
1887	11,953	4,811	16,764
1888	10,913	7,439	18,352

*Approximate.

Note: During the later years some of the contract coolies were Javanese who came to the East Coast through the recruiting offices in Singapore.

Source: Reid 1970:306.

world, the government threatened to prohibit their export to Sumatra's East Coast in view of the bad reputation that that region had acquired in China. Similar reports in the Chinese-language press in Malaya also had a deterrent effect. The Deli Planters Committee reacted sharply by publishing an article in Singapore in which it sought to refute such accusations (Cremer 1882). Another disadvantage was that a number of planters reneged on their earlier agreement not to pay the recruiting offices more than a certain sum per coolie. Their breaking of the accord in this way raised the broker's premium to rise to unprecedented heights (Romer 1885:418).

Deteriorating economic conditions in the area of origin led to accelerated expulsion of migrant workers, much to the delight of the planters whose labour problems were thus temporarily relaxed. 'Fortunately, the supply of Chinese workers was very large that year [1887] due to the famine that was rife in China' (Schadee 1919:44).

The planters had noticed with interest the swelling flow of migrants from British India bound for the overseas colonies, where they were mostly put to work on the plantations. In Southeast Asia they mainly went to the Straits Settlements, from where a small number trickled down to Sumatra's East Coast. Use was made of these 'Klingalese' when the first plantations were being laid out. The employers preferred the labour skill and energy of the Chinese, but the Indians—mostly Tamils from the Coromandel Coast—distinguished themselves favourably because they were cheaper and, according to the planters, were more even-tempered and less rebellious. The fact that under British rule they had become accustomed to social discipline and a regular administration, was also not to be despised (Wiselius 1884:325-6). In view of reports that mentioned persistent famine in Madras and Mysore, Cremer was optimistic about the possibility of tapping southern India as an important new coolie reservoir (Cremer 1885).

In 1880 the Indian Famine Commission reported that in South Hindustan there were 16 million people who earned on average $2\frac{1}{2}$ cents each per day, in good times 5 cents, reckoned in our currency. Many go to Ceylon where the planters pay them 35 to 40 cents per day, but if they were given a little help and if the conditions were favourable, thousands would be prepared to emigrate (Broersma 1919:237).

In a slow but steady trickle so many came, independently, to the East Coast that it was considered to appoint two translators in the Indian languages. In 1876 the planters urged the Dutch colonial authorities to talk the British-Indian government into permitting the recruitment of Indian coolies from Calcutta and Madras. The British agreed on condition that the Dutch authorities allowed the appointment of a British agent in Deli to ensure satisfactory working conditions. The Governor-General found this to be an improper interference in Dutch national affairs and refused. Fresh talks held in 1883 were equally unsuccessful. Again in 1888 an official delegation was sent to Calcutta on the insistence of the Planters Committee to induce the British-Indian authorities to be more flexible, but this mission failed because of the same objection (Van Gorkom 1888; Memorial DPV 1929:62–3).

Meanwhile, efforts continued to attract Chinese coolies on their own front. A direct link was eventually established between the region of origin and the place of employment. A number of plantations adopted the practice of sending special middlemen (*kheh-*

thau) or old hands (*laukeh*) back to their home area after the expiry of their contracts, with the assignment of recruiting new coolies and bringing them back to the East Coast. This system not only saved a great deal on costs, but workers recruited in this way would, it was hoped, come straight from the countryside. Rural workers were rated far more highly than those recruited by the commercial brokers in the market towns and main ports (Bool 1903a:7–8).

To ensure a much greater flow of migrants, however, it was essential for the planters to have their own agency in China. In 1886 a Chinese- language interpreter in colonial government service was sent to China in order to carry out ethnographical investigations. On the request of the Planters Committee he was also instructed to examine ways in which the emigration of workers to the East Coast tobacco plantations could be encouraged. Five of the major companies agreed to meet the expenses involved (Ibid.:8; Van Dongen:113–14). An official Chinese committee of inquiry which visited Deli in 1887 was downright critical of the conditions under which fellow countrymen were employed. Their objections concerned the forced prolongation of contracts, the inadequacy of the leave-pass regulation, the condoning and even encouragement of gambling. Finally, the committee recommended that a Consul should be appointed in Deli (Broersma 1919:238; Bool 1903a:13). The colonial authorities refused to co-operate. A German trading house then took on the task of promoting the interests of Sumatran planters in China and in 1888, with the aid of the German Consul and after bribing local officials, successfully persuaded the Chinese government to agree to the migration of coolies to Deli, abandoning its former demands. The fact that this agreement was achieved without the aid of the Dutch authorities typified the supra-national character of plantation capitalism.

An Immigration Bureau was set up in Medan, under the supervision of the Planters Committee, which carried out assignments for DPV members, kept an eye on the smooth running of recruitment, organized transportation, arranged for workers' savings, if any, to be transferred to China, etc. The government interpreter, Hoetink, was sent to China for a year (1889–90) as proxy for the planters, who paid his salary. His task was to put the coolie migration to Sumatra on a sound footing and to ensure prompt co-operation by the local authorities. Hoetink was seen in China as

a sort of protector of Chinese based in Deli, an impression which
was quite incorrect but which was never rectified. The Netherlands
Ambassador in Peking kept aloof from the whole affair and gave
the distinct impression of being at best lukewarm about labour
migration. He was said to have refused his co-operation in this
'trading in human beings' (Van Kol 1903:96)—an attitude which
did not make him popular among the planters. The German Con-
suls in Canton and Swatow, on the other hand, were decorated by
the Dutch in recognition of their valuable mediation in the recruitment of coolies for Sumatra (Van Dongen 1966:121). Cremer, now
a member of the Lower House, pressed for the appointment of a
Dutch career diplomat as Consul General in southern China. The
first direct shipment of coolies from Swatow to Deli was a complete
fiasco. The coolies mutinied while still at sea; according to planters
sources, they were encouraged to do so by the coolie brokers. As a
result, the contracted coolies refused to go to Deli and left the ship
when it reached Singapore (Memorial DPV 1929:54). Matters improved after this maiden voyage, and once a regular shipping line
was set up, migrants to Deli rapidly increased to several thousands
each year.

Suitable workers for the East Coast plantations were also sought
from within the Netherlands Indies. In 1875 the Deli Company had
brought over a group of Javanese from Bagelen, but this experiment did not immediately increase the supply of coolies very
appreciably. The planters were dissatisfied with the Javanese,
saying that they were lazy and not suited for work on the tobacco
estates. According to Cremer, they preferred to exploit their
women, through prostitution, to working on land (Cremer
1881:41). Chinese field coolies were preferred, and it was only
because the supply, though rapidly increasing, could not keep pace
with the inexhaustible demand, that the planters contracted
migrants from elsewhere.

It was not the employers alone who showed scant interest in
Java as a recruitment area. The notoriously low wages deterred the
colonial authorities from actively stimulating workers from this
densely-populated island to make the trek to the East Coast of
Sumatra. In 1887, complaints were voiced by the district officers
about the grossly inadequate earnings which failed to satisfy the
basic needs of the workers. The Governor-General, acting on this,
wrote to all the Residents in Java, forbidding them to approve

contracts for work in Deli until the monthly wage was brought to a higher level (*Tijdschrift voor Nederlandsch Indië* II:289–91). In addition, the perfidious practices of some of the commercial recruiting agencies in Java, ranging from deception and fraud to kidnapping and naked coercion, had given labour migration a very bad name. An official report written in 1883 spoke about scandalous abuses, and attempts made at a higher level to qualify that statement had little success (*Historical Survey* 1897:72). This gave yet another reason to local government officials to refuse to co-operate. To the Sumatran planters this was a problem that could be overcome, as long as the import from China continued without hindrance. The fact that coolies were recruited there in similar evil fashion was beyond their field of vision, or at any rate did not fall within the formal responsibility of the colonial government. This is exemplified by the shady activities of an official who went to China on government orders to recruit coolies for the tin-mines on Banka. The Netherlands Consul General in southern China wrote about him in a letter to the Colonial Ministry in The Hague:

Mr Van der Stadt gave the manager of the firm of Schomburg & Co. the sum of $500 to be handed over to the above-named Taotai [director of the Office of Foreign Affairs at Pakhoi in South China]. In my opinion he was wise not to proffer this money in person because this would have been far more difficult for him as government official than for a merchant who specialises in the recruitment of coolies (GSA Vb. 19 September 1905, No.32).

The Immigration Bureau in Medan acted as a clearing-house for the Chinese coolies when they entered the country. The affiliated plantations placed an order for so many coolies, and committed themselves to take that number when they had been contracted and put on transport by agents in south China or in the Straits Settlements. The greater proportion of the migrants, however, were coolies who, although they entered the country through the Immigration Bureau, had been contacted by the plantation owners themselves. This was done, as we have seen, by sending a number of trusted old hands back to China each year to recruit strong young peasants from their villages. Soon after the turn of the century, around 5 per cent of the workforce was sent home for this purpose. They took cash with them or a cheque, payable by an agent of the Immigration Bureau, and on return to Deli they were given a premium by their employers for each new coolie (*singkeh*) who came with them. The results were disappointing, however. Not all the *laukeh* did what was expected of them: many did not come back at all, or contracted themselves to another plantation.

The original intention, that sons of the soil would be recruited in the interior who would be happy to go with the *laukehs* in order to work on the same plantation with men from their own village, that intention was not done justice to; the *laukehs* just brought along anyone they could, and complaints by the planters were inevitable (Bool 1903a:47).

In order to keep some control over the selection, many planters started to utilize the services of the *kheh-thau*, i.e. middlemen who held a special position on the plantation as shopkeepers, vegetable growers or as more highly skilled workers, and who had close links with the Chinese plantation foremen, or were foremen themselves. These *kheh-thau* were given letters of introduction and travelled back and forth between Deli and China recruiting coolies for one or more plantations. Hoetink, who went again on a mission to China in 1898 to see how the decrease in migration could be reversed, pointed out in his report that these *kheh-thau* would inevitably turn into professional coolie brokers. As a result, the planters would find themselves in the same disadvantageous position as before when they were still dealing with the commercial recruitment agencies in the Straits Settlements. The planters dismissed his advice regarding an increase in wages when it was found that the fall in the diminishing supply of labour was only a temporary phenomenon, caused primarily by an exceptionally good harvest in China. In the following year, migrants increased to more than the previous average. A survey of the changing origins of the Chinese coolies between 1888 and 1900, according to accounts kept by the Immigration Bureau, is shown in Table 2. It should be noted that the smaller plantations, many of which were still in private ownership and not affiliated to the DPV, continued to recruit their coolies from Malaya. A comparison of the figures for 1888 given in Tables 1 and 2 shows that considerable numbers were involved.

Table 2.
CHINESE COOLIES ON SUMATRA'S EAST COAST, 1888-1900

| Year | Arrival from | | Total | Departure |
	China	Straits Sets		
1888	1152	2820	3972	586
1889	5176	3494	8670	1562
1890	6666	2462	9128	1476
1891	5356	1511	6862	1127
1892	2160	109	2269	693
1893	5152	730	5882	964
1894	5607	857	6464	1350
1895	8163	2142	10305	2140
1896	6661	559	7220	2043
1897	4435	1384	5819	1910
1898	5105	1424	6529	1635
1899	7561	331	7892	1948
1900	6922	4	6926	1835
Total	70111	17827	87938	19269

Source : Bool 1903a: appendix.

Table 2 shows clearly that the majority of the coolies who came to the East Coast were never to leave it again. Life on the plantations was to be of a temporary nature only for about 20 per cent of the Chinese migrants, although they were all originally contracted for a period of not more than three years. Moreover, the great numbers who stayed ought to have increased the Chinese population to a far greater extent than was actually the case. In 1883 at least 21,000 Chinese coolies were working on the East Coast, most of them having come from the Straits Settlements. By 1888 their number had risen to almost 45,000. According to Table 2, which derives from Immigration Bureau figures, almost 70,000 more came between 1888 and 1900, mostly from southern China. Moreover, the latter figure concerned only coolies recruited for DPV-affiliated plantations. In 1902 these represented 75 of the 132 plantations on the East Coast, and included all the larger estates. According to the same source, these plantations then had a total of 36,500 contracted Chinese, or an average of 500 each. If we assume that, at the same time, the other fifty-seven independent planta-

tions employed roughly half to two-thirds of these numbers, it
would seem that at the turn of the century there must have been
15,000 to 20,000 Chinese coolies more than the total registered by
the Immigration Office. Yet in 1900 there were only 59,038 Chinese
under contract to the plantations. I calculate this at not more than
40 per cent of the total that had signed agreements in the previous
twelve years. What had happened to the others? Only a relatively
small number re-migrated, calculated at between 10 and 20 per cent
of the total number of coolies contracted (Reid 1970:300,303). A
handful remained on the plantations as free labourers without
contract. A larger number earned a living in the region as small
shopkeepers or in waged employment. But even this category was
restricted in size because of the difficulties the coolies had to face
when they wanted to settle in the area after the termination of their
contracts. True, the Chinese population outside the plantations
increased steadily, but many of them came directly from Malaya
with the intention of settling in Medan, the coastal towns or the
trading centres without first working as contract coolies. The numbers of 'vanished coolies' included, of course, those who deserted
from the plantations and hid themselves somewhere in the district,
amongst the population as clandestine agricultural labourers, as in
the case of the Javanese (Van Kol 1903:33) or as servants working
for free fellow countrymen as in the case of the Chinese, but always
at the risk of being caught.

Pending more accurate statistical data, which only a detailed
examination of the available records could bring to light, I would
posit that historiography biased in favour of the plantocracy has
formed an obstacle in the diagnosis of the extremely high mortality
that occurred among the workforce. Deaths were far higher than
could reasonably be expected on the basis of age structure (youth,
health and physical strength were important selection criteria) and
the duration of stay. Hidden behind the heroism of opening-up the
new lands, the laborious but continual creation of new plantations
on broken and marshy virgin territory which has been given so
much emphasis in plantation literature, lay the rapid turnover of
the labour force. Malaria, infected wounds on legs and feet, contagious diseases and, last but not least, irrepairable exhaustion
caused by the pitiless working regime combined with inadequate
food and facilities, took the lives of great masses of workers. These
victims were never counted. Based on documentation concerning

the plantation system in other societies of South and Southeast Asia (Breman 1985), however, it seems reasonable to assume that before the end of the nineteenth century one of every four coolies on Sumatra's East Coast died before having served his or her contracted period. This included the unregistered number who did not survive the often gruelling passage.

Reliable quantitative data go no farther back than the last two decades of the nineteenth century (see Table 3). Although the Coolie Ordinance made the registration of contract coolies obligatory, the figures for the initial years are very inaccurate. Nevertheless, they offer sufficient grounds for the conclusion that, between 1880 and 1900 in particular, the plantation workforce not only increased rapidly but also changed drastically in its composition. Almost imperceptibly, the number of Javanese coolies increased from 7 to 8 per cent to almost one-third of the total workforce. Conversely, workers recruited from among the local population on the East Coast dropped from rather more than 10 per cent to almost negligible numbers. Similar figures for plantations associated with the DPV, which guarantees their accuracy for the period 1890–1900, confirm this tendency (Memorial DPV 1929:85).

A variety of factors influenced the coming of more Javanese to the East Coast: uncertainty about the long-term future of immigration from China was probably the least important. The Chinese government, put under pressure by persistent negative reports in the national press regarding the recruitment methods and the working conditions on Sumatra's East Coast, made it known on various occasions that further migration would depend upon the compliance with a number of minimum conditions on the part of the planters. Although these warnings were mere threats, the danger of more drastic measures was not at all illusory. The planters had, after all, refused to meet the Chinese government's conditions. An even greater stumbling block than the demand that opium dens be closed and gambling forbidden (considered by the planters to be intrinsic to the nature of the Chinese), was the insistence that coolies be given a considerable wage increase so that they could transfer part of their earnings to those who remained behind. Equally inconvenient was the demand that the weaker coolies should also be paid an allowance that would enable them to satisfy their basic needs (Bool 1903a:25–9).

Table 3.
SHIFT IN COMPOSITION OF THE PLANTATION WORKFORCE ON THE EAST COAST OF SUMATRA ACCORDING TO ETHNICITY, 1881-1902

Year	Imported from outside			Locally recruited but coming from outside			Inhabitants of Sumatra			
	Chinese	Javanese	Indians	Siamese	Baweanese*	Banjaranese**	Bataks	Malayans	Gajoes, Alas Mandailingers***	Others
1881	15500	1887	1071	36	745	–	2624	894	–	–
1882	n.a.	n.a.	n.a.	n.a.	n.a.	n.a.	n.a.	n.a.	n.a.	n.a.
1883	21136	1771	1528	–	1182	–	–	105	–	n.a.
1884	26620	3217	1747	–	1088	–	–	–	–	–
1885	n.a.	n.a.	n.a.	n.a.	n.a.	n.a.	n.a.	n.a.	n.a.	n.a.
1886	31732	4453	1975	10	1180	269	4248	2910	172	–
1887	33526	6186	1623	75	1020	1087	3905	2211	161	–
1888	44790	9503	2123	–	1353	1853	5521	3078	267	–
1889	n.a.	n.a.	n.a.	n.a.	n.a.	n.a.	n.a.	n.a.	n.a.	n.a.
1990	53806	14847	2461	–	1212	4098	3434	372	324	398
1891	54715	15850	2850	–	1282	4787	3405	351	308	385
1892	39963	10347	2415	–	431	2885	2368	561	248	–
1893	41051	11179	2294	–	708	2823	2317	836	499	–
1894	42876	13443	2272	–	825	3155	2860	1150	780	–
1895	48204	15908	2570	–	833	3036	3232	1134	156	–
1896	48548	17605	2585	–	770	2702	2413	1162	125	–
1897	49407	19291	3139	24	1072	2760	2292	571	289	–
1898	50862	23022	3360	–	877	3085	2101	687	317	–
1899	56000	32000	3000	–	–	–	3000	–	–	–
1900	59038	30484	3295	–	946	3101	1433	289	159	–
1901	54489	29457	4140	–	721	2869	983	409	107	7
1902	55287	34596	3529	–	725	2960	993	378	36	1362

*** Coming from North and Northwest Sumatra.

Of more direct significance was that the planters' original aversion to the Javanese had disappeared, and was replaced by a far more favourable opinion of their work performance. This revaluation initially had to do with the introduction of new cultivation techniques for which Javanese coolies were primarily engaged. In the early 1890s a temporary fall in the demand for tobacco stimulated the transition to other crops. On lands less suitable for tobacco, coffee, in particular, found favour. Serdang became the main area for this crop and thirty-one of the forty-five coffee plantations on the East Coast had been established by 1900 (Schadee 1919:215–16). Due to a lack of experience and unfavourable price developments on the international market, coffee cultivation was not continued. As in the case of tobacco, many coffee planters lacked the minimum know-how needed for a successful enterprise. Most estates ceased to produce early in this century. Nevertheless, this interlude had a long-lasting effect in that perennial crops were now a permanent feature. Coffee disappeared, but was replaced by rubber and later by the oilpalm. In Deli, tobacco continued to predominate other crops. In 1904, plantation owners growing these crops formed their own Planters' Union, which was also joined by a number of smaller and less wealthy tobacco plantations. In 1910 the name of this new employers' organization was changed to the Algemeene Vereeniging van Rubberplanters ter Oostkust van Sumatra (General Union of Rubber Planters on Sumatra's East Coast, AVROS).

The method of wage payment also changed with the introduction of the new crops. It becomes evident from the literature that this was a prime reason for the changeover to Javanese workers. While task work provided the basis for calculating earnings in the tobacco fields, coolies on plantations that specialized in growing perennial crops were paid a daily wage. This obviated the objection to the Javanese coolie who, according to the planters, and in contrast to the Chinese coolie, had never responded to the incentive of a higher wage for greater effort. The Javanese now proved to have even more advantages: employers said that they were docile and placid, albeit indolent. This was a great relief after the restlessness and disobedience ascribed to the Chinese workers. The latter had always complied far less willingly with managerial instructions, and were more likely to rebel against what they considered to be an unjust treatment. Finally, a not inconsiderable advantage

was the lower cost of contracting a migrant worker from Java than
one from China, for whom the recruiting premium and transport
costs at the end of the nineteenth century were very high. Notwithstanding his much greater productivity, the Chinese worker
had become comparatively more expensive (Ong Eng Die 1943:80).
Javanese women workers were paid much lower wages, and since
they comprised an increasingly larger share of the flow of migrants,
this arrangement worked out to be much cheaper on the whole.
Chinese coolies were predominantly young men and preferably
unmarried: the families of married workers had to stay behind in
China when the men left for the East Coast. On the other hand, the
colonial authorities encouraged women to come over from Java by
allowing the planters to recruit them as fulltime workers. In 1905
the 33,961 Javanese contract coolies included 6,209 women. Only a
small minority, i.e. about 6 per cent, of the workforce was covered
by the Coolie Ordinance. During the following ten years their
numbers increased sharply, to 40 or 50 per cent of the number of
male Javanese and rather more than 20 per cent of all contract
coolies (Langeveld 1978:363).

Finally, the open-door policy that had characterized the early
years of labour migration came to an end. In the country of origin,
resistance to the mass export of unskilled and underpaid labour
grew stronger every day, as public opinion became more alarmed
(Reid 1970:310). Conversely, the authorities in the Netherlands
Indies also began to feel apprehensive about the concentration of
an over-large Chinese coolie population on the plantation belt that
had taken shape at the colonial periphery. Cremer concluded his
article in which he urged the large-scale recruitment of migrants
from British India, with the remark that the presence of other races
less inclined to conspiracy, would be in the interest of the state as
well as that of the planters (Cremer 1885:310). Receptiveness for
this argument within the colonial administration was to grow from
the beginning of the twentieth century.

A tax on the import of alien labour finally ended coolie migration
from China. When this occurred (incidentally, not until 1931), the
number of Javanese on the East Coast plantations was double that
of the Chinese, even in the tobacco gardens (Senembah Company
1939:21; Memorial Cremer 1941:86). While, in 1900, the overwhelming majority of the 100,000 contract labourers were Chinese,
by 1919 they comprised little more than 10 per cent of the army of

plantation workers, which by then had grown to 240,000 men and women (Langeveld 1978:300,363).

Increasing population pressure on Java and the assumption that this alone was responsible for the impoverishment of the marginal peasantry, also played a part in the increasingly positive attitude taken by district authorities towards labour migration to the East Coast. Once the 'diminishing welfare'—an euphemism for increasing poverty—had been brought to light in official reports at the beginning of the twentieth century, migration was seen as one of the solutions to this problem. 'The great and assured future of Deli will be in the success of the plan to lay out rice fields on land that has been abandoned for tobacco cultivation, in order to create a sedentary population, preferably from Java' (*Colonial Report* 1891:19–20). This clearly heralds the transition to another system of labour control, i.e. the importation of Javanese peasants, employed on the estates but provided with sufficient land to make them virtually self-supporting insofar as food requirements were concerned.

The growing significance of Java as the supplier of labour made it necessary for the planters to take recruitment into their own hands. At the turn of the century, coolies were brought in at the rate of approximately 7,000 a year (Weigand 1911:132). The commercial agencies that until then had handled the recruitments, had acquired such a bad reputation that it was no longer convenient to rely on them, not least because of the need for smooth relations with the local administration. The plantations on the East Coast stood in bad odour among the Javanese. As Van Kol pointed out in the Dutch Parliament: 'The name of Deli inspires fear among the population in the interior of Java and is considered to be a place of banishment' (Proceedings Lower House, 12 November 1898:168).

To put an end to this evil reputation the plantations decided to open their own recruitment offices in Java, with sub-agencies in various small towns. From this first initiative, taken in 1912, finally resulted the establishment of the General Deli Emigration Office (Algemeen Delisch Emigratie Kantoor, ADEK). Just as in the case of China, individual employers assigned their most trusted workers to the task of contracting new workers from their own home areas. Those sent to Java to ensnare new contract workers had to leave their wives and children behind on the estate so that the planters were assured of their return (Van Blankenstein

1929:53). Labour on the most densely populated island of the archipelago was in abundant supply, and interest in Javanese coolies was growing in Malaya, Indo-China, Australia, New Caledonia and Surinam. Smaller contingents were sent to German New Guinea, Sarawak, the Christmas and Cocos Islands, Reunion and German East Africa; even Mexico was considered at one time. The capitalists of the Netherlands Indies were not pleased with this expansion of the labour market. Press reports pretended that they were concerned with the poor working conditions encountered by the Javanese in other countries (*Tijdschrift voor het Binnenlandsch Bestuur* 1869:295–6). The further course of labour migration from Java is outside the scope of the present study, which stops at the beginning of the twentieth century.

Plantation Profits

The introduction and, later, the maintenance of the Coolie Ordinance resulted not only from the shortage of workers but also from the desire to keep wages as low as possible. Was the latter a consequence of low profits? Apparently not, if we consider the enormous expansion in the number of plantations and in the acreage during the 1870s and 1880s. The initial fear that tobacco could only thrive on virgin soil and could not be planted a second time in the same fields, proved unfounded and production increased sharply as long as the price trend remained favourable. The building of ever more splendid bungalows for the management and the improved infrastructure on the plantations, e.g. the construction of roads, hospitals, permanent worksheds and other facilities, reflected growing prosperity. This expansion came to an abrupt halt at the end of the 1880s. The market price of tobacco dropped from 1 guilder 46 cents per pound in 1889 to 72 cents in 1890. In 1891 over-production brought by the rapid increase in acreage and by more intensive growing methods, resulted for the first time in part of the harvest remaining unsold in the Amsterdam market. Another reason for this was a new import duty levied in the USA. Many tobacco estates had to close down or reduce their production capacity (see Table 4). For the first time, shares of the major tobacco companies on the Amsterdam stock exchange took a nose-dive. Only now did it become clear that the initial expansions had been very speculative by nature. The fabulous profits made earlier (see Table 5) had given rise to a hunt for concessions and to the extension of tobacco cultivation to areas that were not really suitable (*De Indische Mercuur* 1889,12:24, 26, 31; Van Sandick 1892:81-94). When prices fell at the beginning of the 1890s, this proliferation was brought to an end.

In 1890, tobacco shares that had been issued to a total of 12,500,000 guilders were noted in the Amsterdam exchange at 63,290,000 guilders. By the end of that year the value had fallen to 25,770,000 guilders. Great sums of money were won and lost in

Table 4.
GROWTH AND DECLINE OF TOBACCO PLANTATIONS ON
SUMATRA'S EAST COAST, 1864-1904*

Year	Number	Year	Number
1864	1	1887	114
1873	13	1888	141
1874	23	1889	153
1876	40	1891	169
1881	67	1892	135
1883	74	1893	124
1884	76	1894	111
1885	88	1900	139
1886	104	1904	114

*In the initial years there were still a few plantations that grew other crops, particularly nutmeg and coconut, which may have been incorrectly included in the statistics as tobacco plantations. Between 1891 and 1900 coffee plantations increased from 1 to 36.
Sources: Gramberg (1881) for the early years; for the period after 1881, Broersma (1919) and Schadee (1919).

speculations, but this had little to do with the capital on which plantation production was based.

Between 1890 and 1894 twenty-five Dutch and other companies, which together owned fifty-nine plantations, were closed down. It was the smaller enterprises, in particular, which succumbed to the crisis:

Even the biggest companies of those times were shaken to their foundations, and the many independent planters disappeared as snow before the sun. There was a tremendous exodus of natives of all kinds and also of Europeans, and in less than no time cultivation in Deli was reduced to almost half (Marinus and Van der Laan 1929:26).

In an area that had only lately been developed and where the soil was less suitable for tobacco, only one of the seventeen plantations managed to continue production. The contraction went hand-in-hand with the large-scale dismissal of coolies. Almost 25,000 became superfluous, and the subsistence rights that they had been guaranteed now proved utterly worthless. The employers apparently had little difficulty in extracting themselves from the obligations that they had accepted when the work contracts were

Table 5.
DIVIDEND PERCENTAGES (1881-90), AND FALL IN SHARE VALUE OF MAJOR COMPANIES (1890-91)

Year	Deli Co.	Arendsburg	Amsterdam Deli Co.	Deli-Batavia
1881	37	23	-	9
1882	65	25	10	11
1883	101	50	30	45
1884	77	60	30	26
1885	107	100	70	34
1886	109	100	50	35
1887	110	152	80	63
1888	45	120	25	40
1889	35	145	43	35
1890	79	112	41	62
Highest Exchange Market Quotation 1890				
	755	1035	510	460
Exchange Value 31 December 1891				
	340	400	177	224

Source: Van Sandick 1892.

signed, namely, to provide work for which they must pay a wage. Small wonder then that they did not meet the condition of returning the redundant coolies back to their places of origin at the expense of the plantation (Bool 1904:80). As involuntary deserters, the coolies roamed through the region in gangs, searching for food. How they survived this crisis has never been described. A small proportion went abroad, to the plantations that were being started elsewhere in Southeast Asia: Malaya, Thailand and Eastern New Guinea. The grandiose plans for the colonization of Borneo came to nothing. Nevertheless, the colonial authorities refused to give a German planter the permission to recruit large numbers of coolies for tobacco plantations in East Africa (Schadee 1919:210). It would seem that this request was frustrated as much because of the fear of a possible competition as the desire to retain a labour reserve in anticipation of better times to come. And it came soon. In the early 1900s there were approximately 160 plantations on the East Coast, most of which still cultivated tobacco, but with an increasing number growing perennial crops.

In the closing decade of the last century in particular, the government tried to diminish the importance of foreign capital on the East Coast—interests that were to become even greater after the introduction of perennials—by announcing that in future non-Dutch nationals and companies that had their headquarters outside the East Indies would be excluded from land concessions. This decision was a rash one and had to be retracted a year later, when it became clear that the plantation economy could not manage without foreign capital. The following figures show why the pressure probably exerted for repeal of the measure had such a rapid effect.

In 1894, forty-four land concessions were granted to twenty plantations belonging to corporations that were established abroad; fifty-six went to twenty-one plantations belonging to non-Dutch nationals established abroad; thirty-seven to thirteen plantations belonging to non-Dutch nationals living in the Netherlands Indies; and finally, 138 concessions were granted to sixty-four plantations belonging to corporations established in the Netherlands or in the Netherlands Indies (Broersma 1919:178). In the early twentieth century, foreign investments in Sumatra's East Coast continued to grow. The lukewarm interest shown by the Dutch in the early years of rubber cultivation led to an initial preponderance of British and American capital. As always, the Chinese were not allowed to take part in this multinational agri-business.

The recession of the early 1890s has been discussed extensively in colonial literature on Sumatra's East Coast with the aim of showing that profits were highly variable in the long run, and that, in general, the plantation economy was subjected to violent fluctuations. Yet the crisis lasted only for a short time; not more than two years. Market prices soon started to rise again, although the total volume of tobacco produced did not rise appreciably above the 1890 level (De Waard 1934:218). Recovery was speeded up by measures that were taken collectively by the planters. The most significant of these was the prevention of over-production by systematic opposition to the free labour by which it had been stimulated.

The former contract coolies, who were now free workers, became helpers, tobacco leaf hangers and, when the change was made from cutting whole trees to picking the leaves, leaf collectors. Leaf gathering greatly augmented the use of these free workers. These *menoempangs** who worked on short contracts or without any contract at all, assisted the field coolies who were employed and managed by the plantation according to the rules laid down in the Ordinance, but why shouldn't they work independently and thus increase the harvest, if they were able and wanted to do so? One could see that this would lead to a revival of the former free *kongsies* of whom the united planters, in mutual consultation, had rid themselves. And wasn't it precisely the *menoempangs* who, around 1895, had caused such big harvests? Here was yet another reason to do away with illegally-employed riffraff: this in itself would result in lowering the yield (Broersma 1919:130–1).

The DPV advised its members that it was in their collective interest to keep production costs as low as possible. The argument was that only through close co-operation, aimed partly at opposing any attempt to force up wages, could the industry stand its ground on the international market (Memorial DPV 1929:70). Tobacco cultivation retreated to the area most favourable to it, in the centre of the East Coast: in Deli, Langkat and part of Serdang. This was a region of 200 by 80 kilometers in the close proximity of Medan, from where the expansion had taken place in those years of over-

---

*On Java, menoempang was the name given to a dependent worker or tenant who was employed by a land-owning household; on Sumatra's East Coast, however, the term was used for a free worker who worked on the tobacco plantation alongside contract coolies. In Billiton's mining industry, noempang was the name given to a self-constituted team which worked a particular plot of land (Stecher 1905:3).

confidence. The principal characteristic of the crop became the very high intensity of labour on only a small part of each plantation. Tobacco production was only possible by leaving the land fallow for long periods and, conversely, by devoting the greatest possible care on that small part that was momentarily under cultivation. A precondition for this cultivation technique was the low cost and availability of land, and labour in sufficient quantities. De Waard has calculated that, although the tobacco area totalled about 270,000 ha, not more than 7 per cent of that was planted each year.

The question of whether it would be technically possible to maintain the high quality production that had been achieved if more intensive use was made of the land, has never been solved and in the past has always been answered in the negative. So far, it thus seems that one of the preconditions for growing a high-yielding crop is that only a small part of the acreage should be used. It must not be forgotten, however, that in the past it has never been necessary to seek greater intensification (De Waard 1934:261).

The same author has pointed out that the capital intensity of tobacco cultivation, measured according to the gross product, was quite low. Although it decreased steadily, the ratio between the monetary value of the crop yield and invested capital was exceptionally high: 160 per cent in 1880, 130 per cent in 1890, 76 per cent in 1900, and 99 per cent in 1905. Up to the end of the nineteenth century, including the crisis of the early 1890s, gross profits were even higher than the working capital. De Waard has rightly observed that production techniques remained unaltered for a number of years (Ibid.:260). In view of these facts, it is hardly surprising that employers made every effort to keep wages, i.e. the greatest cost factor, as low as possible. The land had to be prepared each year anew, and this was done almost exclusively by hand. Clearing the fields, planting, weeding, harvesting and curing the tobacco on the plantation, i.e. the drying, fermenting and sorting of the tobacco leaves, required a huge army of workers. The plantation production of tobacco could be characterized as a form of large-scale industry that was based on manual labour. The crisis at the end of the nineteenth century did bring some change to its organization and management. Reduced to the original core region, the tobacco acreage was to remain fairly constant during the next decade or so. The number of plantations continued to fall due to the extension of scale, mostly at the expense of the small single-owner enterprises. The figure of the planter-owner increasingly made way for that of the manager, appointed by the Board of Directors of an agri-industrial corporation which owned a number of plantations (see Table 6). The changes in DPV's membership give a good idea of the progress of this trend towards concentration.

Table 6.
MEMBERSHIP AND ESTATES OF THE DELI PLANTERS
ASSOCIATION (DPV), 1879-1900

Year	Number of members	Number of Estates
1879	41	61
1884	42	76
1889	43	105
1890	37	98
1891	33	93
1892	25	74
1893	23	71
1900	22	74

It should be noted that the short-lived recession only helped to accelerate this development. The tendency towards rationalization had already manifested itself, and the era of the plantation owner who managed his own business was coming to an end. More often than not, private planters were tied hand and foot to the big corporations that handled the sale of the crop in exchange for providing credit. The manufacture of wrapper leaves needed an investment of 750 to 1,000 guilders for each tobacco field. At an average of 400 fields per plantation, this meant a total investment of 300,000 to 400,000 guilders. The smaller planters who did not have sufficient financial resources of their own, borrowed the money from their bankers or from a larger company against a harvest contract.

By doing so the entrepreneur is obliged to hand over his ready product to the creditor who arranges to sell it on commission. This provides the creditor with security for his capital and, in addition to that, interest, commission and compensation of costs. By way of guarantee for the fulfilment of these conditions, the creditor is entitled to the standing crop which is not yet harvested, to the infrastructural facilities and to the enterprise itself (Weigand 1911:31).

The financial straits in which the small plantations found themselves in the early 1890s caused ownership rights to become concentrated in the hands of a small number of companies which steadily increased in size, and which were already closely associated with the big commercial banks such as the Dutch Trading Company (Nederlandsche Handelmaatschappij). The Deli Company took the lead. When it was founded in 1879 this enterprise owned 7000 ha; by 1920 this had increased to 180,000 ha (Memorial Cremer 1941:30). Those plantations that were taken over did not remain in their original state but were gradually merged into complexes of much larger estates, a trend that was to continue in the twentieth century (Volker 1928:31). The course of events on Sumatra's East Coast in the last quarter of the nineteenth century can be measured by the history of the company which in 1889 was to become the Senembah Company. In 1871 a German and a Swiss, both of whom had been merchants in Sicily, came to Deli on the advice of a friend who had already settled there as a planter. They were given a concession for slightly more than 5,000 ha, which they first planted with nutmeg before switching over to tobacco. These businessmen expanded their property and by 1889 they had at their disposal over 22,000 ha, largely obtained by opening-up new land, on which a number of plantations were established. They specialized in the production of a particular variety of tobacco leaf, the value of which fell at the end of the 1880s as a result of changing consumers' tastes. To convert to another kind of tobacco would mean time and money, and the two owners wanted to return to Europe. Following a suggestion by the Deli Company, which had acted as their banker since 1875, they put all their properties into a limited holding, issuing half of the shares on the Amsterdam stock exchange. Nienhuys and Cremer were among those who joined the new management, board of directors and shareholders (Senembah Company 1939:5–7). This illustrates such inter-related interests, particularly in view of the agreements that were made with regard to the organization, size of production and market outlets, that it savours strongly of the formation of a cartel. The example shows that industrial concentration had yet another effect, namely, that managerial control was gradually transferred from the colony to

Europe. That this did not happen without a struggle is spelt out in a number of memorial volumes, for example that of the Deli-Batavia Company:

The idea of transferring the headquarters of the company to the mother country was first discussed in 1888, a plan that at first was received so unfavourably in the Netherlands Indies that it seemed that nothing would come of it. In fact, the idea had originated among a group of shareholders in the Netherlands who, while expressing that wish, also gave voice to a number of grievances against the way in which, in their opinion, the plantation business in the Indies was being managed. These charges were considered on the other side of the ocean (Memorial DBM 1925:28).

Capitalist interests proved decisive. In 1893 the head office was moved to Amsterdam, which also became the seat of the board of directors where shareholders' meetings were henceforth held. But was it not only natural that those who provided the financial capital should want to exercise control over it? That argument is based on the idea that the money needed for opening-up and expanding the plantations originated in the Netherlands, in line with the continental idea that new industries in the colonies were financed after the mid-nineteenth century by western capital. Cremer, for example, has stated that the opening of plantations on the East Coast was funded by savings made in the mother country (Cremer 1881:45). This is the complacent image of the pioneers paving the way for European capital (*Sumatra Post*, 5 May 1913). On closer examination this notion is not borne out by factual evidence. Indeed, quite frequently the colonial economy itself provided the resources with which capitalist industry was begun. Also, further expansion of that industry largely came about on the basis of the surplus that was extracted from its labour force. In comparison to the stock market value of tobacco shares, actual working capital was of modest dimensions, even less than the amount that was soon put into the reserve fund.

The profits made in the colonies were transferred abroad; only a small portion being ploughed back into business. But the expansion to which this re-investment gave rise was of a fairly static character: acreage enlargement and greater labour intensification rather than technological renewal.

With the exception of a few recessional years, the plantation economy on the East Coast greatly prospered in the long run, and population growth reflected this favourable trend (see Table 7). Set backs such as those of the early 1890s were of a passing nature and in fact contributed to the rationalization of the industry.

Table 7.
POPULATION GROWTH ACCORDING TO ETHNICITY ON
SUMATRA'S EAST COAST, 1850-1905

Year	European	Indonesian	Chinese	Other Oriental races	Total
1850	-	-	-	-	150000*
1880	522	900001*	25700	2533	n.v.
1888	1160	n.a.	55596	n.a.	182414
1890	1528	191000*	75325	4236	285.000*
1900	2079	306035	103768	9208	n.a.
1905	2667	450941	99236	15573	568417

*Approximate figures.
Source: Dootjes, 1938–9;50; Van Gorkum, 1888; Population Census 1930, Vol. VIII, 1936:71, 91.

Around the turn of the century, production flourished, and was reflected in the really enormous profits made by the largest tobacco corporations which together controlled by far the largest share of production (see Table 8). At the end of 1901 the exchange value of tobacco shares had climbed to 102 million guilders. During that period, the Deli Company distributed profits that were more than 100 per cent in some years and which averaged 53.8 per cent (Schadee 1919:192). On a working capital which ultimately amounted to 25 million guilders, profits distributed between 1870 and 1927 totalled 16 million guilders (DM 1929:27-8). The respective annals show that the profits made by the Deli-Batavia, Arendsburg and Senembah companies did not lag far behind. Between 1893 and 1910 the former paid its shareholders an average dividend of 45 per cent, with peaks of far more than 100 per cent; Senembah's profit between 1890 and 1913 averaged 31 per cent. In the light of these figures it is difficult to accept the statement that, at least until the end of the nineteenth century, capital moved from the Netherlands to the East Indies instead of the other way around (Bosch 1948:81-2). Plantation business from the very beginning seems to provide solid evidence for proponents of the 'drain

Table 8.
TOBACCO PRODUCTION ON SUMATRA'S EAST COAST, 1864-1900

Harvest Year	Number of Bales (each 158 kg)	Price paid per 0.5 kg (Dfl)	Sale value (Dfl)
1864	50	0.48	4000
1869	1381	1.29	250000
1874	12895	1.50	2850000
1879	57596	1.19	10350000
1884	115496	1.44	27550000
1889	184322	1.46	40600000
1890	236323	0.72	26000000
1892	144682	1.26	26700000
1894	193334	1.19	35000000
1899	264100	0.82	33300000
1900	223731	1.11	38000000

Source: Schadee, 1918 Vol. I: 186; 1919 Vol. II: 20, 181.

theory' which became a famous issue in the intellectual debate on the effects of colonial rule. It was with perfect justification, therefore, that in his pamphlet published in 1902, Van den Brand spoke of 'The Millions from Deli'.

III

THE PLANTATION INDUSTRY AS A MODE OF CAPITALIST PRODUCTION

The European Management

The focal point of the plantation (*kebon*) was the 'emplacement'. This was the central area formed by the administrative offices, the fermentation shed, the bungalows of the European staff, the permanent coolie barracks, the shop (*kedei*) and Chinese temple, the stables and other buildings. The industrial hierarchy was immediately apparent from the way in which the complex of houses and workplaces were organized and from the pattern of the roadways. The bungalow where the manager (*tuan besar*) lived was most prominently situated, in a central place but at the same time made inaccessible to the workforce, obliged to keep a respectful distance, completely in accord with the system of social relations on the plantation.

Towards the end of the nineteenth century the figure of the planter-owner had largely made way for the manager, appointed by a board of directors abroad, which was personified in the *tuan maskapai*. Sometimes the manager reported directly to the Board, but in the case of a major company owning a large number of estates he was usually subordinated to a chief manager/superintendent (*tuan kebon*) who supervised a number of plantations from the head office in Medan. The origins of the managers varied considerably, not with regard to their nationality alone. 'It was a peculiarity of the world of the Deli planters that in those days they included people from many professions: former army officers, engineers, merchants, etc. but very few agriculturalists' (Schadee 1919:28).

This quotation described the situation in the early 1890s when there was a strong adventurist element among the planters. Many of those who went to the Netherlands East Indies around that time undoubtedly departed again quite speedily, for it took far more than a land grant and sufficient capital with which to make a successful enterprise. Tobacco growing, which at first could only be learned through bitter experience, gradually acquired a more scientific character. In 1894 the Planters Committee set-up a crop research station. As a result, increasingly higher requirements had to be fulfilled, not only for specific agronomical expertise, but also for quality in industrial management. The progressive concentration of plantations into the hands of just a few major corporations, made it possible to entrust them to the care of managers who were chosen on the basis of professional skill that had been acquired on the same or a similar plantation. On occasions, a planter who had become bankrupt or whose plantation had been sold but who enjoyed a good reputation, would be kept on as manager by the new owner. Frequently, however, the advantage gained in continuity of management was not sufficient to compensate for the high-handedness with which such people customarily behaved. The pioneers then increasingly had to make way for people who had begun as employees and had successfully worked their way up the managerial ladder.

An appointment as the manager of a plantation was preceded by many years of service as assistant (*tuan kecil*). From the beginning these employees were as heterogeneous with regard to nationality and social origin as the planters themselves. There was an enormous need for 'sturdy young men', but they were difficult to come by. In the early years they were mostly fortune hunters and transients from Malaya or from other parts of the Netherlands Indies, temporarily and unintentionally stranded on the East Coast. Gradually, however, the recruitment of European staff was shifted to the mother country. Clerkx, in a penetrating sociological analysis of novels written about the plantations of Deli early in the twentieth century, points out that none of the white men appearing in these stories was actually born on the East Coast. Almost all had gone to Deli at about the age of twenty, with the intention of returning to their homeland as quickly as possible after having earned a great deal of money (Clerkx 1961:ch.II). But however heterogeneous the staff might have been, the Indo-Europeans had little chance of being accepted into their ranks. They rarely climbed any higher than a clerk's position in the plantation office, assuming that they were found suitable even for that. Admission to the managerial level continued to be reserved for whites only, who were expected to return eventually to their own country. 'Java had and still has the advantage for the Eurasian youngster that he can find a post on the plantations, but on Sumatra's East Coast a youngman of mixed colour will only exceptionally be given a job' (Broersma 1922:231).

Familiarity with the country and people was certainly not a pre requisite for expatriates who came to the Netherlands East Indies, and was perhaps not even recommended. However, they very often lacked even those qualities and virtues necessary to make their mark back in Europe.

... it was obvious that the most suitable elements at home did not give preference to a career in Deli, and that those who offered themselves as candidates for employment were people who had gone into trade after leaving school but had not achieved the success they wanted (Senembah Company 1939:26).

To become a successful tobacco planter does not need any particular expertise, apart from having had a good modern education. But a good physical condition, a strong will and sound judgement are essential (Westerman 1901:6).

The assistant, who would have been twenty-two to twenty-five years of age when he came out, had to prove his worth and did not start by being given the benefit of a doubt. On the contrary, it seems from the few references in the literature that such people included a surprising number of misfits and black sheep who were either forced by misfortune to migrate to the colony or were sent into exile there by their families.

What difference in conduct and in influence over the Chinese labourers there must have been among these adventurous young men, exiled or given a last chance when faced with a work force with which they were completely out of tune. Among that army of raw recruits how the sedate-ness of the Dutch must have contrasted with the French vivacity! How differently the stout-hearted Swiss and the stern German must have felt and behaved in the face of ignorance, powerlessness, unwillingness on the part of subordinates than the Dane or the Russian!, Comparisons without all the necessary facts can only lead to unfair judgement; if nevertheless only incidental mention is made here of German accuracy and organization, then that is not only because the German element was very considerable in old Deli, but also because the drawbacks of harsh discipline have to be set against the advantage of successful work (Broersma 1919:53–4).

Thus arose the popular image of plantation assistants, fellows who were inexperienced and hard to please, lacking in self-control and who in effect thought themselves to be too good for the task they were given, i.e. to supervise the work of the Asian coolies in the fields and sheds. Their high-handed behaviour made 'accidents' inevitable, but it was argued that, however regrettable, such incidents could not be avoided.

Deli was a hard training school. The best men stayed and improved their future prospects; the remainder either left of their own accord after some time, or were declared unsuitable for the work and dismissed. There was considerable mobility among the Europeans, partly because the terms of employment offered little security to an assistant. In the pioneering period, it was very exceptional for a new employee to be given a written contract providing some security; only a manager could claim any such right in the early years (Ibid.:52). This sort of loose arrangement which went against the European staff seems ironic indeed when one remembers that not a single coolie was allowed to work without having first signed a formal agreement for a specified period.

The starting salary was anything but generous in comparison to the cost of living. In 1878 it amounted to no more than sixty to eighty dollars per month. Around the turn of the century the monthly salary fluctuated between eighty and a hundred dollars (Westerman 1901:270), a scale which became standard on all estates. Salaries increased according to the length of service: after six years an assistant was paid 200 dollars per month. Fringe benefits also improved gradually. After six years an assistant had the right to home leave; starting in 1899 this included free passage to Europe and back and half-pay for six to eight months. After 1892 assistants with more than six years service received a bonus in addition to their salary, a fixed amount which could be as much as 1,000 dollars per year (Senembah Company 1939:28–9; Broersma 1922:232).

Soon after the beginning of the twentieth century the biggest companies started to reserve a fixed percentage of the profits for their European staffs: the higher their rank and the longer their employment, the higher the bonus, thus causing the manager and his assistants to show maximal interest in increasing production and lowering costs. Junior employees were not only excluded from these benefits, but were also subjected to restrictions that had a drastic effect on their private lives. For example, they were forbidden to marry during the early years of their stay in the East Coast, even if they could afford to, financially, because the circumstances under which they lived and worked, during the pioneering era in particular, almost prescribed a bachelor's existence. This situation changed only gradually until the more senior assistants were allowed to find European brides during their home leave. The unmarried (*boedjang*) status of apprentice assistants (*singkehs*) continued, however, even though the ban on marrying was formally rescinded (Memorial Cremer 1941:114–15; Broersma 1922:233–4). It seems probable that, in their recruitment policies, the company managers were guided by the idea that a junior assistant without any family obligations would be more 'energetic' in his handling of the workforce than older employees who might show more circumspection due to fear for their personal safety (Endt 1919:170).

The strictly hierarchical organization entailed unconditional obedience at all levels permiting the disciplining of the coolies, to begin with. This was perhaps the most important quality required of the assistants who formed the bottom link in the chain of European management, as is shown in a manual written for them on how to deal with the Asian workers.

A man might theoretically be the best planter in the world, or might know everything on how to cultivate tobacco and to care for it, but he will be useless in Deli if he does not know how to exact obedience. The prestige of the assistant or of the planter in general is the heart of the matter (Dixon 1913:20).

In turn, however, the assistants had to behave submissively towards their superiors, and were expected to be guided by absolute loyalty to the company. Novels on plantation life and work underline the power that the manager exercised over his European staff (Clerkx 1961:23–7). It was not until 1895 that the assistants had an organization to care for their interests. A few years later, in 1898, something like a trade union was set up which, much to the disapproval of the management at higher levels, published its own journal.

The Planter protested against the arbitrariness shown by the managers and the directors; demanded that assistants should be given a better share of the profits, and had its own manner of describing the clashes between the assistants and the coolies. The assistant had no protection at all against high-handed treatment other than by making it known in the association's periodical, once this had been started, but the impartiality of reports that appeared in it was often doubted (Broersma 1922:231).

Membership of this Association of Assistants in Deli remained small, due to opposition from above. In 1909 a new organization for wage-dependent Europeans was set up which adopted a less militant attitude towards the higher management. The inaugural meeting was attended by the President of the Planters Committee, and one of the organization's initial activities was to petition the Queen of the Netherlands for allowing more stringent punishment to workers who violated the Coolie Ordinance (Memorial DPV 1929:141). The legal position of the European staff showed little improvement until 1922 when, on intervention by the colonial authorities but against the wishes of the employers, a special decree was passed which regulated the working conditions for assistants on the East Coast of Sumatra (Ibid.:196–7, 224–5). The intention was not only to standardize terms of employment but also to reduce the pressure to which the workforce was subjected, in the hope that the frequent attacks by the coolies on the assistants would subsequently decrease.

The number of staff on East Coast plantations, were only a few dozen at first. In 1876 there were forty-six managers and sixty-nine assistants working in the tobacco region (Gramberg 1881). Their number increased over the course of time to about 2000. They peaked in 1929 with 403 managers and 1953 assistants (Langeveld 1978:329). In other words, there was then one manager to about five assistants, a very different ratio to that of half a century earlier. The growth in size and number of the plantations was only partly responsible for the increased number of European staff. A more significant factor was that, towards the end of the nineteenth century, the assistants started to take over tasks that had previously been carried out by the foremen who were selected from among the coolies.

Where there were no assistants the *tandils*, or Chinese foremen, had more influence and sometimes greater latitude, unless the plantation was so small that the owner or his manager could exercise daily control over all the work. That was the usual situation during the early years after which the numbers of non-owner managers and assistants slowly began to rise (Broersma 1919:51).

The background to this downgrading of Asian foremen by the European staff was the management's wish to strengthen its control over the plantation's workforce.

The Asian Foreman

When the first plantations were being laid out, the owners chose a few coolies who were given the task of dividing the workload among the rest, and of supervising the execution of the work. *Tandil* and *mandur* are the Chinese and Javanese names for the middleman between management and workforce. The literature has little to say about the background of a foreman. His appointment was based on the expectation that he could direct a gang of about twenty to forty workers. In contrast to what was common practice in other plantation societies, such as Ceylon, the coolies were not recruited by the foreman in his own home area. Initially the employers on the East Coast handed over the task of engaging coolies to the commercial agencies. As long as recruitment continued to be concentrated principally on the opposite coast of the Strait of Malacca, were these firms established in Penang or Singapore. When south China and Java began to emerge as labour catchment areas, however, growing use was made of recruiting offices in Chinese and Javanese ports and of the networks of agents who operated in the hinterland. This is not to say that the coolies migrated as an undifferentiated mass. Informal leadership quite probably played a role already at the recruitment stage. The later appointment of a coolie to the position of a foreman may have been based on earlier prominence in the home situation. To my knowledge, however, the labour contractor who, as in Ceylon when the first coffee and tea estates were planted, brought his own gang with whom he worked for a particular period of time, did not make his appearance on the East Coast. In the previous chapter we have seen how the planters eventually set up their own recruitment bureau in order to cut costs and to put an end to the malafide practices of the professional labour brokers.

Even then, however, the recruitment of coolies and the supervision of their work continued to be distinct spheres of operation. The employers adopted the habit of sending old hands (*laukehs*) or trusted middlemen (*kheh-thaus*) back to their natal regions in order to pick up new workers, but they were only given a premium for their trouble and were not appointed as overseer of those they brought back with them. The foremen naturally had a vested interest in the expansion or replacement of the workforce: not only because they were out to acquire as great a share as possible of the commission paid, but also because they wanted to get an immediate hold over newcomers to the plantations. The Chinese head *tandils* did this by giving money themselves to the *kheh-thaus* for the recruitment of new coolies. Hoetink, who went to China on the planters' behalf in 1898, ascertained that these middlemen were in fact confidantes of the Chinese foremen. He pointed out in his report that if this system were to be continued, the recruitment of new workers threatened to become a purely Chinese affair.

... when head *tandils* and their henchmen take the place of the planters, the question will simply become one of who can bring the fattest purse to the market; Deli's industry will then risk seeing the management of emigration taken out of its hands, and will then be in the same unpleasant position that it was in previously with regard to the Straits-brokers, a predicament which made Deli decide to embark upon direct emigration. To have freed itself of the Straits-brokers only to become dependent on *kheh-thaus* and suchlike in China would be a sorry result of all the trouble and expense that have been devoted to direct emigration for many years now (quoted in Bool 1903a:49).

Did Hoetink's warning have any effect? I have not been able to check whether new coolies were subsequently contracted without the mediation of the Chinese foremen, but in view of the way in which recruitment was organized it seems reasonable to assume so. If the foreman's role was restricted mainly to work on the plantations, then that was certainly due partly to the firm action taken by the colonial government against Chinese secret societies which fought for hegemony over the coolie population. The head *tandils* played an important role in this fight (*Colonial Report* 1889 : 14).

What made a coolie eligible for appointment as foreman? Familiarity through experience with the work on the tobacco plantation, and a sound knowledge of what happened on the other side of the line which divided the workforce from the world of the management. But however necessary, these conditions were not sufficient in themselves because the foreman was not just an intermediary in a two-way traffic. The two spheres between which he operated were linked to each other in a relationship of dominance and subordination. The linkage ran primarily from the top downwards. The colonial economist Boeke has correctly pointed out that the foreman was nothing other than a tool which carried out the planters' objectives (Boeke 1955:157). As far as the white management was concerned, there was little need for his representation of interests in the reverse direction, as the following quotation clearly shows: 'The *tandil* or *mandur* of a group of contract coolies is chiefly responsible for keeping peace and order in his team, he has to ensure that they do their work properly, and must pass on orders on behalf of the assistant to his non-Malay speaking coolies' (Dixon 1913:16).

The key position held by the foreman was due to his working knowledge of the language of his superiors. But the problem of communication was not the only or even the main reason why interaction between the workforce and the European staff came to be institutionalized in a separate role. Although not independent, the foreman had some latitude as regards the disciplining of his workers, thus obviating any necessity for direct confrontation between the assistant and the coolies. For this reason the middleman could be assured of more lenient treatment and of some restraint on the part of the assistant, as the same manual for instruction of the European staff clarifies.

It is bad practice to abuse a *mandur* in front of his coolies. In doing so it is all too often forgotten that, as head of his gang, a *mandur* holds a position of some responsibility and thus has to maintain his status in the *kongsi*. If the *mandur* is scolded in the presence of his coolies then his position is undermined. This man is shamed before his coolies and loses his self-respect. The immediate result is that he starts to hate the European who treated him in such a way. He will now keep his superior less informed or perhaps not informed at all on the mood of the workers, and might even stir up his subordinates against the planter. But the coolies will also lose their respect for their *mandur* when they see a *tuan* rant and rave against him in this way. Their behaviour will become more insolent and the *mandur* will now have even more difficulty in getting them to obey him (Dixon 1913:33).

Clerkx, on the basis of quotations taken from a number of novels, gives an evocative description of the terror exercised by the foreman over members of his team during their working hours, taking this much further than the European assistant, who usually stood by as eye witness of such brutal behaviour (Clerkx 1961:76–9). Violence was not the only method by which the foreman could impose his will, however. In another quality, he has been portrayed as a man who looked after his team of workers and in return enjoyed the respectful affection of his subordinates.

As the link between the workforce and the assistant, living and working each day with their coolies, they are as it were the fathers of their *kongsi*. It is thus of the greatest importance that they should be men in whom the planter can have complete faith, but they must also get on well with their workers and have the necessary authority over them (Dixon 1913:19).

The dual role played by the foreman, trusted by his superiors but also a representative of the gang he worked with each day, was one reason why the European staff avoided a close relationship with him. Too much familiarity might result in an excess of self-esteem. Moreover, the assistant was told that the foreman had his own sympathies and interests which sometimes made his attitude incomprehensible, if not unreliable. Outwardly, they could be recognized by their clothing and behaviour, which differed from that of the ordinary coolies.

They are usually only distinguishable from their subordinates by a ridiculous European hat, a pair of shoes that are far too large, and a stick as a token of their dignity; they must also be able to shout loudly because a Chinese respects that and is impressed by it (Westerman 1901:113).

The greatest motivation for adopting a forceful stance by the foreman was that his earnings were dependent on the achievements of his coolies. Instead of a fixed wage he was paid a commission of 7.5 per cent of his gang's earnings. But his authority was far more extensive than the work in the fields. The barrack in which the coolies had to live also accommodated their foreman, and it goes without saying that responsibility for the maintenance of peace and order lay with him. Each coolie barrack was shared by thirty to forty workers. The combination of a gang boss and a barrack manager meant that the foreman had his coolies within easy reach by day and night. And that was not all. He also acted as moneylender and banker to his coolies. Although the plantations had started the opening of individual accounts paying the coolies directly even before the end of the nineteenth century, this did not prevent the foreman from controlling their financial affairs. If they had money in hand, he kept it for them.

Payments and deductions by *tandils* and *mandurs* are quite rightly forbidden by law, but that prohibition is occasionally ignored. It thus sometimes happens that *mandurs* keep small shops on the estate and force the coolies to buy there at prices that are above the market value (Broersma 1922:237).

More than anything else, the dependency of the coolies was an inevitable consequence of the small loans that the foreman disbursed among the members of his gang whenever the need arose. These advances had to be repaid on the main payday that was held at the end of the season. All too often, however, the coolies had to begin the new year with a debt held over from the previous season.

In his daily task the foreman was a subordinate to one of the assistants, but was also accountable to the head foreman. The latter's special charge was to gather information on everything concerning the workforce on the estate. He reported directly to the manager, who regarded him as his right-hand man.

A head *tandil* will first have worked for a number of years as a coolie on Deli and then as minor *tandil*; he will have some money and thus influence. He has to keep a close watch on every thing that goes on among the Chinese on the plantation and must daily report to the manager and to the responsible assistant. He is concerned not so much with growing the crop as with

Chinese affairs (*perkaras*) and could often be compared with a police officer but without the latter's power to mete out punishment. The lesser *tandils* have to keep him informed about the mood prevailing among the coolies, and he has his own spies to check those reports. Such an accurate intelligence service is necessary because the Chinese have an innate delight in intrigue and are masters at plotting and conspiracy (Dixon 1913:18).

The head foreman not only reported on the coolies but also on the activities of the assistants. His information enabled the manager to form an opinion as to the suitability of his immediate subordinates for the tasks assigned to them. Did the work get finished on time? Was its quality satisfactory? Were the coolies able to take advantage of the assistants, and did the latter behave in their free time in a manner that was appropriate to a member of the European staff? Naturally enough, the assistants considered such snooping contemptible, but there was little they could do against the head foreman (Haarsma 1889:22–3).

It will be clear from the above that a man who wanted to become a foreman had to satisfy even one more condition, that of being on good terms with the head foreman. Primarily, this meant having the latter's interest at heart, even more than those of the plantation. In addition to being a man of consequence, whose intercession with the manager was of decisive influence, the head foreman's pay approximated that of a member of the management rather than that of the coolies. A commission of 5 to 7 per cent of the picking wage of his gang constituted a regular part of his income. This provided him with about 250 dollars annually (Westerman 1901: 113). He also had various other sources of income, legal or otherwise. Lacking any definite information, I can only surmise that the foremen also expressed their 'gratitude' to their head by giving gifts of money. It seems conceivable that the head foreman's support would have to be bought if one were to be raised to the rank of a foreman. This was not done by way of a one-off payment it should be understood, but in the form of regular remuneration. The head foreman also lent money to the coolies. His agents, i.e. the foremen, settled accounts on the coolies' main payday. The head foreman could collect a net sum of 8,000 to 10,000 guilders on that occasion (Broersma 1922:126).

Finally, the head foreman profited financially by providing the coolies with the opportunity to gamble. In exchange for payment, he obtained a licence from a Chinese who owned all gambling rights in the region. The majority of plantations had a gambling shed which always did brisk business. Agents of the head foreman held the bank and were always willing to advance money to the coolies, who pledged their future earnings as security. Similarly, the head foreman paid the man who held the opium monopoly for the right to sell the drug on the plantation. Altogether, these sources of income meant that the head foreman was often a very wealthy man. His influential position also gave him power and respect far beyond the plantation boundaries. Head foremen kept in touch with one another and met at regular intervals in order to co-ordinate their interests. For example, in an effort to curb unhealthy competition amongst themselves, they agreed to impose a maximum limit on the fee for recruitment of a coolie in China (Ibid.:133-4). This understanding, which they reached in 1912 and in which fifty-five head foremen were involved, makes it clear that they continued to be involved in the engagement of new workers. Indebtedness was the principal means by which coolies already employed on Sumatra's East Coast could be forced to continue to work after the termination of their initial contract period.

The power of the head foreman and his agents was not restricted to the plantation but extended outside it, and coolies gave the name of the head foreman under whom they worked rather than the name of the plantation on which they were employed (Haarsma 1889:22). There was an increasing apprehension that too much independence on the part of these intermediaries would be detrimental to the interests of the plantation. This new mode of thought which became prevalent around the turn of the century suggested that the white management should exercise control more directly. Implementation of this change of policy was based on the argument that the coolies should not be victimized by their own foremen.

For the Chinese workers the head *tandil* is frequently the silent extortioner. He is a powerful man who rules the entire workforce with the help of his subordinate *tandils*, even if only because he knows how to make himself understood by both the assistant and the labourer. His authority is needed for the smooth running of affairs, but he extends that authority in a direction that is undesirable; he knows various ways by which to benefit himself at the expense of the worker, and he becomes a very rich man.

Neither the manager nor the assistants can be aware of all the activities of
the head *tandil* as he manipulates the coolies more or less fraudently to his
own advantage (Broersma 1922:236).

Indeed, unrest among the workforce was not infrequently
caused by usury practised by the foremen. On payday the coolies
had to hand over so much money to their creditors that they did
not have enough left to meet their own living expenses. When
requests for increased cash advances, made on the instigation of
the foremen, were refused, this could be sufficient reason for the
coolies to down tools and to rebel. The planters lived in continual
fear of coolie riots, and to ward off this threat the European staff
inevitably had to become more intensively involved in the actual
payment of the wages of the workers.

... each coolie was given his own heading in the ledgers, and the accounting
was done in such a way that everyone would be able to check it before the
annual settlement of accounts took place. In this way the management of
the plantation has come closer to the individual coolie (Senembah Company 1939:22).

This source continued with the remark that a more personal
relationship would have been desirable, but that this was
precluded by the inability of the European to master Javanese or
any of the Chinese dialects. For this reason the use of the foremen
had to be continued, but without the great latitude that had characterized their former role.

Between the workers and management there was another
category about whom far less has been written. This comprised the
clerks (*kranis*) who worked in the plantation offices and carried out
simple managerial tasks. The clerks literally formed an intermediate class, made up of Chinese from Penang who had been
educated, and of a combination of various races who, if they were
of partly European stock, were known as half-castes or *Sinjos*.
Although downgraded and slighted, they were indispensable in
the day-to-day running of the plantation. The white leadership
delegated all sorts of routine tasks to the clerks. 'They are mostly
very useful, alert and handy people who can be of considerable
benefit to the manager, but on the other hand they should not be
trusted too much. A strict eye should be kept on them in order to
prevent malpractices' (Haarsma 1889:23).

Although there is no evidence, it seems reasonable to assume that this lower administrative class, together with the foremen, were responsible for numerous illegal activities that were disadvantageous to the workers—an alliance that was shared, furtively, by members of the European staff. Fraud and corruption, mostly at the expense of the coolies, thus ensured that bridges were built over the strictly-drawn colour line.

The Workforce

Facts and figures, or any concrete data, about the bottom of the plantation hierarchy are difficult to come by. The records of agribusiness and other colonial sources provide very little information about the social background, life and work of the coolies. Clearly, however, the workforce did not represent a homogeneous mass but was made up of various segments. The field coolies undoubtedly formed the chief category, each being assigned a field for the cultivation of tobacco plants. The quantity and in particular the quality of the crop depended on the effort put into it. The reputation for industriousness that was so admired, especially in the Chinese coolie, applied primarily to these tobacco growers who worked according to a contract system (*borongan*).

The Chinese field coolie is out before dawn to look after his young tobacco plants, to water the seedbeds, to search for caterpillars, or to prepare the soil for planting. He continues to work until after sunset, with only one or two hours rest at midday. If there is a full moon, the coolies will frequently continue to work on their tobacco, long after normal hours and after a strenuous day. A Chinese may seem a not very likeable fellow due to his loud-voiced and noisy behaviour, but every planter has to respect his zest for his work and his achievements (Dixon 1913:41).

Sometimes an almost idyllic picture is drawn of the diligence and devotion to work shown by the Chinese coolies (Haarsma 1889:120). The field coolies were helped by the *kongsikang* (co-workers) made up of inexperienced labourers who had to prepare the soil for cultivation and to look after the fields while the plants were growing. This category of auxiliary workers included not only beginners, but also coolies who had the reputation of being unsuitable, lazy or unwilling. Men who were unsatisfactory as field coolies or who for some reason or other had incurred the displeasure of the management, would be degraded to the status of these helpers. As a result, *kongsikang* came to be seen as a term of abuse. Its members were referred to by the planters as 'stinkers', a term that came into common usage in the 1870s and referred to the stinking leg wounds, acquired during the heavy ground-clearing work, by which these auxiliary workers became recognizable (Ibid.:25). The original meaning was lost but the name, as an expression of the planters' contempt, remained in use. Such coolies were also governed by other working conditions, and were being paid a daily wage which was docked by the management if, in the opinion of an assistant or a foreman, they had not worked hard enough. The actual tobacco growers, working according to a contract system, are presented in the plantation sources as petty entrepreneurs.

In planting and caring for the tobacco the coolie is to a certain degree independent, and he who is considered suitable to cultivate a field feels himself to be much better than the *kongsikang*, who is paid daily (Comments on Van Kol's articles on Deli in the *Soerabaiasch Handelsblad*, SEC coll. RTI).

After gaining sufficient experience the daily wage labourers could improve their position. If considered suitable they might be allocated a number of tobacco fields on which they had to tend and pick the plants. Very little information is available on how such a promotion came about or whether it caused any change in the composition of the work gangs, but it is certain that the foremen had an important voice in the matter.

The *tandils* always had to ensure that sufficient coolies were available on time, to choose from among those who were to be re-engaged for the next crop year, or from among those with whom an agreement had already been reached even though their contract was not yet ended, and the manager added to this number other coolies or newcomers (*singkehs*) from China (Haarsma 1889:99).

The literature does not make it clear whether there was rivalry among the foremen of the different gangs. Indebtedness was undoubtedly an important tool by which coolies were tied, preventing them from taking the initiative to join another work team.

It is interesting to note that men from certain regions of China were automatically labelled as being unsuitable, and were registered as second or even third-rate coolies. The immigration bureau sold these inferior workers to the plantations at a much lower price (Bool 1903a:54). It is difficult to trace how these assumed differences in quality, officially codified in the regulations of the immigration bureau, originated. Moreover, opinions could change, both over time and from place to place. It thus sometimes happened that indentured workers who were classed as second-class on migration, were sold to the plantations on arrival as first-class coolies (Ibid.:37).

Besides the field coolies, the plantations had various other categories of workers. Tree felling and field clearance, which had to be done each year, were assigned as piece-work to special gangs who had their own foremen. Although an assistant kept an eye on this heavy preparatory work, these workers enjoyed a much greater degree of autonomy than the field coolies. In contrast to the latter, they had no long-term contracts. They committed themselves to doing a particular job on the basis of an advance that was paid to their foreman; after completing that task they were perfectly free to seek work elsewhere. Road construction and the digging of drainage ditches were contracted out on a similar basis. Still other gangs specialized in the building of drying and fermentation sheds, storage places and barracks.

Work on the plantation was essentially divided along ethnic lines. I have already mentioned that coolies from certain regions of China were considered to be good agriculturalists. But they were also ascribed other traits which found less favour among the planters, making it difficult for them to weigh advantages against disadvantages.

A Hailokhong is boisterous, hot-tempered and flares up easily; Keh and Macao calmer and more forbearing although more inclined to kill anyone they hate, or to make plans for doing so. The Hailokhong is usually considered to be the best cultivator, is stronger and better able to do heavy work than the other clans who, on the other hand, are more careful and neat although slower workers (Dixon 1913:40).

According to another stereotype the Javanese were indolent and hardly ever responded to material incentives such as were

provided by piece rates. At first this was even considered sufficient
reason to debar them from work on the plantations. They performed better when paid a daily wage, on the understanding that
they were given their money only after the completion of a task.
Supervised by a *mandur*, they were mostly involved in clearing the
land, digging trenches, and other unskilled fieldwork. Towards the
end of the nineteenth century, however, they started to be used
more and more in the actual cultivation process while preserving
the mode of wage payment to which they were accustomed. As
experience demonstrated, they matched the Chinese coolies who,
although perhaps more industrious, were also more expensive.
The Javanese brought their families with them, increasingly with
the passage of time, which was an added advantage enabling the
planters to mobilize extra labour power in the peak season without
having to pay extra during the slack periods.

The additional advantage of married workers, especially if the women also
signed the contract while in Java, was that their wives and even children
could work in the fields; but in particular they could also be used in the
drying and fermentation sheds in the bundling, sorting and stacking of
tobacco (Westerman 1901:22).

The profile of the Javanese thus gradually underwent a change
(cf. Stoler 1985:30), and they came to form an ever-greater part of
the total workforce. Nevertheless, the preference for Chinese
coolies continued even when, later in the twentieth century, they
had decreased to a minority among the tobacco growers.

Right from the beginning, Bataks and Malays from the coastal
plain and the immediate hinterland had helped the planters in
clearing the jungle. They lived in hamlets on the plantation and
were the first to be called upon for tree-felling and other tasks
involved in clearing the land. Local peasants who refused to work
on the plantation when there was a need for their labour power,
could be forced to do so by denying them the use of the harvested
fields on which they grew their food crops. Their small numbers,
however, made it necessary to call in other groups. For land
clearance, and also for road construction and waterworks, Indian
Klings were usually employed under their own foremen (Kling
tandils). The Indians, a not very sizeable category, included many

bullock-cart drivers. Each ethnic component thus had its own more or less specific work.

... Javanese are employed for digging and road construction, Boyans prove to be good builders of drying sheds and coolie barracks; Klings are useful for digging but especially as cart drivers; Bandanese and Siamese (of whom there are few) team up to build drying sheds and Malayans are prepared to become coachmen. The Bataks also come down from their green hills and try to earn some money with building and tree felling. However, the majority of workmen are Chinese (Naudin ten Cate ed. 1905).

The racial division of work was thus based on assumed group characteristics that could usually be traced back to historical circumstances. They could be due, for example, to different work traditions: when working the land, the Chinese would carry the earth in two baskets hanging from a carrying pole, while the Indians would carry it in a basket on the head. The main factor perpetuating this racial division of work was undoubtedly the planters' view that, for optimal efficiency, heterogeneity in the workforce was desirable, even if it did not facilitate collaboration among the coolies. For example, there were major contrasts among different Chinese groups and these antagonisms were fortified by the secret societies into which they organized themselves according to their region of origin. Disagreements regularly exploded into fierce quarrels.

... Clashes between the Chinese of different tribes and *kongsi*, quarrelsome as they are, were inevitable. The planters tried to avoid any particular tribe from predominating in the region. Statistics drawn up in 1883 for this purpose showed that no one tribe was especially dominant. In 1882 the Kehs and the Macao-Chinese submitted a request to the Resident to be allowed to have headmen belonging to their own tribes, and subsequently a head of the Kehs was appointed in Medan and a head of the Macaos in Labuan (Broersma 1919:252).

Ethnic diversification of the workforce was a common principle of recruitment, as the following quotation concerning coolies employed in the tin-mines of Banka shows.

It was in these years of ample expansion of the workforce that attempts were made to recruit Chinese tribes other than those to which the Banka Sinkehs mostly belonged. One tried to bring Chinese from different regions to Banka, so that a particular tribe or a group of related tribes would not predominate over the others (Schuurman 1922:167).

It seems reasonable to conclude from this that labour control was made easier by a diversity of coolies among whom there was some degree of dissension. It is not inconceivable that ethnic rivalries were even encouraged.

During the pioneering period women were not even considered to be a possible source of labour power, and their numbers continued to be almost negligible as long as the Chinese element dominated. The planters showed no interest at all in the importation of women from China, and this was also not plausible at a time when the jungle had to be cleared which made heavy demands on bodily strength and endurance. Later, it was argued that there were numerous legal and social barriers in China against the emigration of women and against their return if they ever did go overseas. The experience gained with the few women who did accompany their husbands in no way encouraged the employers to try to change the sex ratio.

Searching for caterpillars, raking, stringing (tobacco) leaves, are useful activities for the plantation which Chinese women have carried out just as Javanese women and children have done in other places. But a plantation owner is little pleased if the wife incites her man to leave as soon as the contract ends in order to settle elsewhere as a greengrocer or an artisan. Society on the East Coast of Sumatra might benefit from it, but even they must reject it if the Chinese woman comes there in order to lend money at extortionate rates of interest or to quarrel with the other half of her husband's neighbour or workmate. It is still noticeable that among the women who migrate, the wives of *tandils* and of old hands are in the majority, and those of *sinkehs* in the minority (Broersma 1922:136–7).

In short, Chinese women were not sufficiently docile to bring over to the East Coast in any great numbers. They displayed a business instinct that was not suitable for plantation workers. In that respect, the Javanese women caused far fewer problems. If they lacked sufficient means of livelihood they were forced to prostitute themselves, a type of business that complied much more with the needs of the plantation (cf. Stoler 1985:31-2). In 1896 a plantation doctor ascertained that a newly-arrived batch of women coolies included a number of girls of no more than ten to fourteen years of age (Tschudnowsky 1899:44). He was only too well aware of the fate that awaited them and referred approvingly to a newspaper report which cried shame upon such traffic in children. But the commotion really started only when Van den Brand broached the subject in his pamphlet. He pointed out that the habit of importing to the East Coast some hundreds of unmarried women and young girls each year, started by the major plantation companies late in the nineteenth century, had the result if not the intention of satisfying the sexual needs of the male coolies (Van den Brand 1902:66-70). A former Resident, in answer to these accusations, remarked that the majority of women coolies were prostitutes who were no longer wanted in Java. He had been told, moreover, that in the Javanese *desas* girls of twelve years of age were in fact no longer virgins (Kooreman 1903a:37). The wage paid to the women was far below the amount necessary even for the most elementary living expenses. In complete contradiction to their obligations under the Coolie Ordinance, the planters paid nothing at all to them on days on which there was no work.

The percentage of women in the coolie population gradually increased until, around 1930, they represented about one-quarter of the total (Langeveld 1978:362), after being a mere 8 per cent early in the century, according to DPV data. Even then, however, they had formed a far greater proportion of Javanese indentured labour: about 30 per cent (Memorial DPV 1929:85). In Serdang, the new coffee plantations gave preference to women coolies, who were paid according to the quantity of coffee beans picked. This piece rate decreased as production rose, and increased as the yield declined. Anyone who picked unripe beans was fined. These new wage modalities indicate that women were being discovered as the cheapest workers available to the plantations. However, their absorption into the labour process was restricted by a clause in the Coolie Ordinance which said that they might do only light work: the sorting and bundling of tobacco leaves in the sheds; the weeding of seedbeds in the fields; sweeping the roads on the estate and other jobs that were not fatiguing and needed patience rather than heavy physical effort. Van den Brand was to point out that women actually did much more than just this: 'It is a fact that women are repeatedly used for work which in the Netherlands is performed by navvies. Dredging gravel from the river, breaking stones, taking away sewage barrels from the Chinese and emptying them, etc.' (Van den Brand 1904a:39).

Women coolies had the most miserable existence of all. Even more than their male companions, they were exploited and oppressed by the management and foremen alike. A few managed to achieve the rank of *mandur* and, like their male colleagues, walked around with a cane: the instrument that the supervisory staff always kept with them to protect themselves and to impose their will on their subordinates (Hoetink 1902:73). These were the exceptions, certainly among the women, the bulk of whom lived in a state of perpetual exhaustion. But this, as the doctor quoted above was informed by the plantation manager, was because the women worked day *and* night: in the daytime with their hands and during the night with their bodies (Tschudnowsky 1899:44). He described their hopeless situation which gave rise to despair sometimes taking extreme forms. A few women, including one who had been compelled to leave her children behind when she was shipped to Sumatra, lost their sanity.

The Organization of Work

The Coolie Ordinance permitted a ten-hour working day. At 5 a.m. or even earlier, one of the watchmen would beat the gong in front of the coolie barracks to wake the workers. At morning roll-call the foremen reported which members of their gang were absent and why. Illness was the sole acceptable reason, and if the assistant doubted the genuineness of the complaint, the coolie would be forced to work. The gangs went to the fields before dawn in order to start work at 5.30 a.m. or at 6 a.m. latest. At 11 o'clock they had a one-to two-hour break, after which they worked until 5.30 p.m. or 6 p.m. In actual fact, they worked for far longer hours. For one thing, the fields were usually at a considerable distance from the coolie barracks: nevertheless, they had to reach their workplace on time and were given permission to leave only when the task assigned to them (*borong hari*) was finished (Endt 1919:85). The work norm had been laid down by the management, not according to average, but maximum achievement with the result that the authorized ten-hour working day was exceeded considerably: one or two hours longer was the rule rather than the exception (Minutes

A CHART
ORGANIZATION OF FIELDWORK ON A MIDDLE-SIZED TOBACCO PLANTATION AROUND THE TURN OF THE CENTURY

Work distribution	Unit	1 bahu (0.7 ha) = 1 field	100 bahu (70 ha) = 1 division	400 bahu (280 ha = 1/10 of estate land = 1 enterprise
management			1 assistant 3 foremen	1 administrator, 4 assistants 1 head foreman, 12 foremen
field coolies (mainly Chinese)		1 grower assisted by a fieldhand	100 growers (borongan) assisted by an unspecified number of fieldhands (kongsikang)	400 growers assisted by an unspecified number of fieldhands
labour for clearance and maintenance (mainly Javanese, in addition Bataks a.o.)			± 50 coolies under their own foreman	± 200 coolies under their own foreman
others (Chinese, Javanese, Indians, Coastal Malayans a.o.)				cartmen, messengers, servants, guards and other non-field labour permanently under contract and daily wage labourers (shedbuilders, woodcutters etc.) intermittently employed.

Source: Colonial Reports 1877-1903

of a Regional Government meeting 1902, SEC coll. RTI). This also applied to coolies who worked on a piece rate basis. Their rates of pay were so low that they could achieve a minimum income only by working very long hours, sometimes until late at night. Overwork was also very common during the noon break (Van den Brand 1907:412). At harvest time, in particular, it was not unusual for men, women and even children to work in the drying shed through the night, stringing the harvested leaves. The planter's praise of the Chinese coolie for continuing to work in the fields after dark by the light of the moon or of an oil lamp, has to be seen against this background.

The planted area of a medium-sized plantation consisted of about 400 fields, each with an area of slightly less than one bahu (0.7 ha), i.e. 60 x 900 feet. Each field came into use once in eight to ten years; in other words, such a plantation needed to have not less than 2300 to 2800 ha at its disposal. The 400 fields that were cultivated each year were divided into four sections, each of 100 fields. At the head of each division was an assistant in charge of three foremen who together put 100 coolies to work. In addition, the *kongsikang* helped the actual tobacco cultivators. Apart from these workers who, around the turn of the century, were still almost exclusively Chinese, each division had about fifty labourers, principally Javanese, who worked in gangs under their own foremen to prepare the new fields for the next season. This meant felling trees, constructing roads, building sheds and digging drainage trenches. Extra workers could be mobilized locally on a temporary basis for other sorts of work. When calculated in this way, it seems that there was roughly one extra worker for each tobacco grower, showing that a plantation of some size must have had a workforce of 800 to 1000 (cf. Westerman 1901:112). Statistically, the average labour force numbered about 600 workers, a figure that approximates the total of 160 plantations and a labour force of 100,000 coolies on Sumatra's East Coast at the beginning of the twentieth century (Hoetink 1902:1).

Labour was thus the main factor of production in the plantation economy. The greatest possible care had to be taken to prevent any damage to the tobacco leaf, both during its growth and during transport and in the subsequent processes of drying and fermenting. The delicate character of the various activities made tobacco growing extremely labour-intensive. Moreover, with the exception of draught animals that were used for ploughing, even the very heaviest work involved in clearing the land had to be done by hand. Even in later years, mechanization of work in the fields and sheds was very rare. Tobacco growing was a predatory form of cultivation in which a large part of the acreage lay fallow for several years while a comparatively small area was very intensively worked. In particular, land clearance, which had to be done each year, was heavy and unhealthy. Either disease or injury invalidated a large part of the workforce. Still, the following description gives the impression that the European staff were the ones who suffered.

In the tangle of lopped-off lianas, branches and dead trees, soaking wet or half-wet all day long, plagued by large numbers of leeches and mosquitoes, accompanied solely by a couple of Javanese or Klings, stakes had to be placed accurately to show the correct direction of the future road, while the gangs of workers who followed on behind cleared the dry patches (if there were any!) (Naudin ten Cate ed. 1905).

More scientific methods of cultivation was to increase labour intensity even further. Better land tillage, more care for the seed beds, a higher pace of planting and harvesting and control of insects and weeds, all caused the labour force on the cultivated acreage to be increased (Senembah Company 1889–1939:23). Only since the beginning of the twentieth century has the labour intensity of the plantation economy declined due to the transition to perennial crops. In the 1920s tobacco growing required four workers per ha of planted land, while rubber needed only one; later, rubber was to need only one man per 4 ha (De Waard 1934:217). From the technological viewpoint, however, agri-business on Sumatra's East Coast continued to be a fairly primitive mode of production. That certainly applied to tobacco growing, for which the labour factor represented a very large proportion of total production costs, notwithstanding the extremely low level of payment. In 1885 the preparation of 100 tobacco fields cost approximately 30,000 dollars, and according to a detailed budgetary account, roughly two-thirds of that amount went to the coolies (Römer 1885:423). The crop not only required a great deal of attention, but also demanded meticulous care and regularity. Mechanization and a general increase in capital outlay were not seriously considered as long as labour continued to be abundantly available and lowly priced. For the same reason, it was possible to maintain a reserve stock of labour.

It is imperative to have coolies in reserve, not only for the many activities for which field coolies have no time, but above all in order to train the *sinkehs* to become suitable field coolies for the coming year and to replace field coolies who fall ill (Westerman 1901:115; see also Haarsma 1889 :105–6).

The realization that they could tap an almost inexhaustible supply of labour was one reason why the planters showed more concern for their crops than for the coolies in their employ. The presence of more labour power than was strictly necessary meant that some could be expended in the production process without endangering the crop yield.

The year was divided into two seasons: the field period and the shed period. The first of these lasted for rather more than eight months. The preparatory work on the fields was done primarily by gangs of Javanese, Klings and locally-recruited labourers. They made the land ready for the new planting: clear-felling, digging and levelling the soil, laying-out plant lines, digging drainage ditches, building drying sheds and temporary coolie barracks. These yearly activities began in August and continued until far into January. At the beginning of the new year, once the divisions had been demarcated, it was the turn of the more experienced Chinese coolies who drew lots for the fields for which they were to be responsible. They would then burn off the land after the rainy season, dig it over a number of times and rake and clear it. They also looked after the seedbeds that would be started at this time. After six to eight weeks (March-April) they began to transplant the young seedlings, approximately 16,000 per field. Farming out the work to the field coolies in this way was a striking feature of the early plantation system. At the end of the cycle the plantation paid the tobacco growers according to the number of plants delivered to the drying shed. An intrinsic part of this work organization was the so-called *tanggung* system:

... whereby an experienced worker took over from the planter the responsibility for the employment of one or more new workers. The older coolie
would pay the debts of the younger and thus assure himself of the other's
earnings. He would also guarantee the other coolie a certain amount of

profit in the hope that this would prove to be greater, and for this purpose took over the other's debt to the plantation (Senembah Company 1939:21–2).

This system, with its relations of mutual dependence among the coolies, was abandoned when a new method of harvesting was introduced in 1895. From then on, the field coolies were paid not by plant but by leaf, plucked at the moment when it was fully grown. Simultaneously, the *kongsikang* (or *menoempang*) was withdrawn from their direct control (Memorial DPV 1929:8; Senembah Company 1939:23). The new way of harvesting the tobacco, said to be an important improvement resulting from a more scientific approach, was in fact the same as that which the Bataks had traditionally practised (Pelzer 1978:42). Harvesting started six to eight weeks after transplanting and lasted for roughly the same amount of time. By the end of August all the tobacco fields would have been emptied.

Every five to six fields had a drying shed where the leaves were delivered by the tobacco grower. In the shed, which rotated every year together with the tobacco gardens, the leaves were strung together in bundles and hung up to dry. The crop then went to the fermentation shed, built in the central compound of the estate, where the greater proportion of the workforce was concentrated once the plucking season was over. At this time also, special gangs of coolies would be put to work to clear land for the next season's crop (Westerman 1901:231; Weigand 1911:52–75). Processing the leaves in the sheds lasted for three to four months, from October to January. The coolies worked together, sorting and tying the leaves into bundles, and finally stacking them in bales, for which they were paid piece rates at the end of each day.

The Chinese field coolie, and also the Javanese woman, has an admirable capacity for making the necessary gradations. Negligence can occur, however, sometimes because of the effort to do as much as possible and thus to earn more, or because of drowsiness due to insufficient sleep and a great deal of exertion. In the delivery room, the responsible assistant, helped by a small number of carefully selected Chinese workers and Javanese women, examines the bundles of each sorter, rejects those that are found to be faulty and gives them back to the worker, who thus loses time and money. A bookkeeper writes down on the spot the number of bundles delivered by each worker (Broersma 1922:117; see also Taukeh 1906 :118–19).

This work was also carried out on contract. The sorter chose his own bundler with whom he came to an agreement regarding the division of the day's earnings (Haarsma 1889:196). The management claimed that the workers quarrelled frequently while working in the sheds. It was naturally easier for them to grumble to their own workmates than to a superior.

But once the fieldwork is done and the shed time has begun, they can expect to spend three months in the fermentation shed. The active life in the fresh air is over. The inevitable sorting and bundling does not require the physical effort that makes the peace of the evening so enjoyable, but it strains the nerves. It is a constant peering at the colour of thousands of fermented leaves, with the chance that the work will be rejected and returned again with the consequent shrinking of the meagre wage. The field coolie's temper runs high during the work in the sheds. He becomes irritable, touchy, and small disappointments or adversities are puffed up into major injustices and the direst calamities. If he loses at gambling in the evening then his humour will worsen even further. And if he thinks that his bad temper and misfortune have been caused by someone in particular, then he will arm himself to kill; evil deed resulting from perpetual desperation (Broersma 1922:126; see also Taukeh 1906:126–7).

The conflicts that erupted were not as arbitrary as this quotation would suggest. Foremen and coolies who had loans outstanding among their fellow workers seized upon the daily wages that were paid during the shed work in order to square accounts. Understandably enough, this caused a great deal of tension. The plantation literature is inclined to link the fights in which many coolies were simultaneously involved with the fact that gangs of very diverse composition had to work together, day in and day out. The police and even the army had to be called upon repeatedly, to restore order (Schadee 1919:45). Group antagonisms could certainly play a significant role in these clashes, but other sources show that discontent over work and wage was largely to blame for unrest which could degenerate into coolie riots so feared by the planters. The months spent in the sheds gave the workers an excellent opportunity to discuss their grievances with one another, at least insofar as talking was permitted. The fact that hundreds of coolies had to work together under one roof made it all the more necessary that strict discipline was observed.

Here follows a catalogue of what a coolie may or may not do in the shed. He must come exactly on time and may not leave too early. He must not talk loudly, and preferably not at all. [This zenith of human effort was usually only achieved when the general manager came to inspect the work.] If he is accustomed to wearing a Chinese *rottan topi* (head covering) then he is forbidden to bring it into the shed, or, if the employer does not forbid this, then he has to put it away so that the tobacco leaves do not come in contact with the sharp points of the *rottan*. If he wears shoes, he must take them off and put them away in such a way that they do not constitute a hindrance to the foremen who oversee the work, walking up and down the rather narrow passage. Smoking in the shed is strictly prohibited. He may not tread on the tobacco or damage it in any way; on no account may he take away any tobacco, even if only a small piece of leaf. Above all, he may not fall asleep (Hanegraaff 1910:9–10).

When the time in the sheds was finished, the coolies were again split up into gangs and they returned to the temporary accommodation in the fields.

Wage Formation

The greater proportion of the plantation coolies were paid on task, job or piece-work rates. Insofar as any were paid by daily or monthly rates, this was also tied to a previously fixed amount of work which had to be finished by the end of the day. 'The whole process of tobacco growing, all the work of the Chinese involved in preparing the fields, planting, caring for and harvesting the tobacco, is arranged on contract and the sum fixed by the estate takes the place of the monthly wage' (Bool 1904:24–5).

The same applied to the processing that the leaves underwent on the plantation after having been plucked: drying, fermenting and sorting. This modality of wage payment assured the planters of maximum effort on the part of the workers, both in intensity and length of the working day. To achieve even a minimum income the coolies had to devote utmost care to the crop and frequently work far longer than the ten hours laid down in their contract. Sub-contracting combined with strict supervision determined the character of work discipline on the tobacco plantations during the early capitalist stage.

The abuses to which the piece rate system gave rise soon attracted the attention of the Protector of Chinese in Malaya, whose co-operation was indispensable in the recruitment of coolies. In 1881, the Protector lodged an official complaint with the Dutch colonial authorities about the low wage level, the nebulous way in which payments were calculated, and the inadmissible practices of the foremen on Sumatra's East Coast. In vain, the Protector attempted to urge the government of the Netherlands East Indies to introduce a monthly wage system. The planters reacted by saying that this would provide insufficient incentive for the good coolies, while bad workers would merely be encouraged to default (Cremer 1882:3–11).

Wage levels were fixed by the planters in consultation with one another and the workers themselves had no say whatsoever in the matter. Immediately after DPV had been set up, its members agreed upon a maximum payment of eight dollars per harvested tobacco plant. Plantations that were already paying more than that amount—nine dollars for the best quality was not exceptional—were instructed to put an end to this 'abuse which eventually could have very unpleasant effects' (Memorial DPV 1929:11). Such measures, which tried to forestall demands for wage increases followed by labour scarcity, were wholly successful. During the next few decades, as the supply of new workers surpassed even the rapidly growing demand, the recruitment premium paid to the labour brokers increased but not the price of labour. Early in the twentieth century, i.e. a quarter-century later, the price per tobacco plant had still not risen above eight dollars. Moreover, the majority of the plantations threw all risks of cultivation onto the coolie by paying not according to the number of seedlings distributed but by harvested plant. Bad weather, unfavourable soil, plant diseases and numerous other circumstances over which the cultivator had no influence, meant that incomes fluctuated considerably: not only from year to year but also among gangs working on the same plantation and even among members of one and the same gang. The assistant fixed the price of the harvested leaves brought to the drying shed. Around the turn of the century that price averaged seven dollars, but on plantations that were not associated with the DPV it was even lower (Broersma 1919:231). Multiplying this amount by the total number of plants received, only gives an approximate idea of the gross earnings on which the tobacco grower could count after more than eight months' drudgery. The actual sum was considerably lower because of a number of deductions made by the management which is discussed in detail in the next section. Suffice it to say here that they were truly incredible and included the wage payments of the auxiliary field-workers and various kinds of production inputs, such as implements, seedlings and fertilizers.

During the cultivation cycle, which lasted about eight months, all these deductions meant that the net earnings of the field coolie could not possibly have risen above seventy-five dollars. When the lower-paid work in the fermentation shed after the fieldwork period is considered, this meant that around the 1900s the most skilled category of coolies had an average annual net income of hardly more than one hundred dollars (cf. the cost specification given in Römer 1885:423).

It is striking that the remuneration paid to the inferior part of the labour force, i.e. the *kongsikang*, was deducted from the amount that the field coolies received for the product they supplied. I would suggest that this method of wage payment contributed to the exacerbation of mutual antagonisms among the different sections of the workforce. According to the planters, the gradual change-over to another method of tobacco harvesting, i.e. per leaf and no longer per plant, had brought a not inconsiderable rise in wages. After 1895 the field coolies were paid a standard rate of one dollar for the plucking of 8000 leaves and stringing them together for the drying shed. Referring to this new practice, the employers rejected Hoetink's advice after his visit to China in 1897, that emigration should be made more attractive by giving the coolies the prospect of earning a higher income (Bool 1903a:32). The employers invariably answered complaints about low wages with the argument that the workers were still able to save part of their earnings. Considerable amounts were transferred to China each year. According to Van Kol, however, this averaged a mere thirteen guilders per coolie. Moreover, he stated, this sum should not be taken as the average because by far the greater part of the money was remitted by the foremen (Van Kol 1903:98). An official of DPV confirmed that most coolies who went back to China left as penniless as they had come (Stecher 1905:24).

The lowest wages of all were those of the auxiliary fieldworkers and other contract coolies who, due to inexperience, unsuitability or unwillingness, were not put to work as tobacco growers. They were paid a mere 20 cents per day and even that only if they adhered strictly to the foreman's instructions; that is to say, if they did their work satisfactorily. Deductions for failing to report for work, for arriving late, for 'laziness', lack of skill and other shortcomings, were all too common.

The employer could dock from the wages of the Javanese and *kongsikangs* if, in his opinion, they had not done the work properly. But such deductions frequently amounted to at least a half-day's wage, even when the shortfall in assigned work was less than half. ... That the employer found himself on a slippery slope with these deductions is shown by the fact that the agreed wage sometimes was only partly paid on the grounds of recent arrival in the country and the consequent inadequacy of the coolie's work performance (Broersma 1919:281).

On many plantations, according to the same source, far less than half the Javanese coolies earned the full monthly wage. Until 1900, this amounted to six dollars, yet fines with a penalty of ten cents were imposed on such a variety of things that the yearly income of these lesser skilled coolies was probably nearer sixty than seventy dollars. And that applied only to the men. Javanese women had to be content with half the wage of male coolies, i.e. three dollars for a full month's work, and were only able to earn enough for sheer survival by prostituting themselves. This caused the planters to suggest that these women, rather than work hard and properly, preferred to earn their living in an 'easier and pleasanter' fashion (Mulier 1903:143–4). As Van den Brand stated in his pamphlet, the plantations included such side-earnings in their calculation of labour cost and income. However, Van den Brand's estimate had included the wage increase that major companies were forced to implement in 1900 in order to guarantee the supply of new workers from over-populated Java. The pauperization of the peasantry, there, due to the economic depression of the 1880s had just begun to filter through to the colonial authorities.

It should also be mentioned that, in 1900, in reaction to multiple complaints voiced in Java, the Association raised the customary minimum wages of Javanese men and women, from six and three dollars per month respectively to seven and four-and-a-half dollars, in the hope of thus partly satisfying the agents' complaint that it was becoming increasingly difficult to recruit Javanese workers for Sumatra's East Coast at the wage rate obtaining previously (Memorial DPV 1929:88).

Planters who were not associated with the DPV did not increase the price they paid for labour but for the time being kept it at the old level, although they did raise the amount of the advance made at the time of recruitment. Van den Brand calculated that a woman coolie earned barely eleven cents net per day although, according to shop prices in Medan, she needed thirteen cents for food. On the plantation, where everything was more expensive, the cost of living came at least to fifteen cents (Van den Brand 1902:68-9). A local newspaper considered this nonsensical and said that Van den Brand had grossly exaggerated, not as regards the wage, but in calculating the amount of money that a coolie needed in order to survive, or at least to eat: '... we too have mounted an investigation and have found that a native can live on eight cents per day. With a little forethought it can be done on even less' (*Sumatra Post*, 27 November 1902).

This line of argument constantly recurs in the colonial literature. It was tantamount to saying that nothing needed to be done about wages as long as the needs and productivity of the Asian worker stagnated at a low level.

The sluggish wage developments on Sumatran plantations during the last quarter of the nineteenth century inevitably lead to the conclusion that the Coolie Ordinance with its penal sanctions was instituted not only to assure the employer of a sufficient supply of labour, but that it was also introduced in order to pay the workers at a level which barely exceeded, and was frequently less than the costs of reproduction.

Finally, in addition to the political motive which gained increasing currency during the twentieth century, the low wage strategy formed an important economic reason to replace Chinese by Javanese workers on the East Coast. The gradual rise in the number of women coolies was also a part of this objective. The industriousness of the Chinese coolies was much appreciated by the planters, but not to the extent of having to pay 30 per cent (for the men) to 50 per cent (for the women) more than the amount for which the Javanese coolies could be put to work. The employers managed to increase the productivity of workers recruited in Java to a very acceptable level by changing to other working and payment methods. The wage rate for women coolies that Van den Brand mentioned was actually on the high side. According to a confidential letter written by the former Resident Van der Steenstraten to the Minister of Colonies, male coolies who had never been absent from work received 4.60 guilders and women 2.30 guilders net per month, or fifteen and seven-and-a-half cents per day respectively. For the feeding of prisoners, added this colonial official who had just resigned his post, the government paid sixteen cents per day. He had tried in vain to persuade Serdang's coffee planters to increase the wage rate for female coolies.

One of them had the impertinence, when I called his attention to the fact that an unmarried woman receiving only 2.30 guilders could not possibly feed and clothe herself, to remark that women always had the opportunity to earn more; through prostitution, of course. When I reported extensively on this subject to the Director of the Civil Service and requested him to forbid officials in Java to approve such contracts in future, I was told that the government considered that wage determination was a question of supply and demand, with which the authorities could not interfere (Personal letter to Minister Idenburg, 11 December 1904, in GSA, Vb 28 January 1905, No. 6).

Despite constant exhortations to officials in the region over several decades to protect the workers against the conditions imposed on them by the planters, the colonial authorities, nevertheless, consistently refused to introduce a minimum wage. Ex-Resident Van der Steenstraten received no reply to his comment that the argument given above could not possibly apply to contract coolies who were sentenced to forced labour for refusing to work for a starvation wage. The authorities made no attempt to intervene in wage negotiations and wished to avoid giving the impression that they exercised control over such matters (District Circular 31 March 1903, SEC coll. RTI).

Payments and Deductions

The plantations paid the wages on fixed dates (*hari besar*), usually the first and the fifteenth or sixteenth of each month. The coolies did not receive remuneration for these two days when all work on the plantation was at a standstill. The system used for paying field coolies was different from the daily payment made to other workers. The first category, the actual tobacco growers, were paid a maintenance allowance of two to two-and-a-half dollars per month on paydays during the fieldwork period, and were expected to manage with that amount. The piece-rate work in the sheds was paid once a fortnight. Accounts were settled at the end of the working year on the big payday when the field coolie was told how much he had left over from his tobacco growing during the previous season, as numerous expenses which will be considered later, were docked from his pay. Accounts were settled with the remaining coolies on fixed days throughout the year, according to a far simpler method of bookkeeping. They were paid only the wage for the previous fourteen days, but that amount was also cut by all sorts of expenses and advances. Payment was in dollars, first Mexican and then in Straits dollars, or at least was expressed in that currency. The gradual shift to labour import from Java was one of the most important reasons why the dollar remained the regular currency for wage payments on Sumatra's East Coast. Until 1890 the exchange rate for one Mexican dollar was 2.20 Netherlands Indies guilders. It then fell to 1.25 NI guilders, and stayed at that level until the beginning of the twentieth century. When recruiting in Java, the coolie brokers stated the wage in dollars, at the earlier exchange rate of two NI guilders.

Advances were then paid on this basis, suggesting that the value of the dollar on the East Coast differed very little from that of the silver *rijksdaalder* (2.50 guilders) used in Java. This misleading impression also arose from the fact that both the coins had the same name: *ringgit*. It was a deceit which the coolie realized only after his arrival in Deli, when it was already too late. In local financial transactions on the East Coast the dollar was actually more or less equal to the NI guilder (Endt 1919:132). The cost of living was no lower than in Java and in some respects even decidedly higher. It was for this reason that the plantations started to pay the salaries of their European staffmembers in guilders.

Another form of fraud practised by the planters was that the coolies were not even allowed to spend their meagre wage as they saw fit. Many plantations paid their workforce partly in their own 'money': paper coupons or metal discs that could only be used in the plantation's own shop (*kedei* or *kedeh*). The planters said that they had decided to issue company money because of the shortage of small change on the East Coast. The dollar was divided into 100 *koepang* or 1000 *doeits*, both known as pennies.

It has sometimes happened that a planter, to prevent an outburst of discontent, cut out round discs from biscuit tins, put figures on them, and paid his Chinese with them, pretending that they could be used on the other coast. The Chinese crossed over and returned again after a few days disappointed. But the ruse had succeeded, because in the meantime the planter had been able to provide himself with dollars and other necessary coins (Broersma 1919:147).

This story has a double meaning. It is meant to illustrate the adroitness of the employer as well as the ease with which the coolies could be duped. What it boiled down to was the truck system. The planter leased the right to keep a plantation shop, usually to a (head)foreman who delegated its management to his wife or another member of his family. The coolies were forced to buy their daily necessities at that shop. This applied particularly to the rice coupons with which part of the wage was usually paid. The employer contended that he did this to prevent the coolies from gambling their wages away or from spending their money on opium. They also professed to purchase the rice at a higher price than was paid by the coolie. In their calculations, however, they omitted to include the difference between the wholesale price at which the stores were purchased, and the retail price at which they were sold in the *kedei*. The shopkeeper readily gave credit, but charged prices that were higher than those in the market of the local town for the limited stock available in his shop. The coolie could use his coupons or discs only in the plantation store, but received a far lower cash value in return. This was frequently the only way in which he could obtain any ready money.

The *kedei* was just one of the links in the network of indebtedness that imprisoned the workers, and now and again their discontent came to a head. In 1902, for example, the coolies on one plantation attacked the manager when he paid them only in the company's store money instead of partly in silver or copper coins and partly in coupons, as was customary. A commentator in a local newspaper called it incomprehensible that 'this rabble' should commit such a deed for such a trifle (Van den Brand 1902:51). Coolie raids on company shops were a regular occurrence.

Employers took little notice of official urgings that wages should be paid in accepted coinage. By issuing estate and/or *kedei* coupons they strengthened their grasp on their workers, and the forced purchasing at company shops continued (W. 1905:86; Van den Brand 1907:412).

Although wages were not allowed to be paid through the intermediary of the foreman, he was always present (Taukeh 1906:96), so that he could immediately collect his due. Yet it was the employer who laid the first claim to a part of the coolie's earnings in the form of charges that had little to do with work output as such. In the first place, the costs involved in clearing and further preparing the tobacco field were reckoned at five to ten dollars. Then the coolie had to pay for his own tools and for their eventual replacement. The wage of the auxiliary field-workers, the *kongsikang*, during the cultivation cycle, together with the cost involved in seeking the help of women and children in the drying sheds and looking for caterpillars in the field were deducted from the wages of the tobacco grower. Finally, he had also to pay for the seedlings and, until the end of the nineteenth century, for the cost of fertilizing his field (Haarsma 1889:101, 127, 138; Bool 1904:23). By relying on the *borongan* system, the management pretended that the plantation employed tobacco growers who worked at their own risk but who were supplied with unskilled workers, material and other inputs. The workers sold their yield back to the planters, according to this point of view. In addition, the plantation charged a coolie for his sleeping mat, pillow and even the wooden planks of the bed, together with other personal equipment, and the tools needed for fieldwork that were handed out to the coolie on his arrival. He had to pay even for the ledger in which the account of his work was kept. He was also charged for the expense of the plantation's barber and for a proportionate share of the wage of the cook and of the watchman of the coolie barrack. Further, the plantation paid in advance the industrial tax levied on the coolies and charged a commission of 8 per cent on the amount recovered from the workers. Women coolies were usually exempt from this tax because the paucity of their wage kept them below the minimum level. Unjustifiably but nevertheless quite frequently, miscellaneous charges were made, for medicines or housing, for example (Broersma 1919:255). It was quite permissible, however, to make runaway coolies pay the reward that was put up for their capture and for other expenditure made in sending them back to their employers. The injustice involved in this practice could not be concealed from the local authorities. In 1903 the Resident wrote in a memorandum that many planters did not suffice with the customary sum of two to five dollars, but multiplied that amount (ten to twenty dollars) so that deserters remained perpetually in debt (District Circular 27 August 1903, SEC coll. RTI).

Many managers of plantations in this region seem to be of the opinion that, without further evidence and without the knowledge of the government, they might deduct from the wages all costs, however great, that they have made for the finding and catching of an indentured worker who has left the plantation on days other than his holidays, even if he has not been brought before the Magistrate for desertion (Bool 1904:63).

The most important deduction, which constantly appeared in the monthly accounts, was undoubtedly the gradual recovery of the advance paid to the worker at the time of his or her recruitment. Around the turn of the century this entailed for Chinese coolies an amount of twenty-five dollars (1st class) or fifteen dollars (2nd class), and for Javanese twenty-five dollars (men) or sixteen dollars and fifty cents (women). This initial debt usually increased because the employers customarily advanced a new loan on the occasion of Chinese New Year or of other important festivals. Among the field coolies, who were almost exclusively Chinese, debts were settled once a year when they were paid whatever they had in credit on the great payday at the end of the time in the sheds. The other workers repaid their advances in monthly terms of two dollars for the men and one dollar for the women. Many of them found it difficult to work off their debts incurred during the three years of the contract: 'It was most difficult for the "stinkers", coolies who are lazy whether through aptitude or weakness, and therefore earn less' (Broersma 1919:257).

The pressure that indebtedness represented for the coolie's budget is shown by the directive that was introduced early in the twentieth century to the effect that at most half (!) the monthly wage might be retained as an instalment in repaying the advance. The pressure was made even greater because the advance that was received by recruitment and supplemented on later occasions, was recorded in the plantation's accounts at the earlier exchange rate rather than at its actual value. Certainly, the coolie received his credit balance at the fixed exchange rate of two NI guilders on completion of his contract, but in the main this was an empty gesture. Savings, if there were any, were in most cases hardly worth the name. After all, the wage paid for gruelling labour for endless hours increased little if at all in the course of a quarter-century. Moreover, the chance was considerable that the coolie, for a variety of reasons, would fail to achieve the very high work norm: a failure that was ruthlessly subjected to a miscellany of fines. Apart from the extra deductions made by the plantation's management, the coolie was exposed to various unofficial but no less effective levies made by the foreman. Against this background it is understandable why government officials in the region suggested that the Coolie Ordinance should include a clause to the effect that deductions might not be so high that they left less than the absolute minimum for subsistence (Bool 1904:62). In another way this constituted a plea for a minimum wage, a subsistence guarantee which the higher colonial authorities consistently refused to introduce.

Working Conditions

Housing. The workers were housed in coolie barracks which served as communal dormitories. A *kongsi* house provided accommodation for one or two gangs of Chinese together with their foremen, who appropriated a corner that was partitioned off from the rest, and were responsible for maintaining order among the coolies even outside working hours. From the managerial point of view, this was by far the cheapest and most simple way in which to house the workforce. Plantation literature gives the impression that the Chinese themselves preferred this arrangement, being accustomed, it was said, to living in an extended family. 'Separate dwellings for the Chinese workers are not desirable, even from the moral point of view. They will not lose their vices. In China the people live together in large houses and this should continue to be done here' (Mulier 1903:129).

It proved impossible to maintain this pretention in the case of the Javanese. The *pondok* in which they were housed could in no way be compared with the way in which they were accustomed to live in Java. They saw the barracks to which they were allocated as a punishment that was inherent in the work on the plantation (Ibid.:179; Versluys 1938:173).

The coolie lines were built in rows one behind the other, or in a rectangle around a yard containing the cooking-places. The stench and filth of the environment in which they had to live was made even worse by refuse and stagnant water, which were serious sources of disease (Tschudnowsky 1899:50). For latrines they had to use open pits dug close to the barracks. The barracks themselves had mud floors, wooden walls, and roofs thatched with dried leaves (atap). The interior of the barracks was extremely frugal, consisting almost entirely of sleeping benches on which the coolies also had to eat their meals. The Javanese pondoks were similarly furnished with one continuous wooden bed. The coolies were not even allowed a cupboard in which to keep their few personal possessions: a wooden box was said to be all that was necessary. The lack of any ventilation meant that the buildings were very stuffy and polluted by grime and soot. The poverty of such accommodation contrasted sharply with the wealth and elegance shown by the bungalows enjoyed by the administrative staff, especially those of the managers. To point out that pioneer Nienhuys had lived under the same roof with his coolies might rather rashly give the impression that social relations in the pioneering years were characterized by an intimacy resembling almost that of a family. Even then, however, the distance between the planter and the coolie was immeasurable, although patriarchal tendencies were not unknown. As the control of the plantations changed hands, i.e. as the planter-owner made way for estate manager, and as the workforce increased from a few dozen to many hundreds, the personal element colouring the former relations between the employer and his subordinates, disappeared. The coolies became little more than numbers, unrecognizable as individuals in the eyes of the European staff. The difference in accommodation was a visible sign of the separate worlds in which they lived. While the coolie barracks continued to be as wretched as they had always been, the housing of the higher personnel became increasingly more comfortable as confidence in the future of tobacco cultivation increased and prosperity grew.

Once future prospects became better, a spacious wooden house, two meters above the ground, would be built. This would have an atap roof and a lot of bamboo would still be used in the interior. In 1871 Jonkheer Leyssius on Gedong Johor replaced his bamboo house by a large house built of wood, and in the same period a prefabricated wooden house came from America for Arendsburg (*Kloempang*). The ironwork and locks were bought in Singapore (Broersma 1919:148).

This was very different to the first planter's house, which had cost no more than eight dollars (Naudin ten Cate 1905). Later still, the managers built imposing bungalows of stone, surrounded by gardens and with their own driveways, which are pictured in the memorial volumes of the plantation companies in all their variations. These stately mansions could and did compete with those of the highest-ranking government officials in the region; primarily, however, they were intended to overawe the coolies who worked on the plantation.

A large part of the workforce was not housed all the year through in the compound. These barracks were too far from the divisions where the tobacco was being grown in rotation. The coolies were consequently housed in temporary sheds during the fieldwork period. Drying sheds that had become unsuitable for their original purpose through leakages, were sometimes used for sheltering coolies, but they could also be put into a block of smaller sheds among which the foreman took up a commanding position.

The coolies are accommodated in two to four sheds, with ten to twenty men per shed; the *tandil's* tenement stands in the middle. The sheds front the road on one side, and a communal kitchen is built on the other side, with an eye to the risk of fire. The kitchen is an open shed in which each Chinese cooks his own little pot of rice and vegetables a couple of times a day, above a fire of wood that he has first gleaned (Ibid.).

'Kitchen' is rather too grand a term for the open place where the coolie had to prepare his food. Sanitary facilities were entirely lacking: why should not the coolie manure his field with his own waste? When cultivation in a particular division ended, all the sheds and huts were pulled down and taken to the new clearing. In this way, the coolies circulated through the plantation acreage as new fields were opened-up. During work in the drying and fermenting sheds, however, they all returned to the compound, where barracks provided a more permanent though scarcely better accommodation.

The members of a gang were together by night as well as by day, a communal mode of living which precluded any form of privacy.

Notwithstanding the rising number of Javanese women coolies, they were not usually given separate accommodation. Even unmarried girls and women had to live in the same barracks as the men (Van den Brand 1902:69). Couples tried to ignore the proximity of the others by screening-off their part of the shed with old sacks. Very few plantations had taken any notice of the recommendation that partitions should be built into the *pondoks* so that married coolies could have something like privacy. Only on a few estates and by way of experiment, had detached huts been built that to some extent met the style of living to which the Javanese were accustomed. It was not the lack of housing for the Javanese women which caused concern to the management, so much as the behaviour that resulted from it. Strict instructions were issued in the interests of maintaining discipline and decency.

... non-observance of the order that Javanese women are not allowed to stay in the Chinese *kongsis* at night, or conversely, that the Chinese may not show themselves in the Javanese *pondoks*, will give rise to punishment. Such conduct, especially when married Javanese women are concerned, can be the cause of disorder and even worse (Bool 1904:55–6).

Food and Health Care. The workers had to provide their own meals, and the maintenance allowance which the field coolies received twice a month was almost completely used for their basic food needs. The morning and evening meal consisted primarily, if not solely, of rice, often bought on credit from the plantation shop. They were neither allowed the time nor the land to plant vegetables or rice. Only the local peasantry might grow a rice crop for one season only on the harvested fields; the plantation's own coolies were not permitted to do so. The fact that coolies on the early plantations were allowed a piece of land on which to grow foodcrops in their spare time, shows that in this respect too the work process had become gradually more capitalistic.

To give paddy fields to permanent workers or contract coolies, however much one would like to do so, is not to be recommended because the time that they needed for planting, caring for and harvesting the rice could mean that they would absent themselves from plantation work (Westerman 1901:210).

Meat was eaten only on very special days when the management had an ox slaughtered for the benefit of the workers. The foreman often regulated his gang's housekeeping, naturally looking to his own advantage (Senembah Company 1939:22). The meals were prepared by the *kedei* keeper, by the foreman's wife, or by a *kongsi* cook who was especially engaged for the purpose. In the latter case, his pay was charged by the management to the members of the gang or gangs for whom he catered. Quite commonly, however, no such arrangement would be made: when the coolies returned to their shed at the end of an excessively long day there was no food ready for them, and each one individually then prepared his or her own meal.

In view of the wretched living and working conditions, disease and death must have been daily occurrences towards the end of the last century. Plantation literature likes to give the impression that after the arduous pioneering period when many thousands of coolies lost their lives in converting the jungle into cultivable ground, the situation improved considerably. The biggest plantations employed their own medical personnel. Initially they were medical orderlies who mostly came from India and were recruited in the Straits Settlements. To these were gradually added European doctors, twelve of whom were employed by 1889. These were charged with the care of 700 Europeans and tens of thousands of plantation coolies (Naudin ten Cate 1905). The memorial volumes almost all include photographs of the plantation hospitals, some of which dated from long before the turn of the century. After all, was it not in the employer's own interests that the workforce should be well looked after? This seems rather doubtful, in fact, given the fairly low cost of replacement once the plantations were assured of a continual supply of new labour. Nevertheless, the few health statistics that became available around the turn of the century give the impression that the mortality rate had dropped to less than 10 per cent per year. The most extensive information that is available concerns the plantations of the Senembah Company, where the number of deaths dropped from 60.2 to 45.1 per thousand between 1897 and 1901 (Schuffner and Kuenen 1910:20). When we consider that the plantation population consisted mainly of young men who were selected for their physical strength and who, moreover, underwent a medical examination immediately on arrival, this figure is still unacceptably high; nevertheless, it was far lower than that of the earlier period. Two doctors explained the decrease in mortality in terms of the reduction of epidemic diseases, malnutrition (in 1891 and 1896, for example, cholera and beri-beri had caused enormous numbers of deaths) and easing of the onerous work regime so that Chinese coolies no longer literally worked themselves to death.

This favourable trend seemed to apply to the entire East Coast of Sumatra. According to official data, at least, the mortality rate among the Chinese coolies in 1901 was 5 per cent and among the Javanese coolies 3.3 per cent. There is good reason to distrust these statistics, however. The source from which I have derived the information also mentions that the plantations were not obliged to report the number of deaths (Hoetink 1902:51–2). Moreover, coolies who migrated from their home regions but did not reach their destination were not registered. High death rates aboard the ships in which indentured coolies were transported from China were not in the least exceptional. More than 7 and 11 per cent of the contracted coolies died on two transports around the turn of the century, either during the journey or shortly after arrival (Mulier 1903:100–1). Tschudnowsky noted in his diary that cholera had broken out in 1896 aboard Chinese ships anchored in the harbour of Belawan. He stated that the coolies were transported like *atap* leaves, piled one on top of the other. There was no better source of cholera infection, he went on, than the hold of a ship which could accommodate barely forty people but into which 102 were forced. A few days later he noted that fifty-one of those 102 had died. But they were not the only deaths because bodies had earlier been seen floating down the river. The worst of all were the sufferers who, on arrival, were forced to stay on board: they lay side by side on the deck, under the burning sun, without food, and were forbidden by the coolie broker to complain to the authorities (Tschudnowsky 1899:63). Had the time really gone when, as one manager candidly admitted, 'roughly a third of the contracted scum perished?' (Rookmaker 1904:811) When a health inspector visited a mining company elsewhere in Sumatra in 1900, he discovered that 23.76 per cent of the workforce died each year. Similar conditions were probably also prevalent in the newly cleared areas of Sumatra's East Coast which lay outside the actual tobacco belt.

When new plantations were laid out for coffee and, somewhat later, rubber, the same primitive conditions which prevailed earlier in the Deli region occurred (cf. Proceedings Lower House 1902-3, App.B:67–8). A somewhat cryptic report is to be found in the memorial volume of the Senembah Company, which in fact prided itself on its health care facilities.

In 1890 we suffered very heavy losses that were ascribed to the poor quality of the new coolies from China. Years of satisfactory health conditions now alternated with others in which we had Beri-Beri epidemics or, due to prolonged heat or over-abundant rainfall, Cholera and Dysentery which were horrifyingly rife and claimed many, many victims. Among the causes of death, Anaemia and Malaria played a great part, while on the higher plantations with their uneven terrain most complaints were about the sickly constitution of the coolies, and dysentery was a common phenomenon (Senembah Company 1939:30).

Figures mentioned by Van Kol show that in the newly–developed areas in 1901 the death rate was far above 10 per cent (Van Kol 1903:100). The conditions that prevailed in 1909, when a region in Asahan was opened-up for rubber cultivation, have been listed in an official report, summarized by Endt.

At the point of destination there was no accommodation whatsoever. Mud and dirt were their mattress. Many were starving because they had sold their rice rations to some sly Malay. There were no permanent houses or *pondoks*. In the makeshift hospital no vaseline, iodine or castor oil was available. Mortality was high, reaching as much as 30 per cent, because of appallingly poor washing facilities (Endt 1919:149).

The original Coolie Ordinance had made medical care for the coolies compulsory, but on its revision some years later the words 'proper' and 'free' had to be added. That the coolies were not given what was theirs by right is clearly shown in a medical paper which Tschudnowsky published together with an extract from his diary. Dysentery, malaria and tropical ulcers were listed as the most common complaints by this plantation doctor, who worked in Deli from 1894 to 1896. According to Tschudnowsky, another important cause of the high mortality rate was the fact that many coolies were physically and mentally unable to cope with the harsh life on the plantations and very soon collapsed under the heavy work regime. Similar facts have been registered by other authors writing about plantation life on Sumatra in the early capitalist stage.

In general, these physically weak people seem to be overcome by a sort of apathy; many seem to lose all desire to live; they can be seen, frequently still quite young, indifferently waiting for death. Investigation of their past would probably bring to light a long sequence of misery and deprivation; these people are all too often the victims of grinding toil and insufficient food. Their blank faces, their staring eyes —I can still see them in front of me whenever I think back to my visit to some of the Deli hospitals (Van Kol 1903:101).

An obvious reaction was to deny that the coolies had got into this situation while employed on Sumatra's East Coast and as a result of the treatment to which they were subjected. The former harbour master of Belawan, for example, declared that the Javanese in particular looked wretched when they arrived: 'badly fed, anaemic and haggard people' (Wintgens, in Rookmaker 1904:816). He was not surprised that many of them proved unable to cope with the new milieu to which they had come and died an early death, but this fate would probably have been equally unavoidable in their own country. But even the Chinese who, as he admitted, seemed healthy and strong on arrival, underwent a similar metamorphosis. After just a few months they looked quite different, with a pallid, yellowish complexion, very emaciated, their legs covered with ulcers and with abscesses over their entire body (Tschudnowsky 1899:49). Anyone who is familiar with the lack of hygiene on the plantations and with the bad state of health of the workforce, will never again touch his lips to the famous Sumatran wrapping leaf, this doctor informed his readers.

Why did a coolie continue to work even when he or she was not fit to do so? In the first place because a coolie who absented himself due to sickness received no pay. If illness made a coolie unable to work for more than thirty days, originally intended to be consecutive but taken by the management to mean the total number of days throughout the entire contract, he or she was obliged to serve that time after the termination of the contract. This imposed yet another penalty for bad health, even though this resulted from the heavy work that they were forced to do under horrible conditions and primitive facilities. In the second place, the coolie continued to work because of the poor conditions in the plantation's infirmary. Tschudnowsky has described how it was only with great difficulty that he could procure any food for his   patients. He found it necessary to appoint a special watchman to help him in sharing out the daily ration. The patients frequently depended on support from outside the infirmary for their meals, either on other members of their own gang or on the foreman, and this form of help was converted into a debt relationship. If the plantation provided their food then it was debited to their account, notwithstanding a prohibition by the Resident (District Circular 16 April 1894, SEC coll. RTI). The planters simply cannot bring themselves to realize that proper medical care of the coolies would be in their own interest, said Tschudnowsky (1899:44). That realization was not to grow until many years later. Schuffner and Kuenen (1910:42) have justifiably pointed out that, paradoxical though it may seem, the increase in hospital attendance from 39 per cent of all workers in 1897 to no less than 76 per cent in 1906, did not signify an increase in the rate of illness but an improvement of medical care. On the other hand, this fact illustrates how wretched the lives of the coolies must have been. But indifference regarding the fate of their workers was not the only reason why employers at first refused to introduce even the most elementary facilities. They believed that the majority of those who reported sick were shamming and that better medical care would only encourage that 'loitering and marauding'. According to Hoetink, patients who complained that their food rations were insufficient showed a healthy appetite that hardly befitted a sick person. He advocated that the hospital doctors should be given the right to apply disciplinary methods to unwilling and troublesome coolies and thus to expedite their recovery (Hoetink 1902:35). This recommendation, made by the official who was to become the first head of the Labour Inspectorate, is in sharp contrast to the reports drawn up late in 1901 by the Regional Health Officer on the orders of the Resident, after he had visited some of the plantation hospitals.

Dr Maier described how he had found patients in a state of total filth, with no medical care whatsoever and even without food. When he visited one infirmary, a woman who had already been there for three weeks, begged him to give her something to eat. Against all the regulations, the plantation management had not provided food. Taking as his basis an ill-health percentage that was grossly under-stated, Maier calculated that the hospital accommodation available was far below even that norm. When he discussed this situation with some of the managers, they declared that illness rarely occurred on their plantations and that no special medical facilities were required. Maier's story clearly shows why the coolies often over-exerted themselves to avoid having to go to the hospital: plantation doctors, were paid 25 to 30 cents per patient per day on top of their very generous monthly salary of 1,000 to 1,300 guilders. Although this was intended to cover nursing costs (medicines and food), the doctors tended to consider this daily allowance as a source of extra income and therefore to economize as much as possible on any expenditure. Neglect was also evident in the absence of even the most elementary facilities that belonged to any hospital. The lack of a washplace meant that bathing was only possible for those patients who were able to walk for five or ten minutes to the river. There were no lavatories or even a chamber pot, no lamp to provide light at night, and no drinking water. Men and women shared the same ward; even the gravity of the disease (whether or not it was contagious) was no reason for separation. The beds, made of wood or of iron, had no mattresses and were covered only by a sack made of jute, usually without any pillow or sheet. The medical care was hardly worth the name. The doctor was responsible for many plantations and could only visit them once or twice per month. Very often there was not even an orderly to look after the patients. Frequently, the door of the room in which they stayed was closed on the outside by a chain. The condition in which Maier found the sick coolies was so bad that, while still on his tour of inspection, he asked the junior official who accompanied him to ensure that the most seriously ill patients would be immediately transferred to the central hospital in the nearby town. Maier censured the indifference shown by the doctor in charge, called the treatment revolting and cruel, and considered that there was evidence of premeditated neglect. The following passages taken from his report illustrate this.

A woman who was seriously ill lay on a frame of steel wire on four legs; as mattress she had only a piece of a gunny sack. There was no pillow and, with her head on the iron frame, she was forced to lay her head on one of her arms. She suffered from a venereal disease and also had catarrh of the bladder; a purulent discharge dripped from between her matchstick legs onto the floor. There was no bowl or any other receptacle in which to catch the discharge, around which the flies gathered repulsively.

Another woman was lying on her deathbed.

... her pulse could no longer be felt, her nose and ears were icy-cold, her eyes were broken; she was unable to answer when I spoke to her. Her extremities were cold, she was disgustingly filthy and unwashed. She had a wound on her left buttock, most probably caused by bedsores. Her right foot was completely stripped of any skin, and sores were forming on her back. This suffering woman had lain there for about a month. She wore an old, filthy *sarong* and *kabaya*, and lay on the wooden planks on a dirty gunny sack, without a pillow. Faeces, dirt and urine were found under her; neither of her wounds showed any sign at all of any medical treatment!!! (Maier 1901, SEC, coll. RTI).

The coolies had very good reason to consider the infirmary as an augury of death. And when they died, what happened? As early as 1889 an official memorandum urged the planters to set aside a piece of land as a burial ground. It was customary on many estates to shovel their dead coolies (the report mentioned an average figure of forty deaths per year on each plantation) into the ground on some piece of waste land, with no thought for the religious practices of the various ethnic categories. From Tschudnowsky's remarks (1899:45) it seems that this official recommendation was not complied with. Before his arrival on the East Coast, dead coolies had simply been thrown into the *alang -alang* fields close to the hospital. In later years such revolting practices continued, as is shown in a report on the state of affairs in a gold-mine in 1900.

When a coolie dies, the administration provides ten ells of white cotton in which to wrap the corpse, after that the burying is left to a couple of coolies. As a result, the grave is so shallow that wild pigs have little trouble in enjoying its contents. In this way, a dead Chinese costs the plantation only two and a half guilders (Redjang Lebong 1901).

Van den Brand would later justifiably bring such practices to the eyes of the public (1902:43–7).

'*Rest and Recreation*'. The two paydays per month were counted as official work stoppages, but there was no question of the workers having a day off. In the early morning hours they were given odd jobs to do, such as road sweeping, clearing away any rubbish near the buildings etc., before the half-monthly settlement would start.

No payment was made for this extra work. The coolies could do as they wished for the rest of the day, within certain limits; but at least on this day they had permission to leave the plantation in order to visit the nearest town. On a normal working day, free time was unknown. The coolies did not return to their barracks until after dusk, and sometimes continued to work in their fields in the evenings. Moreover, who would have any business away from the plantation at night? Management valued the wholesome effect of an early bedtime.

If the workman leaves the plantation after completing his day's task this can only be exceptional for a permissible purpose; even if he does not intend any mischief, he will be better off staying at home and, through tranquil sleep, strengthen his body for the work that tomorrow will be demanded of him (Hoetink 1902:47).

They were not allowed to leave the coolie barracks after nine o'clock in the evening (Haarsma 1889:113). In other words, the coolie had no freedom of movement. He could leave the plantation only after obtaining permission from the management. If a worker dared to ask for leave, this was almost always refused. Although the Coolie Ordinance laid down that coolies should be given leave-passes, very few plantations ever did so. It was argued that the worker was apt to lose such an identity card or would use it for deceitful purposes. The real reason, however, was fear that the coolie would run away, whether or not incited to do so by others. 'The evil of absconding was widespread, crimps were always active and no manager would encourage running-away by giving unnecessary leave at a time when a wave of desertion plagued the East Coast' (Broersma 1919:254).

The police in the region were intimated in advance when paydays were held on the plantations, and on those occasions the workers were apparently not required to identify themselves. Foremen were sent to the towns to keep an eye on things. On a normal workday, any coolie encountered outside the plantation was automatically considered to be infringing the regulations unless he or she could provide proof to the contrary. By refusing to issue leave-passes the employers hampered the labourers' freedom of movement outside the plantation, and that was precisely their intention.

Thus, entertainment, such as it was, had to be enjoyed on the plantation itself. Towards the end of their work in the sheds, as the great annual payday approached, the workforce was treated to a *wajang* performance or to Chinese theatre. It was a great festivity for which a troupe, sometimes brought over from Malaya especially for the performance, was engaged at the cost of the management or of the head foreman. They could easily afford the expenditure and, besides, the new season was just around the corner. A show of goodwill at the time when contracts had to be renewed could do no harm.

Gambling provided a much more important break for the coolies in the awful monotony of their existence. Even this relaxation, however, was officially restricted to the period that they spent working in the sheds. After complaints by a Chinese delegation which visited the East Coast in 1887, the authorities at first intended to forbid all gambling on the plantation. They changed their minds after a protest by the planters who feared that the coolies would otherwise visit gambling dens outside the plantation on paydays and there become easy prey to the crimps (Memorial DPV 1929:57–8). According to the employers, it was far easier to check such practices if gambling was restricted to the premises of the plantation.

All gaming franchises in the region belonged to a wealthy Chinese who sold the right to gamble to the head foreman of each plantation, with the concurrence of management, for one thousand guilders a year. In 1908–9 the head *tandils* of twenty-three plantations belonging to the Deli Company together paid 40,080 guilders in gaming leases. Their own gambling debts were considerable.

I noticed on a couple of occasions that some of the head *tandils* employed by the Deli Company, who were in Medan in their free time, gambled with cheques worth three to four thousand guilders. When I went through a ledger belonging to one of them, I found an item of 12,000 guilders, lost in one evening (De Bruin 1918:88).

The head foreman made over his gambling right to some of his trusted subordinates, who then held the bank in the gambling shed (Broersma 1922:122).

The opium franchise was contracted-out in the same way, and the foremen similarly benefitted from encouraging its addiction (Senembah Company 1939:35). Such practices enable us to map the relationships which linked the Chinese headmen in the region to the foremen of the plantations. The Chinese headmen who acted as opium franchisers, gambling licensees, and brothel owners in the towns, were appointed by the colonial authorities. The colonial government also had a financial interest in gambling and opium smoking. In 1879, for example, profits from the sale of these leases brought in almost as much money as all other forms of taxation in the Residency combined (e.g. import and export duties and alcohol tax). The result was a not insignificant surplus on the regional budget as a whole. To put it differently: the costs of the civil service, of the judicature and of the army all together could be defrayed entirely from the opium franchise (Broersma 1919:139), and were therefore paid by the coolies themselves. By the turn of the century, this situation showed no change. In 1901 government expenditure in the region amounted to 2,200,000 guilders, while total income grossed 5,300,000 guilders. A breakdown of this latter amount shows that taxes and excise duties, paid mostly if not entirely by the coolies, provided the lion's share of the government's income. Levies on opium, dicing and arrack, industrial taxes, and the registration fees on contracted coolies, brought in a sum that far exceeded the government's expenditure. In 1901 and 1902 the opium franchise and the gambling tax came to 2,259,500 and 2,321,980 guilders respectively, causing the East Coast to tower head and shoulders above almost all other regions of the archipelago (Mail Report 546, 1902).

More than anything else, it was in the interest of the plantation that the workers should have to spend more for their 'recreation'. That was why the management stimulated the use of opium by giving the coolies a subsidy of 20 per cent of the price (Hoetink 1902:14). It is misleading to use the term 'stimulant' for a medicine that brought some relief to the coolie's suffering and ensured that he continued to be productive until he was destroyed in the work process. Opium helped the coolie to keep going until the end, but it also made him poorer. Cremer, an unimpeachable source as a spokesman of the planters lobby, pointed out that the government encouraged the vices for which the Chinese coolies were infamous.

Without mentioning that the planters had an even greater interest in ensuring the addiction of their contract coolies, he continued:

... that by far the larger majority do not bring their greatest defects with them, particularly opium smoking and gambling, but learn them after their arrival in the colony which gave them plenty of opportunity to do so, not in order to meet an existing need but to create one, to the advantage of the government's treasury (Cremer 1881:39-40).

Tschudnowsky also states that, in general, the Chinese coolies started to smoke opium after their arrival on the East Coast. Its use accelerated the deterioration of their labour power but, on the other hand, it provided solace in intolerable circumstances (Tschudnowsky 1899:49).

The employers' wish to keep gambling within the confines of the plantation also arose from the opportunity that this offered to force the workers, through indebtedness, to renew their contracts. The foreman did not act on his own initiative, but was encouraged by the management.

The head *tandil* purchases a licence that makes it possible to gamble at the time when accounts are settled in the permanent or temporary gambling shed on the plantation, and the coolies need no encouragement to play until all their money has gone, after which they avidly take the advance that ties them anew to the plantation (Hoetink 1902:19).

This brings me finally to a discussion of the ways in which coolies could be forced to stay on after their contracts had expired.

Termination and Renewal of the Labour Contract

After a three-year term a coolie would have fulfilled his obligations and his contract with the plantation would be automatically terminated. But when had it started? The formal criterion was the date on which the contract had been signed. The Javanese did that when they were recruited in Java. The Chinese signed the contract soon after they disembarked from the ship that had brought them to Deli, or after reaching the plantation, when the coolie held the pen with which the assistant made him put a cross by his name. This was an almost ceremonial happening, certainly for illiterates, and impressed upon the coolies the irrevocability of the agreement into which they were entering. The labour contract became effective after being registered with the regional authorities of the East Coast. This was purely an administrative procedure, usually completed at the office of the local civil servant acting as a magistrate of the administrative division in which the plantation was situated. The formality was intended to allow the officials to ascertain whether the labour contract was in agreement with the provisions of the Coolie Ordinance. In principle the registration had to be done shortly after the coolie's arrival, but in practice there was frequently quite a long delay. In calculating the length of service, however, the planters started from the date of registration, even though the coolie might already have been at work for some considerable time. The planters also nearly always held on to coolies who had served their time until the work in the sheds was over, even if that meant exceeding the contract period to a significant extent. Although all this was contrary to the law, the employer could do it with impunity due to the lack of any government control over the stipulation that each coolie, after the termination of his contract, was to be issued with a notice of discharge. Planters who were caught out, more or less by accident, merely replied that the coolies in question had not asked for such a notice. The few workers who had the effrontery to do so were all too often punished (Hoetink 1902:51). If, ultimately, they received that coveted piece of paper, which they were unable to read, it frequently included remarks that turned it into a certificate of bad conduct (Bool 1904:70). Without a letter of discharge the coolies were not allowed to leave the plantation. If they did do so, they ran the risk of being arrested for vagrancy (Van den Brand 1903:12).

The coolie contract was valid for a maximum of three years. Although the wording left the possibility of a shorter term, in practice this never occurred. Interim dissolution of the agreement was permitted if the coolie had discharged all his obligations, i.e. if he had succeeded in repaying all cash advances and further allowances. This was little more than hypothetical, however, and it was far more likely that a coolie had to continue to work after the expiry of his contract. Absenteeism from work due to illness or desertion were the most common reasons for extending the contracted time period. It was the practice of the planters to count all the days on which a coolie was absent due to illness. If these totalled more than thirty, as was the case more often than not, they insisted on the coolie working for an equal period of time. Absenteeism among women, due to menstruation problems and pregnancy, was higher than among men. Hoetink mentions the case of one woman who, at the end of her three-year contract, was told that her employer claimed another 565 working days (Hoetink 1902:67). Similarly, the coolies had to make up for the days that they lost due to desertion and for the length of the prison sentence that they were consequently given.

Nevertheless, the employment could not be protracted endlessly. If the work contract had been fulfilled and they were not in debt, the coolies were free people again. They could not be prevented from leaving the plantation, either to offer their services elsewhere or to return to the place from where they came. The authorities discouraged them from settling as free men or women on the East Coast, fearing that if they were to remain there without signing on for a second term with the same or another plantation, the number of paupers in the region would steadily increase. This concern, expressed in various government reports (Ibid.:53), tells us all we need to know about the condition in which coolies were unleashed on society after discharge. The employer was expected to pay the cost of returning the coolies to their places of origin, not least because they were all too often unable to bear the expense of the journey home. But it rarely got that far. Before the end of the nineteenth century only a minority had returned to China or to Java. The greater number of those who survived their first term of work had to sign on for a second stint: not voluntarily, but forced to do so by the indebtedness from which they were unable to free themselves and into which they would fall once again.

All in all, the contract coolie has a considerable chance of still being in debt at the end of his contract. On the one hand the coolie thinks that he cannot go away as long as he is in the red in his master's books; on the other hand the employer wants to retain him, and as long as the latter can ensure that the coolie remains in debt, it is easy enough to persuade him to sign a new contract (Ibid.:21).

The method usually adopted was to encourage those coolies whose contract expired during the shed work to spend more money than they had earned during the preceding months. At this time, prostitutes were allowed on the plantation, plenty of opportunity was given for games of chance, and the smoking of opium.

On this occasion the head *tandil* enjoys almost unlimited credit with the plantation because the management knows for which purpose the money will be spent. Although it is not always explicitly put into words, it is a tacit condition that the cash will be lent to the coolies whose employment contract has expired or whose future profits [the balance between what they received in advance during their fieldwork and the sum that they were paid at the end of the season] is greater than their debt to the plantation (Van den Brand 1902:64).

Coolie fiddling was the name given to the signing of a new contract. The labourers were able to square their debts to the gang boss with the advances received from the management. However, they were then once again in the red with their employer, and for a long time wages increased little if at all due to the custom of putting-out work at a fixed rate. The situation of the coolies therefore showed no fundamental improvement.

The local authorities were also expected to register the new agreement, but this was frequently done just as carelessly as the first time. Instead of drawing up a new contract, the employer merely mentioned that it was prolonged (Bool 1904:42). It is obvious that the contract formed a trap for the unwary. If the coolies rose to the bait, there was almost no way back after the three-year term. Apart from the two purposes of the Coolie Ordinance that we have discussed earlier, i.e. to keep a sufficient workforce available and to maintain its price at the lowest possible level, there was also a third. The employers were virtually assured of the extension of a contract if they so wished. The assertion that a coolie contract was of a temporary character applied only to those whose presence was no longer needed or who were able to break away from the enormous pressure that was brought to bear on them.

The situation was quite different, of course, if coolies became 'redundant'; that is to say, if due to company closure or the sale of the plantation to another corporation, the workforce became partly or wholly superfluous. In such a case, the terms of their contract gave them the formal right to discharge and to go back to their place of origin. In actual fact, however, they were treated as merchandise, transferred to a recruiting office by the employer against compensation for the amount still outstanding to him for advances. Subsequently, the coolies were resold to new buyers, naturally still in a state of indebtedness (Hoetink 1902:53–4).

IV

LABOUR CONTROL AND RESISTANCE

Bondage

The rigid regimentation of the workforce was one of the most striking features of plantation life on Sumatra's East Coast around the turn of the century. The plantation system was arranged along military lines, and the confinement of the coolies to their own premises befitted such a disciplinary system. Those who had to serve out the term of their contract usually had no alternative but to resign themselves to a labour regime that deprived them of any mobility. The few who succeeded in breaking away had no choice but to leave the region. Together with the employers, the authorities did their best to discourage former contract coolies from settling outside the estates. 'Stray' coolies represented a risk that had to be prevented to the extent possible.

The bondage of the workers could not be denied: after all, that was the actual objective. According to the reasoning that prevailed in colonial circles, however, the coolies entered into the arrangement voluntarily in the expectation of deriving material benefits from it, whether immediately or later. That those advantages failed to materialize, mostly due to their own shortcomings, was deplorable, of course, but was not there any reason to doubt as to whether they had signed the contract of their own free will? Reports about deception and fraud began to be heard almost immediately after the recruitment started. In Malaya, rumours were soon heard that people had been kidnapped and taken by force to the Sumatran plantations. Chinese coolies invited to a *wajang* performance had been rounded-up by armed men and forcibly shipped out to Deli (Van Sandick 1909:23). As we have already seen, the appointment of a Protector of Chinese in 1877 was a direct result of regular complaints about such abuses.

Even as early as 1871, the streets of one of south China's harbours were hung with posters protesting against the forced shipment of coolies from the Straits Settlements to Deli, the authorities in Singapore were informed by the British consul in Swatow. Reid, who mentioned this, quoted another source dating from 1875 which confirmed that:

There exists, in the Chinese labour market, a perfect hatred of the name of 'Deli', which operates not only inimically to that particular place, but also as regards the whole Island—so much so that the Chinese who will ship willingly to Langkat or Serdang, in ignorance of the precise 'locale' of those places, will become perfectly mad if the word 'Deli' be heard on board (quoted in Reid 1970:299).

Once the flow of coolies from Java really got into its stride, the number of complaints about fraud, kidnapping and other nefarious practices of the recruiting agents began to increase. In 1882, only two years after the proclamation of the Coolie Ordinance, an inquiry held among the newly-arrived coolies brought these abuses to light (Bool 1904:45–6). The complaints were to be repeated persistently well into the twentieth century, but without much result. Indebtedness rather than force was primarily the means with which men, women and even children were wrenched from their homes and intimidated into emigration. Under such circumstances, it is nothing other than a colonial fantasy to maintain that a contract was entered into voluntarily. Until the end of colonial rule, rumours that jobbers were active in several parts of Java caused panic among mothers, who would not allow their children to leave the house. The outcome of government investigations were invariably defensive, saying that such rumours were baseless, and that complaints were out-dated, ill-founded, etc. Immediately after recruitment the coolies were kept in detention penned up in depots like convicts. They made the journey from the interior of Java to the coastal ports under constant guard so as to minimize any risk of escape.

They had no say about their final destination. 'This was decided by the emigration office and determined by hanging a card around the neck of the migrants before their photograph was taken; strangely enough, these people did not seem to mind their arbitrary selection . . .' (Stecher 1905b:5).

Even the most elementary facilities were lacking on the ships that brought the coolies to Sumatra. Many had to remain on deck, tightly packed together and exposed to wind and rain, during the journey which lasted several days. Below deck the passage was worse. Accommodation for sleeping was not at all necessary, wrote a medical inspector in 1906.

It is enough to paint coloured lines on the floor of the ship's hold and to keep some passages open for inspection. ... Any additional facility will not increase comfort but will contribute to filth. One must think of the fruit peels, the chewing of betelnuts and the effects of sea sickness (Kuenen 1906:22).

Small wonder that the coolies reached the East Coast in a state of disarray and exhaustion. It was only fitting that they should be booked as freight (Stecher 1905b:35). Their reception on reaching the East Coast harbours and the inspection procedure that followed after a compulsory bath and selection in the depot, could only lead to one conclusion, namely, that the migrants had lost all say over their labour power. On the final leg of their journey, from Belawan port to the plantations in the hinterland, they travelled in railway vans like cattle (Rothe 1946:328). Freight and cattle, the associations were not incidental. From the time of their recruitment the coolies were systematically dehumanized in order that, even before their work started they would be degraded effectively to resemble a labour commodity, pure and simple.

The distribution of each coolie transport depended on demand. The employers in mutual consultation regulated the sending of new batches to the plantations, where they would be confined for the length of their stay. The strongly hierarchical structure of the industry went hand-in-hand with systematic subjugation of the imported labour force. This began immediately on the coolies' arrival at the plantation. They were housed in barracks and split-up into gangs headed by foremen who, after working hours, acted as warders entrusted with maintaining discipline. Each estate also had its own watchmen in charge of security, whose task it was to register everything that might seem suspicious from the viewpoint of the management. They had to prevent coolies from deserting and, conversely, to keep away any undesirable intruders such as coolie crimps.

These were Bengalese, Penang Malays, Javanese or Klings. The first are mostly discharged soldiers from British India, or former policemen from one of the states of the Malay peninsula. These are preferable to all others in that they have learned to shoot, something that can be very useful in the event of riots (Westerman 1901:42).

Once absorbed into the plantation regime, it was well-nigh impossible for the coolies to break loose. This was also the moral code impressed upon them. Intimidation which slid into the use of force was not the only way in which the confinement of the coolies to the plantation was ensured. The contract was initiated on a basis of indebtedness, and the impossibility for a coolie to free himself of that debt was undoubtedly the most important reason why the contract endured. The prominent part played by the Asian foreman in all this has already been described. Insofar as the plantation literature discusses the more objectionable sides of the foreman's role, it should be remembered that such practices were tacitly accepted or even actively promoted by the management. It was an economical way in which to ensure work discipline and one which, moreover, was defrayed by the workers themselves rather than by the employers.

Around 1900 the first generation of Javanese coolies born on the estates made their appearance in the work process. This development was against the will of many planters who steadfastly refused to allow their coolies to have families on the plantations because of the wage increase this would inevitably involve. Apart from that, the planters were delighted with the quality of these *anak Deli*. They had become accustomed at a very early age to earn a few cents by picking tobacco leaves and thus to look after their own requirements (Hoetink 1902:41). It was not unusual for children to start working at the age of seven.

... they help the women with watering the plants, they search for insects, a job which is particularly suitable for children who need not stoop down and who, with their excellent eyesight and nimble fingers, catch many caterpillars and other insects; these little caterpillar catchers are a common sight in the tobacco fields of Java and Deli. This is all work that does not harm the children's health (Rothe 1946:345–6).

Such statements were intended to soothe and also to imply that it would be nonsensical to criticize these practices as being exploitative of children. But ultimately, that was what it was all about. At that time, there was no question of a stable labour force which would renew itself on-the-spot through reproduction. This was not to become the dominant policy until later in the twentieth century, eventually bringing a halt to the import of new labour that had characterized the first half-century of the plantation system.

Conditioning of the Plantation Coolies

It would be incorrect to assume that pure force was the only way of putting coolies to work and keeping them at it. In fact, informal mechanisms played a significant role in the everyday routine. The absorption of contract labour into the production process depended on experience and attitude. Newcomers who displayed the necessary qualities of industriousness, obedience, punctuality and deference to their superiors, were soon allocated a field on which they had to carry out all the tasks necessary in a crop cycle. An ingenious system of cash advances and piece-work jobs kept them tied in a state of dependence on the one hand, but spurred them to maximum effort on the other. Those who turned out to be unsatisfactory, were considered to be inefficient, lazy or troublesome, and they continued to work as helpers in the field (*kongsikang*) or were demoted to that rank. The work target was set very high, leaving the coolies with little time or energy for anything other than work. Many were worn out in the production process and were not considered eligible for a second term after their contract ended, even if they themselves wished to stay on. The planters preferred to rely on fresh workers, partly because their training needed very little time, and in any case the coolies themselves had to meet the costs incurred on that score.

Work was organized on competitive lines. For example, if a field coolie was unable to complete a particular task, he obtained the help of a gang-mate who had already finished his own work for that day. However, the extra reward that the latter received for his assistance was deducted from the pay due to the coolie who had been deficient. Another common occurrence was that a coolie who had spent or gambled away his fortnightly allowance would work during the night on another's field in return for a meal (Römer 1885:421). Finally, trusted old hands were given a bonus to return to their homes and ensnare fellow villagers in the same trap into which they themselves had fallen a prey. The result was a systematic contractualization of relationships between the coolies. Moreover, the recruitment pattern fostered the emergence of differences among the workers. Ethnic fragmentation hampered horizontal solidarity and facilitated the outbreak of violence among different *kongsis* or between the Chinese and the Javanese. The 'quarrelsome nature of the workers' provided the planters with yet another justification for maintaining order and discipline with a heavy hand.

Coolies known to be reliable and trustworthy were considered for promotion to the rank of a foreman. The price they had to pay was unconditional loyalty to the estate's management. The foremen formed the lowest and at the same time the most important link in the chain of discipline. These low-ranking bosses not only carried out the orders from above, but were also charged with reporting back about what was going on at the bottom level. Through this channel, and through the head foreman, the manager was also able to form an idea of the European assistants' ability to command, and of their willingness and capability to adapt themselves to plantation life. There was a hierarchy of loyalties, which was strongly compartmentalized. To the coolies, their obligations to their own foremen were probably of overriding importance rather than to the demands made by the European staff, with whom they had little to do and even less to share.

All these informal mechanisms with their partly binding, partly divisive effect, enabled the management to keep a grip on the workers. The Coolie Ordinance was indispensable in this respect, providing planters with a prominent instrument with which to discipline the labour. By exerting pressure on the colonial government to keep a tight hand on the free movement of the workforce at a time of extreme labour scarcity, the united planters succeeded in insuring themselves against the risk of imported labour cancelling their contracts which, according to the legal fiction, they had entered into 'voluntarily'. The influence of the planters lobby, pre-eminent champions of free enterprise, was of decisive significance both in the proclamation of the original Ordinance as in its preservation in later years. In addition, the colonial authorities helped the employers to systematically block the transition to a system of free labour when such tendencies became manifest on the East Coast. Earlier, the regional authorities even tried to halt the growing practice of employing more specialized workers as free casual labour on a piece-work basis.

According to an official memorandum written in 1883 to the managers of plantations, it was no longer permitted to employ '... sawyers, tree-fellers, *noempangs* etc.' without a registered contract, because they included disreputable elements and many deserters and registration would make it possible to exercise control over them (Bool 1904:17).

This regulation was in compliance with the measure agreed upon by the planters as long ago as 1879 to put an end to the so-called free *kongsis*, in the hope of thus doing away with what was said to be a major cause of desertion. With the 1889 revision of the Coolie Ordinance, it did become theoretically possible to employ on a casual basis, coolies who had come from other parts of the colony, in contrast to those coming from abroad. This was due to the realization that there were Javanese around who were willing to work on the plantations but not as contract coolies. The Resident wrote that such an optional measure would certainly find favour among the parties concerned (Van Hamel 1892:81). As far as the planters were concerned, however, this was a miscalculation: they adhered uncompromisingly to binding the coolies, whether Chinese or Javanese, with the aid of a contract to penal sanctions. It should be noted here that employers in British India reacted in exactly the same way when the colonial authorities similarly attempted to relax the coercion of the labour force (Guha 1977:17). The planters on Sumatra's East Coast backed up their refusal to make use of the new regulation by stating that such a mixture of free and tied labour on the plantations would lead to insurmountable difficulties.

The cause of the change from the imperative direction included in the first Ordinance to an optional one was the unlawful presence of considerable numbers of natives on the plantations where they were willing to work, but not as contract coolies. This first test of the so-called option system has had little success. The plantations continue to work almost exclusively with contract coolies (Proceedings Lower House 1918–19, Appendix 397.1:3).

During the early years casual labourers had represented a

minority of 10 to 20 per cent, but in the subsequent decades they had declined to almost negligible proportions of 4 to 5 per cent, as can be seen from Table 9. This clearly illustrates the fact that the 1889 revision of the labour law had no effect whatsoever. The casual labour force included only very few Chinese, Javanese and

Table 9.
CONTRACT COOLIES AND CASUAL WAGE LABOUR ON THE
PLANTATIONS OF SUMATRA'S EAST COAST, 1881–1902

Year	Contract coolies	Casual Wage Labour	Total
1873	1525	358	1883 *
1881	23080	2877	25957 **
1882	24003	5332	29335
1883	25722	5732	31454
1884	29704	6230	35954
1885	35600	7900	43500
1886	39330	7619	46949
1887	43119	6675	49794
1888	58675	9813	68488
1889	64396	8001	72397
1890	74722	6230	80952
1891	75975	7958	83933
1892	53109	6109	59218
1893	54882	6825	61707
1894	59049	8312	67361
1895	67201	7872	75073
1896	69421	6489	75910
1897	72949	5896	78845
1898	77893	6418	84311
1899	87000	7000	94000
1900	93987	4758	98745
1901	89306	3876	93182
1902	94337	4303	98640

* Only coolies employed by the Deli Company.
** The total number does not correspond with the same figure in unreliable data supplied by the *Colonial Reports* of the respective years.
Source: *Colonial Reports* 1877-1903.

Indians, and was made up mostly of Bataks and Malays, i.e. local inhabitants who were never affected by the Coolie Ordinance.

In 1895, in an effort to combat the 'evil' of free labour, which never disappeared entirely notwithstanding the persistent attempts to the contrary, the Deli Planters' Association once again prohibited all its members to employ coolies who were not bound through the customary contract. The recent adoption of new harvesting methods had caused an enormous expansion of the *menoempang* system, i.e. gangs of casual labourers who offered their services to various plantations and in the busy season in particular, had no difficulty in finding sufficient employment. The smaller plantations that were not associated with the DPV probably took little notice of the prohibition, but the bigger companies which accounted for the major and ever-increasing part of production, adhered to it scrupulously. For example, the Deli Company employed contract coolies exclusively: this business giant alone, which included twenty-one plantations, employed 62,000 of the approximate 100,000 coolies working on the East Coast at the beginning of the twentieth century (Hoetink 1902:3). Once again, the Resident agreed to help in making the ban on free labour as effective as possible (District Circular 11 January 1896 SEC coll. RTI; Memorial DPV 1929:80).

There was very little difference of opinion as to whether the Coolie Ordinance should be retained, almost a quarter of a century after its proclamation. If the regulations were to be made more widely applicable, other regions could also profit from it. Extension rather than abrogation seemed necessary. An advice brought out by the Council of the Netherlands Indies in 1903 on this subject, started with this argument.

... the primary condition for the development of the Netherlands Indies is to establish agricultural and industrial enterprises on islands outside Java; those establishments will not be able to survive without workers brought in from elsewhere. The supply of such workers is attended by great expense for the planter who, in return, may justifiably require and, in order not to endanger the survival of his enterprise, expect and even insist that he be given the greatest possible assurance that those workers will remain at his disposal during a period previously-determined (Hoetink 1904:2).

Nevertheless, the motivation had changed to some degree.

Justification for this system of forced labour was no longer sought primarily in the chronic shortage of workers, i.e. the problem of quantity, but above all in the inability or the total reluctance of the coolies to work in the way to which they had contractually committed themselves. The quality of labour, so ran the general complaint, left a great deal to be desired. The Asian coolie, alas, was not a truly economic being, and only strict discipline could condition him or her to regular labour and proper productivity. Maintenance of discipline and order was thus more than merely in the interests of the employers: it was a medicine which, in the final resort, would be of benefit to the workers themselves. This reasoning fitted into the morality of uplift-the-natives-in-spite-of-themselves which became popular around the turn of the century together with the Ethical Policy.

But what happened if coolies managed to adapt so well to the work regime to which they were subjected that they were able to repay the debt on which the contract depended, and to quit their job? Then they would no longer need to be educated or protected against themselves, as it were. True, but their employers would still need to remain protected against the dishonest practices of other planters.

There is a danger, however, that the opportunity to terminate a contract would be misused to cajole workers to leave their employer, thus giving rise to a situation that in many ways would be counter-productive and which would, at the same time, pre-empt the rationale for the existence of Coolie Ordinance. An industrial enterprise needs above all a stable workforce. It is organized on an insecure footing and will be unable to meet the demands made on it if the number of workers does not remain more or less constant (Hoetink 1904:26).

Even against the will of the coolie, therefore, extension of the contract was justified in order to prevent any damage to industrial interests. The contract coolies could only be required to make such a sacrifice, however, because in return, they could claim certain rights. When those rights were met, according to Hoetink, there was no reason why the workers should want to withdraw from their contract. On the contrary, they would probably have been in a far worse situation without it. The reverse side of this protection was the coolies' punctilious compliance with everything to which they had bound themselves. If they did not do so, correction would be automatic for,

... the workman who failed to meet all his obligations or who did things that were contrary to the order and discipline that necessarily had to be maintained on a plantation, the imposition of a prison sentence was almost always the only effective method by which to make him understand that he could not arbitrarily ignore a signed employment contract and all the consequences that stemmed from it (Ibid.:35).

It is not accidental that Hoetink has been cited so extensively in the pages above. In 1902 he was ordered by the Director of Justice to investigate the working conditions on the plantations on Sumatra's East Coast, shortly before the publication of Van den Brand's controversial pamphlet. Some time earlier, and for the same purpose, Hoetink had visited a number of mining enterprises elsewhere in the Netherlands Indies which also employed principally Chinese coolies. In 1904 he was to be appointed the first, for the time being temporary, head of the Labour Inspectorate, whose work was in the first instance restricted to the plantations in the most prominent of the Outer Provinces. In his official capacity, Hoetink drafted a new Coolie Ordinance, basing his work on the results of his recent investigations. His point of departure was that reasonable demands made on the coolies should be compensated by decent treatment and fair payment. Although improvement in many respects was urgently needed, Hoetink judged the situation as a whole to be not unfavourable. As future Labour Inspector, he wrote:

I cannot consider the obligations that rest upon the immigrant to be onerous, and in my opinion, if the labour contract is strictly honoured and the Coolie Ordinance is fully applied, those obligations should be more than offset by the rights that are due to him. It is the task of government to see that those rights are not curtailed (Ibid.:10–11).

According to Hoetink, government officials ought to take care that the coolies obtained their rights. Over many years, the owners and managers of plantations had managed to interpret or to distort the loosely-formulated regulations to their own advantage. Such selective use of the labour regulations had been possible because the employers had been allowed far too much latitude. Government intervention, in his opinion, should be far more intensive and effective than it had been in the past.

Although the detailed regulation which Hoetink drew up in close consultation with the planters and the authorities in the region was never put into practice, at long last it probably had a corrective effect. His 'constructive criticism' was certainly not received with any gratitude. The planters lobby continued to find him acceptable, however, because he made it known without further ado that he would not meddle with the spirit and principles of the Coolie Ordinance or become too much of a nuisance for the employers. On the contrary, after his tour of inspection in the Sumatran plantations, Hoetink even suggested the deletion of the clause which said that a labour contract should be optional (Ibid.:2).

Reactions from the planters' circles nevertheless showed increasing irritation about what was seen as uncalled-for government interference. The employers had become accustomed to exercising almost unlimited control over their plantation workers. If, by way of exception, a local authority visited a plantation in an official capacity, he came and stayed as a guest of the manager. In the company of the latter he might possibly meet some of the coolies, but only while acknowledging and confirming the hierarchical relationship that existed on the plantation. Seen from that viewpoint, the acknowledgement of government responsibility in the sphere of labour relations appeared as an almost intolerable intervention in internal business management. On whatever good intentions it might have been based, the retention, once again, of the Coolie Ordinance and of the harsh work regime it entailed were not questioned. The idea that a government agency might be able to function in any other way than as an extension of the power of the planters, signalled a fundamental break in the earlier collusion between planters and officials. The need to render accountability to the government as a third party could easily degenerate into labour unrest, resulting in the erosion of the already damaged managerial authority.

The Rule of the Planters

Very little had changed since the beginning of the plantation system, when employers had arrogated all policing and judicial power from the sultan's administration to themselves. The minute size of the regional administration had prevented anything more than a cursory supervision over the implementation of the Coolie Ordinance, and this situation had continued. However, it would be a distortion to assume that the inequality of justice was due to a lack of sufficient officials. It may even be said that the government apparatus was meant to remain thin in order to give the planters the latitude which they demanded. Moreover, to be able to punish the workers on the plantation also obviated the need for the employers to have to lose their 'disobedient' or 'recalcitrant' coolies who were serving terms of imprisonment.

The autonomy of the planters was not only extremely effective, but it also allowed the coolies to be disciplined at little cost. This tacit agreement between the planters and the government ensured the supremacy of the former in their own house, while outside the plantations the authorities made it certain that the coolies behaved in accordance with the Ordinance. The plantations were surrounded, as it were, by a 'cordon sanitaire' which safeguarded the day-to-day management from undue interruptions. The colonial government machinery was not intended to provide contract coolies with even elementary protection, but rather to ensure that the plantations retained their unrestricted control over the imported workers. Police and government officials, who also acted as magistrates, saw to it that coolies did not leave the plantations without permission, took suitable action if they stealthily managed to do so, and when asked, punished any obstinate coolie on whom an application of the plantation's own sanctions had no effect. Only a very small percentage of the many abuses practised by the planters ever penetrated to the offices of the colonial government on Sumatra's East Coast, let alone to Batavia. And even when this did occur, the planters were seldom prosecuted. If complaints were ever received, they were usually hushed up. One feature of this practice, known as *toetoep* (Van den Brand 1902:15–16), was that those who brought the complaints were intimidated or bribed while witnesses were spirited away. If matters ever came to a judicial trial, the accused planter was given plenty of notice and he managed to avoid the due course of law and subsequent punishment by leaving the district. '. . . if he received notice that an order for his arrest had been issued, he departed to Penang or Singapore and might, if he so wished, take his leave of the Resident since the latter could not detain him' (Kooreman 1904:74–5).

The Chinese headmen were also involved in the colonial power complex in this region, dominated by plantation interests. Provided with a salary and a military rank (major, captain or lieutenant) as was customary also in other parts of the colony, their primary task on the East Coast was to keep an eye on the movements of plantation workers. They checked whether arriving and outgoing Chinese coolies at the port were in possession of valid identity papers, and special searchers were appointed to track down run-away contract coolies. The Chinese headmen were also at the centre of the network which gathered information on the mood of their compatriots working on the plantations.

The safeguarding of production, however, began and ended on the plantation itself. It was partly for this reason that the employers attached so much significance to the formalization of what they had already achieved informally: control over the workforce, in particular the authority to take their own disciplinary action without government interference. The estate workers in Java went back to their own villages in the evening. Work and life were neatly separated into two distinct spheres. Not so in the East Coast where the coolies did not leave the plantations at the end of the working day. Was it not obvious, therefore, argued the employers in Sumatra, that the management should have the same jurisdiction over its coolies as that given to a village headman in Java? (Kooreman 1903a:21). Even having a plantation police force was considered. According to this plan, which originated with the Government Secretary who came to the region in 1883 to reorganize the judiciary system, each owner or manager was to be empowered to appoint a number of officially recognized constables responsible for the security of the plantation. The government ultimately considered that this was going too far, and an adaptation of the same idea submitted by the Resident in later years also found no favour. Plantation regime continued as before, on an informal footing. The regional government invested plantation management with police powers. What was officially not permitted, was nevertheless tolerated reasonably well.

The situation thus remained the same. Within the boundaries of the estate the manager and his assistants acted as upholders of order and safety. In the case of burglary, murder, fighting, etc., they immediately investigated the crime, the guilty party was promptly detained and sent to the nearest government official. This also occurred for infringements of the Coolie Ordinance and in the event of encountering suspicious strangers (Bool 1904:99).

The planters made use of their room for manoeuvre to arrest and to lock-up workers as they saw fit; the majority of plantations had a so-called guardroom for this purpose. Frequently, however, the culprits were then not sent on to the District Officer, acting as the local magistrate in the area. With the extenuating remark that a more informal sentencing was in the interest of the coolies, Resident Scherer nevertheless found it necessary in 1886 to check the autonomy of the planters to mete out punishment by ordaining that detention on the plantation should not last longer than twenty-four hours. He also made it conditional to bring coolies guilty of any misdemeanour before the District Officer. On the same occasion, the Resident expressly prohibited the exercise of any pressure on contract coolies who wanted to lodge a complaint by deterring them 'in one way or another'. The very broad interpretation that was given to this circular suggested that the planters were free, at any time, to keep a coolie shut up for a day and a night without having to account for their actions. What it amounted to was that the employers used the right to take their coolies into custody as a form of punishment. They paid little if any attention to the directive that transgressors might not be tied-up except in the case of a serious crime, that preventive detention might not last more than twenty-four hours, and that pardoning after an arrest was not allowed. Government officials in the East Coast tacitly resigned themselves to what had been common usage since the pioneering days and had now been given the appearance of legitimacy by Residential instruction. Retrospectively (1904), former Resident Scherer (1886–9) defended his instructions as follows:

... I considered them to be justified, and many officials, including the judiciary, apparently shared my opinion. Be that as it may, the objective was to restrict and counteract abuses and to protect the coolies against mistreatment, without making tobacco cultivation impossible, which would have been the case if regulations had been strictly adhered to (Kooreman 1904–5:73).

Shortly after the turn of the century, a proposal not only to consolidate but even to extend the policing powers of the planters was made in view of the small size of the regular constabulary. In

1897, when it seemed too expensive to increase the force, the Resident again suggested the appointment of a corps of security guards who need not be paid by the government. A year later, his concrete request that this should be put into effect in order to combat theft was turned down at a higher level of the colonial government. When he argued its desirability again, he was not even given a hearing. Objections voiced by the Attorney-General in Batavia who at that time was confronted with growing numbers of criminal proceedings against planters who had taken the law into their own hands, ultimately caused Scherer's 1886 memorandum to be withdrawn. The planters were finally told: '. . . that the apprehension, confinement or tying-up of a suspect by you or by one of your subordinates is not permissible and will be severely punished' (Bool 1904:104).

The Planters Committee reacted indignantly. The government would have to back up the prohibition by opening a police post on each and every plantation. How else would it be possible to keep the rowdies among the workforce in check? The Committee petitioned that the regulation should be modified so that,

the managers of plantations in this region could be given the authority, in the event that a man is caught red-handed in the act of committing a crime or a breach of the peace, to have the guilty person, either handcuffed or tied and taken to the magistrate. And, if this is not immediately possible because the day is already too far advanced, to detain the suspect until the following morning (Bool 1904:105).

The repeal of the regulation which dated back to 1886 had almost no effect whatsoever. Even before the end of the year the Resident wrote that culprits were still being locked up. He drew the attention of his subordinates to the fact that the plantations had their own prisons (District Circular, 18 November 1901, SEC coll.RTI). Under pressure, however, the Resident eventually bowed to the demands of the employers. In polite language, it was said that, after careful consideration, he had decided that the right to detain and if necessary to lock up a guilty person until the following day was indispensable to peace and order on the estates. The official annulment of the Scherer memorandum was an error of judgement, so the Resident verbally informed the Planters Committee. In 1902 he agreed that the Committee should inform the plantation managers

10 to 44 per cent of the violations of the Coolie Ordinance were concerned with breaches of peace, refusal to work, and other manifestations of protest (Hoetink 1902:56). This theme forms a pivotal element in Ann Stoler's work, although she is concerned primarily with a later period than that covered here (Stoler 1985:47–92).

The manner in which the disciplining of plantation labour was organized left almost no latitude for collective resistance. Apart from the systematic intimidation and terrorization to which the contract coolies were subjected, the diversity among them, such as their ethnic heterogeneity, their division into workgangs, the strict control exercised by their own foremen, and an excessive contractualization of mutual relations among coolies formed a significant structural barrier to joint action. It was all the more surprising, therefore, that spontaneous eruptions involving large numbers of workers were a fairly regular occurrence. The planters greatly feared such riots in which their inferiors showed that they were willing and able to oppose the management, however shortlived that opposition might be. One local incident was quite sufficient to involve the workforces of many other plantations in lawlessness and rebellion. Each riot, however minor, could be the spark that would explode the powder barrel. Tales of how coolie rows originated and progressed missed the vital point about a common front reached on the basis of shared experience. This lack of understanding was due to various reasons. According to one kind of explanation, it was often suggested that a riot might have been caused by an incident that in itself was quite trivial, such as a reprimand, a slap or a fine. Trifles such as these would usually have no consequence, but due to a combination of circumstances, a coolie, who correctly or incorrectly considered that he had been treated unjustly, might become so agitated as to incite his workmates. In similar fashion, debt caused by uneconomic behaviour might lead to increasing indifference and recalcitrance, and trap a coolie in a spiral of disobedience. Another variant stressed the latent tension among the various ethnic categories and workgangs which could surface at the most unexpected moments.

... usually due to kindled racial hatred and based on a futility, a quarrel about a piece of cloth, affection for a woman, and suchlike. From the fight in which the Europeans have to intervene in order to restore order, come first the irregularities and taking the shape of open revolt (Mulier 1903:66).

The second kind of explanation lay stress on the fact that the coolies' resentment was not directed against the European staff but against their own foremen, who did not hesitate to deceive their own fellow countrymen and members of their workgangs. Although the management had nothing to do with such quarrels, it was its duty to pour oil on troubled waters.

Of the 100 coolie uprisings which the Europeans (the planters) tried to prevent by going with a fine contempt for danger into the crowd to calm down tempers or to take firm action against one of the ringleaders armed with a heavy *jankol* or other weapon, 99 are *not* directed against the company and 95 *not* against the European personnel. No, most of the Chinese insurrections are aimed at the Chinese themselves and in particular at the gang leaders or work bosses, the *tandils*, often also against the head *tandil* and against the shopkeeper on the plantation, the *kedei* holder (Ibid.:65-6).

To investigate the background of coolie riots, why and how they took place, was a virtually hopeless task. It was, after all, literally impossible to talk to the Chinese. Moreover, they kept their mutual affairs (*perkaras*) and their ultimate objectives hidden from the outsider.

According to yet another kind of argument, the planters tried to minimize the significance of the quarrels. Such events started unexpectedly and ran an erratic course, but they did not amount to much. 'Many of these rows in the shed time are at first little more than tiffs, mischievous expressions of an occasional need to kick over the traces' (Ibid.:50).

By emphasizing their unpredictability and uncontrollability in this way, such incidents took on the character of a natural phenomenon: a continually threatening thunderstorm which sometimes erupted over the estates. However, peace did not always return immediately. Occasionally, the manager was unable to keep a riot within the confines of the plantation. In such cases the assembled workers streamed out in a procession to the nearest government office to complain. But then a great deal must have happened, because penal sanctions were inevitable if contract coolies dared to leave the plantation *en masse*. By doing so, orderly workers became styled as 'rogues' and 'agitators'. Such collective resistance was injurious to the name of a plantation precisely because it was known in advance as to who would be the loosers. Perhaps even more important was the loss of face suffered by the management, which had demonstrably failed in what was considered to be a primary requirement: to maintain law and order with the company's own means and manpower.

This occurred, for example, in 1903 when 300 coolies from one plantation marched to Medan to complain about the settlement of their accounts, and would not wait until the District Officer of the area in which the plantation was situated had investigated the affair, but went on to Medan. The ringleaders were punished (Bool 1904:55).

Although the planters were always worried about the possibility of an escalation, they usually managed to prevent it, or at any rate to squash it without delay. The network of informers which every manager maintained, was pivotal in this respect. Reports of conspiracy were rewarded generously and trustworthy informers who thus showed their loyalty to company interests, could ultimately count on promotion to the rank of a foreman. As we have seen, the coolies primarily vented their anger on the gang bosses: not only because of their deception but perhaps even more because they formed the lowest level of the management and, in that capacity, had the first responsibility for discipline and were, on the other hand, both physically and socially the immediate target of revenge.

Was the foreman really nothing more than a willing tool in the hands of the management, a pawn who blindly implemented all the orders given by the management? In effect that was the case but, like all middlemen, he tried to gain some room for manoeuvre, undoubtedly for his own advantage. In the disturbances of 1877, for instance, it was found that the workers' discontent on several plantations had been instigated by the *tandils* who feared that they would lose their outstanding loans due to a more thrifty regime introduced by a new company manager (Broersma 1919:266). The increasing number of complaints voiced against the excessive authority of Asian foremen caused some of the biggest plantations to appoint more European assistants. This clearly did not result in the elimination of the foreman as a go-between, if only because of the language which formed an insurmountable barrier in day-to-day encounters. More than ever before, however, the white staff were exposed to close contact with the workforce, with the inevitable consequence that the latter's rancour and aggressiveness was now aimed directly at this middle level of the management. In the first decades of the twentieth century the number of attacks on assistants were to rise steeply while, on the other hand, the foremen were driven back into the ranks from whence they originally came. It was certainly not coincidental that the trade union movement in the plantation belt on the East Coast, as in similar enclaves in South and Southeast Asia (Breman 1985:77–8), was to expand primarily through these foremen. Growing doubts regarding the trustworthiness of the *mandurs* and *tandils* began long after the turn of the century. But the Asian foremen had always been characterized by a dual identity. When all was said and done, they themselves were also locked into the coolie milieu. This position, which made them ideal informers, for the same reasons set bounds to the treachery that they could perpetrate. Sympathies and antipathies of a purely personal nature would have played an important role. The fact that, within the context described above, they were known as 'squealers' and 'stool pigeons' rather than as ringleaders of coolie riots, tells us little about their actual behaviour once they were outside the visual and verbal control of the European management.

In government jargon towards the end of the nineteenth century, coolie riots fell into the category of serious crime. And rightly so. The minimal preparation for even a spontaneous outburst required a form of organization which meant at least the temporary negation or neutralization of both the industrial hierarchy and of the dividing lines that split the workers on the plantation. The measures taken by the regional authorities were intended to prevent any disturbances from spreading to other companies. Police and the military were rapidly brought in to localize the resistance and to restore order, with the use of arms if necessary.

A row is a refusal which starts with the intention of perpetrating acts of violence. Such outrages can only be prevented by stern action with the aid of a strong police force. If the ruffians become masters of the terrain for even one moment, they will be capable of the most horrible mischief (Kooreman 1903a:54).

The remedy was sought not in eliminating the causes of the riots, which was impossible given the presuppositions discussed above, but in exemplary punishment. To combat the evil of agitation, the Resident on the East Coast asked the central colonial government in 1890, for much harsher sanctions than those provided by the Coolie Ordinance (Bool 1904:86). With this comment on the revisions of the Ordinance, he made himself the mouthpiece of the employers, who also urged for more rigorous measures.

Individual Forms of Coolie Resistance

It is impossible to estimate the percentage of coolies who rebelled independently of each other against the plantation regime. Since the maintenance of security on the plantations was in practice left to the planters, most of these acts of rebellion and certainly those that were concerned with the plantation, were kept out of the public eye. From the sources that are available, it is possible to deduce the nature of individual resistance but not the degree to which it occurred. Dependent on the action taken, it is possible to draw up a classification ranging from passive resistance to desertion, the latter sometimes being preceded by violent behaviour. The first type was undoubtedly the most common and took the form of a deliberate failure to complete the task assigned and in general the tendency to ignore the directives given at all managerial levels. Passive resistance had a thousand-and-one variations, from simulated incomprehension to tardiness, inaccurate or incomplete execution of orders, and the like. This was a method of sabotage which caused the white members of the staff to explode in anger. Time and again such behaviour was ammunition for the stereotypes of the passive and indolent Asian and the hot-tempered and aggressive European. In order to extort the prescribed amount of work from the coolies, they were placed under continual and stern supervision by foremen and assistant managers. By failing to meet the work norm, a large proportion of the contract coolies harmed their own interests since their incomes were tied to piece-work. Those workers who nevertheless saw chance to be obstructive, could be called to order with the charge of laziness. The inclusion of this article in the 1889 revision of the Ordinance provided planters with an instrument with which to force unwilling workers back into line. The same applied to a more drastic form of resistance, namely, the refusal of a coolie to work. A contract coolie had the formal right to complain about a foreman to the assistant, then to the manager, and finally, outside the plantation, to seek recourse to the magistrate. Yet, apart from the fact that most of these levels lay far beyond the effective reach of the workers, who would dare think of bringing a complaint over one's paltry wage, long work-hours, lack of decent housing and other elementary facilities, retention on the plantation after the termination of a contract, mistreatment or other abuses? Hoetink's naivety verges on the incredible when he reported on his investigations on fifty plantations in the East Coast, that very few complaints had been submitted to him by the workers (Hoetink 1902:76).

The coolie gained no respite if he said he was sick to camouflage his disobedience. If it had been the intention of the planters, with some favourable exceptions, to turn the plantation's infirmary into a place that was dreaded by the coolies, then they succeeded admirably. Tschudnowsky noted in his diary that a number of women who were running high temperatures insisted that they be allowed to work, and refused to go to the hospital. A coolie agreed to be admitted there only if he was no longer able to stand on his feet, according to this plantation doctor. The patients feared that they would not survive a stay in the infirmary and, once there, they behaved with such hostility that one of his orderlies had asked for permission to carry a pistol (Tschudnowsky 1899:40).

Lacking any acceptable means of legal protest, coolies who were not satisfied with sabotaging the work that was assigned to them had no other option than to take recourse to open rebellion. This could take the form of an act of violence against the lower management, who was usually their own gang boss, but also sometimes against one of the white assistants. The Europeans, who constantly feared such 'coolie attacks', were always armed with a cane with which to defend themselves. The Chinese coolies in particular had the reputation of flying off the handle if they felt themselves to be treated unjustly. An accumulation of grievances could suddenly find release in aggression, but before that happened the management was usually able to intervene on the basis of prior information.

A Chinese is a coward by nature. He will rarely attack someone openly or of his own accord. If he is planning something of the sort, then he will assure himself in advance of the support of a few of his comrades. As soon as these have been found they will enter into a pact of secrecy, sealed by slaughtering a chicken on whose blood they will swear a solemn oath to support each other faithfully in the further action that they have in mind, to suffer together any eventual punishment, and never to betray one another. However solemnly these oaths might have been taken and however binding they might be for a Chinese, the conspirators usually included an informer who, eager for monetary reward, would betray the plot to the head *tandil*, who would then be able in good time to catch the ringleaders and take them into custody (Dixon 1913:49).

Although this clearly shows that the incident was not at all unpremeditated but, on the contrary, was sometimes planned far in advance, it suited the colonial imagery of the coolies to assume that the culprit had acted on impulse. According to this interpretation, the coolie who perpetrated such an infamous deed lived in a twilight state and it was impossible for any normal thinking person to imagine the forces and emotions that then possessed him. In this connection one talked of 'the complicated and secretive native community' and 'the very superficial and peculiar thought process of the native' (see Langeveld 1978:349).

Much more often, a coolie ran away without having recourse to violence. What drove him to do so? If we are to believe the literature, it was almost never due to injustice inherent in the work regime because a willing, well-behaved and hard-working coolie had absolutely no reason to leave the plantation before the termination of his or her contract, and not even then. No, the reason was again to be found in the immediate environment of the contract coolie. Almost always it was due to a gambling debt, women, quarrels among the workgang, dissatisfaction with the foreman, or strictly personal grievances. In the knowledge that desertion on impulse was anything but easy and that, once outside the plantation, the fugitive would need the help of others to reach to safety, the assistant took his precautionary measures. For this purpose, the plantation's information apparatus was of crucial importance.

With the help of *tandils* and other spies he should be kept fully informed about the prospect of desertion among the coolies. At the same time an eye should be kept on the suspects and on their money, clothing and purchases. In the event of desertion he should immediately have the deserters followed by a few trusted watchmen or coolies provided with the necessary chits, and should also inform the manager of what has happened, who will then take all the necessary steps (Haarsma 1889:213).

To encourage vigilance, plantation managements frequently held the foreman responsible for the debt left by the deserter (Dixon 1913:17). It was only logical that the foreman in turn would apportion the amount of the claim, made up of contract premiums that had not been repaid together with any further advances that had been given, among the members of the deserter's workgang. In this way, the manager not only passed-on the financial risk, but he encouraged the coolies to be extra alert because they themselves would be victimized if any of their work mates managed to escape. If desertion was not the result of circumstances for which the coolie had only himself to blame, then it was said to be due to physical debility, namely, a weak constitution which prevented him from performing adequately.

The so-called deserters, both as concerns the Chinese and the Javanese, consist mainly of two categories: first, those who are in debt to the *kedei*, *tandil*, *mandur*, or Bengalese moneylender; second, of fairly healthy but generally physically weak individuals who cannot cope with the work, who then stay away (for a few days) and return again. The common deserter who goes away for good, on the other hand, is a robust individual (Mulier 1903:87).

Evidently, the coolies were quite frequently in danger of collapsing under the plantation regime, and ran away in despair at that realization. At a meeting of the regional government held in 1902 the officials present said that 'starvation wages' were the principal cause of desertion. The coolies hoped that if they absconded they would go to prison where they would receive better treatment than on the plantation (Minutes of Regional Government meeting, 8 September 1902, SEC coll. RTI). They set off actuated by need rather than any clear idea as to their ultimate destination. Another source referring to defection implied that the majority of deserters were either overtaken immediately or, due to the lack of any alternative, soon returned voluntarily to the plantation, sick and wretched after their wanderings in the jungle (Dixon 1913:31). Stronger workers, who made suitable preparations and left the plantation with the determination never to return, could choose one of several courses of action. During the early years, when the majority of coolies came from Malaya, it was self-evident that deserters would try to return there. The planters blocked off this escape route, in close co-operation with the authorities, by appointing 'searchers' who worked under the supervision of the Chinese headmen. Vessels patrolling the coast would stop and interrogate the passengers and crew of smaller boats making their way to the other coast. In the region itself, the growth of the plantation sector had given rise to various ancillary industries and establishments that were also in need of workers. However, if a Chinese vegetable grower or pig farmer took a deserted contract coolie into his employ, then he also was guilty of breaking the law; the police kept a close watch to ensure compliance with the prohibition on sheltering deserters.

The least guarded escape route was that towards the hills in the thinly-populated and inaccessible interior of the East Coast, but from the point of view of safety and survival, this option was most unattractive. This was the territory of the Bataks who, since the beginning of the plantation system, had enjoyed the reputation of being premium-hunters, the premiums being offered by the planters for the tracing and returning of contract coolies. There is a well-known story in plantation literature about deserters who were returned to their employer like hunting trophies, tied upside down to a pole carried by two Bataks.

The greatest stumbling block for the freedom-loving coolies was not getting away from the plantation but leaving the East Coast. Since most such efforts were bound to fail, the only way by which a deserter could avoid the police and the plantation's watchmen was usually to sign a new contract that would bind him to another plantation. Quite often, in fact, the foremen of other plantations would incite workers to desert, with or without the prior knowledge of the management. The deserted coolie then used the cash advance to buy false papers needed for a new identity. It was no secret

that many *tandils* traded in letters of discharge by preferably employing deserters from other plantations and by giving them a dismissal chit which had to be paid for out of the cash advance. In 1889, 63 coolies were apprehended on a plantation in Serdang who had been taken on on the basis of invalid letters of release; 38 of them were immediately claimed by other estates and the Planters Committee circulated descriptions of the other 25 among its members (Broersma 1919:239).

When such malafide practices were 'discovered' the planters came to a gentlemen's agreement as to who had the first claim on these workers who, as it were, sold themselves twice over. In the majority of cases it meant that the coolie had to serve his time with both planters consecutively.

Coolies who ran away did not do so in the hope of being able to break through the numerous barriers that separated them from the land of their birth. For many of them there was, quite literally, no longer any place at 'home'; they were only too painfully aware of this fact, which was actually the reason behind their entering into a contract to go to Deli in the first place. What drove them to flee from the plantation was the hope of being able to settle elsewhere in illegal freedom. Only a small minority succeeded in doing so. These ex-coolies lived on the periphery of the plantation system and ran the danger of being re-captured for many years after running away (Stoler 1985:35–6). The fact that, notwithstanding this, so many attempted to escape gives a sufficient idea of the state in which contract coolies were forced to work and live. Worse conditions were scarcely conceivable and many were inspired by the thought that a better fate might await them elsewhere under a different foreman and a different manager. Coolies who were found without any identity papers, were taken into custody without fail. The Resident opined that their status as deserters could be deduced from their attitude and outward appearance (District Circular, 11 January 1896, SEC coll. RTI). He ordered that these suspects be circulated around the prisons in the main towns of the region. Their descriptions were published in the local press and a planter who thought that the description fitted one of his deserted coolies could collect him from the prison. One such notification ran as follows:

Persons detained in the Government prison at Tebing Tinggi, who do not have identity papers.
Maroon, Javanese tribe, age 28 years, height 163 cm, distinguishing marks: white scar right ankle and right knee.

Timah woman, Javanese tribe, age 20 years, height 152 cm. distinguishing marks: birthmark under right eye and 2 scars right cheek.

Ng A. Soen, Teotju tribe, age 25 years, height 167 cm, distinguishing marks: scar on right shinbone and left knee, birthmark above left nostril.

Tan A. Teong, Heilohong tribe, age 29 years, height 161 cm, distinguishing marks: scar above right knee and birthmark on back.

Djapar, Javanese tribe, age 20 years, height 159 1/2 cm, distinguishing marks: scars on left and right shinbones. (*Sumatra Post*, 14 November 1903)

Marked by scars, very often caused by the brutal punishment inflicted upon them, the plantation workers were easy to identify. These personal characteristics, i.e. sex, race, age, height and noticeable physical debilities, anticipated the dactylographic registration that was to be introduced some decades later.

What happened to the coolies who remained unidentified and were not claimed by any employer? On the orders of the Resident they were also punished, just to be on the safe side, and then expelled from the region (District Circular, 11 January 1896, Ibid.).

One can only make an approximate estimation of the actual numbers of deserters. All quantitative statements pointed in the same direction: it was the most frequently occurring offence. Hoetink concluded on the basis of his investigations that in a few districts 10 to 44 per cent of the breaches of the law with which local magistrates dealt in 1901 were concerned with desertion; in some districts, in fact, the percentage was even higher (Hoetink 1902:56). Yet even these figures are under-estimated, since by no means all cases of desertion were made known to government officials. The planters preferred to settle their own accounts with the run-away coolies who returned voluntarily or who were tracked down by the plantation's own security guards. Apart from the satisfaction that it gave to take the law into one's own hands, punishment meted out on the estate had a deterrent effect on the other workers. A last resort for the coolies who saw no other way out was to opt for self-directed violence. That suicide frequently represented such a solution is incontestable. The refusal, in a condition of extreme depression, to accept any food and to fast until death followed, was one way in which such an escape occurred. More frequently, however, they would take more active ways of ending their lives: by hanging, drowning, or an over-dose of opium. Tschudnowsky gave several examples in his diary: they included the case of a man who was seriously ill, refused to take any medicine and crawled out of the hospital, determined to die. Another succeeded in putting a piece of cord around his neck and to pull on both ends until he strangled himself. 'You must then really want to die', commented the author (Tschudnowsky 1899:39, 42, 44–5, 51, 67; see also Van Kol 1903:104). It is not difficult to believe Tschnudnowsky when he says that, after dysentery and malaria, suicide was the most frequent cause of death.

Punishment

The most common form of punishment was wage reduction or extra work for coolies who did not show sufficient zest, follow orders, or in other ways were considered to be disobedient. Managers used their own discretion in applying this sanction. Foremen and European assistants had the permission to call individual coolies to order, but could also assert their authority against an entire workgang. As extra punishment, a coolie who had deserted would be held accountable for all expenses incurred by the plantation in hunting him down and bringing him back, such as the bounty for information of his whereabouts, the fee for arresting him, and the expenditure of the watchmen sent out. As his debt grew, the contract coolie's immobility also increased. The workers were given to understand that they might only terminate their stay on the plantation if they were free of debt, even if that meant exceeding the agreed contract period. The fact that payment was so low, the workload so heavy and the coolie's life so precarious, meant that such financial penalties had only limited effect. Moreover, they were usually contrary to the provisions of the Coolie Ordinance, which instructed that punishment of the coolies should be left to the authorities. Ever since penal sanction was introduced, the planters had demanded the right to detain coolies who were suspected of violating the Ordinance on the plantation until it was possible to send them on to the magistrate. This arrangement signified the formalization of a long-existing practice. The planters attached considerable importance to this, not only because it legitimized their authority but because it convinced the workers that the planters acted as an extension of the government.

Minor infringements were disposed of by the police. In 1877, before the introduction of the Coolie Ordinance, the Resident of Sumatra's East Coast held special monthly sittings in order to pronounce sentences on coolies on the basis of complaints submitted by the employers. '"The numerous convictions that followed soon became generally known, and made the Chinese coolies realize that they were not lords and masters in this country", stated a satisfied ex-Chief Inspector of the Deli Company' (*Sumatra Post*, 5 May 1913).

On the days on which the District Officer held session, planters who fell within his area of jurisdiction sent coolies to him under escort with a chit mentioning their names, the misdemeanours and the punishment they considered to be appropriate (cf. Van den Brand 1902:22; Van Blankenstein 1929:11). Invariably these were the very sentences which were proclaimed. Refusal to work and other forms of disobedience to superiors could be punished with twelve days detention and employment on public works; desertion was an offence for which coolies had to suffer a month's forced labour. If they repeated this crime, punishment would be more severe (Hoetink 1902:56).

The category 'crimes' included murderous assaults on foremen: in 1901 two coolies in each thousand were guilty of such misdeeds. The number of contract coolies who were brought before the authorities each year for the violations of the Coolie Ordinance were far greater (see Table 10).

Hoetink found in his investigations that in districts where there were strong concentrations of plantation enterprises, almost half the sentences meted out by the local magistrate were concerned with desertion. Crimes perpetrated by coolies were brought before the Divisional Courts which were established in the main towns of the large districts into which the region was divided. There were four such courts at the beginning of the twentieth century.

The planters and the Chinese headmen were represented on this tribunal as examining magistrate (Van den Brand 1902:19). If he so requested, a planter who was personally involved in a particular case could gain permission to be on the panel. Any appearance of objectivity in the sentencing was thus completely lost. It was practices such as these that led Van den Brand to assert that no justice was administered on the East Coast of Sumatra, only punishments (Ibid.:55). That critic was equally justified in observing that of the actionable offences perpetrated by the Europeans against the coolies, and they were never mere bagatelles, not even one per cent was considered for prosecution. These cases came before the Residency Court in Medan, but this tribunal had a very limited authority. Even the very few cases that eventually reached

Table 10.
MISDEMEANOURS AND CRIMES COMMITTED BY COOLIES ON
SUMATRA'S EAST COAST AROUND THE TURN OF THE
NINTEENTH CENTURY

Year	Coolies convicted for misdemeanours*	Crimes**
1894	n.a.	148
1896	11314	n.a.
1897	11704	n.a.
1898	12974	189
1899	12227	n.a.
1900	n.a.	236
1901	n.a.	209

Source: * Kooreman, 1904–0532.   ** Van Kol, 1903:99.

the Court of Justice in Batavia rarely resulted in conviction. That
was the reason why Van den Brand argued that a Court of Justice
should be set up in the region. The trading houses in Medan had
earlier petitioned for such a court to allow civil suits to be handled
more quickly. They had eventually withdrawn that request under
pressure from the principal plantation companies which wanted
to keep the judiciary as much as possible out of the region.

In 1904, during a debate in the Netherlands Parliament, the
Minister of Colonies frankly admitted that the administration of
justice on the East Coast was far from satisfactory.

... it seems, and I say this with regret, that the magistrates, that is, the
officials of the civil administration, who are charged with jurisdiction in
cases of violation of the Coolie Ordinance by the workers, have more than
once considered themselves not to be governed by the provisions concerning legal evidence, and that their judgements often demonstrate major
shortcomings in that respect. It has also been shown that civil service
officials have sometimes acquitted cases contrary to their instructions and
that they have often managed to get complaints withdrawn before these
have been considered. The officials in question have not always acted
against Europeans with sufficient severity (Proceedings Lower House, 30
November 1904:317).

Irritated by the shock caused by the negative publicity over abuses
during his rule, Kooreman, who had recently resigned as Resident
of Sumatra's East Coast, defended himself by saying that the

situation had improved a great deal during the past few years. When he had been posted there as Secretary of the Region from 1884 to 1886, everything had been far more brutal. 'Police roll-calls were often held around the table in the club, and those punished were hired out to the planters on a daily basis. Their wages were used for the purchase of various requirements and for embellishing the place' (Kooreman 1904-5:25).

Much had changed for the better when compared to the harsh regime that had prevailed not only on the plantations but also outside them. More is the pity, complained the planters. From their point of view the workers had become too presumptuous due to the generous and accommodating treatment shown to them by the authorities. Sentencing by the magistrate did not bring the sinners to see the error of their ways but often had a contrary effect. The coolies undergoing punishment were only required to work nine hours per day, and not at all on Sundays. They were also given more and better food than that to which they were accustomed: the cost of prison meals was actually 50 per cent more than the amount that the coolies expended when on the plantations (Hoetink 1902: 58). What had happened earlier might have been below par, but it was really not necessary to give the coolies a rest cure! This presentation of affairs did not agree at all with the reports of less biased observers. According to Tschudnowsky, the level of hygiene and medical care was such that, when released, the majority of detainees suffered from beri-beri or dysentery, diseases that were almost impossible to cure. The coolies who knew what awaited them therefore dreaded the idea of being shut up in a government prison (Tschudnowsky 1899:38-9). Compared with the conditions prevailing earlier, however, the chances of prisoners remaining barely alive at the end of their sentence, increased. During his first posting on the East Coast, according to ex-Resident Kooreman, the number of prisoners was far too great for the space in which they were confined. So many died among those awaiting trial that very few of them needed to be sentenced (1904-5:25). Kooreman was apparently not satisfied with the improvements made towards the end of the nineteenth century. In 1896, during his term of office, he circulated a memorandum,

in which it was announced that detainees called *krakal* [forced labour] a holiday in that they did not have to work so hard as on the plantation and 'could eat all they wanted while in prison'. The Resident therefore instructed the District Officers to make the prisoners work hard, especially with a view to counteracting desertion. Furthermore, he requested the District Officers to investigate whether the fining of good workers, who felt very slighted by being paid less wages than they had expected, would not be a more effective punishment than *krakal*, bearing in mind that those who managed them would have to be prepared to advance the fine (Bool 1904:94).

Although even in 1901, 13 per cent of the detainees in the state prison in Medan were to die while in confinement (Van Kol 1903:106), the planters did not conceal their dissatisfaction regarding the laxity and leniency shown by the government officials. According to the employers, the increasing intervention by the colonial authorities with matters concerning the estate management, had encouraged the workers to rebelliousness rather than obedience. They argued that punishment on the plantations was a necessary evil. Who would dare to guarantee the maintenance of discipline and order when all autonomy was taken away from the planters? Everyone was immediately prepared to admit that the treatment of the coolies was anything but gentle. But even in this respect it was said reassuringly that the situation at the turn of the century had drastically improved specially over the first few decades. Drawing on his own memory, ex-Resident Scherer (1886-9) told about '. . . coolies being caned with a rotan until they collapsed, and numerous other tortures, so hideous and dreadful that I prefer not to describe them here in detail' (quoted in Kooreman 1904–5:24).

   Even the officials of the judiciary were guilty of such violations. One magistrate had the habit of hitting with a cane any Chinese coolie who did not understand his pidgin Malay. This was known as the cure of the miracle cane, because its use magically brought an end to problems of communication during the trial. Even Chinese workers who called on him with some sort of complaint were likely to be given the same treatment if it proved that they had not paid the industrial tax which was levied on contract coolies coming from abroad (Ibid.:36). The later generation of planters may have been guilty of a casual smack or blow with the cane—though with not much more force than a horse would get from his rider, as one of them said reassuringly (*Sumatra Post*, 3 October 1903)—but this paled into insignificance when compared to what had taken place earlier. Only a hard hand inspired proper humility and deference—the sources maintain discrete silence about kicks—and respect for plantation management came before anything else.

If this is undermined or is insufficient then there will soon be no peace and order in a district or on a plantation. Neither people nor goods will then be safe (Dixon 1913:20).

The Assistant who has prestige will be assured of the support of his foremen, while friction with his workers will now and then occur, it will nevertheless be exceptional (Hanegraaff 1910:11).

To prevent any loss of prestige, it was necessary for the workers to clearly understand that orders could not be flouted. To show who was the boss implied keeping the coolies at an arm's length. Not to talk but to order, was the rule, which was usually coupled with much ranting and cursing. But that kind of language was all that the contract workers understood. According to current opinion, the coolies were the scum of the society, wherever they came from. The recruitment of Chinese coolies, principally in seaports, showed that a large percentage of them had already left the villages in the countryside, broken adrift before they reached the plantations of Sumatra. The planters' society had just as unfavourable an opinion of Javanese men and women.

The men belong mostly to the dregs of the Javanese nation. The majority are discharged and deserted convicts. The deserters are characters who understand quite well that only through emigration can they avoid the criminal judge; or else are vagabonds of whom their fellow villagers would like to be rid and who decide to emigrate under pressure from their village headmen. Ordinary villagers, the sort of people best liked by the planters, those for whom emigration is an attempt to escape oppressive taxes, corvee labour and other obligatory communal services, and to improve their lot, are seldom encountered among the emigrants (Kooreman 1903a:35–6).

The employers provided a service to society by ridding the hinterland of this scum, so ran their reasoning. In this way, employment on the plantations assumed the character of a large-scale social rehabilitation (Van Blankenstein 1929:46). Was it surprising, then, that contacts with such crude people had a coarsening effect on the European staff? Anyway, the coolies could stand being knocked about and were not likely to complain if at times things got a bit rough. The tenor of all these reports was that there was no question of real violence and that those who were dealt a few blows fully understood and accepted such behaviour. 'The truth of the matter is that they would rather be given a hiding if they have deserved it than a lengthy reprimand accompanied by abusive language, or perhaps extra work, and worst of all, a cut in their wages' (Kooreman 1903a:53).

Sometimes the entire management, from top to bottom, found itself in a situation where a coolie could only be brought to reason by a good hiding. The foremen were first in line here since they were in close contact with the coolies from early morning until late evening, and carried prime responsibility for them. The gang boss knew better than anyone else what sort of men he was dealing with. He might be able to achieve results with kind words with one, but only with the aid of paternal severity with another. Who could blame him if his hand or foot sometimes slipped and if he chastized a coolie who proved hard of learning? It did not go much farther than that, as Hoetink reported after investigating working relations in a tin-mine.

It was not in the nature of the Chinese to immediately castigate or mistreat their subordinates. They would rather use their tongue than their hands, and although it naturally occurred that a foreman (*thai koeng*) would thrash a coolie, the coolie would not complain (Hoetink, 24 June 1902, in GSA, Vb., 31 March 1903, No. 34).

When things did get out of hand and a case of mistreatment occurred that could not be hidden from the outside world, it was always possible to blame an Asian foreman who had carried his zeal a little too far. In other words, an industrial accident was almost inevitable under the given circumstances. Splinters are bound to fall where trees are felled. Hoetink only came across one serious incident during his investigation of the East Coast plantations, namely, that of a foreman who had smashed a coolie's arm rather badly (Hoetink 1902:75). This was impermissible of course, but nevertheless nothing to match the treatment to which Chinese were accustomed to in their own country.

While, in his own country, for the smallest offence, he would have been handcuffed, chained, put in the stocks, tortured, mutilated or, for more serious offences, be put to death after being tortured, here he comes off the train to a decent dwelling where he hears the strangest things from his new friends. Men are never hanged, or almost never, the mandarins in white suits do not torture, do not cut off your hands or ears if you lie or steal. But they have a different set of ideas which is difficult to explain to a Chinese but could roughly be translated into Chinese as 'western notions' and which, if matters are carried too far, they enforce with the aid of a single blow (Mulier 1903:49-50).

In view of practices as barbarous as these, what did it matter if the European staff sometimes hit or kicked a coolie? According to the standard view, this occurred spontaneously when necessity arose, as a form of non-verbal communication. It was the most powerful but also, in fact, the only way in which the assistants could demonstrate their dissatisfaction with the coolies. Yet one must note that this physical contact was remarkable precisely because the white bosses in all respects, except the sexual, kept the greatest possible distance from the workforce. This was a logical consequence of the very different world to which the top of the plantation industry belonged, a difference that was maintained by strictly hierarchical relations.

But was it not in the interest of the planters that their workers should be well cared for? Employers liked to pride themselves on their paternalistic attitude. The approved image of the plantation was that of a family enterprise with which all concerned felt strong ties, based on rights and obligations that accompanied particular positions. It was undeniable, however, that some contract coolies refused to adapt to this image, in spite of all effort to make them do so. They not only created problems for themselves, but involved others in their deviating behaviour. What was to be done with these troublesome customers who would not listen to reason? Only a handful of coolies behaved like bad sheep and ultimately the only thing to do was to discharge them from their obligations and to send them back to their places of origin. That, at least, was the version customarily given. What the literature does not report is that the planters used quite different methods of settling accounts with these recalcitrant elements who proved insusceptible to correction. Was it surprising that the coolies feared their employers so much that they preferred a stay in the state prison? 'In prisons I have heard coolies beg, not to be given the sort of freedom for which they had no taste, but to be allowed to become a convict, if necessary for many years, doing forced labour in chains' (Rookmaker 1904:810).

The explicit preference shown by tobacco planters for Chinese contract coolies, at least until the first few decades of the twentieth century, has been already discussed. Apart from the fact that they worked harder, the Chinese were said to behave in a way that their white masters found easier to understand: amenable to reason although hot-tempered if their sense of justice was offended. Such a reaction was predictable and could also be checked because, in such a case, stern measures usually achieved the desired result: 'a Chinese, who is not one of the bravest of men, always respects spirit and pluck' (Dixon 1913:49).

Javanese coolies had a name not only for indolence, but were also said to be docile workers. They rarely caused problems, but their behaviour was far more enigmatic. A trivial incident could arouse them to blind anger, and such unpredictability made them untrustworthy.

Normally, they are sturdy, taciturn and apparently quiet workers who will follow orders well and willingly to the best of their own understanding, judgement and manner of work; a dangerous customer can thus pass as being peaceful sometimes for many months, before his true character becomes known (Ibid.:26).

Group stereotypes of this sort were not deeply rooted and could change according to the circumstances. Once the Javanese men and women had been exposed to the plantation environment for some length of time, they apparently underwent a metamorphosis, and the differences between them and their Chinese counterparts faded away. Little was left of the compliance and humility which characterized the Javanese when they were still fresh from the villages. The planters soon began to complain about the 'boldness' of the coolies, regardless of their ethnicity (Memorandum Tobacco Cultivation in Deli 1883:204). Such transformation was linked to the status of the contract labourer, i.e. someone who had lost his or her freedom.

He feels himself uprooted, separated from all the old customs and traditions, brought to an environment which is entirely alien to him, in a country where no-one speaks his language or understands his customs. Held in contempt by his fellow countrymen, among companions who have long put aside all politeness and subservience such as he had learned in Java, he became an entirely different person (Dixon 1913:30).

In the opinion of the planters, it was certainly not a change for the good. Noteworthy in this respect is Hoetink's remark that new-comers from both China and Java were said to be quiet workers but that, on the contrary, old-timers were seen as being troublesome. Contract coolies who had signed on for a further term were more likely to show a tendency to disturb the peace and to resist their betters than were workers who had less experience with life and work on a plantation. This explains why recruiting agents in Java were instructed to reject old hands who wanted to sign on again (Stecher 1905:5, 24). Ideally, workers should be young males coming directly from the villages in Java and China.

Newcomers from China are in general submissive and quiet. However, the longer a Chinese works on a tobacco plantation, the more difficult he is to govern and the more easily he will resist his superiors or even attack them. On a plantation where Chinese old-timers (*lau-khehs*) are primarily or exclusively employed, the task of a European supervisor is twice as difficult (Hoetink 1902:73).

Hoetink's statement throws an interesting light on the effects of the discipline to which the employers attached so much significance. It also explains why the planters wished to ensure a continual supply of fresh workers. The circulation of labour might be more expensive, but even this disadvantage could be neutralized by charging its costs to the migrants themselves.

One incident mentioned in the Rhemrev Report has stuck in my memory as a striking example of the bold behaviour of the ex-perienced plantation coolie: a number of women pulled up their sarongs and turned their bare bottoms to an assistant when he ordered them to get to work (Rhemrev 1987:350). It is a classical gesture of contempt, even when they risked being struck with a cane, as indeed they were. Examples such as this vividly illustrate the insolent attitude, in both word and deed, of the plantation workers. Their behaviour was not that of a timid, defenseless mass, but gave witness of the indifference and defiance of those who had nothing more to lose. It was the demonstrative silence that I would call characteristic of a raw industrial proletariat. Apart from the planters, government officials were also offended by such behaviour. During a meeting of the regional government in 1902, the assembled district officials urged that violations of Article 10 of the Coolie Ordinance, concerning offences such as refusal to work, rebelliousness, etc., should be punished more severely.

Towards the end of the nineteenth century, a sultry climate prevailed on the plantations of Sumatra's East Coast. The same arsenal of violent means that provoked individual or collective protest among the workers, was used by the management to keep the coolies on a tight rein. The result was a spiralling of violence of which outsiders had little if any understanding due to the enclosed nature of the estate world. Moreover, many people who ought to have known better due to their involvement or even direct responsibility, showed a noticeable lack of interest. Such detachment also made it possible to consider 'incidents' that came to light as being indeed incidental. That is to say, they could be brushed aside or even excused; in any event, awkward questions as to their extent were not asked. I shall discuss this bond of silence and secrecy in greater depth in subsequent chapters.

The planters themselves were certainly aware of the exploitation and oppression to which they subjected their workforce and, more than that, they could guess at the feelings of frustration or even hatred that existed among the victims. The tone echoing throughout the documents that originated in the plantation milieu gives the impression of living on a volcano. Emphasis lay in the loneliness of the life of the manager and his assistants on the remote plantations, surrounded by a mass of coolies: one European to approximately 100 Asian workers, who had more than sufficient reason not to be well-disposed towards the management and who threatened to revolt at any moment.

With this horror always in mind, it is understandable that employers worried so much about their own security. In the last instance they could not rely on their own means of defence, whether legal or illegal, but had to depend on the assistance of the authorities. This was the background to the incessant complaints about the meagreness of the police apparatus and its inferior quality.

To put it colloquially, we pity the uniformed native who diligently tries to imitate a being whom he has never yet seen in the flesh: a European police constable who has been properly trained for his task. So let's say nothing more about him, he can't help being what he is (Mulier 1903:41).

It does not seem too far-fetched to assume that such denigrative expressions hide the suspicion that, at the critical moment, the non-European police force would probably make common cause with coolie agitators. Over the years, the strong arm of the government machinery had been considerably enlarged (see Table 11). In 1881 there were only 148 armed policemen in the tobacco region; in 1887 and 1898 respectively, they were joined by another thirty and fifty men (Kooreman 1903a:17–18).

The number of administrative and judicial authorities also increased gradually over the years. Improvements that were introduced in the road system and the communication network were important not only for production, but also for the security of plantation managements. Yet none of this went far enough for the planters, who were thinking in terms of new police-posts, at company expense, at which personnel would be stationed for short periods, in a constant cycle of rotation

because the Malay or Javanese guards would, before long, become immensely good pals with the Javanese *kampong* population, both men and women, and the situation would soon become an easy-going routine mess, quite different to what the legislator would have in mind (Mulier 1903:55).

Table 11.
POLICE FORCE ON SUMATRA'S EAST COAST, 1864-1905

Year	Constabulary
1864	2
1872	13
1876	28
1881	148
1887	178
1898	228
1905	456

Source: Deli, In woord en beeld 1905; GSA, Vb 19-9-1905, no. 34.

The author of the above quotation worked out an elaborate plan for the setting-up of a special mobile unit for the plantations: to present a show of power in times of peace, and to act as troops in times of riots. This crack corps—indigenous mercenaries led by European officers—were to be housed in barracks in a central location and would have telephone connections to all plantations to facilitate their mobilization, on cycle or horseback, in the case of an alarm. Mulier even gave thought to the possible cutting of telephone lines when riots broke out: in such a case, signals would be fired from the roof of the manager's bungalow, the number of signals conveying the seriousness of the situation (Ibid.:56–64). From scenarios such as these it is obvious that the planters considered themselves to be pent up in a hostile environment. This fear psychosis in itself provoked violence. But even the best precautionary measures were of no help when coolie riots broke out on all sides. After all, the police could not be in various places at the same time! The result was that '. . . the planters were in a sense driven to maintain their prestige in an illegal manner, because they knew that their lives would be lost if authority was lost and a fight broke out on the plantation' (Ibid.:61–2).

This statement cannot be seen as anything other than an attempt to justify the violent treatment of the coolies. It was reasoned that they had only themselves to blame for being ruled with an iron hand, and that they would not meet their contractual obligations if the cane were not used. Some planters (or perhaps most of them once in a while?) did not know where to draw the line in their treatment of the 'disorderly' and 'unwilling' work force. Given the necessity to maintain strict discipline, excessive brutality, although it could not be condoned with, was sometimes considered to be unavoidable. After all, one cannot make an omelette without breaking eggs! The customary reasoning ran that rare cases of torture and manslaughter that might occur were exceptions and should not be seized upon as a reason to condemn all planters.

It should by now be clear that, such an explanation of the violence on the plantations based on economic rationality, is a perversion of the facts. A more fundamental conclusion, and one which is justified by abundant data, is that the coolies were systematically terrorized and that their exploitation was accompanied by maximum oppression. The presupposition was that, since the contract coolies were by nature disinclined to work, they had to be forced to do so. Threats in themselves were not sufficient. Castigation in varying degrees of intensity had a dual objective: punishment of those Asian workers whose work was inadequate and, to prevent this, intimidation of others. As we shall see later, atrocities committed against the coolies by no means always originated in the work sphere. Moreover, violence that caused temporary or permanent invalidity or even death of the victim, was a form of chastisement that was not compatible with sound economic logic in that it led to the destruction of a production factor of which scarcity was the most noticeable characteristic. Taussig takes this feature as his point of departure in his analysis of the horrifying treatment of the Indians in the Amazon region, meted out by rubber gatherers in the early decades of the present century (Taussig 1987). In a fascinating study, this anthropologist explains his thesis that violence became an objective in itself, rather than a means with which to force the autochthonous population to provide labour. The 'culture of terror' was based on a mixture of contempt, envy (for the inability to dehumanize them) and fear. The contempt was a logical consequence of the degradation of the dominant race to a status of total inferiority. The attitude that was thus adopted went much farther than a 'Verdinglichung' (objectification) of the underdog, its reduction to a commodity. What it amounted to was abomination, negating the human value of the other by attributing him with bestial behaviour. The climate of violence to which this gave rise was accompanied by a technique by which people were tortured to the verge of death. The infliction of physical pain was also intended to cause mental torment to the victim, to make him realize that he could lose his life at any arbitrary moment, and that the tortured person had no say even in the matter of his own survival. It is characteristic that the examples mentioned by Taussig also occurred in Sumatra's East Coast: repeated immersion in water until the victim almost drowned; protracted hanging-up of Chinese by their pigtails so that, even in that stretched position, they could barely touch the ground; withholding food and water until the victim became unconscious; flogging a coolie who was bound in a crucified position, and applying other methods of torture such that death would have meant a welcome release.

In reading the scarce literature that is available on plantation and mining enclaves in French or British colonial Asia, I have found remarkable similarities in the techniques of torture. The rubbing of red pepper onto the sexual organs of female coolies, tying a coolie in a crucified position to a stake in front of the planter's bungalow, occurred not only on Sumatra but also in Assam and Cochin China, for example. The case mentioned by Rhemrev of a female coolie who was given shock treatment has also been reported as a method by which to penalize disobedient coolies on the tea estates of Assam.

Those who were subjected to such treatment, were declared to be animals, and given what they deserved: bestial treatment. Contempt was mixed with frustration, caused by the feeling that the Asian coolie did not respond spontaneously and willingly to 'normal' economic incentives, was insensitive to the self-compulsion which resulted in an adequate labour performance. It was a form of escape which gave rise to fierce aggression among the white employers.

The deeper cause, which in my opinion is correctly stressed by Taussig, was the fear of those who were oppressed and trampled upon. In Brazil that fear was directed towards the mysterious power exuded by the natural environment, with which the autochthones were so closely linked. On Sumatra's East Coast the planters were far more intimidated by the social milieu that they themselves had created, that of the sea of coolies in which they thought they would drown. This led to nightmares and to forms of possession which the planters tried to exorcise by taking refuge in the use of terror. What are we to think, for example, of the case of a female coolie, reported by Rhemrev, who was first beaten to death and subsequently hanged from a tree?

Given the impossibility of raising the workers to a higher level of civilization, any contact with them held the risk of the planters lowering themselves to the same level of primitiveness that typified the character and nature of the coolies. Violence then had the function of creating the necessary distance between them. The intermediaries employed by the planters, such as the overseers and other agents, were expected to collect information on whatever was going on among the coolies. They kept the fear of their employers alive by reporting on turmoil, ill-will, disobedience, sabotage, conspiracy, treason, etc. By confirming the fear that already existed among their employers with such stories, they proved that they were indispensable and also enabled the planters to find an outlet for their partly genuine, partly imaginary feelings of intimidation. The tension to which the planters were daily subjected sometimes turned into an almost hysterical feeling of insecurity. In other words, the excesses that occurred were inherent in the plantation system, rather than an aberration that was limited to a few sick minds.

... the colonists and rubber company employees not only feared but themselves created through narration, fearful and confusing images of savagery; images that bound colonial society together with the epistemic murk of death. The terror and torture they devised mirrored the horror of savagery they both feared and fictionalized (Taussig 1987:133).

Contempt, frustration and fear together formed the basis of the racism that permeated colonial society and which did not come to an end even when the outside world had been made aware of the coolie scandals on the East Coast. The colonial literature, which formed the breeding ground for racial superiority, continued to exist. Moreover, I reject the supposition that what happened was restricted to that region and that it was caused by inadequate supervision on the part of the government. In opposition to the tendency to emphasize exceptional circumstances which occurred only in a remote corner of the colony, I would maintain that the plantation milieu represented an intensified form of a situation to which the colonized population in the Netherlands Indies as a whole was subjected. I intend to return to this thesis in the final chapter, but shall now first examine the contrast between planter and coolie as an extreme variation of the relationship between European lord and Asian servant.

V

PLANTATION SOCIETY AND THE COLONIAL ORDER

Plantation and Frontier Society

Plantation society as it existed on Sumatra's East Coast had a completely unique character. Its determining characteristics were the late opening-up and the region's peripheral situation within the colonial domain, the rapid rise of plantation agriculture as a predominant factor and, in principle, the temporary presence of both employers and employees. I shall first examine these features and subsequently discuss their effects on labour relations. The hegemony enjoyed by the planters and the violence that coloured their relations with the coolies were inherent in the frontier system which had crystallized on Sumatra at the end of the nineteenth century. The 'Wild East' seems to be an appropriate term for the social climate prevalent in the region.

The opening-up of this Outer Province—a name which in itself is significant—represented an important step in the demarcation of the colonial empire of the Netherlands in Southeast Asia which neared its completion at the end of the last century. The remarkable factor was that, in the first stage, both top (the employers) and bottom (the workers) of the plantation formation came almost entirely from outside the colony. The initiative definitely stemmed from private entrepreneurs who used the strategic position of this thinly-populated region, rich in land, to establish a new mode of production, little troubled by any pre-capitalist structures. In addition to economic motives, there were important reasons of the state. In the first half of the nineteenth century, Sumatra was disputed between the Netherlands and Britain. With the opening of the Suez Canal the distance to western Europe was considerably reduced and this was even more significantly so with regard to the world market. The rapid development of Malaya as a colony suited to exploitation and also based on plantation agriculture, together with the growth of Singapore as a transfer point in the Pacific, alerted the Netherlands Indies government to action. The passage to East Asia, where great changes were taking place, lay close to Sumatra's coast. Only by being effectively present could the Dutch authorities prevent the surrender of the region to British interests.

In the 1860s London's protests were neither firm nor immediate enough to prevent Holland's advance in the East Coast of Sumatra. The increasing interest of the more dangerous powers in the area made it seem desirable that Holland should be allowed effectively to occupy the island which the 1824 Treaty had seen as its 'sphere of influence' (Reid 1969:284).

Nevertheless, competition with a foreign power was not the only reason that drove the colonial government to fill the vacuum at the periphery. There were also considerations of internal policy why the claimed territory should have been effectively occupied and protected. The urge for expansion, was also due to the increasing awareness that Java was over-crowded. Its peasant population was hopelessly immobile and continued to stagnate at a sub-economic level. This, at least, was the view adopted by the colonial authorities. Was it, therefore, not far more attractive to direct infrastructural efforts, both technological and managerial, towards the Outer Provinces, where the development of empty land seemed likely to open-up new perspectives? During the course of the twentieth century, advocates of this school of thought, who had a strongly geo-political streak, were to plead increasingly that the focus of colonial development should be moved from 'exhausted' Java to other islands of the Netherlands Indies where natural resources were still abundantly available, without the deadweight of a mass of small peasants with whom nothing could be done. The planters who pioneered on Sumatra's East Coast during the 1860s can be seen as the forerunners of a capitalist policy of exploitation. Their success was a considerable source of inspiration to adherents of this late-colonial development ideology (De Waard 1924:1035–7).

A significant difference with the classical plantation societies of Latin America and the Caribbean region is that plantation industry on the East Coast emerged at a much later stage of capitalist and also of colonial transformation. Elsewhere in the Southeast Asian region, particularly in Ceylon, India (Assam and Nilgiris), French Indo-China, Malaya and the Philippines, plantations were also a fairly late phenomenon. None of them date back much farther than the middle of the nineteenth century, while the majority of the estates did not attain full growth until the turn of the century or shortly thereafter. Thus, the process which had taken some centuries in America, was completed within a few decades in Asia. The bringing together of western management expertise and Asian labour power in large-scale establishments formed the basis for a new mode of production which passed by the peasantry on whom colonial exploitation had earlier been founded. In all cases the new industry was concentrated in enclaves peripheral to the colonial state of which they formed a part. These salient similarities as well as the existing or emerging differences, have never been subjected to any systematic comparison. This has chiefly been due to the orientation of the colonies to their own mother countries, a tendency which also gave a bias to their historiography.

It cannot be coincidental that the first limited liability company in India (the Assam Company set up in 1845) and also in the Netherlands Indies (the Deli Company in 1869) was a plantation enterprise. Both companies were to achieve gigantic size and to rule their areas of operation in a way that was more than a match for their respective colonial governments. When it became certain, around 1885, that tobacco production on plantations was not a temporary but a permanent phenomenon, both the entrepreneurs and the government proceeded to make expensive investments that later became a necessity: roads, railways, ports, hospitals, government offices and, in general, an improvement in the level of infrastructural facilities and an institutional framework appropriate to a more regulated and developed society. Medan, for example, grew into a highly westernized urban centre and became more attractive in appearance. The advance of modern civilization brought an end to the primitive conditions for which Deli had previously been notorious. This progress was also reflected on the social life of the area, and by the end of the nineteenth century social life had become refined and fashionable. 'Society on the East Coast is not degenerate, it is not an undisciplined rabble; conditions were like that earlier, but in the course of time it has changed for the better' (Kooreman 1904–5:55). Cremer has given a fascinating account of the new bourgeois culture that arose in this area.

Visiting, associating with ladies, dressing correctly, going for ex-
cursions to the hills, frequenting theatre and music concert halls,
all of which made their appearance in the European community
in the 1880s were to be found here now (Cremer 1889:56–60).

Uncertainty of an entirely different nature however had to do
with the sales of the product in the world market. Similar to every
other mono-crop, tobacco was extremely sensitive to fluctuations
in the international economy. Very few of the original planters
were able to retain their independence. After the boom of the 1880s,
a brief but severe recession in the early 1890s gave rise to a first
reorganization which ushered in the transition from an early-
capitalistic industry to a fully capitalistic one; a transition accompanied by the replacement of mercantile enterprise by corporate
business interests. By 1925, only fourteen of the 129 tobacco companies remained on the East Coast, and those fourteen owned a
total of seventy plantations (Volker 1928:31). Tobacco growing was
now confined to the Deli district and its immediate neighbourhood, i.e. the land that had first been cultivated for that
purpose. In other parts of the Residency new perennial crops, such
as rubber, sisal and oilpalm, were to be introduced which would
eventually far surpass the tobacco crop in importance. This
diversification of agri-business, however, was to occur mainly in
the course of the twentieth century, which is beyond our scope.
(For a survey of this later period, see Stoler 1985.)

The strongly international atmosphere which had been typical
of Deli since it was first opened-up, continued to prevail. The
orientation to the other coast of Malaya dated from pre-colonial
times. From the economic point of view, even in the nineteenth
century, this relationship had been mediated by the Chinese rather
than by the British traders. The advent of the Dutch administration
was inspired partly by the fear of the British extending their
influence through Chinese agents in the coastal states (Reid
1970:291). In the pioneering stage of the plantation system, these
agents became very powerful as economic brokers. In 1876 the
Resident reported that trade was virtually a Chinese affair, controlled by businessmen who operated from Penang and Singapore.
They acted not only as traders, but initially also showed interest in
agricultural production, as we have seen in Chapter I. The main
reason why the Chinese did not take this any further was not the
lack of capital or technological capability, but rather the lack of

willingness to allow any other than the European planters to take up plantation agriculture. The Chinese were speedily excluded as producers because the Planters Committee feared that,

if agricultural land rights are given to alien Orientals, particularly to the Chinese, many coolies now working for the tobacco planters would leave the plantations after the expiry of their contracts in order to work on other lands to be employed by members of their own race even though, according to the Committee, that would sometimes be for a smaller wage because a Chinese prefers to work as a free man under another Chinese than as a contract coolie for European planters, however better off he might be by the latter (Bool 1903b:24).

Access to market operations, was similarly defended against this alien, Asian, competition. Intervention of a non-economic nature thus ensured that the capitalist industry acquired and retained a European identity. On both sides of the Strait of Malacca, the Chinese, who formed a rapidly growing economic minority, were forced back into the retail trade and commission business, both of which they pretty well monopolized (Van Langenberg 1977:59; for a particularly interesting survey of the nature of such business, see De Waard 1924:1047–9).

The Chinese circuit played an important role in preserving contacts with the other coast. Everything needed by the Europeans on the East Coast, in the beginning, including their daily provisions, had to be imported from Penang; Nienhuys obtained not only his merchandise but also his coolies from there. The initial capital for opening-up the new land was provided mostly from the Straits Settlements. East Coast produce reached the world market through the same route. Shipping connections to and from Deli continued for many years to run through Penang and, increasingly, through Singapore. At first, it was almost impossible to reach Sumatra from Batavia: the journey to Riouw took five days, and that was only the first part of the passage. From Riouw a boat sailed once per month to the port of Belawan.

In those days, Deli could really be considered as an isolated region, which had little or nothing to do with the rest of the Netherlands Indies and which was oriented exclusively towards the Straits and to Europe. Even the currency commonly used 'on the other coast' [i.e. Malacca] became the standard means of exchange in Deli. In succession, this was the Mexican dollar, the Japanese dollar and the Straits dollar (Marinus and Van der Laan 1929:46).

An interplay of various national and colonial interests underlay this mercantile orientation. In exchange for the recognition of Dutch sovereignty over Sumatra's East Coast, the British Government expected and obtained unrestricted economic access to the region for its subjects.

Intervention by the colonial administration otherwise played only a modest part in the dynamic development experienced by Sumatra's East Coast. Private industry started there with a considerable measure of autonomy and, encouraged by the region's peripheral situation within the Netherlands Indies, was far less inclined than employers elsewhere to allow government officials to lay down the law. The planters belonged to a great variety of nationalities and, for that reason alone, had little connection with the Dutch authorities. The labour system was organized along lines that had already been introduced in Malaya. The ties between the European community on the East Coast and Malaya were very close, not only economically but also socially. Penang was known as the 'Kurort' of Deli: quite literally so, since shares in the English-Dutch sanatorium were mainly owned by Delians. The planters went to Penang on leave and in order to get away. 'One is able to walk there without getting warm or in the least tired, one feels refreshed in the cool air of the evening, and one sees neither coolies nor tobacco!!!' (Westerman 1901:300).

In the course of the twentieth century, the government of the Netherlands Indies was to become increasingly successful in setting limits to the hegemony of the planters. The economic climate gradually became more protectionist, with consequences for investment policies and trade (Allen and Donnithorne 1957:218). The intensity of relations with Malaya gradually decreased. Towards the end of the nineteenth century the Dutch element among the tobacco planters became stronger. This was due not so much to a narrow-minded nationalism as to the fear of foreign employees, mastering the profession, and starting plantations of their own, financed with funds from their home country. The Dutch companies did not want to promote such competition. Cremer himself is said to have ensured the departure of German assistant managers from Deli Company plantations under his management, and a number of other large corporations did not hesitate to follow his example ('A Word', *De Indische Gids* 1904:1554: see also the note in *De Indische Gids* 1901:1385–6). However, it would not be correct to draw more general conclusions from the concentration of Dutch capital in tobacco growing. Due to the rise of perennial crops at the beginning of the twentieth century, of which rubber and palmoil in particular brought a strong input of European (British, French and Belgian) and North American capital, the planters' milieu on Sumatra's East Coast continued to be an international one. However, the colonial government demanded that its subjects be loyal to the political system within which they operated. In the initial stage it had been impossible to make even that demand. It seemed then, in fact, that the pioneers could dictate to the government: support in their efforts to obtain and keep sufficient workers, legislation which assured them of unrestricted access to land, and little if any taxation. Planters were even heard to say that if these wishes were not complied with, then a political union should be sought with Malaya.

The planters—and they included various foreigners such as Germans and English—announced that they made Deli what it was and what it could become; that *they* had brought money, prosperity and the entrepreneurial spirit. And now it was their opinion that the Netherlands Indies Government was slighting them, was not doing anything for them; even the Resident lived far away, in Bengkalis, in a region that was of far less importance than Deli. But when the government also began to levy moderately high taxes, then things really went wrong. People made no secret of their feelings and said aloud that the government only considered Deli good enough to glean, to fleece and to milk, but that it did nothing in return.... Thus there was something brewing. Some seemed not to dislike the idea that it would be much better for Deli if it became a part of the neighbouring British territory. England at least did something for its colonies, Holland only bled them white (*De Hollandsche Revue* 1903:560–1).

The planters thus used what room for manoeuvre they possessed in order to pressurize the colonial administration and, in view of the results, they seem to have been very good at it.

Finally, a particular feature of the colonization of Sumatra's East Coast was that those who went there had no intention of settling down permanently. Both planters and coolies assumed that their presence was only temporary. In the classical plantation societies of the New World, workers and planters also largely originated elsewhere; nevertheless, they came not only to work but usually also to stay. This was definitely not the case in the East Coast of Sumatra, nor in many other colonial societies in Asia where plantation agriculture was introduced. Even after the difficult pioneering years, Deli continued to be a transit-station for the white staff, all of whom wanted to earn as much money as possible in the shortest time feasible and then to return as wealthy men to Europe. The great captains of industry, such as Nienhuys and Cremer, had set the example. The latter was only thirty-four years old when he returned to the Netherlands, to further his career as business tycoon and politician. The coolies also signed on for a limited period only, in principle no longer than three years. Many of them died before the end of that term or were worn out by the exhausting pace at which they had to work, combined with a low wage, bad living conditions and inadequate health care. Others stayed on, at least for a second term: not of their own free will, but through indenture, they were forced to do so. Yet plantation managements actually preferred a continual flow of labour, i.e. a constant supply of fresh workers who paid for their own disciplining and who needed little training for the work assigned to them. Free settlement outside the plantations was forbidden to the coolies; work remuneration made no allowance for family formation or for the coming of non-working family members. Labour reproduction had to take place overseas, in the peasant hinterland, and the cost involved also had to be found there. The planters were only interested in tied labour for a certain length of time, a situation which was to continue into the first decades of the twentieth century.

The following case shows how many managers still continue to fear the idea of a free labour market. Sixty Chinese whose contracts had expired, had requested and obtained from a District Officer the permission to stay in the country. They were men of irreproachable behaviour. Nevertheless, angry protests were immediately voiced by the planters. 'In this way', they said, 'there will be a free labour market in Deli.' As though that was a self-evident evil! (Van Blankenstein 1929:48–9).

Data on the rate of labour circulation are almost non-existent. One source only reports that a tenth of the workforce was sacked each year and replaced by fresh workers (Schuffner and Kuenen

1910:23). It would be inadmissible to draw more general conclusions for the total area for the whole period covered by this
study. The figure mentioned above referred to the plantations
belonging to one company some years after the turn of the century.
The temporary presence of the plantation population of all levels
helped to exacerbate the interrelationships among them. The
restraining effect that emanates from an entrepreneurial class and
a workforce both rooted in or near the place of employment was
lacking in the East Coast, due to the particular way in which
plantation society was organized. In a lecture to the School of
Tropical Agriculture in Deventer, The Netherlands, one man of
practice explained to his audience why it was that plantation life
on Java was far more attractive than that on Sumatra.

There is no drudgery or quarreling; one works with willing, though not
very diligent people, instead of with the ill-natured, insolent pigtailed
Chinese. People go to Deli with the firm idea of leaving again as quickly
as possible; this is different in Java. People are more reconciled to their
environment, they feel more at home. After some time one learns the
language of the people and becomes more interested in their family
life—things that are inconceivable in Deli because people rarely if ever
learn Chinese and the Chinese do not have a family life (*De Indische
Mercuur* 1894:527).

Long after the establishment of the plantation economy was
completed, the East Coast of Sumatra continued to have the character of a frontier society, with a thin upper stratum and a broad
base. Two worlds with a gulf between them, polarities which have
to be comprehended in their antagonistic opposition to one
another.

The Plantocracy

Sumatra's East Coast really came into existence as one huge plantation, with the Deli Company as the biggest shareholder. It is
indicative that this company chose Medan as the seat of its headquarters, and that Medan only subsequently became the administrative centre of the region. Not without justification, the
planters considered Deli to be their own creation and property. The
main infrastructural works, such as roads, railways, telephone and
telegraph connections, water supply, hospitals etc., were financed

and executed by agri-business. Medan was situated in the heart of the plantation country and reflected its character.

Medan is therefore the new town, with white, fresh buildings, situated among green, fresh lawns, whose origins are due to the busy plantation life which surrounds it. It is entirely unique in our Indies; you will never again find its equal, not on Sumatra, nor on Java. It is modern and European; it has a flavour of England; the vicinity of Singapore has undoubtedly been of influence to Medan. 'The White Club' (so aptly named), Post Office, Town Hall, Javanese Bank, Hotel de Boer and the Medan Hotel, the imposing offices of various companies (Harrison and Crossfield, Deli Company, Deli Experimental Station, Deli Railway Company, Van Nie and Co.), all stand there in the exceptionally fresh green of rain-washed palm-trees, fig trees and jemaras. They stand as white buildings of prosperity, of successful work, of admirable western effort (Couperus 1924:33).

Medan, the centre of the plantations on the East Coast, is filled with a spirit of daring and nerve, of getting to grips with things. This has dominated the history of the plantations, and the spirit continues amongst all those who belong to this population. People here do not like inertia; they have to be active. The population is international, the principal element being western (Blink 1926:128).

In these twentieth-century descriptions, the emphasis is on the non-indigenous character of the town. Coolies did not belong there but to the plantations. Even the government kept a low profile. The numerous companies that were affiliated with the Deli Company gave the latter the aura of a state within a state. The man who stood at its top was looked upon as the king of Deli. 'For a time it carried out the administrative functions of the government in the territories leased from the sultan. It was, indeed, an empire builder as well as a great commercial and agricultural enterprise (Allen and Donnithorne 1957:99).

This situation seemed to change when the staffing of the administrative apparatus was strengthened from the 1880s onwards. The number of officials and agencies gradually increased, but even after the pioneering era, the hegemony of private enterprise was not visibly weakened. Of decisive significance was the common stand taken by the planters who realized fairly quickly that collective action would be to their advantage. The regional government, which was required to operate at a great distance from the centre of colonial policy-making, was confronted by a powerful and closed front of plantation enterprises. Moreover, government officials stayed in the region for only a couple of years after their appointment—they circulated even more rapidly than planters and coolies—which was mostly at the beginning of their careers. Young District Officers wielded extensive powers in their capacity as magistrates, but proved incapable of using their prerogatives impartially. When on a tour of inspection through their district, they spent the night on one of the plantations (Hoetink 1902:77–8). The generous hospitality so freely offered made it difficult for them to form an independent judgement. Van den Brand deprecated the servile attitude shown towards the planters by even senior officials. Similarly, Van Kol, as member of the Socialist Party, commented disparagingly in the Lower House on the covert bribery with which this was accompanied. Before leaving the area to take up a new post elsewhere, they used to sell off their furniture and other personal belongings to the highest bidders.

I refer to the auctions held by the Residents, Assistant Residents and District Officers on Sumatra's East Coast, especially in Deli. I am well aware that a similar situation exists in other parts of the Indies, but it is nowhere so aggravating as in Deli. It is well known that in this way Residents in Deli have received as much as thirty to forty thousand guilders, because they knew how to get into the good graces of the planters and therefore did not properly do their duty (Proceedings Lower House, 19 November 1902:121).

The Chinese headmen and the indigenous aristocracy were co-opted in the alliance that ran affairs on the East Coast, and also promoted the interests of the planters with great vigour. In this connection, Van den Brand spoke of,

the three groups that benefit from laxity on the part of government and somnolence on the part of the law: the native princes, the Chinese headmen and the planters. The high prices fetched at such an auction often serve to show the successor what he might expect if the conception of his task proves agreeable to that of the interested parties (Van den Brand 1904a:41).

We have already discussed the position of the Chinese headmen, who played both a preventive and a repressive role in the disciplining of their fellow countrymen on the plantations. They originated from the trading middle-class whose members were found in large numbers in the chief towns and ports of the region, operating as agents of Chinese firms whose headquarters were in Singapore or Penang. They formed an essential link in the distribution network, whether legal or illegal, the latter included the smuggling of opium, the sale of deserted coolies, the supply of prostitutes. The most prominent of these Chinese belonged to Deli's leading citizens. The majority, however, were simple artisans and shop-keepers who had come from Malaya or from Java. Although they were of far better standing than the coolies, the planters neverthe-less continued to handle them with some arrogance.

Anyone who knows the Chinese only as a trader, or as an ever-polite, ever-smiling *baba*, will find that the Chinese field coolie in Deli is an altogether different being. The former (*baba*) has been born in the Indies, has acquired some superficial politeness through his lengthy contact with the Europeans and due to his trade relationships. But the latter, who has been imported from the Chinese hinterland as a coolie for a plantation in Deli, is cast in a very different mould (Dixon 1913:39).

The native administration operated solely in the shadow of the colonial bureaucracy. The original rulers had allowed themselves to be deprived of their power in exchange for a considerable annual allowance and now played an almost decorative role in the region. The coolies did not fall under their jurisdiction, but they tried their own subjects if these dared to shelter or to use the labour of deserted plantation coolies. The native elite also had an important source of income in the issuing of land concessions. Any planter who bought land for clearance had to make allowances for the lesser native authorities, who demanded a financial reward for their co-operation.

He will go first to the most influential of the sultan's High Officers, a Datu, Tungku or Sibajak, to obtain his co-operation and intercession with the Sultan, on which occasion he will drop some *baksheesh*, perhaps a couple of hundred dollars, with the promise that, if he gets his contract, another thousand dollars will follow. Then he makes an appointment to see the sultan. It does not matter which of the sultans or princes is approached. The one which is more co-operative than the others, or asks for less money. It depends not only on the size of the contract and the price which the sultan asks for the land, but also on whether there is demand for the land in H.H.'s region. We will assume, however, that the sultan is satisfied with 10,000 dollars and, after much complimentary talk, the planter will take his leave. But next comes the sultan's *Krani* [writer] who has to draw up the contract in quadruplicate, and who naturally also has to be given *baksheesh* (Westerman 1901:86).

Officials had to be bribed, even into the office of the Resident, a subject on which the sources touch with great delicacy (Ibid.:87; Kooreman 1904–5:25). Questions raised in the Lower House regarding the enormous amounts of money that were pocketed by the Sultan of Deli, remained unanswered. Van Kol, who had recently been given a cordial reception by the sultan, who acted on the assumption that Van Kol was a crony of Cremer's, ventilated his criticism in no uncertain terms.

The princes used to live in Labuan Deli where they had settled and gradually acquired their present territory. They have simply usurped the fertile land of the Bataks, which they now own. Moreover, this Sultan is a fanatic Muslim who has even had the nerve to declare, in the presence of a District Officer of the Civil Service, that he would strenuously resist any missionary work in the Batak lands and would not tolerate any headman who embraced Christianity. He has acquired his significant influence simply through the support of capitalism, given in exchange for the concessions that he has issued to the tobacco planters. He has been saved by the tobacco monopoly. Deli tobacco, with its fine texture and strong fibre, has become a monopoly article that, by pure accident, has made him very wealthy. For the rest he is an absolutely useless old man who lives in luxury and is flattered and made much of by the tobacco growers who hope in this way to get new concessions from him. He has been given the title of sultan to gratify his vanity, since his real title is *'sutan'*. Enormous sums of money have accrued to him in exchange for his ceding of land, and although the lands belong to the people, he has not given a cent of the millions that he has received to the benefit of the community, but uses them all for his own pomp and circumstance. A ridiculous splendour rules in that marble palace, which is scandalous in view of the wretched circumstances in which the people live (Proceedings Lower House, 25 November 1902:193).

Medan was not only an administrative and economic centre, headquarters of government services, trading houses and the ancillary industries, but was also the place where the planters came for rest and recreation. To the outside world the emphasis was on the sense of comradeship and closed ranks among the planters. But a number of dividing lines ran right through the class of employers. The foreign element, for example, was not distributed more or less evenly among all companies, but was found in strong concentrations in particular firms. The Senembah Company, for example, showed a distinct preference for German-Swiss employees who lived together 'as members of one large family' (Broersma 1919:170). This applied to their fellow countrymen who belonged to the 'Deutsche Verein' and who retreated into this circle in order to keep alive their ties with the fatherland (Senembah Company 1939:28). Rank and standing also existed among the staffs of the various companies.

In Holland the Deli Company is the best known tobacco company and it was then anything but easy to be taken on as assistant. Supply far exceeded demand and the directors in Holland made good use of the opportunity to choose the best. Consequently, the employees of the Deli Company considered themselves with some justification to be the elite of the planters, and they rather looked down on colleagues who were not employed by the company (Van den Brand 1904b:61).

Of far greater importance than these status distinctions, however, were the differences between juniors and seniors in the management. Assistants who had just come out to Deli hardly counted in social life. In the club they sat together at the bachelors' table in the corner, without ever thinking of mixing with their betters on an equal footing. Relations were hierarchical, but rough and jovial rather than formal and distant. Naturally, decorum must never be forgotten in front of the workers. Perhaps it was all the more eagerly observed for which, the new employees were ragged when the planters were by themselves, as in the club. The young assistant had to put up with a great deal, but on the other hand had the right to seek some variety for his lonely existence. Who begrudged him his occasionally boisterous behaviour during his few leisure hours?

The assistant, who lived in isolation and, due to the lack of transport, seldom found his way to the inhabited world, was only likely to coarsen his habits since he had to associate daily with an indifferent lot of coolies, to whom he had to show his teeth in order to keep discipline and order. In those days the assistant's house was little better than a present-day *mandur's* dwelling. Small wonder that the assistant of those days sometimes kicked over the traces in his behaviour towards the workers and was exuberant to say the least on the few days in the year that he found himself in Labuan and Medan in the company of his peers (Broersma 1919:149–50).

He sought his amusement in hunting, with the natural adjuncts of horse and rifle. Eye-witnesses at the turn of the century reported that the rougher aspects of the planter's existence were gradually being smoothened out. Manners and social intercourse became more polished, and a new type of planter made his appearance which showed a greater degree of poise. This new generation was called 'Salon planters' by the remaining old-timers (Kooreman 1903:24). Such observations seem to have been made rather too hastily. If we are to believe the contemporary novels written about the plantations, wild drinking parties, coarseness and vulgarity continued to characterize the lives of the Europeans in Deli during the later colonial period (Clerkx 1961:20–1). The clubs in which the planters sought their leisure were also frequented by the government officials. Gone were the days when the latter passed sentences on coolies guilty of misdemeaners, while sitting in the club. However, their association with the plantation management showed the same mechanics as were manifested in the auction system: the hegemony of the captains of industry, to whom the government personnel were a willing tool.

The strong under-representation of the female element fitted the image of Deli as a frontier society with a macho-culture. Men dominated all levels of the plantation system, from high to low. In 1884 the 688 Europeans living on Sumatra's East Coast included 540 men and 148 women, a ratio of almost 4 to 1 (Schadee 1919:41). In 1900 the ratio of the sexes was almost unchanged: 1,578 men out of a total of 2,079 Europeans (*Sumatra Post*, 5 May 1913). Kooreman observed that almost all officials, many officers and the majority of senior managers were married men (Kooreman 1903a:24). Assistants, who were forbidden to marry, had the status of bachelors (*boedjang*). If they sometimes behaved over-boldly or boastfully, this was excused by referring to their solitary existence.

Women also constituted only a small minority among the

workforce. At the beginning of this century, the total force of 62,000 coolies employed by the Deli Company included only 5,000 women, all of whom were Javanese. The men belonged almost entirely to the younger age categories, in the prime of life. Was their life on the plantations deprived of sex? The Chinese coolies were said to be indifferent about women. The few sources that broach this delicate subject suggest that they preferred 'unnatural lewdness', showing a particular partiality for young lads who were little more than children. These were known as little calves (*anak djawi*), and the foremen had the first claim on them. Murderous assaults due to male love affairs were quite common, reported Van Kol (1903:35,99). This is hardly surprising since the affair was enacted before numerous eyes. The young male prostitutes in the coolie barracks draped their own beds with curtains and baubles (Tschudnowsky 1899:52).

Pederasty is common among the Chinese in settlements where there are no women or only very few, as in so many not only in our region, but also in the Straits Settlements. I do not believe that on any plantation a Chinese has ever complained about the shortage, or lack, of women (Kooreman 1903a:39).

The position was quite the reverse as far as Javanese men were concerned. According to the same source, they could not endure life on a plantation without women. The men were said to be easily satisfied and, the female coolies became attached to the plantation where they lived, as soldiers' wives became attached to the barracks.

Unmarried Javanese women can easily find Javanese men on the plantation who will co-habit with them or marry them, because it is astonishing how little discrimination the Javanese shows with regard to women, how little he is interested in their earlier life and outward appearance, even their age. Those who are not so fortunate, do their work, and for the rest are free to continue their former trade of prostitution (Ibid.:37).

Relationships were just as easily broken as they were entered into, and this contributed to the rapid spread of venereal diseases. In view of the firm conviction held in and around planters circles that most, if not all, women who came from Java to Sumatra were syphilitic, Tschudnowsky's report is significant that not one of the new consignment of women whom he had to examine medically suffered from this disease (1899:54). The evil was thus really linked to life on the plantations. Van Kol's statement (1903:93) that women sold their *kebon* children to the highest bidder, which meant to the Chinese purchasers, is supposed to illustrate the debauchery that ruled among the plantation workers. Anything like marital faith was said to be unknown among couples. Competition was immense, and the few women on a plantation would pass from one to the other. This, at any rate, is the impression given by the literature on plantation society (critically reviewed by Stoler 1985:32-5). The reputed immorality enabled the management, in contravention of the Coolie Ordinance, to separate man and wife whenever this was opportune: that is to say, as punishment, or to suit the sexual convenience of a foreman or an assistant. To avoid hindrance from the clause stating that married coolies were not to be separated from one another, the planters refused to recognize any marital unions entered into by the coolies during their stay on the plantation. They sometimes even introduced an explicit prohibition on marriage (Hoetink 1902:40; discussion on the First Report of the Labour Inspectorate, *De Indische Gids* 1912:1326). Coolies were taken on as individuals. Co-habitation was permitted only under due observance of this principle, which formed the basis of the labour system.

The resentment caused by sexual interference on the part of the assistants or foremen was one of the causes of coolie attacks on the managerial cadre. Rhemrev reported on coolies who pelted a club building with stones when an assistant started an affair with a Javanese woman who lived with a *mandur* (Rhemrev 1904:406). The planters also held strong opinions about the sexual proclivities of other ethnics who were not Chinese or Javanese. It sometimes happened, for example, that a number of male coolies of Indian origin set up house together with a woman who cooked for them and with whom they also shared their beds.

By no means all the Klings are married, but they try to compensate for this social lack by at least obtaining a share in a woman. In this way, three or four of them will take over a good-looking Kling woman from another, and this, particularly if the partners are drunk, frequently causes fairly serious trouble (Haarsma 1889:35).

Statements of this sort throw an interesting light on the racist prejudices that were inherent in the plantation environment.

Given the scarcity of women, how did the European males satisfy their sexual urges? The emphasis was on macho-behaviour and the planter presented himself as a young, aggressive and rugged male. This self-image and the strong social restraints to which they were subjected, precluded any open demonstration of homosexuality between white members of the management and Chinese or Javanese coolies. I have not found a single source that even indicates the possibility of such a relationship, but this naturally does not mean that they did not occur. On the other hand, to live together with an Asian woman was accepted and even found fitting in that male society. It was taken as a matter of course that the white staff should have the first choice whenever new female coolies came to a plantation, but naturally only as a temporary affair. 'Formerly, it was taken as axiomatic that assistants might not marry; even married managers were very few in number. Then and now the men must make do with a native or Javanese manager, the good examples of which were really excellent housekeepers' (Dixon 1913:77).

'Housekeeper' is a very detached term to use for the Javanese concubine (*njai*), who was ideally, beautiful and docile, but also said to be temperamental and inscrutable. This combination of attraction and repulsion must also be seen in the light of strongly racist relationships. Current opinion had it that all female coolies were prostitutes or inevitably became so. Nevertheless, the planters, actually in competition with the male coolies (apart from the 'dissolute Chinese', of course), made use of these 'contract sluts' to satisfy their sexual needs. Can the feelings aroused by such practices perhaps explain the sadistic practices to which female coolies in particular were subjected by white superiors, and which Van den Brand, for example, dared to mention in his publication?

Racism

In the plantation system, white superiority encountered the structure and culture of inferiority imposed on Asian workers. The colonial situation, a fertile soil for virulent racism, thus brought even greater tension to labour relations on the plantations. To all concerned, this particular coloration of the domination-subordination relationship was an established fact with which all

incoming planters and coolies were rapidly familiarized. 'The
army of workers is always formed by orientals of the worst sort.
Supervision is in the hands of men who are conscious of racial
superiority, all of them living under a tradition of patriarchal
relations' (Broersma 1919:263).

The worker possessed no characteristics that would make him
into a person, but by definition represented all the traits of the
collectivity to which he or she belonged. Group prejudices which
were principally negative, such as 'stinkers' and 'contract sluts'
were recorded entirely as a matter of course. A number of these
platitudes have already been considered: a Chinese was said to be
an arch-deceiver and too bold; a Javanese was slow, lazy and
temperamental; and a Kling was boisterous and unclean (Westerman 1901:23), or childish, cowardly and inclined to tell tales
(Haarsma 1889:34). Moreover, in the eyes of their masters, the
members of each race all looked exactly the same: 'At first, it is not
easy for a *singkeh*-assistant to tell all those yellow mugs apart'
(Dixon 1913:48).

The sources make no mention of stereotypes in the other direction, i.e. those that the coolies held with regard to the whites. The
emphasis was always on colour. There could be no intermingling
between white on the one side and brown or yellow on the other.
This explains why there were no Eurasians on the Deli plantations,
in contrast to Java. Even amongst government officials there were
few representatives of this intermediate class. Such a mixture of
different races, known as *Sinjos*, could never be good. Although
less attention had apparently been given to skin colour during the
pioneering era when taking on staff for office and other supportive
work, by the end of the century this intermediate stratum on the
plantations had been purified of all non-white elements.

In earlier times in particular, use had been made of these half-castes, but
this practice has gradually been reconsidered. Although they are useful
people in many respects, they did not always keep the desired distance
and they exercised a bad influence over their insubordinate workforce.
They have mostly inherited only the vices of the Europeans, and this has
anything but a favourable influence on their natural bent. They are particularly susceptible to 'bribery' (Westerman 1901:19).

In its postings of civil servants, the government made allowances for the exceptional circumstances of the East Coast, which meant the racist milieu (Marinus and Van der Laan 1929:47–8). The *dokter djawa*, appointed towards the end of the nineteenth century for the treatment of their countrymen, were forbidden to dress in the same way as their European colleagues. They had to articulate their ethnicity by wearing the *sarong* (Tschudnowsky 1899:43). Only the whites counted, as ex-Resident Kooreman made clear when he spoke about 'the Deli community which consisted of 1,700 people' (Kooreman 1904–5:82). The class of European planters in the region was notorious for its exceptional arrogance, even to outsiders, and expected its workforce to show a servility that went far beyond what was customary in similar societies elsewhere (Reid 1970:320). But even in this respect a distinction has to be made between a more good-natured and a malicious variant.

In the first case emphasis was placed on training the workers to be virtuous and some indulgence was shown towards their shortcomings. The planter acted as an omniscient and energetic father whose word was law. 'People so often say: "coolies are like big children". In my opinion, too little emphasis is given to the fact that, even if they are indeed "big" children, they still have their troublesome moments' (Dixon 1913:47).

According to this line of thought, the coolies had childish ideas, behaved somewhat simplistically, which meant that they were stupid, naive and feeble-minded; but at the same time they could be troublesome and had to be called to order. Such infantalization of the workers acted as a mechanism with which to justify their subordination to white authority. A show of servility emphasized the relationship which at best might be one of familiarity but which was never intimate. The Javanese automatically squatted on their heels whenever they were close to one of the assistants, and whenever the workers passed by the bungalow of the manager they were required to bare their heads. Hoetink reports on a number of Chinese whom he found in a plantation's lock-up because they had found this mark of respect rather too much to ask when they passed the house of their master while carrying heavy loads (Hoetink 1902:56).

In this relationship, the distance between the coolie and the planter was extenuated to some degree by a form of paternalistic responsibility. In the other variant, however, the distance between them became almost unbridgeable. The white superior had no interest whatsoever in the happiness or misfortunes of his subordinates. There was no need for any communication between them at all. The coolies were unable to speak Dutch, which in any case would have evidenced an unheard-of impudence on their part (Hanegraaff 1910:13). Conversely, the European management showed no inclination to learn the language of their workers, excusing themselves from doing so by saying that the diversity of the workforce made that a hopeless task. If an assistant had shown any desire to learn the language of the workers, that would have meant his wanting to bridge the gap between them; in other words, to lower himself to the level of the workers. And who was likely to take it into his head to express himself in the same way 'as a troup of cackling Chinese'? (Kooreman 1904–5:40; Dixon 1913:24). Malay was the convenient lingua franca, and even then the foreman acted as the intermediary. As far as the Europeans were concerned, however, even the knowledge of that 'dialect' seldom went further than a few sentences and exclamations, strung together with curses and obscenities. This was also the image of the planter with which the newly-arrived assistant became familiar.

... who angrily shouted orders, hurriedly obeyed by the brown and yellow coolies (Dixon 1913:9).

... on the East Coast plantations almost no-one knew the language of the contract workers, and the European employees—as I repeatedly saw during my investigations—seldom spoke to them in anything other than a snarl in bad Malay, which was said to be necessary for their prestige! (Rhemrev 1904:345).

In the eyes of the planters, the lack of understanding usually shown by the workers in their bewildered reaction to the botched and garbled directions that were shouted to them, was proof not only of their dullness and stupidity but also of flat obstinacy. Under such circumstances, was it not understandable that the assistant or the manager, whose patience was so sorely tested, should explode in rage? As the regional authorities also believed, those who would not listen had to feel the weight of authority physically.

At the club table, in the presence of his superior, a young District Officer ascribed the fact that the coolies were so often beaten to the fact that the planters and their assistants understand as good as nothing of the different languages spoken by them. 'Do you talk to your horse if it refuses to trot?' asked his chief. 'No', answered the District Officer. Well, said his chief, neither do you need to talk to the coolies (Kooreman 1904–5:25–6).

The ex-Resident referred to this example from earlier years in order to illustrate that during his term of office, shortly before the turn of the century, such unqualified racist remarks were no longer made. There are many cases, however, that prove that his statement was definitely untrue. In the malicious variant that I have distinguished the coolies were certainly considered to be 'Untermenschen'. Their dehumanization began at the time of their recruitment and their shipment to Deli as so much merchandise. The more critically-minded literature repeatedly makes the association with the transport of cattle. Plantation workers were alienated in a double sense: they were not only denied access to the means of production, but even to a human identity. In referring to the Rhemrev Report, a ministry official remarked in an advisory memorandum to the Minister of Colonies that in Deli the coolie was seen as a living machine, not as a human being. Among the European elite of Deli a commonly-held opinion was that the only restraint that needed to be shown to an Asian worker was due to the recognition that even an animal had the right, not to humane treatment, but to treatment by a human being. Were not the sexual habits of the workers more bestial than human? The following effusion, taken from a local newspaper published in 1903, is a striking expression of the racist trend of thought that was common among the planters.

Are Chinese tobacco coolies people? They are animals that look a little like people! Don't talk to me about your altruistic concepts; they are absolute nonsense. And if Chinese coolies are like animals as regards their morals and mental faculties, that doesn't mean that people should mistreat them because an animal should not be mistreated. But no-one has ever heard that an animal could take the stand as a witness and make sworn statements, with burning incense, mumbled prayers, cow's milk, Koran on the head, or whatever other idiocies they might perpetrate, which serious people in Batavia watch and even seem to find significant (quoted in Van den Brand 1904b:17).

Utterances of this sort go much farther than is usual in a colonial system that is based solely on peasant production. The racism

inherent in the plantation environment was not only a result of, but
also a precondition to, the enslavement of the workforce. Contacts
across the colour line were unavoidable, but for that reason were
strictly formalized and had to occur according to strictly defined
rules. A surprisingly large number of the gruesome cases of torture
reported by Rhemrev were not due to any transgressions while
working, but to 'liberties' taken by the coolies in the social sphere.
By labelling the coolies as beasts (cf. Stibbe 1913:20), and by denying them any human qualities, any sort of action against them
could pass as being legitimate.

If the limits of humanity were thus violated, those who were
guilty of excesses were said to be the victims of tropical madness.
Anyone who suffered from such a state of mind was unable to
control his passions and committed deeds for which he could not
be held responsible. This was a syndrome which had first been
described as such in the German colonies of Africa, but which
occurred everywhere where Europeans, and males in particular,
were compelled to live in a tropical climate in the midst of the
native population. The phenomenon was quite familiar in the
Netherlands Indies, and was described by a colonial author of the
time as follows: '... all those acts of bestiality, sexual indulgences,
physical torture and murders, together with expressions of
megalomania' (Kohlbrugge 1907:167).

While collective characteristics were thus ascribed to 'the
natives' in general and the coolies in particular which cast doubt
on their human qualities, Europeans on the other hand were only
deficient as individuals in maintaining the norms and values that
were considered to be desirable or proper in social intercourse.
That which was stigmatized as group behaviour for the one party
was said to be exceptional for the other, a decline into excesses
caused by a nervous disease, for which, moreover, the Asians and
the social environment were naturally said to be responsible. It was
this difference in the assessment of human traits in particular
which illustrated the fact that racism was woven into the colonial
situation.

A Climate of Violence

The evil practices for which the East Coast plantations had always
been notorious were not changed by the Coolie Ordinance. Yet the

legal protection which the contract coolies would derive had been a principal motive for its introduction in 1880.

It was obvious that a real reign of terror had ruled on many plantations. Whipping and torture and unauthorized imprisonment had been the order of the day and could not always be prevented by the government which did not, and could not, know what happened on the more distant plantations. Moreover, it was necessary to keep a low profile with regard to other countries, especially England, since coolies were recruited by brokers in Penang and Singapore (Bartelds 1894:13).

The few reports which got through to the outside world at that time indicated that the planters continued with their autocratic behaviour and the mistreatment of their coolies, and these conjectures were confirmed by casual comments in papers such as the annual *Colonial Reports*. Attempts to bring a halt to such excesses by a stricter formulation of the orders and prohibitions had little or no result, or even had the opposite effect. It was no longer possible to gloss over the fact that the exercise of violence was a conspicuous and endemic feature of the plantation and mining industries in the Outer Provinces which had large numbers of coolies in their employ. After a series of articles on the miserable plight of plantation workers in Deli had appeared in the *Java Bode* in 1886, the Resident of the East Coast was instructed by Batavia to punish clear cases of ill-treatment more severely. Towards the end of the nineteenth century the subject invariably came up for discussion in considerations of the budget for the Netherlands Indies in the Lower House of the Dutch Parliament. A riot among Chinese mine-workers on Banka in 1898 brought to light that coolies were being branded, for reasons of identification, although, as the Minister reassuringly said, the burns did not leave any permanent marks (Proceedings Lower House, 28 November 1905:238). In China, the authorities who had to give permission for coolie recruitment, spoke of their surprise that nothing more was ever heard from the coolies who departed to Banka (GSA, Vb. 19 September 1905, No. 32). With regard to the island of Sikep (Riouw), one official wrote: 'the coolies die here like rats'. In some years deaths among the Javanese coolies in the tin-mines of the Straits Settlements was as high as 50 per cent. According to reports made by a former medical officer, conditions in the gold-mine of Redjang

Lebong (Central Sumatra) were so inhumane that many indentured labourers fled into the jungle, inviting certain death: even
sick people took to their heels, driven by hunger. One ex-Resident
seized on this affair to write an indictment, in a romantic- realistic
style, which ended with the assertion that his reconstruction
reflected a situation that was common on many plantation and
mine industries (Winter 1900). His story was not believed but he
had probably not exaggerated, as can be seen from the cases of
torture on the East Coast which Van Kol referred to in the Parliament in 1900. For example, how a coolie who was suspected of
having caused industrial trouble, was belaboured by a doctor with
a red-hot branding iron, under the pretext of physiological tests, to
force him to confess; and how the corpses of coolies who had died
in the hospital were thrown into the *alang-alang* fields. Van Kol had
obtained this information from Tschudnowsky who, after returning to Europe, had spoken about these abuses before a medical
congress in Paris (Proceedings Lower House 1900–1:415–20).
Tschudnowsky wrote that he himself had come across cases in
which physical punishment had resulted in the death of the coolie
(1899:19). Minister Cremer would believe none of these stories and
in his reply called Van Kol the 'ally of a Polish doctor of little
credibility' (from Tschudnowsky's writings it appears that he was
of Russian origin), with which remark he dismissed Van Kol's
indictments as slanderous (Proceedings Lower House 1900–1:415-
–20). This was quite incorrect, as was shown by a former Dutch
medical officer who, at about the same time, published an article
which was perhaps more elegantly worded but which nevertheless
contained the same message.

And in view of the fact that exploitation was of more importance than
humanity and health regulations, the latter were completely neglected in
favour of the former. Mistreatment of a pecuniary nature, but no less of a
physical nature, was common (Van der Burg 1898:742).

The newspapers in the Indies regularly printed reports of new
coolie scandals, thus keeping the affair in the eyes of the public. In
the official world of the Netherlands Indies, a typical bureaucratic
state, news very easily leaked out, although the informer or source
usually had to remain anonymous. Around the 1900s, therefore,
notwithstanding the lack of any political forum, the activities of the

colonial authorities were studied with some criticism, even though in the wake of the sensation stirred up around the persons involved, the events behind these affairs often remained obscure. These criticisms apparently did not penetrate into official reports. The version upheld by the authorities was that all interested parties had an extremely favourable opinion of the effects of the Coolie Ordinance (*Historical Survey* 1897:128).

I have pointed out in the Introduction to this book that Van den Brand's accusation certainly did not represent a stone cast into a millpond. Some of the most serious abuses perpetrated in Deli had eventually reached the Court of Justice in Batavia. In this centre of colonial control, the legal authorities were undoubtedly aware that it was customary for such cases to be quashed at source, and could therefore be certain that the few cases that did reach them represented no more than the tip of the iceberg. Probably with the idea of finding out more about these matters, the Director of Justice engaged in 1900 an official for Chinese Affairs, Hoetink. This was probably done on the instigation of W.J.M. Michielsen, a prominent member of the Council of the Netherlands Indies, who had known Hoetink during his posting as Resident on the East Coast in the early 1890s. Hoetink was given the assignment to familiarize himself with the operation of the Coolie Ordinance in a number of mining and agricultural concessions in the Outer Provinces which principally employed Chinese coolies. For this purpose, Hoetink made a number of short tours of inspection between 1900 and 1902. His first report, on the mining industry Redjang Lebong in southern Sumatra about which much had been written in the East Indies press, confirmed the horrendous state of affairs which had been related by the industry's former medical officer (GSA, Vb., 1 April 1903, No. 48). On his second visit, Hoetink found that the management had in the meantime made many improvements. It was true that the mine-workers complained about the doctor, saying that, when he was in a bad temper, he struck and kicked the patients and also caused unnecessary pain, but Hoetink did not give much credence to the reliability of this information. If the complaints were well-grounded, it could do no harm to tell the doctor that in future he must control himself but, Hoetink added, it would not be right,

... if the reputation of a European doctor should be put at risk by giving publicity to unproven allegations by Indonesian and Chinese coolies who are usually not very particular as regards the truth and, like all Orientals, are inclined to exaggerate (GSA, Vb., 14 February 1902, No. 25).

Hoetink was far more shaken by the conditions that he found in the Redjang Sulit mine, exploited by the same company, where the mortality rate was no less than 37 per cent. 'Horrifying' was his description of the stories of how, in times of many deaths, the corpses were simply thrown into the earth like dogs—*seperti andjing* the coolies said literally—or were sometimes just flung into the river. Early in 1902 Hoetink reported on his visits to a number of mines in the eastern part of the Netherlands Indies. The Soemalata Company which had 851 contract coolies in its employ, had less than half still alive after a period of eighteen months: 169 (20 per cent) had died, eighteen had deserted, and 132 had been sent back home, at least according to the information provided by management. The contract coolies were paid a wage of six cents per day; even Hoetink found this to be so scandalously low that he actually praised the coolies that they submitted to it. Those who worked less than twelve days in a month (the morbidity rate was very high) were given no wage on payday, but were tied to a stake and whipped. Towards the time that the coolie contract was due to expire, the management pressurized the worker to continue by refusing to dismiss him: unwilling workers were beaten and refused any food until they gave in. When the local government official, a junior District Officer, visited the mine, the head *mandur* who acted as his translator and as the mediator between him and the coolies was the same man who thrashed the coolies each month. As a result, the workers were not informative, remarked Hoetink laconically. His report was sent by the Director of Justice to the Governor-General with an accompanying note in which he wrote that, with a view to effective protection against arbitrary treatment by the employers: '. . . some control, independent of that which is supposed to be exercised by the heads of regional government, seems desirable' (GSA, Vb., 31 March 1903, No. 40).

The idea of something like a Labour Inspectorate for coolies employed on the agricultural plantations, first urged by Brooshooft in his 1901 publication, was now apparently also considered in the colonial government circles. The Director of Justice, who had asked Hoetink to make further suggestions based on his findings elsewhere in the Outer Provinces, wrote a few months later that Hoetink was drawing up his report on the working conditions on the East Coast plantations, and later in that same year would go to Borneo (divisions Southeast and West), Banka and Billiton, with the intention of drafting a new Coolie Ordinance in the light of the experience gained (GSA, Vb., 1 April 1903, No. 48). The Director proposed the addition of a new division to his department, under the leadership of a Chief Inspector whose rank would be equal to that of the heads of the regional government and whose task would be to ensure that the Coolie Ordinance was complied with (letters Director of Justice to Governor-General, 11 February 1902 and 3 June 1903, in GSA, Vb. 28 January 1905, No. 6). Thus things were moving behind the scenes, even before 'the Deli scandal' gained the limelight.

The abuses continued to be hidden from the outside world, certainly after 1897 when Cremer who himself was an ex-planter and leader of the planters' lobby, became a minister. When Van Kol questioned him in the Parliament in 1898, Cremer stated emphatically that the life of the plantation coolies left nothing to be desired. He was supported by MP Pijnacker Hordijk who had recently visited Sumatra (Proceedings Lower House 1898–9:167–8, 188–91). A year later, when Van Kol as a Member of the political opposition accused the East Coast officials of a dereliction of duty, he was severely reprimanded by the Minister. In the subsequent discussion of the budget for the Netherlands Indies, Cremer said arrogantly that the Member's annual Deli speech bored him. Did not the fact that large numbers of coolies were prepared to sign on for a new term indicate that they enjoyed excellent treatment? In 1900, as we have seen, Minister Cremer vehemently denied the accuracy of assertions about mistreatment. At a party congress, the socialist spokesman on colonial affairs complained about the coolness and disparagement that he encountered in the Parliament. 'Even the Minister laughed when the speaker told of the most horrifying cruelties' (quoted in Tichelman 1967:269). Van Kol refused to be discouraged, however, and continued to pursue 'Deli's man' with new facts and queries regarding scandalous practices.

A great deal also remained hidden for critical outsiders. For example, the findings of the investigation made by the Inspector of the Public Health Department, Dr A.G. Vorderman, of the conditions suffered by forced labourers on the Ombilin coalfields in Sawah Loento (West Sumatra) were quite staggering. Some years later, on an inspection tour through the Netherlands Indies, Van Kol visited this infamous place which was cursed by the coolies as a hell. What he had to say was bad enough, even though the mine's management had refused to provide more detailed information (Van Kol 1903:29–37; letter Chief Engineer Delprat in GSA, Vb., 27 March 1903, No. 13). Vorderman announced in his report that the health of the delinquents left much to be desired. When the coolies were ill they preferred to treat their own ailments rather than trust the inadequate medical care which was provided for them. Thus, it sometimes happened that coolies suffering from a wasting bowel complaint accompanied by loss of blood, would eat pieces of coal. In the mine's hospital, the medical orderlies, who were themselves forced labourers, would frequently mistreat patients under their charge. The medical inspector gave a number of poignant examples to illustrate his statement that the relations among the workers in this penal colony were ruled by callousness. Not all, but the majority of the mine-workers were convicts doing forced labour, and desertion among them was unprecedentedly high. In 1900, more than half of the approximately 2,500 delinquents in this state mine, where work went on day and night, deserted. Nearly all of them, 1,309 of the 1,331 who deserted in 1901, were very soon caught again, either brought in by the local inhabitants for a cash reward, or forced to return to the mine because of the impossibility of surviving in the surrounding jungle. The few who managed to remain undetected would with only a few exceptions have died in the hostile terrain. The crime of desertion was punished with the cane. According to the District Officer's reports, 1,570 forced labourers experienced such punishment in 1900. In other words, this was more than the total number of deserters, showing that corporal punishment was very widely used as a means of maintaining labour discipline. The local government official, as an efficient bookkeeper, had kept notes: twenty lashes with the cane in 1,194 cases of desertion and possession of knives or other sharp objects; fifteen lashes in 246 cases of desertion but voluntary return; ten cane lashes in 130 cases of idleness during working hours. A native physician (dokter djawa) confirmed to the Medical Inspector that on the average he had to inspect four coolies per day for enduring this punishment. Vorderman wrote in his report that he had seen how, in his leisure time, a police guard practiced hard and accurate hitting against a banana stem that was tied to the caning stake. It was hardly surprising that, according to his calculations, one out of every seven coolies who were caned in this way ended up in the hospital and frequently died of his wounds or became a permanent invalid. And that was not all. The foremen of the mining gangs had themselves risen from the ranks of convict labourers, being detainees who, in the eyes of the higher ranks, had distinguished themselves by 'good behaviour'. Against their fellow prisoners, above whom they were elevated like barrack leaders in a concentration camp, they could only hold their own by energetically beating them, which often caused broken bones. They did this without any authority but also without being forbidden to do so. In the autumn of 1901, only a few months after Vorderman had visited Ombilin, Hoetink arrived there on his inspection tour of the mining and agricultural industries in the Outer Provinces. It was typical of this official that he gave a far more favourable opinion of conditions there. Hoetink did not confirm the story of a missionary who had spoken of 'a valley of death where Satan rules'. His report did in fact start with this pronouncement, but everything that followed amounted to a negation.

In the first place I was struck by the fact that the penal system for the Indigenes shows here to full advantage. At Sawah Loento the prisoners are forced to do regular and useful work. It doesn't agree at all with the nature of the native to find regular work a pleasant thing, and when he is forced he will try to avoid it (GSA, Vb., 27 March 1903, No. 13).

Corporal punishment was barbaric, admitted Hoetink, but it was indispensable if order and discipline were to be maintained. Needless cruelty must not occur, of course, and he ordered that cane lashes should be given in such a way that they only caused pain but no injury. Hoetink showed as little sensitivity as the mine management to Vorderman's argument that the assumed consequence was in fact the cause, by explaining that mistreatment led to desertion and that punishment by caning therefore had an adverse effect. In Hoetink's opinion, there was no such direct connection. He described desertion as a sort of epidemic which took on enormous proportions even on Deli's best tobacco plantations: an evil which, according to him, was just as infectious as suicide. And as regards the high-handed activities of the foremen, little could be done. They had to use the cane in self-defence. Those among them who used excessive violence, laid themselves open to revenge which might cost them their lives. It did indeed occasionally happen that a *mandur* would be murdered even though he had not been guilty of mistreatment. Hoetink ascribed this to causes for which the convicts were likely to take one another's life, which was a covert allusion to homosexual relationships. He finished his report with the remark that conditions in Ombilin were no worse but were in fact better than those on other plantations that he had visited. In his opinion, there was no reason to take special measures, an opinion which was fully shared by his superior, the Director of Justice. A colleague of this high official in charge of trade and industry, wrote that the urge towards desertion could be mitigated if those who were condemned to forced labour, in addition to an iron ball on their feet, were also given an iron chain around their necks (Bruinink-Darlang 1986:117).

In an earlier report, Dr Vorderman had advocated the abolition of punishment by caning for convict labourers who were guilty of desertion. The medical officer had studied the way in which this chastizement was carried out in ninety-six institutions on Java and Madura. He had been shown exactly what happened, up to and including the tying of the prisoner to the punishment stake. By using a special sort of rope which left weals, especially-prepared rattan of a certain thickness and length which was moreover soaked in water, and a caning technique that was calculated to achieve maximum effect, i.e. by concentrating on a few particular places so that bloody wounds were caused after just a few lashes, the punishment gained the character of torture. The heads of the regional government in the East Indies, when asked for their opinion, said without exception that they would not want to lose this means of punishment, particularly because of its deterrent effect. They dismissed the accusation of unnecessary high-handedness, and that was the end of the discussion as far as the officials were concerned.

The lesson that I have drawn from the above is that the circumstances under which contract coolies lived and worked on the plantations were not very different to those suffered by the convicts. The former were considered to be potentially as criminal as the latter had proved themselves to be. The attitude towards both categories was in effect the same: only with cast-iron discipline could these 'native scum' or 'useless scoundrels' be put to work and kept there. The punishment stake which played such a major part in disciplining the workers on the plantations was not only used there. It had not been invented by power-hungry employers, but was a tried and trusty tool with which the colonial government forced rebellious workers back into line.

A Negligent Government

Initially, the most common form of defence was simply to deny the accusations that became more and more numerous. When this no longer worked because of the mounting evidence that so much was amiss, the responsible policy-makers tried to evade the issue by pleading ignorance and by promising to seek information from the authorities directly in charge. When this delaying tactic proved only partially successful, the colonial government sought recourse in suppressing embarrassing information. In this connection, it is interesting to note that crime statistics for Sumatra's East Coast are lacking since 1897. Until that year each *Colonial Report* included such information and, as ex-Resident Kooreman did not fail to point out, the data were certainly provided, although not for subsequent years (Kooreman 1904–5:54). What he avoided saying came out in the following discussion in a more open fashion. From the time that Cremer, ex-planter and, in his role as a politician, the principal advocate of the interests of agricultural estates on Sumatra, became the Minister of Colonies (1897–1901), the *Colonial Report* kept silent about the more murky aspects of Deli.

Refusal, in the interests of the state, to provide information about conditions in the colony, was always a last resort but one which was taken surprisingly often. The number of reports that never saw publication for this reason was legion. However, the most common response was to play down the abuses whenever clarification was sought. The authorities tried to dispel the impression that there was any reason for concern regarding the working conditions on the East Coast plantations. Van den Brand was said to have exaggerated grossly. It was not as bad as it was made out to be. This reassuring pronouncement was backed-up by the following arguments.

First, however deplorable many cases might be, the seriousness and also the number were negligible when compared to conditions that formerly prevailed on the plantations. Kooreman, ex-Resident of the East Coast who had retired just a few years earlier, exerted himself to show that great progress had been made during his period of office. His successor, Van der Steenstraten, wrote in a similar vein in a confidential letter to the Minister.

You are probably aware that I have served on the East Coast of Sumatra first as a District Officer (1884–9), and then as an Assistant Resident (1897–1902). I therefore know from experience how very bad affairs were on many plantations in the earlier years, and in comparison I find the situation during the latter period to have improved considerably (Letter, 11 November 1904, GSA, Vb., 28 January 1905, No. 6).

In other words, things were getting better and better all the time. That observation had also been made in the past. As long ago as 1882 the Resident had reported: 'Both the treatment and the quality of the workers are improving daily' (*Historical Survey* 1897:72).

Second, with all the criticisms that were voiced, it should be remembered that the majority of the contract labourers were of inferior quality. In order to maintain adequate standards of efficiency, the application of strict discipline was inescapable, and in operating the Coolie Ordinance the planters needed greater latitude than those employers who could manage without forced labour. The proposal made in 1903 that contract coolies should be forced to work another term if their past record showed them to have been lazy or unwilling, was called 'reasonable' by the Director of the Civil Service of the Netherlands Indies. While formerly only coolies who had been absent for more than a certain number of days due to sickness, desertion or punishment might be kept on after the completion of the contract, a planter could not force contract labourers to continue in his employment if their work performance left much to be desired (GSA, Vb. 3 March 1903, No. 7). It is interesting that he came to this conclusion on the basis of the existing practice on a mining enterprise in the eastern part of the archipelago, which had made itself infamous for such bestial treatment of its coolies that even Hoetink had shown himself to be aghast.

Third, the majority of the commentators agreed that the conditions on the plantations of the major companies that were associated with the Deli Planters' Association provided no cause for complaint. It was only on the smaller and more remote plantations which were often still privately owned that all kinds of iniquities occurred which would not bear the light of day. Hoetink suggested in his report that it would be better for the coolies if agri-business on the East Coast was controlled by large corporations (Hoetink 1902:26). Even the socialist MP Van Kol found that the situation of workers on the larger tobacco plantations was quite satisfactory (Proceedings Lower House, 21 November 1902:172), a pronouncement which the Minister of Colonies Idenburg gratefully acknowledged in the parliamentary debate.

Fourth, insofar as violence still occurred it was due primarily to the hot-headed actions of the Asian foremen. Both the Javanese *mandurs* and the Chinese *tandils* would hit out vigorously in order to show their authority. Back in their own country the Chinese coolies in particular were accustomed to much rougher treatment. This gave rise to the suggestion that violence was more or less the order of the day among the Asians and thus actually represented a continuation of traditional practices from which the whites were largely excluded.

Fifth, it could not be denied that the European managements were sometimes also guilty of violent behaviour, frequently in reaction to provocation or in self-defence against actual physical aggression by the coolies whom they had to control. This occurred mostly among junior assistants who had only recently come to Deli and did not know how to cope with dangerous situations. In this respect, Cremer pointed out that the planters included a fair number of Germans with distinctly Prussian tendencies.

Young men with German military opinions regarding discipline and obedience (the recently-disclosed atrocities at St Cyr had taken place on a plantation that was under German management) in his [Cremer's] opinion do not belong there, and he feels that the planters should exercise strict control over the young men whom they send out, and should ensure that only civilized, educated and humane employees come to the plantations (*De Hollandsche Revue* 1903:560).

There would always be wrong-doers, of course. The Europeans inevitably included a small number who abused the power they held and were guilty of cruelty. But these were individual deviations. The racism underlying the explanation of these excesses is indisputable. The blind anger which sometimes flared up among the coolies, called 'running amok', was ascribed to the irrational characteristics of their ethnicity, but the sadistic excesses of the Europeans were never labelled as a pattern of collective behaviour. In fact, such individual misbehaviours were blamed on the environment of which the people concerned formed a part at that particular moment. This pattern of behaviour was facilely called 'tropical madness'. In any event, these disgraceful elements were said to be the exceptions only.

It is inconceivable that, more than a thousand Europeans of varying culture, character and temperament, coming into daily contact with Chinese and native coolies of sometimes very questionable character, should not now and then get out of hand and indulge in excesses. Even if the government was represented in every part of each district—which is certainly not the case—it would not be able to entirely prevent distressing outrages against the coolies. In evaluating conditions on the East Coast of Sumatra the common mistake made is that everybody is judged alike and all are measured against the actions of a few; while those facts that are brought to light are often inflated into crimes and given an exaggerated qualification (Hoetink 1902:71).

Sixth, there was the accusation, voiced by employers, that the government itself had caused the established abuses in that, for many decades, the administrative machinery and in particular the police and the judiciary had been undermanned. At first sight this argument seemed to imply that, if the ineffective administrative infrastructure had been timely expanded, the planters would not have shown such disgraceful arbitrary behaviour. But what the entrepreneurs were really saying was that the colonial authorities were not giving them sufficient support in their efforts to control the workforce. The government had intervened not too little but too much in plantation affairs, with the result that the authority of the management had been irretrievably impaired. Just a few trouble-makers on one plantation were sufficient to arouse a spirit of rebellion, and the assumption that the coolies could gain a hearing from the District Officer with their fancied grievances only caused further escalation of unrest. Seen from this viewpoint, labour conscription did not go nearly far enough. This was also the irritable reaction of the management of the Redjang Lebong mine to the report in which Hoetink denounced the iniquitous conditions there. Their reply ended as follows: 'Finally, we cannot refrain from observing that the Coolie Ordinance does nothing but award rights to the employee and lay obligations on the employer and that the employer is absolutely powerless against lazy and unwilling contract coolies' (GSA, Vb., 1 April 1903, No. 48).

This opinion was commonly held in entrepreneurial circles. Not more, but less government intervention was needed in the labour system. It was a misunderstanding to assume that the Coolie Ordinance caused the labour migrants to become helpless victims. On the contrary, it was the employers who suffered when the regulations were incorrectly applied. The labour shortage actually benefitted the contract coolies, and as long as this condition continued, legal protection of the workers was quite superfluous.

... labour inspection to protect the employee against the employer does not have much sense in Deli because workers there enjoy the best, the ideal, protection in the self-interest of the employer. The law of supply and demand favours the worker in Deli, and is unfavourable to the employer. If there is any injustice and abuse of power it is to be feared from the side of the workers to the disadvantage of the employer (Memorial DBM 1925:50).

This was a point of view which found more understanding than contradiction among official agencies that were directly involved. Ex-Resident Kooreman made it known that, between 1894 and 1899, only a few cases of death through 'imprudence' had occurred, and he therefore concluded that cases of maltreatment were exceptional (Kooreman 1903a:24,56). In his report on the East Coast, Hoetink warned against unnecessary tampering with the planters' authority. In the wider colonial interest, it was necessary that agri-business be allowed to develop uninterruptedly. Incidents were no more than that—regrettable deviations from accepted norms and practices. To place too much emphasis on abuses that, in his opinion, were only venial, would all too easily distort the image of the plantation system. Hoetink apparently thought it his task to correct this tendency, to counter what in his opinion were excessive criticisms voiced by uninformed outsiders. Was not what he had been told by the coolies themselves the best proof that there was no reason at all for alarm?

On the plantations that I have visited, when I have asked about their treatment, Chinese coolies have only by exception complained about high-handedness by a European master. Some have smilingly admitted that they were beaten when they did something wrong, but did not appear to mind (Hoetink 1902:75).

If we are to believe Hoetink, this was roughly the reaction of naughty children who knew that they were being punished for their own good. The Minister of Colonies read this passage from Hoetink's report to the Lower House in an attempt to undo the damage caused by Van den Brand's pamphlet (Proceedings Lower House, 21 November 1902:173). Van den Brand stood to his guns, however; in new publications he rejected one by one all the arguments that had been put forward to refute his accusation and to defuse public opinion. He pointed out that the cases which he had described had not happened long ago but were of very recent date. Moreover, he said, the most horrifying cruelties were perpetrated by the Europeans; the Asian foremen maltreated the coolies only when ordered to do so, frequently in the presence of their white superiors. Cremer's suggestion that German employees in particular might be merciless in their actions, was said by Van den Brand to contradict reality. The most shocking cases had occurred on plantations that were staffed almost entirely by the Dutch. And finally, there was no basis at all for the claim that conditions in the larger companies which had plantations in the immediate environs of Deli, were better than on smaller, privately-owned plantations that were farther away. He spoke in this connection of a myth which, unfortunately, had gained an appearance of truth due to a remark made by Van Kol in the Lower House. Above all, Van den Brand contested the opinion that what was at stake could be discounted as a handful of excesses, violations of the Coolie Ordinance which, if not prevented, could be curbed by stricter control. 'In contrast to what is usually the case when regulations are concerned, the evil is not in the people. . . . The system is wrong, impermissible, immoral; the atrocities are only the symptoms of the disease' (Van den Brand 1904b:57).

By calling the proven abuses a logical outcome of the Coolie Ordinance, Van den Brand forthrightly denounced this regulation of labour relations on Sumatra's East Coast. In drawing his conclusion he was undoubtedly fortified by his familiarity with the

Rhemrev Report from which he quoted a number of passages. It is relevant to note here that Rhemrev had uncovered so many crimes that he decided to stop making an inventory of them because, without more judicial assistance, he was unable to bring penal action against the offenders (Rhemrev 1904:341).

The Use of Violence in Labour Control

At the beginning of this century and for many years later, neither what Rhemrev had written nor the facts that he reported could see the light of day. The report of this legal official was therefore kept secret which is the immediate reason for the present study. A reading of what Rhemrev had to say brings some understanding of why the responsible Minister, notwithstanding strong pressure from within and without the Parliament, stubbornly refused to publish even a short abstract. The highest policy-makers in the colony and in the mother country were naturally acquainted with the contents of the Report. Their reactions to the document, the conclusions that they drew from it, and the immediate results of the report, are subjects that will be discussed in the final chapter. At the end of the present chapter I wish to consider the problem with which Rhemrev was also preoccupied, i.e. the question of the causes of the manifold cases of maltreatment.

After the Rhemrev Report, it became evident that the violence directed towards the workforce could no longer be explained as being merely incidental. Intimidation, corporal punishment, imprisonment and torture formed successive gradations of a more general pattern in the uncontrolled exercise of power which characterized relations between planters and coolies. The determining factors of violence are analysed in more specific detail below.

To meet the local shortage of labour power, the original pioneers had to depend on a supply of workers from elsewhere. Coercion was needed in the first place to persuade sufficient numbers of migrants to come to Deli; in the second place to keep them at the place of employment; and in the third place to spur this new proletariat towards regular work. Government intervention in the labour system was unknown except on the pretension of providing workers with support and protection. The introduction of the Coolie Ordinance with its penal sanctions was intended primarily to enable the employer continually to expand production by ensuring the import and incarceration of sufficient numbers of contract coolies. The labour conscription that thus came about need not be accompanied by violence, but it certainly was conducive to such practices.

The plantations employed a circulating labour force which mostly performed unskilled work. The opening-up of enormous, almost inexhaustible reservoirs of labour, first in China and then on Java, implied a fairly low cost per coolie and a fairly easy replacement. Unsuitable or worn-out contract coolies could be got rid of without much fuss and exchanged for fresh victims. The low wage rates made it possible to maintain a labour reserve. The planters thus did not have to bother about a coolie more or less. Labour was so cheap that employers had little economic incentive to treat their workers with any decency. The very fact that in principle both employers and workers were there only temporarily contributed to the dehumanization of the labour regime. To both sides, the plantation remained an alien environment. The coolies lacked the security brought about by having roots in familiar surroundings, and they could not fall back on traditionally-acknowledged rights. They found themselves confronted by bosses who, due to the impermanence of their own stay, had no interest in the fate of their coolie and showed no scruples in exploiting them to the maximum.

In the course of time, the plantation system had experienced considerable enlargement in terms of scale. The original pioneers had employed only a few dozen coolies for a contracted period of not longer than one year, over whom the planters themselves exercised control. The plantations increased in acreage, but the technology of cultivation did not keep pace. In the last decades of the nineteenth century, the labour intensity of tobacco production increased further. Rhemrev, who visited all the major plantations on Sumatra's East Coast with few exceptions, counted the number of coolies on each plantation. It appears from his data that a total of 91,928 coolies were employed on 145 plantations, an average of 634 men and women per estate (see Table 12).

As agri-business became more large-scale in nature, the character of the industry changed. The ownership of estates shifted from an individual planter to control by a manager. As a result, the distance between the top and the bottom levels of the plantation hierarchy increased, and the relationship between the two became more impersonal. As a new-style planter, the manager maintained no direct contact with the many hundreds of coolies who

Table 12.
DISTRICT-WISE DISTRIBUTION OF THE PLANTATION
WORKFORCE IN 1903

Administrative division each estate	Number of coolies	Number of estates	Average number of coolies on each estate
Deli Langkat	58835	74	796
Serdang	15459	43	368
Padang, Bedagei Batoe Bahra and Asahan	17634	29	608
Sumatra's East Coast	91928	146	634

Note: Not included are the coolies who did not turn up for roll call held by the legal officer when he visited a plantation. He observed that a large number of coolies were dismissed shortly before his arrival in order to cover up all sorts of malpractices.

Source: Rhemrev 1903.

populated his plantation. A strict industrial hierarchy came about in which, at an intermediate level, the European assistants occupied a focal position. Extension of the chain of command ending abroad, resulted in higher demands being made on the quality and quantity of work as one went down. The increase in the 'cases of beating', an euphemism for explosions of violence and counter-violence between staff and workers for which Deli became notorious, was a direct outcome of the pressure of these constantly increasing demands, as was to be acknowledged some decades later.

When the planters first appeared on the scene, government officials were conspicuous by their absence, and in the following decades the land was opened-up at a far greater rate than that of the expansion of the administrative apparatus. The frontier character which the East Coast long retained meant that private industry in this region was given, or rather took, police and judicial powers which it did not have elsewhere in the colony. The government offered hardly any resistance when planters took the law into their own hands. The cost of public administration could be kept low because the government in effect acknowledged the autonomy of the planters within the sphere of their own plantations and to some extent also outside them. In case of need, the planters could always seek refuge in legal methods in order to keep the workers in harness. The regional authorities co-operated by punishing the coolies in accordance with the directives provided by the management, and did so more severely than was permitted by the Coolie Ordinance. Conversely, the authorities refrained from imposing sanctions on the planters when they violated labour regulations, by declaring accusations to be non-admissible, by not registering or persecuting crimes, dismissing charges, and helping to get rid of troublesome witnesses. Rhemrev confirmed all these 'irregularities' and among other things ascertained that ex-Resident Kooreman, who had hit out against Van den Brand in such righteous indignation, had as magistrate been guilty of a number of very reprehensible actions. Consequently, the collusion between the planters and the government was an established fact for the coolies. Coolies who dared to complain to the local government official about their treatment were likely to be punished by that same official for desertion. Even Rhemrev himself, who faced a closed front of planters and administration during his investigations, had to proceed with care. Is it surprising that, as a representative of that government, he did not really succeed in breaking through the wall of silence?

Migrants who entered into their contracts voluntarily were not able to withdraw from them. Once they had been put to work on the plantation, escape was next to impossible. One characteristic of the Coolie Ordinance, emphatically re-confirmed by the Minister of Colonies Idenburg in the Parliament, was that the deserting coolies were returned to their plantations by the strong arm of the law. In other words, a penal sanction was attached to ensure compliance with a civil law contract (Proceedings Lower House, 30 November 1904:319). On occasions, coolies were made to sign forcibly (Rhemrev 1904:351). Contract coolies worked and lived on the plantation, constantly under supervision and unable to withdraw into family life or the village sphere at the end of the working day. Such institutions, which screened-off workers from the all encompassing authority of the employers, did not exist in the case of plantation coolies. Their subjugation went further than that of free workers in an industrial production process and was all but exhaustive. Rhemrev made this clear by saying,

... that the relationship of the employer to the contract coolie is, shaped in such a way that the former always has felt himself to be the lord and master over the worker, and that the latter has always held the conviction of being entirely dependent on the employer. He had, in his opinion, sold himself to the employer body and soul: '*soedah djoewal djiwa dan kapala*', as he was wont to express it (Ibid.:403).

Employers regarded the coolies as a commodity over which they could exert rights of property or even ownership. Rhemrev supported this observation by referring to a correspondence in which the manager of a plantation demanded, that a District Officer return a deserted coolie: 'we ask for the release of our property (coolie) and we shall apply to the Resident to claim our ownership (coolie)' (Ibid.:344).

Labour was reduced to a production factor which, like raw material, could be processed in the industrial cycle. A study of the long list of maltreatment cases shows that they were usually caused by something fairly trivial and also that they often had nothing to do with the actual production process. The most objectionable cruelties, sometimes resulting in death, were surprisingly often due to some personal grievance which caused the planter to explode in blind rage: pepper in his food, the irritation caused by an argument between a servant and his wife, a request for a drink of water, the provision of one sack of hay for the horses instead of two, etc. In all this, the arbitrariness was obvious. While the plantation sources expatiated at great length on the unpredictability and unreliability of the workforce, the coolies in their turn could never be sure when, why and how the management would be likely to punish them. However capitalistic planters were, in the exercise of power they shared many traits with feudal lords. The non-economic subjugation of labour was accompanied by their use as servants, messengers, beaters for the hunt, etc., and the sexual exploitation of the female coolies. In Rhemrev's words:

Misuse of power on the one side, slavish submission on the other side. Callousness, insensitivity, cruelty by the master, servility and spiteful vengeance by the workman. And this led to revolting scenes. Here a manager who refused a coolie leave to bury his child, and an assistant who misused his power by sending the coolie to gaol so that he could take possession of the man's wife—there the cringing worker who did not dare to resist (Ibid.:403).

Nevertheless, resistance did occur. The coolies did not suffer their exploitation and subjugation passively but took action, whether individually or collectively. Their brutalization was intended both to prevent and to break such resistance. Violence was used in a number of standardized ways which implied the presence on the plantation of a number of implements or appliances. Rhemrev has mentioned prison sheds, wooden blocks to which coolies were shackled, iron chains, handcuffs, posts to which they were bound, rattan canes, ropes of various thicknesses and lengths, a whip made of rhinoceros leather, and a machine for administering electric shocks. The principal techniques of torture, which were often used in combination, included: incarceration without food and water, running the gauntlet, tying-up in various positions (standing, sitting, laying on belly or back, crouching, hanging), standing in the sun for a fortnight (*didjemoer*, 'airing'), binding them hand and foot, water immersion, bastinado in a crucified position, dragging them behind a horse with the hands tied, beating them with leaves that caused itching and then drenching them with water so that the body swelled, having slivers of bamboo driven under the fingernails, rubbing finely-ground pepper onto female sexual organs, hanging Chinese coolies by the pigtail so that the victim could barely touch the ground with his toes, and clubbing them to death. These punishments were often not meted out in secrecy but rather in full publicity, showing that intimidation of the workforce was an important motivation.

To gain a proper understanding of all these practices, it is necessary to emphasize the racism that characterized the plantocracy. The contract coolie did not count as a human being. Corpses of deserted coolies who had died of starvation were left to rot in the fields, to be eaten by dogs, or to serve as fertilizer for the coffee crop. If a coolie was absent from work due to the death of a child he would be punished because, as a planter maintained to Rhemrev, this was no reason for absenteeism. The appointment of a '*rattan tandil*', a foreman charged especially with the caning of coolies, was typical of the systematic way in which these outrages occurred. Corporal punishment was not always delegated to the Asian foremen: many planters did the job themselves. As a variation of racism, many cases of physical punishment were based on sexual sadism. Cruelty was more than merely instrumental; that is to say, it went further than punishing the victims or intimidating the rest of the workforce. Tying a male or a female coolie to a stake in front of or under the manager's house also had a symbolic significance. It is surprising how similar methods of torture were in the various new plantation regions of Asia. The following quotation is taken from a report written in 1887 about Assam, and it could be supplemented with numerous other examples: '. . . in the case of women they were tied to a post in the porch of the Manager's house, their clothes lifted up to the waist, and beaten on the bare buttocks with a stirrup leather' (Chandra 1966:368). Enslavement of the coolies, i.e. their personal subjugation to the white members of staff, was an end in itself. Rhemrev relates how, on their return to the plantation, two female coolies who had been picked up for desertion, were whipped naked through the coolie barracks. One hung herself for shame; the other was beaten to death by the foreman and then hung up on a coffee tree in front of the manager's house (Rhemrev 1904:362). It was undoubtedly only a minority of the planters who were cursed with the sadistic tendencies that gave rise to such excesses. Yet the racism was characterized by the fact that the planters' milieu had no moderating effect on such deviant behaviour. Since the coolie had no right to humane treatment such barbarism could remain hidden to be repeated again and again. It was far more important to maintain the *esprit de corps* among the planters than to provide even the most minimal protection to the workers in accordance with the directives of the Coolie Ordinance (Ibid.:322). The exercise of naked power was intended to demonstrate the superiority of the European masters and, at the same time, to imprint on the Asian subordinates the consciousness of their worthlessness. The planters were dependent on the coolies but yet could not bear their presence: a paradox whose solution they sought in violence.

Both circulation of labour and coercion were basic elements of the labour regime in East Coast plantation society towards the end of the nineteenth century. During their stay, which was for a minimal period of three years, the coolies were immobilized on three levels. Firstly, in the work-cum-living situation. The gang to which they belonged did not represent a continuation of traditional social relationships but was a new form of organization that was adapted to an early mode of capitalist production. Informal mechanisms of control, partly coercive in nature, played a pivotal role. Secondly, on the plantation, the management did not permit a coolie to withdraw into a private domain, but demanded unconditional preparedness and obedience, day and night. Planters' autocracy was the principal method with which to maintain his or her subjugation to the forced labour regime. Thirdly, on the East Coast of Sumatra, a contract coolie who left the plantation without permission from the employer was outlawed. Legal violence embodied in the so-called penal sanctions was used to track down absconders, to punish them and then to return them to the workplace. The Coolie Ordinance acted as a link connecting the three levels of discipline which, each in its own way, was accompanied by the application of naked force. Coercion did not conflict with, but was integral to the way in which colonial capitalism was developing on the East Coast (cf. Stoler 1985:45). Abandonment of the bonded labour regime and adoption of free labour would undoubtedly drastically transform the plantation economy; according to those in authority, however, the pre-conditions for such a restructuring did not exist in the first few decades of the twentieth century.

VI

THE COOLIE QUESTION

Publicity and Public Opinion

The pamphlet which Van den Brand published in 1902 almost immediately gave rise to heated discussion. Reaction on the East Coast of Sumatra was naturally enough the most severe and also completely negative. Businessmen in Medan placed advertisements in the local press to the effect that they wished to have nothing to do with Van den Brand, fearing the loss of their clients (*Deli Courant*, 23 November 1903). 'My life here is intolerable', Van den Brand wrote to his brother in The Netherlands, who then approached the Minister of Colonies with the request that the safety of his brother in Medan should be guaranteed (GSA, Vb. 6 February 1907, No. 56). The challenged author made it known that he would not react in the local press to all the taunts and slander that came his way (*Sumatra Post*, 28 February 1902). To 'foul one's own nest' in such a way could only result in ostracism and Van den Brand temporarily had to leave the scene. One journalist, familiar with life in Deli, wrote: 'He has been thrown out of the club, banished from the community; he has been deprived of the means to earn a living, boycotted, so that he was forced to leave Deli' (*De Amsterdammer*, 4 December 1904).

The pro-government press in the mother country was hardly less hostile. Numerous ex-planters and former government officials took up their pens or took to the lecture circuit in order to claim their own innocence and to air their outrage. This was not a problem insofar as their audiences consisted of colonialists who refused to listen to anything derogatory about the splendid development work being done on the East Coast. The genre was exemplified by the talk given by Lefebre, the same Lefebre who had entered into a debate with Van den Brand on the occasion of Van Kol's visit to Medan in 1902. 'A dealer in human flesh', Van den Brand had contemptuously called this owner of a coolie recruiting office (Van den Brand 1902: 8). Now it was Lefebre's turn to lash out at his opponent. He gave a colourful description of the care with which the planters cherished their workers.

The speaker has often envied the coolie who, after finishing his work, spends a pleasurable evening with his fellow countrymen in the *kampong* or the coolie barracks, perhaps watching a *wajang koelit* show or gambling, even if the latter were illegal, while the planter, left to himself, spends his few free hours reading or writing letters, or occasionally giving a party for visitors (Lefebre 1903).

Philanthropical measures taken by the colonial authorities had only caused the unrest among the workforce to increase, according to Lefebre.

All these words of reassurance and of indignation about 'undeserved vilification' were not without effect. According to many editorials, Van den Brand had grossly exaggerated and had not provided sufficient evidence to support his claim of coolie maltreatment. The Opposition dailies and weeklies, which were closely allied with the Social Democratic Labour Party (SDAP), were far more receptive to Van den Brand's disclosures. A cartoon by Johan Braakensiek about the Deli scandal, was published in *De Amsterdammer* with Van Kol in a star role and with Cremer as the cynical spokesman of the planters' lobby. This aroused the ire of the bourgeois press, according to which it was not right to sully the reputation of a man with such an outstanding public record merely because of an accusation that was not taken seriously by those experts who were in a position to judge (*Algemeen Handelsblad*, 1 and 4 December 1904). The colonial press, however, had published too many reports in preceding years about abuses throughout the archipelago, for this affair to be declared closed. Moreover, its echo resounded far beyond national frontiers. At a medical congress in Paris the plantation doctor Tschudnowsky, who had just returned to Europe, related all the gory details of how natives and Chinese in Deli were being civilized with the aid of canings, alcohol and syphilis (Tschudnowsky 1899:19). The *Frankfurter Zeitung* published a serial in which Dutch planters were portrayed as brutal tyrants (*De Indische Gids* 1903, I:108–12); and the British authorities in Malaya, under pressure of a press hostile to the planters on

Sumatra's East Coast, threatened to withhold their permission for the further recruitment of Chinese coolies for Deli (W. 1905:90–1).

Political turmoil was inevitable. In its year of publication, *The Millions from Deli* was discussed extensively in the Lower House during its annual deliberations on the budget for the Netherlands East Indies. Van Kol, spokesman for the socialist Opposition, and ex-Minister of Colonies, Cremer, now a Chairman of the standing committee on that subject, acriminously attacked each other soon after the debate began in closed session. According to Van Kol, Cremer had abused his influential position by avoiding questions about the working conditions of the coolies on Sumatra's East Coast, and by omitting from his report critical remarks that had been made on the subject in committee meetings (Proceedings Lower House, 19 November 1902:109–20). Among other things, the MP urged the publication of the reports written by Hoetink on his visits to agricultural and mining enterprises, including the plantations in Deli. A member of the same opposition party, G.W. Melchers, quoted long passages from Van den Brand's indictment in the hope of prevailing upon the Minister to institute a thorough investigation. Far more effective, however, was the pressure exercised by politicians loyal to the ruling coalition. Van Limburg Stirum, a Christian Democrat, was the first to discuss the pamphlet. He considered that the honour of the Dutch government had been tarnished, and asked for clarification. Minister Idenburg's reply was more than reticent. He said that he was opposed to all those who were in favour of abolishing the Coolie Ordinance and would go no further than to hold out the prospect of sharper control over its observance. In his opinion, this actually had already been the case in recent years (Ibid.: 21 November 1902:172–3). Nevertheless, Idenburg undertook to bring the indictment to the notice of Governor General Rooseboom and promised further investigation.

Understandably enough, the Minister's words made little impression on Van den Brand. In a second pamphlet, *Again: The Millions from Deli*, Van den Brand reiterated everything he had said earlier, adding, that he was aware of having embarrassed his Christian-Democratic political friends of the Anti-Revolutionary Party by the disclosures. This was specially so because the widespread abuses on Sumatra's East Coast had caught the public eye after Idenburg became Minister in the autumn of 1902. The truth had to be made known, however, and he had really counted on a more emphatic response from a political ally who had the reputation of being a 'champion of true Christian values'. 'I did expect to hear something different, something stronger, rather less ambiguous, less vague, than what he said during the debate on the Coolie Ordinances in the Lower House' (Van den Brand 1904a:10).

Van den Brand did not despair, however. He hinted that the Minister did really intend to take further action, but just to make sure, he urged that the matter be expedited. The Minister wrote to the Governor-General asking him to investigate the truth about the abuses mentioned by Van den Brand and to take necessary measures. He did not neglect to mention that Van den Brand's pamphlet had made a strong impact and called for effective action (GSA, Vb., 9 December 1902, No. 49). By government decree dated 24 May 1903, J.L.T. Rhemrev, employed as public prosecutor by the Council of Justice in Batavia, was ordered to start an administrative investigation into the accusations made by Van den Brand in his sensational pamphlet. Rhemrev was told to examine whether the allegations of maltreatment, illegal imprisonment and irregularities in the administration of justice on the East Coast could be substantiated. The wording of the assignment was such that the investigation was clearly intended to have a judicial orientation rather than a political one. This was further strengthened by the additional instruction given to Rhemrev by the Procurator-General of the High Court of the Netherlands East Indies to the effect that he should investigate any criminal offences that might come to light and ultimately prosecute the offenders. Rhemrev reached Medan on 8 June 1903 and began his task two days later.

When questions about Rhemrev's progress were asked in the Lower House during the debate on the new budget in the autumn of 1903, the Minister was unable to give an answer. He asked the Governor-General about the state of affairs, implying that he wished to be informed immediately once the results came in (GSA, Vb., 3 December 1903, No. 15/3353). The Minister could not be entirely easy in his mind about the outcome. Perhaps that was why he decided that MPs should be allowed to peruse Hoetink's report, which until then had been kept secret (Vb., 29 April 1903, No. 39). In the critical debate that followed on the findings of this official, the Minister declared that he also envisaged a future without a Coolie Ordinance (Proceedings Lower House, 24 November 1903:458).

Rhemrev's report does not mention when he finished his investigation or for how long he stayed on the East Coast. At any event, he returned to Batavia at the end of 1903 and submitted his indictment early in the following year. Before examining how that document was received and dealt with in the Netherlands and in the Netherlands East Indies, and the discussion it gave rise to in policy-making circles; I shall consider the method that Rhemrev followed in carrying out his task.

Administrative and Judicial Investigations

Initially, Rhemrev adhered closely to the terms of his assignment. Directly after his arrival, Van den Brand, who was then still in Medan, provided him with further details of offences and crimes carried out by planters, whom he named and who had often not been prosecuted. Although proper evidence was scarce or even altogether lacking—not the least because witnesses were spirited away with the help of government officials as highly placed as the Resident of Sumatra's East Coast—Rhemrev reached the conclusion that Van den Brand had by no means exaggerated the facts in making his accusations. Insofar as they could be checked, the latter's descriptions of specific cases were almost always accurate. Only in one or two incidents did the facts appear to have been rather different, which was later disputed by Van den Brand. But in a number of cases, his descriptions even failed to match their dreadful reality.

Rhemrev was faced with the even more difficult task of checking whether or not Van den Brand had been guilty of exaggeration in the more general allegation of unlawful detention and maltreatment, sometimes turning into inhuman cruelty, with which he charged the planters. Attempts to acquire information directly from former coolies who had stayed on in the region met with little success, and Rhemrev realized that the chasm that divided him from these informants was unbridgeable. Although these former coolies were now living in freedom, they had learned not to trust Europeans, planters or government officials.

However unbelievable it may seem, during my investigation into the irregularities in sentencing by magistrates, I frequently found that coolies who had left the plantation in order to complain to the magistrate about their treatment by their employer were punished by that same magistrate for desertion (Rhemrev 1904:334).

Rhemrev decided to use 'spies', i.e. persons he could trust to collect the information that he needed. He decided to recruit several orderlies with long service records who were made available to him by the Resident. Among these were some Chinese who spoke the indigenous languages and who had apparently carried out similar assignments in the past and a couple of casual labourers (a stable boy and a butcher's boy) who had formerly worked as contract coolies. They were given instructions as to how to proceed.

The spies were not to reveal who they were and their task was to pump the coolies on the plantations for information, whether in the *kedeis* or in the fields, during their pauses or in the evening at known meeting places. They also had to get information from people who had formerly worked as contract coolies (Ibid.:334).

The method used by Rhemrev is nowadays a standard one for collecting data by anthropologists all over the world and as such could not have been objectionable. In a situation marked by fierce antagonism, however, such an investigative technique was bound to acquire an almost subversive character. By calling his assistants 'spies', Rhemrev drew renewed attention to the onerous conditions under which he was obliged to fulfil his task.

The information thus obtained soon made it clear that Rhemrev would quite easily be able to cite numerous specific cases in corroboration of Van den Brand's charges. When he wanted to start the interrogation of a worker employed by the St Cyr plantation—a fortuitous choice probably caused by the fact that one of his assistants had served there as a contract coolie—the man was spirited away a short while before the Public Prosecutor could reach the place. Rhemrev took immediate action, bringing to light a great variety of atrocities on this estate which had sometimes ended in permanent disablement or even death. The manager who had been guilty of these crimes stood high in government favour and for years had sat as a member of the Regional Court. Rhemrev could not confine his activities to this one affair. On the basis of the information received, he started prosecutions against various other managers and assistants. In listing these cases, he mentioned

casually that the incidents had all occurred on the plantations in
the vicinity of Medan which were owned by major companies.

Rhemrev was convinced that his approach was the correct one,
and made it abundantly clear that the use of 'spies' was essential
to unearth the truth. Nevertheless, he was compelled to revise his
modus operandi fairly drastically. The primary reason that he gave
for doing so was that the number of crimes brought to his attention
was so large that it was quite impossible to deal with them all by
himself. He estimated that this would take many months, even
years; moreover, he would be unable to get on with the administrative investigation which remained his principal objective. A more
powerful reason was the opposition shown to him on the part of
the planters. Soon after his arrival in Medan, Rhemrev made it
plain that he had no intention of conducting his enquiry in accordance to their wishes. In fact, he did not even try to establish any
contact with them. The displeasure of the planters was considerable and they intervened as soon as a suitable occasion arose. In
strong words they gave vent to their protests in a meeting of the
DPV held in Medan in April 1904[*].

What particularly aroused bad feelings among the planters was
the fact that Rhemrev had started to make use of 'spies'. They gave
him to understand that under no circumstances would they agree
to that course of action.

It is self-evident that such people, brought up in regions where our
Netherlands Indies system of distinguishing between Native and
European residents is not known, and where a Native feels himself to be
the equal of a European, will not behave here in the manner expected by
Mr R. (Minutes DPV in Kooreman 1904–5:9).

It was unheard of that an outsider should turn up on the plantations and insist on speaking to the coolies without the presence of
the management. Notwithstanding the gravity of the criminal

[*] There minutes were published in the *Sumatra Post* and then copied in a number
of other papers (including the *Colonial Weekly*, 6 January 1905) or read aloud, for
example by Kooreman during a lecture (Kooreman 1904–5). The latter source, from
which I have taken the passages quoted, incorrectly mentions 1903 as the year of
that particular meeting of the DPV. There is some lack of clarity regarding the exact
date. According to Kooreman this was 13 April 1904. Troelstra spoke in Parliament
of 19 April of that same year (Proceedings Lower House 1904-5:304).

offences discovered by Rhemrev on St Cyr, his visit there signified a turning point in his investigation. His method of questioning had aroused a spirit of protest among the workforce which immediately threatened to spread to other plantations, according to the DPV leadership.

The next day the manager of a neighbouring plantation came to tell us that, after the inquiry, St Cyr's Javanese had come across to the plantation that he managed, cheering and dancing, calling to the coolies who worked there that the Europeans now had nothing more to say. An official had come from Java to help them, etc., etc. (Ibid.:10).

The press reported growing unrest among the workers. On one plantation they were said to have planned an attack on the manager. This incident was said to be linked directly to the suggestive manner in which the Chinese translator had spoken to the coolies.

They were told that they must immediately go and complain if they thought something was not right; that they should immediately go to the District Officer if they were beaten or if their accounts were incorrect. The Chinese translator even went so far as to say that the former *tuan besar* was in prison in Batavia because he had locked-up a Chinese. Such talk was intended to subvert the coolies, and the spirit of protest that now exists among the Chinese on the plantation can be blamed on these words (*Sumatra Post*, 14 November 1903).

This reaction was exactly what the planters needed to lodge a complaint with the regional government. On that same day, the President of the Planters Committee went to the Resident to complain about the approach taken by the obstinate Rhemrev. The Resident said that he had no authority to intervene, but promised to convey their objections to Rhemrev and said that the latter would change his *modus operandi*. In other words, the Public Prosecutor's investigation was brought to a halt. A few days later Rhemrev met a delegation of the Planters' Committee and, according to the DPV minutes at least, apologized for the inconvenience he had caused. He also declared himself to be open to suggestions as to how to give a different turn to his course of action. The planters' spokesman warned him that to continue along the same road would inevitably lead to coolie riots, and this was immediately backed up by those government officials who were present. The President of the DPV pointed out,

that until now the government had only in very extreme cases taken over the responsibility for peace and order outside the principal towns, and for the rest had left that responsibility to the estate managers. The latter could not be expected to continue to maintain that peace and order if the government suddenly appeared on the plantation, summoned all the coolies together, sent the manager away, then asked if there were any complaints and at the end disappeared again, whilst the nearest police were at one or two hours' distance from the enterprise (Minutes DPV in Kooreman 1904–5:11–12).

The intervention by the planters' organization was intended, quite successfully, to clip Rhemrev's wings. Rhemrev gave in to the pressure and agreed to be accompanied by a representative of the planters' association and a regional government official on his future visits to the plantations. He also had to give at least three hours' notice of his impending arrival, and said that he would ensure that his interrogation of the coolies did not cause unnecessary disruption of the working day. He finally said that he would take care that the respect due to the plantation management was not impaired and that he would not object to the manager being present during the questioning, unless serious charges were brought against him. It was decided that a police squad would be stationed on St Cyr to guarantee the maintenance of peace and order. Rhemrev wrote in his report that he considered the fear of coolie riots to be grossly exaggerated, but all said and done he yielded to the demands made on him. He realized that the planters had formed a closed front against him, united in their wish to thwart his investigation by all possible means. He was told this by one of the managers against whom he had instituted criminal proceedings, and he took care to record the information in the verbal process of the interrogation. Although his adversaries were later to deny this accusation persistently (Ibid.:19), Rhemrev's initial suspicion was strengthened by the new evidence that he managed to bring together. The 'spies', whom Rhemrev had wanted to retain, also disappeared from the scene. Although he did not believe the planters when they complained about the provocation by the 'spies', he could not stand up to the pressure that was brought to bear upon him. He gave in, but not without realizing that he was losing a valuable source of information.

The spies in question had so far given me no reason at all to distrust them. The information provided by them proved always to be consistent with the truth, and there was therefore no reason to doubt the veracity of their version of the facts (Rhemrev 1904:344).

The rumour that Rhemrev did not have a free hand in carrying out his investigation reached the Netherlands. Fock, MP for the Dutch Liberal Party, remarked in the Lower House that the continual presence of a member of the Planters' Committee during the interrogations on the estates conflicted with the requirement of impartiality, and asked the Minister of Colonies to guarantee that Rhemrev would rely on his own judgement. If the Chief Inspector of the Deli Company was his constant companion, how would it be possible for him to acquire complete information, wondered Van Kol as a member of the political opposition (Proceedings Lower House, 24 November 1903:452,459). Nevertheless, Rhemrev proved to be not entirely impervious to the argument that the destruction of the planter's authority over his workforce should be avoided at all cost. When visiting the plantations he never neglected to impress upon the assembled coolies that they owed strict obedience and on no account were they to rebel. He considered it his task to register the transgressions of the Coolie Ordinance, not to change the social fabric of plantation life and work. During his stay on Sumatra's East Coast, all things considered, he agreed with the decree issued by the Resident which allowed planters to detain absconding coolies who were 'caught in the act'. Hoetink had urged this further tightening of the regime in his report. That Rhemrev's investigation would give rise to restiveness among the workforce was no concern of his, an attitude which greatly annoyed the planters.

Rhemrev was quite straightforward about the fact that far more significance should be attached to the first part of his enquiry than to the second part. The entourage with which he was surrounded during his later visits to 145 plantations included the Resident himself; or another member of the civil service in the region; the official in charge of Chinese affairs who also acted as interpreter when necessary, the representative of the Planters' Committee; and, last but not least, the manager of the particular plantation. This fact in itself was sufficient to ensure that the coolies remained silent or only uttered a few grievances after long hesitation, even though they were urged to speak out frankly. Even when a manager voluntarily admitted that he sometimes hit a coolie or detained 'troublemakers', the workers refused to confirm this, let alone submit a complaint about maltreatment. Rhemrev was forced to rely on indirect clues: a building that obviously served as a gaol, indentations in the whipping post from which it could be seen that coolies had been tied to it with ropes or chains. He observed that a surprisingly large number of coolies were sometimes dismissed and sent away shortly before his arrival—in one case amounting to 136 out of a total workforce of 764—undoubtedly in an attempt to prevent them from meeting him. With growing discomfort, Rhemrev remarked that he was finding out less and less in the further course of his investigations, although,

... most iniquities occurred on the most profitable plantations and by the best organized companies. Moreover, it has to be said that, the further the investigation progressed, the fewer were the offences which came to light. But the latter part of the enquiry had been carried out on estates that were economically weak and which were also situated far away from the seat of the government. The poor state of the roads also made them more difficult to reach so that the employer would be more tempted to take the law into his own hands than elsewhere, where communications with the principal town were excellent and the appropriate magistrate could easily be reached (Rhemrev 1904:374–5).

Rhemrev gave special attention to the question of whether the judicial authorities had committed abuses in the application of the Coolie Ordinance. In this respect also, Van den Brand's indictment proved to have been correct. It needed only a written complaint by an employer for a coolie to be punished for alleged desertion, frequently even more severely than was legally permissible. The officials concerned tried to vindicate their behaviour by saying that it had become customary. They admitted that they considered the plantation managers to be their helpers in maintaining the law, as an extension of police authority within their own jurisdiction in this respect. While coolies could be tried and condemned solely on the basis of a charge submitted by the employer, indictable offences committed by Europeans escaped prosecution. Even the most serious crimes, the facts of which could easily be proven, were never brought before the magistrate.

Notwithstanding all the impediments that were put in the way of his investigation, Rhemrev upheld the essence of Van den Brand's charges. His report ended with a devastating summary of the evils that he had encountered on the East Coast. It is significant that Rhemrev linked the sad fate of the contract coolies with the operation of the Coolie Ordinance in principle and practice. In this respect his opinion was clearly different from that of Hoetink, whose criticisms were not only far more moderate but were based on a belief in the essential desirability of the system. While Hoetink tried to soften the effects of forced labour by better protection of the coolies, Rhemrev took the line that maltreatment was the inevitable result of the lack of freedom which characterized the labour contract imposed on the coolie. The technocratic administrator who wanted to improve the rules of the game was opposed by the legal formalist whose task was to demonstrate the discrepancy between official norm and social practice and who, in doing so, had come to the conclusion that the system itself was wrong. Hoetink enjoyed the trust of the planters, while Rhemrev was given a decidedly hostile reception on his arrival. The latter was seen to be an outsider. Hoetink was thoroughly familiar with the problem, having acquitted himself well in his early career by carrying-out assignments in China for the planters. He had since then shown himself to be guided primarily by plantation interests. None could say this of Rhemrev, whose course of action aroused the worst suspicions. The planters' lobby openly surmized that Rhemrev was 'prejudiced' even before he came to Deli. He had, after all, been employed by the Court of Justice in Batavia which dealt with crimes which were more serious and for that reason could not be prosecuted on the East Coast. It seemed reasonable to assume that the legal authorities had formed a thoroughly unfavourable opinion of the conditions on the estates from the files they had received and collected over the years. Finally, there was yet another motive why Rhemrev was unable to meet the planters on an equal footing: as an Eurasian he did not belong to the white milieu on the East Coast of Sumatra. His name immediately identified him as a person of mixed blood. It was customary for the offspring of a white man and a native woman to turn around the family name of his European ancestor; Vermehr thus becoming Rhemrev. Some observers hopefully anticipated that his background would enable Rhemrev to find out more and that '. . . as an Eurasian by birth, he will probably have a sharper eye for the needs and the suffering of the natives'. They abandoned this hope, however, when it proved that, under pressure from the planters, Rhemrev had to change the course of his investigation (Rookmaker *De Amsterdammer*, 30 August 1904). As a lone wolf against a closed front of planters who were imbued with a strongly racist mentality, Rhemrev would have been unable to avoid the feeling that criticisms of his task were in fact also directed against his person. I would assume that this realization made Rhemrev extra sensitive to the demonstrative expressions of dissatisfaction that he encountered during his enquiry on the East Coast and about which he waxed indignant in his report. Confronted with these shocking findings, the authorities had no other option but to give them serious consideration. How was this done and what was the ultimate effect of the judicial investigation on colonial labour policies?

The Colonial Government in Inertia

According to a note written on the last page of the original report, Rhemrev's account reached Governor-General Rooseboom on 18 January 1904 and was almost immediately (on 31 January) sent on to the Minister of Colonies (GSA, Vb., 28 January 1905: No. 6). However, the numerous papers appended to the report, including the verbal processes of Rhemrev's interrogations, were left behind in Batavia. It is doubtful whether these appendices have ever surfaced again, or were even asked for by the Netherlands. In his accompanying letter the Governor-General made no comment at all about the contents of the report, but sufficed with repeating a few concrete suggestions that had been made by Rhemrev and the corresponding action that had been undertaken. The recommendations which he extracted from the report concerned (1) the appointment of officials who would be especially charged with the duty of supervising compliance with the Coolie Ordinance (2) the setting-up of a Court of Justice at Medan (3) an increase of the wage paid to women coolies; and (4) an increase of the police force. The heads of the departments concerned and the Resident on Sumatra's

East Coast were asked to advise. The question also arose of whether steps ought still to be taken against those officials whom Rhemrev had accused of negligence.

The first point was discussed most extensively, i.e. the arguments for setting-up a separate Labour Inspectorate. The Governor-General forwarded a memorandum written by the Director of Justice and dated 3 June 1902, i.e. over a year before Rhemrev was given his assignment, in which he proposed that an office should be set up under the Department of Justice, to exercise control over the correct implementation of the Coolie Ordinance (GSA, Vb., 14 March 1904: No. 8). To give it sufficient leeway, the Director of Justice considered it necessary for the future head of this agency to have a rank equal to that of the Resident, the highest authority of a region. In his opinion, the work could most suitably be done by the officials for Chinese Affairs in the various regions, who were already under his jurisdiction. His profile omitted only the name of the official whom he had in mind, but this could clearly be none other than Hoetink. The Council of the Netherlands East Indies was in complete agreement with this proposal and pointed out in its recommendations that, since the Coolie Ordinance was proclaimed in 1880, at least one-and-a-half million guilders had been charged in registration fees, paid by the contract coolies themselves, but without any expenditure at all on their behalf. The Council proved susceptible to the argument that such control could only be guaranteed if the task was taken away from the regular civil servants in the region and emphatically agreed for that reason that the Inspectorate should be brought under the aegis of the Department of Justice, nominating Hoetink as the Chief Inspector. After all, he had already carried out incidental tasks of this nature, to the full satisfaction of his sponsors.

Mr Hoetink is now 48 years of age, healthy and strong, and full of fervour and dedication to the task assigned to him over the last two years. He has full command over the modern languages, is well-mannered, very intelligent, and is very observant (Advice by the Council of the Netherlands East In dies, No. XX, 17 October 1902 in GSA, Vb., 28 January 1905,No. 6).

One of Hoetink's principal virtues was not listed in this characterization, namely, the planters' faith in him based on previous experience.

After having received these recommendations, the Governor-General made it known that he was prepared to appoint Hoetink, although at a slightly lower rank and within the Department of Civil Service (letter to the Director of Justice, 22 November 1902, No. 4004). In the regional hierarchy this meant that the new official would be subordinate to the Resident. Informed about this suggestion, Hoetink let it be known in March 1903 that he did not find this proposition acceptable (letter to Director of Justice, 16 March 1903, No. 879). He did so in the certain knowledge that the Council of the Netherlands East Indies would block any other construction in which he did not appear. To the great annoyance of ministerial officials at The Hague, the Council twice impeded the enactment of a new Coolie Ordinance, for which the Director of Civil Service had received the approval of the General Secretary (GSA, Vb., 14 March 1904, No. 8). By that time it was no longer a question of whether a Labour Inspectorate should be established, but of its sphere of activity (all the Netherlands East Indies or only the East Coast of Sumatra to start with) and particularly of its status within the colonial apparatus an independent agency, or as part of the Department of Civil Service). The weakness of the Governor-General's position is illustrated by the fact that he was not able to assert his own viewpoint. For the time being no further action was taken until Rhemrev's report arrived. The Governor-General then wrote to the Resident of the East Coast that he would be given the disposal of a special official. He wondered whether a 'retired but still able-bodied officer' might not be suitable for the post.

In a second despatch, sent on 24 July 1904 (No. 1664/3, in Vb. 28 January 1905, No. 6), the Governor-General informed the Minister of Colonies about the steps that he had taken in the subsequent months. A Labour Inspectorate had been set up as a temporary measure, under the leadership of Hoetink who, during his stay in the Netherlands, had been informed by the Ministry that the Netherlands East Indies authorities intended to entrust him with the drawing-up of a new Coolie Ordinance for all the Outer Provinces (GSA, Vb., 14 March 1904, No. 8). The circumstances had forced the Governor-General to yield to a number of conditions made by Hoetink. As Head of the new agency, whose operations were to be confined to the East Coast, the Inspector would not be subordinate to the Resident of that region but would be directly accountable to the Director of the Civil Service. Hoetink had proved impervious to pressures that he should accommodate himself to a position under the Resident, even with the promise that he would be allowed adequate room for manoeuvre in carrying out his task. His firm stand had the approval of the Director of Justice.

An inspection cannot properly be carried out if he who is entrusted with it must in his work await the orders of the Civil Service in the region. I cannot conceive of any properly effective control unless it is assigned to someone who is completely independent and is capable of doing every-thing that he considers necessary in the interests of his task (Report by the Director of Justice, 28 May 1904, No. 7:11; repeated in a different wording in his letter of 11 July 1904, No. 5623).

Hoetink also made it clear that he considered the intention to appoint him as the only official of the Labour Inspectorate as a breaking point. He wanted at least two Assistant Inspectors to share in the work of supervising 170 plantations whose total work-force numbered approximately one hundred thousand coolies. He had his way. It was typical of bureaucratic formalism that cor-respondence between the heads of departments held forth exten-sively on the expenses that the future Labour Inspector would be allowed to claim and on the official uniform that he should wear. Hoetink himself had no hesitation in pointing out that he was better qualified than any other to put things in order.

I believe that I may claim to be rather well acquainted with the situation in Deli and that, on the basis of my record, I can always get more out of the Deli planters than a stranger would be able to do. I also have the advantage of the experience gained during my visits to enterprises in the Outer Provinces in the years 1901–3, and I do not think that I can be accused of any lack of self-confidence or ambition (Minute to the Director of Justice, 11 May 1904:4).

In a later writing he made himself even clearer. The Labour Inspector eventually to be appointed would not be popular on the East Coast. The planters would curse him as a snooper. No-one, including himself, was particularly eager to undertake this thank-less task, but if he should be called upon he, Hoetink, would consider it his duty to agree. He had been on the East Coast from 1880 to 1889 and had returned there on a number of occasions. Hadn't Michielsen, who was now Vice-President of the Council of the Netherlands East Indies but had then been Resident on the East Coast, expressed a very favourable opinion of him in 1892? To be content with less than he had asked for would only detract from the dignity of the office that he was prepared to fulfil (Hoetink to Director of Justice, 6 July 1904). Under such pressure, the Governor-General was forced to drop his opposition, even though he reserved the right in due course to regulate the position of Hoetink's successor with regard to the regional government in a different way. In his order of appointment dated 24 July 1904 he wrote,

... that the inspecting officials shall be particularly charged with direct supervision over the implementation of the regulations regarding mutual rights and obligations of employers and workers in the region in question; with regular visits to the plantations or places where the regulations apply; with control over conditions prevailing there; with receiving possible complaints by employers and workers, and with reporting on their findings and, where appropriate, with submitting necessary proposals (Extract from the Order Register of the Governor-General in the Netherlands East Indies, No. 3, Mail No. 1664/3).

The new inspectorate had to be satisfied with this brief task description. The Governor-General was advised by his counsellors not to formulate and publicly announce any formal plan of operation, undoubtedly in order to prevent the possibility that planters would take umbrage at an elaborate task description with very rigid guidelines. In the meantime, a delegation of the Deli Planters' Association had visited the Governor-General to inform him about 'the peculiarities of conditions in Deli' and to explain why it had been necessary for the employers to assume police powers (Minutes of the General Meeting of DPV, quoted in Kooreman 1904–5:22).

The answer that the Governor-General received to his question about coolie wages is worth mentioning. The Resident of the East Coast replied that these were indeed scandalously low—he spoke of a starvation wage—but that, lacking any power to intervene, he could do little more than to ask the planters to give their workers better pay. 'May I be permitted to remark, however, that I consider it necessary that the government should establish a minimum wage if the extortionate practices of some employers are to be brought to an end once and for all' (letter to the Governor-General, Medan, 2 April 1904, No. 722/4).

There was no reaction to this clearly-stated and well-known opinion. With regard to the question of whether officials who had been found guilty of reprehensible conduct in the administration of justice ought to be prosecuted, the head of the regional government acknowledged the accuracy of Rhemrev's conclusions. But, he stated, deviation from the formal instructions had become customary. In practice it was extremely difficult to provide legal evidence of transgression of the Coolie Ordinance by the workers. What could an acting magistrate without much judicial training do other than to sentence the contract coolies against whom charges were made and who, moreover, admitted their own 'guilt'? Of the 28,588 coolies who had been sentenced by the police magistrate between 1901 and 1903, only a small minority of 4 per cent had denied being guilty of the misdemeanour for which they were punished. If the magistrates had imposed sentences without hearing witnesses, they did so in order to prevent the greater evil of coolie riots. The fault committed by my predecessors, according to the Resident, was that they did not ask for the regulations to be changed. In effect, his argument amounted to saying that it was neither possible nor desirable to maintain the pretence of equality before the law (letter from the Resident to the Director of Native Government, 25 May 1904, No. 35: Vb., 19 October 1907, No. 19). By defending his subordinates in this way, the highest authority on Sumatra's East Coast acknowledged that the Ordinance had been merely a legal fiction insofar as protection of the rights of the coolies was concerned. His superior showed himself in sympathy with this point of view. The deviations were of course not justified, but in view of the prevailing conditions they were excusable. After receiving these opinions the Governor-General decided on a general pardon. No steps were to be taken against members of the administrative corps in the region. Those who had carried responsibility were no longer employed there and for their subordinates the classical defence applied: mitigating circumstances (letters from Director of Native Government and from the Government Secretary, 27 January 1905, 18/A and 23 February 1905, No. 109; GSA, Vb., 19 October 1907, No. 19).

Political Discussion in the Netherlands

The results of Rhemrev's investigation were anxiously awaited in the Netherlands. Public interest in the subject had been kept alive by the reactions to Van den Brand's pamphlet voiced by planters and by officials who had returned from the Indies, and by Van den Brand himself who stood by his accusations in new publications. The manner in which Rhemrev had been subjected to pressure during his stay on the East Coast was naturally not left undiscussed and, as we have seen, even gave rise to comments and questions in the Lower House. Even while he was still working on his assignment, the Dutch and European press published unsubstantiated reports on the abuses that he was said to have uncovered. German papers wrote about 'bloody millions' and 'inhuman cruelties' (GSA, Vb., 12 October 1903, No. 26). The authorities at home and in the Indies did everything possible to avoid drawing attention to the report that he was writing, but some of its contents inevitably became known even before it was discussed in the Parliament. Almost immediately after it reached the Netherlands it was apparently decided that its findings would not be made public. The personal letter that Deen, a journalist on the *Deli Courant*, wrote from Amsterdam in April 1904 to the Director of one of the largest plantation corporations, is very revealing: 'The Rhemrev report is bad, so bad that, I have been informed on good authority, it cannot be discussed or published'. He went on to say that there was reason to believe that continuation of the investigation would bring even more atrocities to light. 'What the report does not say is perhaps the worst of all. It is a miserable business' (RTI: letters and newspaper cuttings). Deen's published story, working as he did for the mouthpiece of the planters lobby, was naturally different. Certainly, the fearsome criticism was not surprising and the planters must take it seriously. But who was likely to attack them, he added, '. . . forced as they are to work with irrational beings, such as the coolies usually are . . .' (quoted in *De Amsterdammer*, 4 December 1904). In later reactions, his defensive argument was to gain the upper hand. Other published comments, however, tried in the first instance to play down the findings of the official investigation. A noticeable example of this was Kooreman's reaction who said that Rhemrev's findings, or what was known of them, were partly unreliable and for the rest provided no new information. He even started by saying that the serious charges made against the magistrates and other officials on Sumatra's East Coast had not been proven. Only some minor shortcomings had (Kooreman 1904–5:1). The ex-Resident clearly felt that his honour was at stake, and he challenged the Minister of Colonies to make the report public. As the situation stood, caustic judgement was about to be pronounced over numerous officials and over the whole Deli society—meaning the white elite—without any of the persons or parties concerned being given the chance to defend themselves. Kooreman tried to tarnish the credibility of Rhemrev's conclusions. He considered the information compiled by Rhemrev with the aid of his 'spies' to be utterly worthless, and he used the minutes of DPV's general meeting to suggest that the first part of the investigation had been a complete failure as a result of this method of data collection. Nevertheless, the tone of noble indignation did not sound entirely genuine. The earlier charge made against Van den Brand to the effect that he had sought publicity without having sufficient evidence to support his accusations, could hardly be maintained in the case of a public prosecutor who had merely tried to comply in a precisely and detailed manner with the task assigned to him. Rather than to demand satisfaction for 'undeserved vilification', the Deli press informed its readers that various 'censurable facts' and 'irregularities' had been ascertained which, although they were not general occurrences, nevertheless gave food for thought. This line of defence gradually introduced other arguments. The shift from denial to acknowledgement that labour relations on the plantations were not in accordance with the law, was accompanied by the warning that the situation should not be judged according to standards applicable in Europe. The way in which a former harbour master of Belawan put this point of view was typical. After pointing out that the planters, in their isolated positions, had to maintain order among massive numbers of 'unruly and irrational coolies', he hoped that the people would understand that, in doing so, the planters sometimes could not but exceed the limits of the law and even of humanity (*De Indische Gids* 1905:27:97–8). This argument, although more nebulously worded, found a wide response in that it suited the colonial thinking about the (non-)economic behaviour of the Asian worker. Seen in this context, the abuses were more understandable and, as a result, less obnoxious. But reactions continued to be voiced in varying keys, running from apologetic admission, 'that's the way it is', to the harsh statement, 'and it can't be done any differently'.

This conclusion anticipates the political discussion and winding up of the affair. To start with, it is noticeable that the secrecy acted as a setback for the investigator and his findings rather than for those who had given him the assignment. During the committee meeting held in preparation for the public discussion on the Indies' budget in the Lower House in Autumn 1904, the Minister of Colonies was immediately asked to produce the report (Proceedings Lower House, 29 November 1904:303). Idenburg refused to comply with this request, denied that the report had been sent for perusal to the Chairman of the Planters' Committee in Deli, and drew attention to the completion of the draft of the new Coolie Ordinance, prepared by Hoetink who had meanwhile taken up his post as the temporary Labour Inspector. The committee members, belonging to various political parties, refused to be satisfied with this statement and again asked for access to the report, whether in summary or in any other form. The Minister continued to voice objections. In explaining his refusal, he first drew attention to the fact that the investigation was partly of a judicial nature. Secrecy was inevitable in view of the criminal proceedings that were in progress or pending. Secondly, the important thing now was to take measures that would put an end to the abuses. Rather than to mark time by what had exactly happened, Idenburg considered it advisable to devote all attention to the proposed reforms. The Labour Inspectorate had already been set up, an announcement about the expansion of the police force was expected to be made in the near future, and the establishment of a Court of Justice in Medan was under discussion. The Minister had woven Rhemrev's principal findings into his own reply.

1. The situation on a number of plantations on Sumatra's East Coast leaves a great deal to be desired as regards relations between employer and contract coolie. During the investigation it was found that [coolies] were hit by hand or with the cane on by far the majority of plantations.
2. Until shortly before the investigation, serious mistreatment occurred on various plantations.
3. Unlawful detention, whether or not accompanied by physical

torture, was a regular feature on Sumatra's East Coast until shortly before [Rhemrev's] arrival.

4.   Europeans have sometimes, but rarely, been guilty of man slaughter; so far, there has not been a single case of murder by a European on the plantations; cases of manslaughter and murder committed by natives and Eastern aliens on fellow countrymen are very numerous.

5.   The relationship between planter and contract coolie is such that the employer has always felt himself to be the lord and master of the workman, and that the latter has always been convinced that he was entirely dependent on the employer. (Memorandum written in respect of the report; Proceedings Lower House, 21 November 1904, App. B, No. 46:69).

This summary, terse though it was, provided the spokesmen of the various political parties with sufficient ammunition for an extensive debate in the Lower House which took place on 29 and 30 November 1904 (Proceedings Lower House 1904–5:301–29). There was obviously a good deal to hide, replied Troelstra on behalf of the Socialist Opposition to the Minister's decision not to publish the report, against the express wishes of Parliament. Troelstra regretted that lack of sufficient information meant that judgements on the measures to be taken had to be less thorough than was needed. He referred to Van den Brand at length. A piquant detail was that, in his most recent publication (*The Coolie Ordinance in Practice* [1904]), Van den Brand, who had provided the impulse for the official investigation, quoted extensively from the Rhemrev Report which somehow had been made available to him. In this way a number of salient data from that report came up for discussion after all. In his reply the Minister repeated why he had to suffice with the conclusions from the report. He had announced these, he said, 'accurately and without concealing anything'. This expression which, as we shall see, was not in agreement with the truth, by and large satisfied the spokesmen of the government parties. They readily capitulated to the Minister who urged them not to look back but ahead, but made it clear that Rhemrev's findings had surpassed their worst suspicions. Fock exclaimed that the Deli planters were a pack of freebooters and demanded to know why the government officials were in such blissful ignorance about the outrageous conditions. Another MP, De Waal Malefijt, fol- lowed this by reminding the Minister that Rhemrev had also been instructed to investigate the activities of the magistrates, and he asked for further information in this aspect. A third speaker, Pijnacker Hordijk, suggested that the local government was perhaps quite well aware of the abuses, but that it had never been provided with the means for closely monitoring what took place on the plantations. The spokesmen for the ruling coalition no longer insisted on the publication of the report. Cremer now also took part in the debate, partly to deny that the regional authorities had ever pressed for more personnel. At any rate, he knew nothing about such a request. In his reply, the Minister cautiously said that the authorities on Sumatra's East Coast did indeed have some knowledge of the abuses which they had tried to the best of their ability to restrain, but that the point of departure had always been to ensure the maintenance of law and order on the plantations through co-operation with the employers. This was seen as being in the general interest. To his regret, the Minister had to acknowledge that the officials in the region had not kept to the rules when punishing the coolies and, on the other hand, had spared their European masters. His answer revealed that, on the previous day, Idenburg had presented Rhemrev's conclusions with less accuracy than he had feigned. Nonetheless, his balanced argumentation made a strong impression, particularly when he said that he was determined to put an end to all malafide and vicious practices. 'Rhemrev's visit has opened our eyes. The government's intention to cease such affairs has been shown convincingly and will be shown convincingly' (Proceedings Lower House, 30 November 1904:317).

It was this passage in particular which aroused the indignation of a number of former government officials. Ex-Resident Kooreman discoursed at length on the information that in the course of time had been sent by the regional government to Batavia. Requests for increases of the administrative and police forces were usually denied, if indeed any answer was given at all. The claim that the higher authorities had not been informed was said by Kooreman to be incorrect and untruthful. Had the authorities in the Netherlands Indies, whether purposely or accidentally, perhaps neglected to send these reports on to the ministry at The Hague? Kooreman was supported by Scherer, his colleague and predecessor on Sumatra's East Coast, who confirmed that the centre of colonial power was well informed about conditions in the region but that it overlooked a great deal in order not to harm the tobacco industry (Kooreman 1904–5:52–69).

The personal involvement of some of the speakers in the Parliament added extra colour to the discussions. Van Kol was given the credit that he deserved: in 1898 he had been the first to draw the Parliament's attention to the coolie scandals and had stubbornly refused to accept the meaningless or evasive replies that he was repeatedly given. Van den Brand was also praised on various sides for what the Minister called his good and humanitarian work. This rehabilitation was not always sincere, however, as can be seen from the report of the debate in the Upper House: 'I do not know Mr Van den Brand at all; snoopers of that sort are sometimes necessary to bring some affairs to light' (Proceedings Upper House, 30 December 1904:164). This rather petty remark by the spokesman of the Liberal Party, Van Houten, was prompted by his annoyance at the fact that the Minister of Colonies had taken the initiative to invite Van den Brand to a meeting when he returned to the Netherlands in the Spring of 1904. But Idenburg had hedged his bets. While he made sure that MPs were well aware of his gesture of good will to the man who exposed the systematically scandalous way in which coolies were treated, he also protected Cremer against the reproaches and derision that were directed at him, now an ordinary MP. Charges were levelled against him particularly by the Socialist Opposition, for the arrogance with which,   when still a Minister, he had waved aside troublesome questions about the abuses that were taking place in Deli. In his defence, this captain of industry-cum-politician, who for the rest of his life was to be saddled with the nickname 'coolie Cremer', got no farther than the lamentable statement that, assuming the validity of the conclusions reached in the Rhemrev Report, he, was in no position to dispute them, '. . . we are dealing here with a breakdown of morality on Sumatra's East Coast and that collapse must have been from a later date' (Proceedings Lower House, 29 November 1904:313). In other words the scandals took place only after his departure. It was a 'Sorry, I didn't know', sort of remark which gave rise to an even sharper criticism. In unusually bitter words, Troelstra settled Van Kol's old score as Cremer had once attacked this party specialist in colonial affairs. He must have had a difficult time. A letter which Cremer wrote to the Director of one of the largest plantation companies implied that the press had reported incorrectly on his speech in the House. In a roundabout way he tried to invalidate Rhemrev's findings (letter from Cremer to Janssen, 17 December 1904, coll. RTI).

Minister Idenburg proved to have taken the right tone in the House, however, and the members of the parties belonging to the coalition among his audience were only too willing to listen to reason. The socialist opposition took a stronger stand in the debate by pleading that the penal sanction in the Coolie Ordinance be abolished. How could a Calvinist Minister of Colonies permit the perpetuation of industrial relations to be based on depriving people of their freedom? wondered Troelstra. He referred not only to Van den Brand, a political ally of Idenburg, but also to ex-Resident Rookmaker who had called the coolie labour contract 'immoral'. The Socialist spokesman submitted a fairly moderately-worded motion in which he suggested that it be investigated whether the labour contract should be subjected to state coercion and that a new system of industrial coercion be designed on the basis of the results of that investigation. Speakers from the ruling parties did not wish to go even this far, and agreed with Idenburg that a repeal of the present regulation would lead to complete disorganization which would not be in the best interests of the coolies. Certainly, said the Minister, he also hoped that coercion would in future no longer be necessary but that day had, alas, not yet come. He pointed out that a similar Ordinance was in force in the Straits Settlements. Under the circumstances, it was unavoidable. After all,

... although it may be true that our western sense of justice rebels to some degree against the force earlier referred to, the fact that breach of contract is punishable does not seem strange to the oriental peoples. Moreover, it should not be forgotten in this connection that the Chinese workers, who are employed in such large numbers on the plantations in Deli, are not all saints, indeed, they have very considerable shortcomings. But in addition, apart from the penal coercion on the worker to fulfil his contract, there is the equally legally enforceable pressure on the employer to fulfil the contract (Proceedings Lower House, 30 November 1904:319).

This was a repetition of the well-known argument that had repeatedly been put forward by the colonial government in the past. Troelstra showed his scepticism, and rightly so. He pointed out that the planters lobby had immediately torpedoed the plan to set up a Court of Justice on the East Coast. To have a judiciary so near home, which undoubtedly would have a deterrent effect, was an idea the planters did not appreciate. It was said that, after this personal intervention by the General Manager of the Deli Company, the Resident of the region had also informed the Governor-General that there was no need for a Court of Justice in Medan (Van den Brand 1904b:63–72). Idenburg made it known that no decision had yet been taken, and expressed the hope that the Coolie Ordinance based on Hoetink's draft would soon be introduced, and again announced a strengthening of the police force. This package was quite enough to satisfy the majority of the members of the Lower House. In a friendly motion they thanked the Minister for the information they had been given and encouraged him to continue along the same path. In the end the Socialist Opposition resigned itself to the inevitable and withdrew its own, more critical motion. The House thus in effect intimated that it shared the views of the Minister and was prepared to go along with his wishes, which was the retention of the Coolie Ordinance with penal sanctions, with improvements but no fundamental differences.

The Ministry

We have described the state of affairs as could be observed by the general public. However, together with the Rhemrev Report, I found in the colonial archives a number of official papers, a few letters that had been received as a result of the parliamentary debates, the informative notes written to Minister Idenburg by the top civil servants of his ministry during the debate on the budget, and even a draft of the speech which the Minister read in the House in answer to the questions put to him. This fortunate circumstance enables us to examine how opinions were formed behind closed doors and which attitude was adopted within the bureaucracy in answer to the criticisms that had been raised.

The Rhemrev Report, which arrived in The Hague early in March 1904 (GSA, Vb., 14 March 1904, No. 8), caused considerable mortification to the colonial policy-makers. 'A sorry tale of suffering and injustice', runs the note made by the Minister and initialled by him, on the first page of the original documents, which I found in the archives. In the knowledge that the publication of the report would be insisted upon, it seems that some consideration was given to releasing the summary given at the end of the document. Not the literal text, of course, which was apparently found to be too embarrassing, but an edited version. How that was to be done is shown by notes written in the margins. Apart from removing all personal names, in some cases the wording was to be toned down by changing or even deleting the sharpest and most damaging passages. Ultimately, however, Idenburg felt he could not risk the publication of this concluding section, even when watered down. As we have seen, when he replied to the parliamentary's committee's urgent request by a letter dated 21 November, he sufficed with summarizing Rhemrev's main conclusions. Was this done 'accurately and concealing nothing', as Idenburg said in the Lower House? Certainly not, as is clear from the letter written to him on the same date by A.E. Elias, Secretary-General of the Ministry.

I would recommend that the conclusions not be taken over in quotation marks but that they should be modified a little, as I have done, for example, by changing the word 'horrible' into 'serious' and by omitting the word cruelties (mistreatment is quite bad enough) (Letter from Elias to Idenburg, 21 November 1904; GSA, Vb., 21 November 1904, No. 28).

The Minister initialled the amendment and adopted it. Even more revealing is the marginal note made by the civil servant who wrote the memorandum with which the Minister replied to questions raised in the parliamentary debate, with reference to the essence of Rhemrev's argument: 'The writer considers it advisable to say nothing about the Coolie Ordinance. In view of what is written in the report, it seems that Mr Rhemrev considers that Ordinance to be the source of all sufferings.' His superior did not agree, and wrote underneath:

I don't interpret it in that way, but neither does his report mention a revision of the Coolie Ordinance, so that for that reason alone there is no reason to mention that revision in this memorandum (Handwritten memorandum concerning the report, 20 November 1904:4; GSA, Vb., 21 November 1904, No. 28).

Idenburg also said nothing in the House about a subject that ex-Resident Van der Steenstraten had raised in a personal letter to the Minister, i.e. the continued refusal by the Netherlands Indies authorities to establish a minimum wage for the contract coolies (letter Van der Steenstraten to the Minister, 11 December 1904; GSA, Vb. 28 January 1905, No. 6). Rhemrev had certainly taken up this point in his report. The Governor-General, in his accompanying letter, had also drawn the Minister's attention to this specific recommendation.

Idenburg further failed to make use of the note written by the members of his own staff with respect to the motion forwarded by Troelstra, to the effect that the establishment of a Court of Justice in Medan would not abolish the legal inequality between the employers and the workers. Crimes perpetrated by the former were only very seldom committed by the latter. Charges made by the planters usually resulted in the instant administration of 'justice', but the coolies were forced to follow a much longer road before they could find anyone even willing to listen to their complaints, let alone to start criminal proceedings. The point at issue was not where, but *how* they could obtain their legal rights. Seen from this point of view, improved supervision was only a stop-gap. The real question that had to be considered was: Coolie Ordinance or no Coolie Ordinance? The Minister of Colonies made no mention whatsoever of these arguments, which all too clearly did not fit his line of reasoning.

Finally, Idenburg's remark in the House to the effect that a similar labour regulation to that of Deli was in force in the Straits Settlements, derived from documents that Cremer had sent him informally in the Spring of 1904 (personal letter with annexes from Cremer to Idenburg, 1 April 1904; GSA, Vb., 28 January 1905, No. 6). The Minister naturally did not mention his source—he was careful to maintain a proper distance from Cremer in public; neither did he think it necessary to point out that a comparison of the two Ordinances with regard to the rights and protection given to the contract coolies, would quite clearly be to the advantage of the Straits Settlements. He also chose not to read the comment made by the person who had collected the documentation in Singapore on behalf of the Chief Inspector of the Deli Company, i.e. that 'such a stupid lot [the coolies] are not fit for free labour of their own preference' (letter from Romenij to H.C. van den Honert, 2 October 1902). It is interesting to note that in regulating the labour system on behalf of private industry on Sumatra's East Coast, legislation drawn up by the colonial government of Malaya was taken as a model both for its inception and for its preservation. This calls attention once again to the multinational character of the plantation economy.

This background material gives some clarity regarding Idenburg's contacts, of whom he made no mention at all in his parliamentary exchanges. On the basis of what has been said above, I conclude that the Minister not only did not give the House complete information, but that he also misrepresented the actual data at his disposal. While he tried to give the impression that he was quite open to any advice that might be given him, the way in which he selected the facts on which to base his argument is sufficient proof that he had already drawn his own conclusions. Immediately after receiving the Rhemrev Report, the Minister wondered whether the entire system on which the Coolie Ordinance was based was not in need of thorough revision. At first he gave the impression that he would take a far more militant stand. Loudon, head of the judicial division (A1) of the Ministry of Colonies, had drawn the Minister's attention in a memorandum to the fact that the management of the Billiton Company attached no value to maintaining the Coolie Ordinance and would prefer it to be repealed (GSA, Vb., 14 March 1904, No. 8). Yet well before the parliamentary hearings started, Idenburg had decided that his own opinions on the labour problem in the East Indies were not the same as those of Loudon. To gain better insight into the matter with which the Minister, in his own words, was not sufficiently familiar, he ordered Loudon to compile a survey and to state his own objections to the policy line taken (Memorandum Idenburg to Head A1, 24 June 1904; GSA, Vb., 28 January 1905, No. 6). Loudon then devoted his attention to writing his report.

He started his exposition by admitting that he had never favoured the Coolie Ordinance. At the time they signed the labour contract, the Chinese or Javanese coolies had no idea of what they were committing themselves to. They entered into the contract in sheer desperation, to ensure their livelihood, but they were completely unfamiliar with both the country and the work for which they were destined. The Ordinance placed an unbreakable bond on the ignorant and destitute coolies, in a social milieu in which they were also discriminated against on racial grounds. Such a labour contract, entered into with a people who could have absolutely no idea of what awaited them, a contract which was indissoluble and compliance with which was ensured with the use of force, in Loudon's opinion, smacked of slavery. The Coolie Ordinance made it possible for the employer to obtain cheap labour. Without relinquishing this objective, it was hoped now that better protection of the coolies would enable some mitigation of the use of force. But even this remedy, he predicted, would not be effective.

After this promising beginning, work on the report was halted for some time, probably due to the heavy workload caused by the parliamentary debate on the Netherlands East Indies budget. Loudon did not continue until 24 January 1905, but his tone was now very different, for which he gave the following interesting explanation.

I shall now continue this report, which I started some months ago, even though the purpose and the point of departure are now quite different. Earlier I thought that the Minister's wish was to have a survey of the labour problem in the Netherlands East Indies *in general*, whereby the question automatically arose: Coolie Ordinance or not? Both on ethical and judicial as well as practical grounds. Now the question is rather: whether the Coolie Ordinances, seeing the ulterior objective of preserving the existing plantations, *eo ipso* should be retained? whether they can be expurgated and how far? whether in that respect we should retain the penal sanction and enforce it with a strong hand (in case of desertion)? (Memorandum Loudon; GSA, Vb., 28 January 1905, No. 6)

In the meantime it had become clear on which side the Minister stood. Although this did not agree with Loudon's own views, he adapted willingly as a good civil servant should. He could no longer take as his point of departure the principle that labour had a value in itself, and that it was the legislator's responsibility to ensure that the economically weak would lead a life of human dignity. No, in the new line of argument priority was given to industrial interests. These had to be protected with all means available such as the Coolie Ordinance, but at the same time the relationship between the employer and the worker had to be made as harmonious as possible. Drawing his conclusions, Loudon postulated (1) that a Coolie Ordinance was indispensable (2) that such a regulation was legally tenable (3) and which precisely described the modality of the Ordinance. Such a study would take a great deal of time and would require specialized knowledge which he did not have. Would it not be far easier, suggested Loudon, if Idenburg were to say that he intended to retain the existing Ordinance and then wait to see what the result of the discussions being held in the Netherlands Indies would be? He accompanied this suggestion with the warning that the Minister must then expect very meager results, over which the Members in the next round of debates would in all likelihood show themselves to be disappointed. Nevertheless, Loudon listed for the Minister all the reasons why, in his view, the need for the Coolie Ordinance had not been firmly established, and did so in a style that suggested close affinity with the Ethical Policy. He also explained how his aversion to this labour regulation had been aroused. As a lawyer connected with the Court of Justice in Batavia between 1885 and 1888 he had been involved in the prosecution of planters from Deli who were accused of mistreating their coolies. The Ordinance, which had acquired its own rationale, had initially been introduced as an emergency measure and, in Loudon's opinion, this made a critical investigation of its tenability all the more necessary. He once again drew attention to the remark made by the General Manager of the Billiton Company in March 1904, to the effect that even without the Coolie Ordinance sufficient Chinese would continue to report for work in the tin-mines. He had continued: '. . . we can manage quite well without that piece of paper; it should be repealed as soon as possible' (quotation included in Loudon's memorandum).

The opinion of a wide range of colonial specialists in the colony should certainly be considered, Loudon acknowledged, but he also warned that they would bring great pressure to bear for the existing situation to be continued. Loudon's memorandum was first sent for comments to Viehoff, Head of the Division of Civil Service and Public Works in the Ministry, under whose jurisdiction the subject actually fell. Viehoff completely disagreed with the line taken by his colleague and hoped,

... that people would not let themselves be propelled by the propaganda music of the social-democratic orchestra in the Lower House in a direction whose consequences for the development of [the colony's] natural resources cannot be foreseen (comment by Viehoff on Loudon's Memorandum, 30 January 1905; GSA, Vb., 28 November 1905, No. 6).

Viehoff did not disguise the fact that the Coolie Ordinance had all sorts of shortcomings, but in his view the prime question was whether further development of the Outer Provinces was necessary in the larger colonial interest. If so, and he left no misunderstanding that this was the only correct answer, then the pacification of their own conscience must take the higher priority. The end justifies the means, noted Loudon in turn in the margin with evident disgust. He also indignantly denied the insinuation that he held socialist views; for a colonial official in those days this was an insult that was obviously difficult to swallow. Loudon said that he only opposed injustice and defended humanity. Secretary-General Elias hastened to tone down the difference of opinion that had arisen between his divisional heads, but carefully avoided taking the side of either. A thorough study of the origins and operations of the Coolie Ordinance, as recommended by Loudon, could do no harm in his view. But the Minister would only be able to make up his mind on this question after having received the advice of the Governor-General. In a final note written on 23 February 1905 in respect of the recommendations made by the principal members of his staff, Minister Idenburg again stressed that the penal sanction was the essence of the Coolie Ordinance. To return a coolie to his workplace with the use of force, as occurred on the plantations on Sumatra's East Coast, was a measure that could only be justified under very exceptional circumstances. Idenburg left open the possibility that a new Ordinance would only apply to certain regions, branches of industry and categories of workers. The exact wording would be an affair for the lawyers, but it had to be based on discussions with 'men of experience' (GSA, Vb., 28 January 1905, No. 6). In a letter dated 24 January 1905, the Minister of Colonies officially informed the authorities in the Netherlands East Indies about the parliamentary debate on the coolie problem. The reply to the principal question, i.e. whether or not there should be a penal sanction, would depend significantly on opinions held in the colony, Idenburg wrote to the Governor-General. Idenburg also asked the Governor-General why it was that the East Coast plantations maintained a regime that was no longer found necessary in the Billiton mines. He urged that the Governor-General should consult interested private citizens in addition to his official advisers, and that he should submit his final reaction within the coming months (GSA, Vb., 28 January 1905, No. 6). The Minister received a fitting reply. On 25 May 1905 the Governor-General informed him that both the Director of Civil Service and the Council of the Netherlands Indies endorsed the recommendations made by the temporary Labour Inspector (Hoetink) and the industrialists on the East Coast (i.e. the Planters Committee and the Planters Alliance), namely, that the coercive conditions in the Coolie Ordinance were indispensable. To abandon these clauses would mean a deathblow for a flourishing industry. The Governor-General also strongly supported this view himself (GSA, Vb. 27 December 1905, No. 65/3737). In the next debate on the budget for the Netherlands East Indies, the new Minister Fock informed MPs that all authorities in the colony considered the penal sanction to be of vital importance (Proceedings Lower House, 23 November 1905:178).

Does all this mean that nothing changed? In my opinion, events around the turn of the century did in fact signify a transition to a new system of labour relations on the plantations. How affairs further developed during the twentieth century is outside the scope of this study. Here, we are concerned only with the immediate effect: what concrete results arose from the Deli coolie scandal? Very few. Did nothing change at all? I think so: the suggestion of continuity stemming from the retention of the existing Ordinance would be misleading.

Impact

After the denouement, the principal players in the whole affair seem quite quickly to have disappeared from the scene. Rhemrev who, as a member of the judiciary, had painstakingly carried out his thankless task, i.e. to confirm that which the colonial authorities did not wish to hear, had nothing to do with the further course of events and there is little to be recounted about him. The bearers of unpleasant news seldom get the reward they are later said to have deserved. But, did the further career of this public prosecutor suffer as a result of his Report? That he was not entirely easy on this point is shown by a remark that he made a short time later. 'If only this ministry continues! Because if the Deli set comes into power again, Cremer will be Minister of Colonies, and my days will be numbered' (Dijkstra 1906:21). Dijkstra was anything but favourably disposed towards Rhemrev, but had earlier been on fairly close terms with him. In 1905, as a government commissioner, Rhemrev had

looked into the alleged irregularities in the Lampung District of
southern Sumatra. The charges had been filed by Dijkstra, a
planter, who even in his own writings gives the impression of
being a troublesome person (see also GSA, Vb., 10 December 1906,
No. 57). According to Dijkstra, Rhemrev the 'Deli Terror', as he
nicknamed him complained of having been passed over for promotion to the post of the Attorney General. He feared that his advancement would be blocked again because he had many enemies
among the highest-ranking civil servants. But how could it be
proven that the appointment was withheld because of the way in
which he had acquitted himself of his task in Deli? Reactions to his
activities in southern Sumatra were also extremely negative. His
report led to the resignation of the Resident of that region, who
then vindictively wrote a *roman clef* in which he assigned a dis-
creditable role to Rhemrev (Neumann 1914). Rhemrev could hardly have enjoyed all these intrigues, and it is not at all surprising that
in 1905, after finishing his assignment, he went to Europe where
he stayed for two years on sick leave. His further service record
was not outstanding: he ended his career in 1910 as Vice-President
of the Court of Justice in Surabaya.

The man for whom Rhemrev had shown so much fear, Cremer,
continued his brilliant career. Although after the coolie scandal he
no longer made himself available for another term in the Lower
House, he later returned to politics as Member of the Upper House.
In 1907 he was appointed President of the Netherlands Trading
Company (NHM), the major colonial bank, and from 1918 to 1920
he was Ambassador of the Netherlands in Washington. The last
years of his life were spent on his estate in Santpoort, the Netherlands, where, according to insiders, he lived in a princely state. The
biographies of this talented captain of industry have not been
blemished by any slur on his reputation (Fasseur 1979:122–5).

And what is there to be said about Hoetink? He had been
appointed Labour Inspector as a result of Van den Brand's publications and Rhemrev's report, the substance of both of which he
had disputed. According to the Council of the Netherlands Indies,
no-one else would have been able to put a check on the coolie
scandal with the aid of a well-reasoned regulation. He had a
powerful protector in Michielsen, a prominent member of the
Council of the Netherlands Indies, who had been the Resident of
the East Coast when Hoetink was employed there as a Chinese

translator (1879–83). Together, they had put up a good fight during the coolie riots, it was said in a somewhat enigmatic explanation of the connection, by the Secretary-General of the Ministry of Colonies at The Hague (GSA, Vb., 14 March 1904, No. 8). The first Inspector of Labour also enjoyed a great deal of credit in entrepreneurial circles, where he had come to be known as a valuable defender of industrial interests. In China he had helped to arrange the recruitment of coolies, an assignment which he had carried out with diligence and dedication. The planters were so pleased with the way in which Hoetink had served them that in 1892 the DPV proposed that he should be appointed Consul General. He listened with cynicism to the complaints of the Asian coolies regarding their neglect and maltreatment, but gave their masters who, after all, were Europeans, more than the advantage of a doubt. In no single case did he recommend that employers be prosecuted, even when his own findings provided more than sufficient reason. His advice was usually that the management should be asked to make necessary improvements, or to urge that legal regulations be complied with. Hoetink was ever the level-headed civil servant who kept an eye on industrial interests. Healthy labour ethics required strict discipline, but he was not in favour of 'needless cruelty'. As far as he was concerned, the labour system might continue as long as it was shorn of the excesses that had developed over time. It was also reassuring that Hoetink had given a far more favourable report of the relations between the employer and the worker on the Sumatran plantations than Rhemrev was to do a short time later. The tone and tenor of Hoetink's inspection reports made it clear that he would be guided primarily by the interests of industry. When he drafted the Coolie Ordinance in 1904, he did so in close consultation with the planters (Com. Vol. DPV 1929:100). They retained their objections on a few important points, but no-one other than the first head of the Labour Inspectorate was prepared to listen to them so patiently and to accommodate them as much as possible. The planters' sources give the impression that the setting-up of the Labour Inspectorate was a black page in the history of the development of the East Coast. In other words, it illustrated the government's growing intervention in business life there. The only ray of hope was that the leadership of the inspectorate was entrusted to someone who was thoroughly familiar with the special character of the region and of the plantation

industry. The regional press was pleased with Hoetink's appointment and greeted him as a reasonable and sensible man (cf. the
Sumatra Post, 24 June 1904). The DPV's commemorative volume
makes no mention at all of the reason why the Labour Inspectorate
was installed, i.e. the accusations with which Van den Brand had
appealed to his Protestant supporters and the formal investigation
made by Rhemrev as a result of those incriminations. This suppres-
sion of information can be equated with the falsification of history.
Hoetink stayed in office for a surprisingly short time: in 1906, only
two years after his appointment, he returned permanently to the
Netherlands. It is questionable whether the Coolie Ordinance
would have remained intact without the protection of the planters'
interests that Hoetink had provided during the years when they
were most threatened. The planters could live with his constructive
criticisms, particularly since their implementation was shelved
indefinitely.

A far more interesting figure was Van den Brand, who driven by
his religious conscience, rebelled against the labour system which
prevailed on the East Coast. He admitted quite openly that when
he first went out, as the editor of the *Sumatra Post*, he shared the
common opinion of the European community there. Lefebre, his
opponent in the public debate held in Medan on 29 March 1902,
made it known on another occasion that only a few years earlier
Van den Brand had defended the planters, and habitually depicted
the coolies as the scum of the Chinese and Javanese peoples
(Lefebre 1903). What had caused his conversion? According to Van
den Brand, it happened in Malaya where he was employed for
some time by a mining enterprise which worked only with free
labour. When he explained the working of the Coolie Ordinance
and recommended it to a British government official as a model to
be copied, the other had said with horror: 'We don't want slavery
here' (*The Colonial Weekly*, 8 January 1903).

In his fight against the injustice that he had exposed, Van den
Brand appealed consistently to the Protestant political parties and
politicians in the Netherlands. In his initial publication, he quoted
Kuyper's statement in 'Our Programme' regarding the principles
of colonial policy: to provide justice to the native who is exposed
to social oppression. His position was in fact far more radical than
that of the Socialist, Van Kol, who, as has only recently become
known, was himself the owner of a coffee plantation in Java and in

his private capacity thus confronted rather than defended the Asian workers. It is thus not in the least surprising that, as a politician, Van Kol showed himself to be in favour of a gradual conversion of the labour regime. Van den Brand, on the other hand, wanted to do away with the Coolie Ordinance, even if it meant the ruin of the region (Mulier 1903:35). Due to his radicalism he came to be known as a Christian Anarchist, which was meant to be a disapprobation and not a compliment. Van den Brand was not interested in what he called the legal splitting of hairs: for example, the question of the exact difference between the Ordinance and the slavery system, and whether or not it contravened the Constitution. Neither would he allow himself to be drawn into a discussion over retaining the Ordinance if the workers were given more protection and there was greater control over compliance with its conditions.

... it is a matter of indifference to me whether planters or companies show a greater or lesser degree of philanthropy and show their workers better or worse treatment or care. The only thing that concerns me is that it is contrary to the honour of God; it is contrary to humanity. Truly, the lack of freedom cannot be recompensed with a nice hospital and a handful of money (Van den Brand 1904a:13).

The fact that Van den Brand derived so much inspiration from his religious belief was a source of embarrassment to politicians of the religious parties. Idenburg himself, as a Protestant MP, had only recently declared that egoism must not be a guideline and that colonial policy should be based on morality and should be diametrically opposed to any system of exploitation (Middelberg-Idenburg 1935:92). If it were really necessary, it was far easier to deal with the Socialist Opposition in the Parliament, adversaries who professed a God-less ideology, than to have to listen to the following exhortation by a member of his own faith. 'The honour of God and of the Netherlands demands that the government intervene immediately and forcefully to establish such law and order in Dèli as will be compatible with the foundations of a Christian state' (Van den Brand 1904a: 42).

Although he was unquestionably disappointed by the meagre effect of his protests, Van den Brand did not turn away from Christian politics. He went to the Netherlands in 1904, with the undoubted intention of continuing his fight against the system of bonded labour on the plantations. His attempt to do this in the political arena was a failure. As a member of the Anti-Revolutionary Party (ARP) he put himself up for election to the Lower House, but did not gain sufficient support. His opinions showed sufficient evidence of religious faith, but were nevertheless too leftist to find favour with the ARP leaders (*Java Bode*, 6 December 1921). There was nothing left to him but to return to the Netherlands Indies, where he again settled in Medan, not in the least intimidated by the opposition that he had experienced and was to continue to face in future years. The treatment meted out to him by the authorities was so hostile that in 1906, at his wit's end, he submitted a complaint to the Governor-General in person. The latter was advised by the Director of Justice that Van den Brand should be ordered out of the region, but it carried a note written down in the margin that unfortunately there were not sufficient grounds for doing so (GSA, Vb., 24 November 1906, No. 62). The secret investigation ordered by the Attorney General and the High Court of the Netherlands Indies in 1907, as a result of the complaint, cannot be qualified as anything other than a defamation of character (GSA, Vb., 26 August 1907, No. 71). To the exasperation of the officials and private individuals alike, Van den Brand's spirit could not be broken, notwithstanding all the insinuations that were made against him. He continued to be at odds with the authorities, and on his death in 1921 a newspaper report spoke of: '... his implacable guerrilla against the BB [Colonial Civil Service] with which, as solicitor and attorney, he was continually at loggerheads' (*De Locomotief*, 5 December 1921). Van den Brand certainly had difficulty in maintaining himself in the white society and, although he never tried to evade the long-lasting campaign that was carried out against him, he did become embittered. For all that, he also had his supporters, as was shown when he was elected to the municipal council of Medan in 1913, though that support was probably linked to the prominent role that he played in the religious life of the town. He continued to occupy himself with the labour problem, although he now used another line of approach. In his legal practice he took up the cause the European staff who had become involved in disputes with the managements of plantations, and with the regional administration. The popularity which he thus gained caused him to be chosen as the Chairman of the Assistant Managers

Trade Union in Deli in 1917, notwithstanding powerful opposition by the employers. In 1918 he went to Europe on sick leave, and after his return in 1920 he devoted himself fully to trade union work. He did this with much enthusiasm, without betraying the coolies' cause that he had earlier served. Their immediate bosses were the same assistants with whom Van den Brand had now associated himself, but in a series of articles published in 1918 in the *Vrijzinnig Weekblad* he made it quite clear that his opinion on the coolie problem was still the same as before. And even more than that. He argued that a workers' trade union ought to be set up as a necessary counter-weight to the power of capitalism and considered that the time had now come for such an organization (Van den Brand 1918:741). Many of those whose interests he defended would have fiercely disagreed with this point of view.

Van den Brand was in office for only a few months as Chairman of the Assistant Managers Trade Union. With the conscientiousness that was typical of him, he had advocated the formation of a fighting fund to provide a stronger basis for negotiations with the managements of plantation companies. The support he gained for this plan was not sufficient, a majority but not the required two-thirds of the members voted for it. He resigned immediately, considering that this result detracted from the reputation of the trade union within the Federation of European Employees in the Netherlands Indies, which in the meantime had chosen him as its leader. In that capacity, he became a member of the Popular Council (*Volksraad*) in May 1921, and this necessitated a move to Java. When he died six months later, a commemorative address made it clear that in pleading for the interests of employees, he had found fierce opposition until the very end of his life (De Banier 1921:578). However, he will always be remembered as the unpaid plaintiff in the coolie scandal of the East Coast: 'whose name for many years was seldom mentioned in Deli planters' circles without anger and hate' (De Taak 1921:822-3).

The reason why the coolie problem on Sumatra's East Coast became a scandal of such magnitude was not due only to the fact of the planters treating their workers so badly. The undeniable truth was that the authorities were also partly responsible for the situation. The affair is instructive for everyone who is interested in the question of how policy-makers behave when a scandal is disclosed. Denial, mixed with indignation, directed against those who set the ball rolling is a predictable reaction. The first action taken by the regional government after the publication of *The Millions from Deli* was to ask the Attorney General in Batavia whether it would be possible to prosecute the author (Van den Brand 1904a:11). This attitude was maintained for some length of time, fanned by reactions from the planters and the former government officials. Gradually, as denial in itself did not prove to have sufficient credibility, the tenor of the argument changed. Certainly, all sorts of abuses had occurred, but they were all in the past. In the last few years things had improved considerably and that development would continue. New incidents still came to light but they were regrettable exceptions, deviations by individuals, and were not representative of the system as such. In extenuation, emphasis was placed on the reverse side, i.e. the intractability of the coolies, and on the impossibility of measuring them according to western standards. Such arguments all had the same intention, i.e. to make it plain that outsiders could not and should not stand in judgement. As new facts increasingly came to light, however, it was no longer possible to dismiss the problem or to keep it out of the public eye. It was far more disturbing, in fact, that what Van den Brand and then Rhemrev had shown to be the nucleus of a coercive and arbitrary system, could have been covered-up for so long. In the last instance, the authorities could do nothing other than admit that a great deal was amiss. This acknowledgement was naturally followed immediately by the resolute statement that permanent steps would be taken to preclude the endurance of abuses. The gratuitous statement that the ultimate target was to introduce a system of free labour was all a part of this policy of camouflage. The embargo placed on the Rhemrev Report made it possible for those who opposed drastic revisions first to ignore its diagnoses and conclusions, and in the next instance to report on them incompletely or inaccurately, and finally to express doubt about the correctness of the material included in the Report and cast aspersions on the true intentions of the investigator. In 1905, when it had become clear that, for its own reasons, the government intended to maintain secrecy over the results of the investigation by Rhemrev, the Planters' Committee in Medan approached the Governor-General with the request that more data from the Report be published. This request was refused (Request Planters Committee, 27 January 1905, and Decision GG, 27 May 1905, coll. RTI). Broersma, who vainly asked in 1917 for sight of the Rhemrev Report, has suggested that its publication was prevented because of the dubious quality of the investigation. For the same reason, he thought it quite understandable that the government preferred to rely on Hoetink (Broersma 1919:274–7; 1922:183–7).

Perhaps the most tender point touched by Rhemrev was that his investigation revealed the close interplay between the government and the industry. It was commonly thought that this was necessary in the interests of the development of the country and the people. In 1899 Resident Kroesen had informed his subordinates that the European planters were entitled to a generous support by the Civil Service. If a coolie against whom a charge had been made was punished too lightly or not at all, the planter would be encouraged to take the law into his own hands. It was often difficult to submit proper legal evidence, but such formalities were not necessary for a police charge. If the judge was convinced, that was sufficient reason to move on to prosecution. This instruction was received with approval and brought to the attention of the wider public (A Memorandum 1899:845–8).

As the legal investigation of Sumatra's East Coast established, local authorities and planters were jointly responsible for a merciless labour regime which kept the coolies imprisoned under duress in a situation of arbitrariness and indigence. For the work that they had to do, arduous even by the standards of those days, they were not given a reasonable wage. The government's direct policy was to keep its distance publicly from the employers and thus to give the appearance of impartiality. In my opinion, this was even the most important function of Rhemrev's assignment. Even in the eyes of the workers, his original working method clearly illustrated the division between the government and the management, and confirmed that the former could call the latter to account. It was this aspect in particular which aroused so much bitterness among the planters. They could no longer act as a master on their own plantations, accountable to no-one. By intentionally undermining the authority of the planters, so ran their criticism, the government also ran the risk of disrupting the entire colonial system. The President of the Planters' Committee, who accompanied Rhemrev on his tours of inspection, put his worry into words with the following striking example.

On another plantation there was even a Javanese who made use of the opportunity to ask the Government Commissioner some questions, and, for example, pointed out that among members of the government there was a distinction between the Europeans and natives who, in his opinion, should be equal (Minutes DPV in Kooreman 1904–5:16).

Pronouncements such as this reflected the militant spirit that prevailed among the plantation workers.

Revision of the labour regulations was a part of the government effort to free itself of the stigma that it was only alive to the interests of the employers. To keep its distance, however, did not imply showing opposition to its former colleague by implementing a policy that was intended to improve the position of the underdog, even though that had been the initial reason for setting-up the Labour Inspectorate. From the beginning, emphasis was placed on countering any excesses while maintaining the existing system of labour relations, including the coercive conditions that accompanied it. The policy's point of departure, however, was and remained that abolition of the Coolie Ordinance with its penal sanctions would bring an end to plantation agriculture on the East Coast of Sumatra.

VII

RESTORATION

Appraisal of the Reforms

What became of all the promises that had been made? The increase in the police force caused the least of the problems, although strong pressure had to be brought to bear by the Minister of Colonies before the newly-appointed Governor-General J.B. van Heutsz went ahead in 1905. A report drawn up by H. Colijn, then Captain in the Military Police Corps stationed on Atjeh and later to become the Prime Minister of the Netherlands, was very significant in this respect. The increase amounted almost to a doubling of members, i.e. from 423 to 770 ranks and officers (GSA, Vb., 19 October 1905, No. 75). For a time, it was thought that the extra expense that this involved could be met from a levy that would be apportioned equally over all the plantations. Although the planters expressed their willingness to pay this, it was eventually decided to meet the expense from the public funds, probably in order not to make the relationship between government control and agri-business any more transparent than it already was. The colonial authorities argued that it would always be possible to cover the extra expense by slightly increasing the tax on export crops (GSA, Vb., 26 October 1904, No. 55). Once again, it was that troublesome solicitor Van den Brand who made it known that the plantation companies had provided labour for the building of new police stations (Van den Brand 1907:416).

It took a long time before a Council of Justice was finally set up in Medan. Although the trading houses established there had earlier urged the authorities to handle civil cases more quickly, they withdrew their request under pressure from the plantation companies. The threat that the latter would in future transfer their business to Penang and would also make all their purchases there, proved very effective. In this case, too, intervention by the Minister of Colonies was needed before the Council of Justice was at last instituted in 1908 (GSA, Vb., 14 February 1906, No. 23; 6 February 1907, No. 56). Certainly, a judge had earlier been stationed in Medan, empowered to prosecute all cases brought against the Europeans. However, the Minister's legal adviser had immediately remarked that this measure would be of little help in ensuring compliance with the labour regulations. As previously, the authorities refrained from intervening in industrial relations. The fixing of a minimum wage that would allow a coolie at least a subsistence living, something which the regional authorities had been urging for years, again remained in abeyance. Hoetink did not object to this lack of action, as he made clear in a statement made many years later (Memorandum from ex-Inspector of Labour B. Hoetink in Proceedings Lower House 1918–1919, Appendix 397.1:34). It was a viewpoint which exposed his partisan stand on the matter.

Finally, an improved Coolie Ordinance was in fact to take shape, and Hoetink's principal task in his new post was to see this through. The draft which he ultimately submitted, a version which was watered- down in accordance with the wishes of the planters, was published in the *Javasche Courant* on 27 September 1904, in order to make it widely known. The reactions to it were not very favourable. Ex-Resident Rookmaker declared that, out of the far more numerous clauses included in the new Ordinance, some did indeed offer better protection to the contract coolies, but that on the other hand, far stricter penalties had been attached to all manner of misdemeanours (Rookmaker 1904:809). In two subsequent re-written drafts, Hoetink tried to meet criticisms from various sides, but when it appeared that the government of the Netherlands Indies continued to hold considerable objections, his design was put aside. There was thus no chance of a speedy introduction of a new Ordinance, as the Minister of Colonies had promised the Parliament. In 1905, still under the aegis of Minister Idenburg, A.F. van Blommestein, Assize Judge (*Landraad*) in Batavia, started work on a new draft which was far more critical of the plantation regime than the previous ones. Van Blommestein was also responsible for the background study which had been urged by the Ministry officials at the Hague (cf. GSA, Vb., 27 December 1905, No. 65/3737a). The ultimate draft which was finalized in 1908, recommended that the penal sanctions be retained only for a part of the workforce and, for that reason, was found to be unacceptable by the planters. They remained adamant even after Van Blommestein had partly complied with their wishes. A new Coolie Ordinance was not put into effect until 1915, retaining the penal sanctions which Van Blommestein had called 'the whip'. The heavy pressure that had been brought to bear by a wide front of employers and officials had once again been success-ful. Cremer was among those who backed the interests of the planters by impressing upon Idenburg, who was now Governor-General of the Netherlands Indies, that penal clauses in the work contract were indispensable (Extract from Cremer's letter to Iden-burg, 29 March 1914, in: Various files on the Coolie Ordinances 1885–1915, coll. RTI). According to the report of the Parliamentary Commission which discussed the new Ordinance, the number of coolies on the East Coast plantations had risen to almost 200,000 by early 1917, doubling the number at the beginning of the century. Free workers, however, represented only 3.5 per cent of the total, even less than that in the earlier period (Proceedings Lower House 1918–19, Appendix 397.1:1–40). Forced labour was, and continued to be, the rule. Anticipating this outcome, Van Blommestein pub-lished a pamphlet in which he accused Idenburg of having sys-tematically taken the side of the planters and of refusing to realize the consequences of his oft-repeated statement that there had to be an end to bonded labour (Van Blommestein 1917). In effect, he charged Idenburg with hypocritical behaviour—an accusation that seemed to be well-grounded.

And what happened to the Labour Inspectorate? It was imme-diately deprived of its sting. The reassuring statement made when the Inspectorate was instituted, to the effect that the government had purposely desisted from describing task and powers with any exactitude, was significant. The course of action in daily practice was left to the Head of the Inspectorate, a man who was recognized to be a level-headed official and who had made it known that he would work in close co- operation with the Planters' Committee (Organisation of the Labour Inspectorate 1904:726). From the way in which the service started operating in 1905 it became immedi-ately clear that very little could be expected from it. Moreover, the prohibition on the publication of the first few annual reports, which did not appear until much later, prevented the outrages that still occurred from becoming widely known. The likelihood of an unfortunate publicity was extremely slight for yet another reason. The guidelines issued to the Inspectorate's officials were so innocuous that the employers had little to fear from their inspection tours of the plantations. No information was compiled without the actual knowledge and help of the planters. The method which Rhemrev had found to be so effective and successful, that of 'the pernicious spying system', was not to be used under any circumstance. The Inspectors were forced to make a forthcoming visit known at least a day in advance, and the management was in principle to be present during all interviews unless there were urgent reasons to the contrary. Under such circumstances, the coolies naturally showed very little willingness to speak out. Many years later, Van den Brand quoted a reliable spokesman as saying that the early retirement of Hoetink and his Assistant Inspectors was due to the lack of co-operation shown to them (Van den Brand 1918:688). When they departed in the summer of 1906, government protection of the plantation coolies seemed to have come to an end even before it had properly started. Early in 1917, a temporary instruction was hastily introduced to ensure the continuation of the Inspectorate. A government decree dated 6 June 1908 brought the definitive establishment of the Labour Inspectorate for the entire Netherlands Indies. As had previously been the case, its sphere of operations for the time being remained restricted almost exclusively to Sumatra's East Coast. It was not easy for the Inspectors to do their work in this hostile plantation milieu. More and more companies introduced the custom of holding some festivity if the workers refrained from submitting complaints to the Inspectorate. It was hardly surprising, therefore, that Hoetink remained ignorant of a case of coolie murder by an Assistant Manager on a Deli plantation, which occurred during the period when he was in charge of the Inspectorate (Van den Brand 1907:410). As in the old days, therefore, anything that could embarrass the employers was suppressed. Nevertheless, the planters continued to be inordinately annoyed by these official 'snoopers' (cf. a planter's anonymous review of the first report of the Labour Inspectorate [First Report 1912] and the reply published some time later by the Labour Inspector of the time [Stibbe 1913]). But they learned how to manipulate the new regulations and how to evade them when necessary. For this reason they registered no objection when, in 1908, the government replaced the temporary regulation of the

Labour Inspectorate by a permanent one (Gazette 400). During the preparatory work for the new Coolie Ordinance which came into force in 1915, the Planters Committee ascertained with satisfaction in a confidential memorandum that the planters' interests were not in danger. In the preceding years, after all, little had come of the proposed sharper control that was to be exercised over the management. Since 1907 there had been only nineteen cases of prosecution of planters who had been guilty of violating the Coolie Ordinance (Views of the Planters Committee regarding the new Coolie Ordinance 1914, in: Various files on the Coolie Ordinances 1885–1915, coll. RTI).

It is difficult to avoid the conclusion that the measures taken bore no relationship at all to the magnitude and seriousness of the coolie scandal on the East Coast. In other words, the authorities who were responsible for carrying out the colonial policy were extremely successful in neutralizing the effects of the scandal.

Looking Back

Those who supported the established order in the field of labour relations, were hard pressed by the public outcry when the coolie scandal became known. Advocates of the ethical trend in colonial policy then had more influence than was to be the case in later years. Looking back, we can see that more fundamental reform would have been possible in the atmosphere of indignation and shock that came about, if only more pressure had been brought to bear at the right political moment, particularly in the mother country. This was also the view of the most critical observer of the coolie problem several years later.

The coolie scandal disclosed by Van den Brand and Rhemrev had a very strong impact in the Parliament and it was the right psychological moment at which to do away with the penal sanctions. If Troelstra and Van Kol had tried to utilize this possibility, the battle to abolish the coercive contract would have been shortened by twenty years (Endt 1919:177).

Why did the parliamentary Opposition resign itself so easily to the preservation of bonded labour, and why was it apparently satisfied with little more than a ministerial promise to see to it that the coolies were given better legal protection? The answer is simply that the colonial policies of the Social Democrats differed

very little from that of the good bourgeois members of the Christian
or Liberal Parties. At the national and international social conferen-
ces, Van Kol's stand gave him the name of being a colonial reformer
who ascribed the European peoples with the historical task of
subjugating and educating those nations 'that were without
civilization'. Some years later, Van Kol also refused to have anything to do with the rising Indonesian nationalism, and in all
manner of important questions tended towards a position that
showed little sign of a sharp criticism. Idenburg, first as a Minister
and later as the Governor-General, was Van Kol's political kin
rather than his opponent (Tichelman 1967:709). The contrasts of
party politics were thus far less vociferous than what was apparent
from the Parliamentary debates.

But if the Opposition had shown a sharper judgement and a
more fighting spirit, would the political result have been any
different? The room for manoeuvre within which those who made
decisions had to operate was perhaps far less than it seemed to be
the case from the outside and was certainly less than it seems in
retrospect. The viewpoints of those who are inclined to base their
premises on the logic of the situation implies that policy-makers
are only able to bring about marginal changes. What they mean, in
fact, is that there was no alternative for the system of un-free
labour. How else would it have been possible to develop a thinly-
populated area on the colonial periphery? Without the large-scale
import of labour which was then bound to the place of employment, the land could never have been exploited. According to this
point of view, the initial growth of the agricultural plantations and
their subsequent consolidation and further expansion, would
never have been possible without the Coolie Ordinance with its
penal sanctions. I find this argument unconvincing, for various
reasons. In the first place, it assumes that a different organization
of production along capitalist lines was out of the question; quite
incorrectly, as we have seen. During the pioneering period it
seemed for a time that others besides European planters would
engage in the cultivation of export crops. These were the Chinese
traders, who had shown interest in the pepper cultivation even
before the arrival of the European pioneers. Several of them, following in the footsteps of the pioneers of western entrepreneurship, started to develop tobacco gardens, at least until the colonial
government put an end to it under pressure from the white

planters. The Chinese were simply denied access to any land and the same treatment was meted out to potential entrepreneurs among the local population who might have been interested in growing tobacco. A retrospective view of the motivations for the setting-up of the Deli Planters' Association, written by its Secretary early in the twentieth century, puts this self-interest into unvarnished terms.

The natives or alien orientals will become prosperous through their profits and will begin to employ other people. These will undoubtedly be coolies who have deserted the European plantations, perhaps enticed away by the native tobacco growers (Memorandum on the agreement entered into by members of the DPV, drawn up by Bool, approx. 1905–6, in coll. RTI).

Another mode of production, which was also market-oriented and which was soon nipped in the bud, was the transition towards indigenous peasant capitalism, for which pepper cultivation had given the first impulse. This alternative process of development was blocked in two ways. Directly, by issuing plantation companies with enormous tracts of land that were far greater than they needed for the crop each year, with the result that most agricultural land was permanently withdrawn from the peasant economy. And indirectly, by the arrangement, that organized western industry would only market tobacco that originated on the plantations which were under western management. The marginalization of the local inhabitants on their own land was thus coupled with forcing peasant agriculture back to food crop production, at the expense of native export crops which might have been competitive with European plantation agriculture (cf. Sinar 1978: 187–8).

An obvious objection to this line of thinking is that an alternative, more internally-based trajectory to societal development would have required the presence of a far greater number of people than were available in the region towards the end of the nineteenth century. This argument, which emphasizes the regional underdevelopment that resulted from a population density that was too low, is in itself quite correct. However, if the large-scale import of labour from distant places did not form an insurmountable obstacle, why should it not have been feasible to bring in peasants producing for the market from heavily-populated regions in Java? It is my belief that the strategy of capitalist development favouring large-scale enterprises such as the ones which emerged in Deli was not a fortuitous one, but was consciously promoted by the colonial administration. This government thus actively helped to safeguard the monopoly of European big industry by preventing other modes of exploitation of the natural resources.

The Coolie Ordinance and its penal sanctions met the employers' need for cheap labour. To this extent there was a direct link between extensive land use and the nature of the labour regime.

Without the penal sanction, the planters needed to obtain their labour force from among free immigrants. Not mere working machines, but colonists with their families would have had to be attracted to Deli, and this would have forced the planters to relinquish large areas to the immigrant population for growing rice. Extensive cultivation would then have to end. The same piece of land would have to be used more than once, which would necessitate the investment of much more capital and the use of modern methods of mechanization. Instead of an unskilled coolie, the worker would become a skilled labourer and low wages could not have been continued. On the other hand, it would not be possible to maintain a penal sanction for skilled labourers. Abolition of the penal sanction would therefore cause an economic revolution in tobacco growing, changing it from a primitive and backward to a more modern industry, but at the same time reducing the abnormally high profits (De Waard 1924:1039–40).

This quotation shows that the assumption of the plantation type of production, by a logic of its own prescribed the continuation of un-free labour, which also found acceptance in the literature critical of the foundation on which western agri-business was built. This seems to make the need for coercion even more plausible. Nevertheless, I am still sceptical. In the first place, there is the intriguing information that the management of Billiton Company—a large-scale mining enterprise on an island off Sumatra's East Coast—did not consider the penal sanction attached to the labour contract to be necessary; in its opinion, even without the Coolie Ordinance, sufficient coolies could be acquired for work in the tin-mines, a mode of primary extraction which was not so very different to the industrial organization of production on the plantations. This information is made even more interesting by the fact that, when the Coolie Ordinance was introduced, the Assistant Resident of Billiton had expressed himself in similar terms (Bool

1904:6). Secondly, and in connection with the above, the planters consciously and systematically opposed the transition to free labour, a trend which the planters at an early stage blocked with the active support of colonial officials. Why? Un-free labour precluded both higher wages and the free settlement or spontaneous mobility of the migrants. The nature of capitalist production on the plantations until the beginning of the twentieth century was such that the planters were not interested in having a permanent and stable workforce at their disposal. On the contrary, plantations were organized on the basis of circulating labour, i.e. a constant supply of fresh workers and the repatriation of those who were worn-out. 'The preference constantly expressed for *sinkheh* labour over that of experienced hands suggests that the planters encouraged a pattern of social and economic relationships which was actually inimical to the development of a stable labour force' (Reid 1970:320).

Such a regime necessitated a tightly formulated regulation which implied the unconditional subjugation of the contracted workers. The Coolie Ordinance with its penal sanctions met this need to perfection. By postponing its abolition, the government helped to perpetuate a mode of production that by the turn of the century was actually out-of-date. Interesting in this connection is the complaint of an industrialist who had vainly tried to introduce a different pattern of labour relations by contracting work out to groups of workers who had entered into a partnership for that purpose. In his experience, Chinese coolies liked to work on a contract basis and were accustomed to doing so in teamwork in their own country. However, the Coolie Ordinance prescribed that a contract had to be signed with each individual worker who must be directly put to work by the employer, and precluded any other working method.

The omission from the contract of clauses that hinder free labour is not permitted, even if both parties should wish it. This legal prohibition on free labour is the reason why free Chinese coolies from the Straits are unwilling to come to the Netherlands Indies to work, with the exception of Banka and Billiton where free labour is not forbidden (Letter to the Dutch Branch of the Netherlands Indies Society for Industry and Agriculture published in Rookmaker 1904:816).

The writer of this letter urged that the industries other than the tin-mines should also be exempted from irksome restrictions which in effect forbade the use of free labour. By far the greater majority of the employers, however, were not interested in the idea. They continued to maintain that there was no need at all for a prohibition since the coolies agreed of their own volition to come to the East Coast. This was a manifestly incorrect version of the state of affairs, as a representative of the main plantation corporation wrote from Hong Kong in 1905. He told his employers in Deli that recruitment was free only by name, and that the owners of the 'shops' where contract coolies were lodged until their transport was ready, employed men especially to submit to questioning if an official arrived on an inspection tour (Stecher 1905). Similar practices meant that in Java, too, both on the road and also in the coolie depots, there was little question of any free will.

Restoring the Alliance between the Planters and the Government

During the first decades of the twentieth century, great changes occurred in the nature of the labour system on the East Coast plantations. It seems natural to ascribe these changes to the exposure of the abuses that took place, first by Van den Brand and then confirmed by Rhemrev in his official report. I have earlier expressed my doubt about this interpretation, according to which politicians and bureaucrats exerted themselves to introduce reforms, under the pressure of perturbed public opinion. Actually, the transformation was based on forces which were entirely different. Moral or even a political revaluation of the relations between employers and employees in the light of the Deli coolie scandal did not inspire the reforms. The gradual transition from tobacco to other perennial crops, i.e. rubber and later sisal and oilpalm, resulted in a different use of the work force, a shift which coincided with the progressive replacement of the Chinese by the Javanese coolies. The planters now tended to give preference to permanent settlement of migrants on the plantation. Thus, the altered basis of the plantation industry gradually appeared to render the system of un-free labour superfluous.

... the main reasons for the stubborn resistance among the tobacco growers to the import of free labour, do not apply to perennial crops. This difference in interest can clearly be traced in the fight that has been going on for so many years to retain the penal sanction (De Waard 1924:1044).

Nevertheless, the coercive and penal conditions included in the Coolie Ordinance were to remain in force almost until the end of the colonial rule. Employers continued to wield the Ordinance as an instrument with which to control their workforce. The manner in which this occurred can be seen in Stoler's excellent recent study which is concerned particularly with the late-colonial and post-colonial period (Stoler 1985). In the course of the twentieth century the formal balance of rights and duties unmistakably moved in a direction that was more favourable for the workers, although atrocious excesses such as those described by Rhemrev continued to occur. One example is the terror to which coolies were subjected in the construction of the Sumatra Road between 1912 and 1914. According to one report, a stake with iron chains stood before the coolie barracks in the work camp, to which men were tied who, in the opinion of a white boss, did not work hard enough. That white supervisor was tried for manslaughter. During his trial it became clear that coolies were regularly flogged and that, as a result of this callous treatment and poor medical facilities, death rate was extremely high (Bruinink-Darlang 1986:104–10). These facts became known only a few years after the abuses on Sumatra's East Coast had been discussed so extensively but, surprisingly enough, no reference was made to them. Such an exceptionally short memory on the part of the colonial policy-makers seems suspect. However, abuses of this nature gradually became more rare and probably became known sooner. I consider this as an indication of the passing away of the primitive accumulation phase, in which the reproduction of labour was given a low priority. The colonial entrepreneurs slowly came to realize that labour, even that of the Asians, was a production factor with its own value, and that its destruction was irrational from the economic point of view. This did not alter the fact, however, that the plantation workers continued to be ruled with an iron hand and that, for the time being, little improvement if any at all was introduced into their miserable daily existence. How did the high-ranking colonial policy-makers account for their biased attitude? In his private correspondence, Idenburg continued to display unease about forced labour. True, his own actions as a minister had made its continuation possible. However, it was a necessary evil which, as far as he was concerned, should be brought to an end as quickly as possible (Idenburg to Kuyper, 18 January 1911, in Brouwer 1958:30–1). His appointment as the Governor-General of the Netherlands Indies (1909-1916) gave him the opportunity to make his opinions effective. In 1913 he resisted the introduction of the penal sanction in Java, which had been urged in entrepreneurial circles, and did not make himself popular by doing so. In a letter to Kuyper, however, Idenburg wrote that he gave more weight to the interests of the native population, an attitude in which he took pride.

... it needs far more strength and courage to resist for many months the daily pressure to do what would please 'capital' and would not be found distasteful by many government officials. But in doing so I should have acted against my own conscience ... (Ibid:31).

By statements such as this Idenburg managed to build up a reputation as an early proponent of the Ethical Policy, and that is how he has become known in colonial historiography. Koch's euphoric portrait of him is a good example (Koch 1960:11). In the meantime, however, he had been overtaken as a leading spokesman on colonial affairs for the Christian parties by Colijn, who took a much harsher line. Colijn considered that abolition of the penal sanction would be catastrophic for the planters and would also be detrimental to the public interest which benefited from the success of the plantations on the East Coast of Sumatra. He recommended that this system of labour coercion be introduced in order to open-up central and southern Sumatra to western capital and industry. It is interesting to note that, in the age of nascent nationalism, Colijn should have been the proponent of an influential school of thought in the Netherlands which advocated an expansionist policy in the Outer Provinces on capitalist lines. He had no trouble at all in reconciling his Christian conscience with the principle of coercion because, he told his party followers that the penal sanction had an educative effect. The mentality of the coolies, who were of low character and had criminal tendencies, made it essential for the coercive conditions to be maintained. As long as the supply of labour could not meet the demand, industrial stability and growth could only be guaranteed in this way (Proceedings Lower House, 15 October 1910:306–7). The link between offence and punishment should be retained in order to train a primitive people for civilization. Colijn made no secret of the fact that he considered the spirit of western enterprise to be the motor of colonial development, just as before him Kuyper had been convinced that the investment of European capital was a cultural-historical necessity. Less than ten years after Van den Brand had repudiated the Coolie Ordinance on moral grounds, Colijn warmly advocated it. This disparity in attitudes, both inspired by the same Christian doctrine—so pliable is religion—helps us to understand why the so-called Ethical Policy on labour relations left such few marks.

Early in the twentieth century the tide had again turned in favour of the planters, with the result that they showed less inclination to make any concessions. With the guaranteed support of the Christian parties, they had no reason to make any arrangements that would be better attuned to the interests of the workers.

Order and discipline continued to be maintained strictly on the plantations. As a Public Prosecutor stationed in Medan, ten years after Van den Brand's charge, observed nowhere in the archipelago were the coolies flogged so hard as in Deli (*De Indische Gids* 1912:803). The aggression which this induced among the workers discharged itself in an increasing number of attacks on European assistants: they had to pay the price for an industrial policy which had gradually restricted the competence of the Asian foremen. As a result, the white staff came to stand in the frontline, directly facing the violent explosions that were inherent in the onerous work regime. The resistance became increasingly collective by nature. More than one coolie was involved in sixteen of the forty-two attacks on European assistants that were registered in 1913 (Statistics of Attacks 1914:576–9). The employers accused the authorities of not acting with sufficient force: 'Formerly, a coolie was sometimes beaten to death by accident, now the planters are murdered with malicious aforethought' (*Sumatra Post*, 5 May 1913). The statement was not intended to draw a comparison between the two deeds, which could not possibly be reduced to the same denominator, but was intended to remind the western public that an improvement in the legal position of the Asian worker only encouraged him in his insolence. This line of thought showed no understanding of the fact that the Labour Inspectorate was set up to put an end to abuses. Rather, the suggestion is that its establishment had put an end to the natural superiority of the employers and had thrown social relations completely out of balance. Such voices were immediately heard. In 1904 the Resident of the East Coast requesting for extra police, tried to explain his position by saying that a spirit of rebellion existed among the plantation workers since the investigation by Rhemrev and the establishment of the Labour Inspectorate (GSA, Vb., 24 October 1904, No. 55). Remarks such as these were caused by a mentality that was very common in the planters' circles and which considered that any appeal by the coolies to a government agency, seeking the legal protection to which they had a right, was equivalent to insurgency. This was a point of view that employers did not give up, even in later years. It is exemplified by the strongly emotional description by planters of the Labour Inspectorate's visit to his plantation. The feelings of mortification that they experienced when *Asian* interpreters belonging to the Inspectorate questioned *their* coolies about the conditions on the plantation were colourfully described. To them, this control by the state signified an infringement of the patriarchal authority which had earlier characterized the relationship between the employers and the estate workers. The interference hindered the planters from maintaining a 'healthy' discipline, with the inevitable result of increasing the brutality of the workers, which degenerated into attacks on the white staff (Hanegraaff 1910).

When evaluating the work regime on the plantations at the beginning of this century, it is obviously impermissible to apply norms and standards that belong to another time and place. Even in the Netherlands, when all is said and done, the Labour Inspectorate had only been set up a few years earlier in 1890, after a Parliamentary inquiry had brought all sorts of abuses to light. Moreover, even the Dutch agency had little success at first due to the opposition of both the employers and the municipal authorities (Hoogenhuis 1981). Is it then reasonable to blame the Inspectorate on Sumatra's East Coast because it did not immediately achieve success? The answer can only be in the affirmative if substantial improvements appear not to have been made even after many years. The reaction which came about in the Netherlands due to growing resistance on the part of the working class which joined forces in its own organizations, was not feasible in the colony, where the government would not permit the interests of the Asian workers to be articulated through unions or political parties. As a result, the plantation coolies were at the mercy of the well-organized employers.

The collaboration between the employers and the government authorities, severed for a time in the public eye for political reasons, was soon restored behind the scenes. The prevailing opinion was that those relations had all too easily been distorted in favour of the unwilling and intractable coolies. It was forbidden to use physical violence, of course, but the authorities showed complete understanding for the planters who resorted to it in a moderate fashion.

... on the other hand, he [the manager] is sometimes faced with a tormenting and insolent Chinese who doesn't care whether he lives or not and who belongs to the scum of the Chinese society, and who at that moment can only be made to see reason by an unhesitating slap or blow. On the other hand he has to be mindful of the legal investigation with all its unpleasant consequences (Letter by Resident, Sumatra's East Coast, 17 October 1910, quoted in Bruinink-Darlang 1986:83).

The head of the regional government, for example, was entirely in favour of the employers' relentless insistence that the coolies who were guilty of violating the Coolie Ordinance should be punished more severely. The usual sentence of forced labour on public works was considered too mild when compared with the work regime to which the plantation coolies were accustomed. He suggested that the convicts should be made to do arduous work such as filling-in marshes, shifting earth, collecting gravel from the riverbed, breaking stones for road metal, all under rigid discipline and with a ban on talking for ten hours per day. In his opinion, demonstrable laziness should be punished with caning. The regional authorities whole-heartedly backed the planters' request to the Governor-General that the coolies who were sentenced to forced labour should be subjected to severe forms of hard labour. Ignoring the negative advice of some of his top officials, Idenburg agreed with this request, and the relevant instruction was declared applicable with priority for the plantation area of the East Coast. The highest authority in the colony showed himself to be so sensitive to the arguments brought to bear by the planters that he personally gave instructions that the convicts were to be given less or more inferior food (Ibid.:90). It is difficult to reconcile all this with the ethical image with which the Governor-General prided himself. When the flogging of prisoners who were condemned to forced labour was again considered for abolition in 1907, it was averted by strong official opposition. In one way or another almost all the heads of the regional government repeated the words of the Resident of Banka.

In view of the almost absolute lack of morality and sense of duty and of any feeling of responsibility or reciprocity on the part of the uncivilized individuals with whom we are concerned and among whom we are expected to maintain order and discipline without too much expense, it is necessary for the administrator to have a hard, strict and very tangible means of punishment at hand (quoted in Ibid.:126).

The earlier complaints by the officials connected with the Labour Inspectorate were also heard in later years. After Hoetink had left, the Inspectorate came under the direct control of the Civil Service, as had been the original intention. On occasion, the regional head of this department on the East Coast would return a report that he found to be too critical of the life on the plantations and insisted that it be replaced by one that was more mildly worded. The acting magistrates also fell back into the disgraceful habit that Van den Brand had censured at the beginning of the century. In fact, with the statement that the post of the judge had been exchanged for that of a henchman, he declared that his earlier accusations were still in force many years later (Van den Brand 1918:688–9). With approval, he quoted from a undisclosed memorandum written by Assistant Resident Tideman, in which the latter denounced the practice of setting industrial interests above social justice. In reply, the planters held a protest meeting at which they approved a motion to the effect that they no longer had confidence in the Assistant Resident (*Indische Gids* 1918, II:1005-6). In 1920, the director of a plantation hospital who drew attention to the malnutrition and maltreatment of the coolies who became this patients, obtained no response from the authorities. His reports were found to be so disagreeable that he was forced to resign from his post (Bruinink-Darlang 1986:99). It seems justified to conclude that the power structure in the region had not undergone any drastic change since the beginning of the century. Van den Brand, more than any other,

was of this opinion, as he made clear in a speech to the Popular
Council, a proto-Parliament, a few days before his death.

The conditions on the East Coast of Sumatra are terrible and it would not
be difficult to write another *Millions from Deli*. Again and again, new
discoveries show variations on the old scandals which will never disappear as long as the Coolie Ordinance is in force (Proceedings Popular
Council, 25 November 1921:156).

The evidence that abuses continued to occur has to be seen in
connection with the virulent racism with which the white top of
colonial society was imbued. Perhaps even more than previously,
feelings of hate and contempt for the dominated race were expressed in exceptionally violent fashion from the beginning of the
present century as the forerunners of the nationalist movement
championed a separate Indonesian identity, socially, culturally
and politically. However circumspectly this happened at first,
claims to their own values and the denial of white hegemony,
caused the greatest possible irritation among vested interests who
were accustomed to speak about 'the natives' in the most
derogatory terms. The proponents of the Ethical Policy, who at
least considered the possibility of education and who had given
themselves the task of bringing civilization to the indigenous
society, were found hardly less provocative in their ideas by the
majority of the Dutch expatriates. The climate of the times is well
illustrated by the discussion which took place at the end of 1910 in
a number of leading newspapers in the Netherlands Indies. The
issue was an article in *De Suikerbond* by J. Fabricius, well-known
author of popular plays, to the effect that the measures taken to
protect the plantation coolies had had a counterproductive effect
on industrial relations. The author argued that the 'Deli coolie
beasts' could not be made into human beings even with the help
of a well-defined set of regulations. People who stood so low on
the ladder of civilization only showed respect for the cudgel, and
there was no other way but to use this copiously by way of
punishment (*De Locomotief*, 10 November 1910). The article gave
rise to many reactions. The first, surprisingly enough, was of a
negative nature. An officer of the Civil Service in Java wrote to the
editor of the paper that he was shocked by the tone of the article.
He drew attention to the ill-treatment of the workers on sugar

plantations which occurred repeatedly in many districts of Java, but without resulting in any legal prosecution. He discussed the one case, with which he was familiar from his own experience, more extensively. It concerned the manager of a sugar plantation who was accustomed to hit a coolie, not only because of assumed or actual shortcomings in his work, but also when the Javanese in question did not show him sufficient respect as *tuan besar*. When the magistrate asked the planter whether he would also treat workers in Holland in such a fashion, he replied that there was a great difference between thrashing a white man and a Javanese. The accused was dismissed with a very small fine while, on the other hand, natives who were guilty of some violation or misdeed were customarily given a very heavy sentence. That in this case the planter was taken to court at all was due to the arrival of a new civil servant who had investigated the case on his own initiative. The Javanese workers interviewed by this official were extremely surprised. Until then, they had interpreted the absence of any official action as a sign that the ill-treatment of the natives was not a cognizable offence. The writer of the letter protested against such a state of affairs, and emphatically opposed the meting out of corporal punishment. Harsh treatment could only result in bitterness and racial hatred (Ibid.: 11 November 1910). His comment found little support. A number of counter-arguments were published to the effect that only the rattan cane could offer any success against the increasingly insolent coolies. These were not impressed by a few days in the cell with forced labour, imposed by the magistrate, according to a Deli planter. Misbehaviour ought to be corrected then and there. Instead of making a charge which would probably be difficult to substantiate, it was better to take the law into one's own hands and to beat the wretch to a jelly (Ibid.: 21 November 1910). The well-known colonial journalist Wijbrandts also took part in the debate. He spoke with contempt about 'Javanese lovers', by which he meant all those who spoke up on behalf of the 'so-called victims'. In his opinion, there was no possibility of any uniform standard of justice. To flog a Javanese and a white man were two entirely different things. He condemned everything that showed any trace of Ethical Policy and would have nothing to do with guidance towards self-government. The 'moral uplift' of the population, a target much valued by all those who believed that it was their work to bring civilization to the people,

was considered nonsensical by Wijbrandts. In his view, an educated native was untrustworthy,

becoming more dangerous and antipathetic as his schooling increased. He told his readers that the small minority of Europeans
could only maintain their position in the colony by acting with
impunity. 'If we want to stay here, then we must retain control. If
we want to be looked up to as Masters, then we have to behave as
Masters' (*Nieuws van den Dag in Nederlandsch-Indië*, 15 November
1910). Unqualified racism caused him to characterize the coolie in
Deli not as a workman but as a beast. In line with such opinions,
some people thought that the Labour Inspectors in the East Coast
should be replaced with plantation police, a corps that should be
led by ex-officers. Only then would it be possible to check the
attacks made regularly on European assistants, sometimes causing
the death of these innocent and hard-working young white men.
The cautiously worded reports, occasioned by a number of recent
attacks, to the effect that violent action against the coolies had
increased rather than decreased during the last few years and that
the coolies only tried to defend themselves against the inhuman
treatment to which they were subjected, made little impression.
This was also the reaction to the intervention of a Javanese Regent
who started his letter by admitting that the plantation coolies were
the scum of society, but who considered that this was no reason to
condemn all natives. He called for the gap between the white and
the brown races to be bridged, and expressed his gratitude to the
supporters of the Ethical Policy who helped to harmonize the
relations between the rulers and the ruled (*De Locomotief*, 24
November 1910). In the colonial climate of the time, such an
attitude which showed very little radicalism, i.e. the acceptance of
white leadership on the way to brown progress, was the most
extreme that could be published. When asked whether the native
population had at least the rudimentary capability to become
civilized, Wijbrandts gave what was essentially a negative reply.
In the western sense, there was no question of it. He retorted again
and again that the preservation of Dutch authority stood or fell
with the readiness to strike fear into the workforce. According to
Wijbrandts, the planter's cane which was used to teach discipline
to the recalcitrant coolie should not be equated with the agricultural tool which the inferior Asian worker raised as a weapon in

revolt against his white superior. To measure with two standards was vital for the continuation of European supremacy. How otherwise could one European stand his ground against a hundred coolies? (*Nieuws van den Dag in Nederlandsch-Indië*, 29 & 30 November, 1 December 1910). A number of letter writers who participated in the newspaper debate even managed to surpass the racist tone of this prominent journalist. One of them said that cowardice was the principal characteristic of the Javanese, and added for good measure, their unreliability, perfidy and relentless provocation (Ibid.: 9 January 1911). The indisputable nadir, however, was when the question was raised whether everything that stood upright had to be considered a human being. Certainly not the native population; and those who argued to the contrary were said to be lickspittles. No other word was suitable for those who took up the defence of these 'half-apes'. Was it not a fact that all the Sundanese women prostituted themselves for a few cents? (*De Locomotief*, 29 November 1910). To be sure, the author of that article was prosecuted for inciting racial hatred, but he got away with a mild fine of two-and-a-half guilders. The Indonesian who shortly afterwards championed the cause of equal justice for the natives and the whites alike, in an indigenous newspaper on the East Coast, was given a very different treatment. On the orders of the regional government, he was sentenced to a term in prison (Ibid.: 20 May 1911). Inequality was the foundation of colonial rule, and any protest against it uttered by the colonized peoples were stifled with an iron hand.

In reading government reports on colonial misdeeds, one is struck by the insensitivity of the people in authority. But what is even more striking is the way in which, embarrassing information was purified of all elements that did not fit into the prevailing opinion, as it went up the government ladder. Once the unwelcome message reached the top, facts which were still unpleasant were neutralized by a selective use of language, which muffled beyond recognition the reality on which they were based. Policy memoranda were tailored in such a way that unprejudiced readers found little if any reason for criticism. The actual state of affairs remained concealed behind descriptions and analyses that gave the impression of deviations from legal or administrative rules as being almost unknown. Wrongs that could not be denied were almost immediately corrected by a just government which kept a careful eye on things.

All this does not mean that the colonial *mise-en-scene* was never subjected to criticism. This was even heard within the government apparatus, although uttered by obstinate officials who risked a great deal by their refusal to keep in step with their superiors. Such deviating opinions by critical insiders gave rise to annoyance, interspersed with derision, or were simply ignored. The sifting, toning down and polishing of information during the route that it had to follow to get to the apex of the official hierarchy shows how the officials sitting behind their desks tolerated the enslavement and murder of coolies, let alone their 'normal' exploitation. It was only outsiders such as Van den Brand who took exception to standard practice and caused a shock effect. They disturbed the peace of the colonial authority and also made its effects obvious. That was startling for a time, but a start was soon made with repairing the damage and the authorized version of affairs again ruled supreme. Exactly the same happened with regard to the coolie scandal on Sumatra's East Coast. The way in which it ended shows that radical reforms were actually made. In my opinion this was due partly to the limited range of colonial critics. With sincere indignation, these troublesome outsiders and a few insiders decried the inhuman regime to which the plantation workers were subjected and denounced the government which condoned or even actively supported it. They pronounced severe judgement on planters and officials, but never exceeded permissible limits with their protests. Notwithstanding all else, the critics were more close-ly linked with their adversaries, who were also partners in the ongoing debate, than with those whom they defended. In their narratives the excesses are given a focal point and far less is said about their context: the miserable existence of the plantation proletariat; their drudgery and slavery; the hardship and bullying that was their daily lot; the loneliness which marked their life on the plantation, and the pitiless fight for survival in which workers competed with one another. Outsiders looked on from a safe distance, and what they saw all too often confirmed the many negative sayings that were in vogue about coolie inferiority. It was clear from the statements made by the socialist Van Kol, for in-stance, that he subscribed to some of the planters' prejudices with regard to Asian workers, even though he advised a different remedy. When he designed a colonial policy for the Social-Democratic Labour Party in 1901, one of the principles on which it was based was the altruistic education of 'the native' towards independence (Van Kol 1901:215). But, he asked himself on another occasion, does indeed every race have the capability to emancipate? (Tichelman 1967:699).

The critics were observers who had no profound knowledge of the issue at hand. With very few exceptions, such as Van den Brand who was able to penetrate more deeply, the world of the coolies was closed to them. Almost incidentally, the plantation doctor Tschudnowsky noted in his diary that the planters hated their workers: a comment which he illustrated with a number of striking examples. The opposite was certainly also true, but we are only able to guess at the feelings of hatred harboured by the coolies with regard to the planters. These have never been recorded, due to the lack of oral history under colonial rule.

It is characteristic of the social system in the Netherlands Indies that those who protested against the East Coast coolie scandal at the beginning of the twentieth century were themselves part of the colonial power complex, or at any rate not personally subjected to its rigidities. I have been unable to find any written reaction that originated among the victims: at that time not even a modest vanguard had been able to develop in any critical sense. This is all the more surprising because similar abuses on the tea estates of India had far earlier been denounced by Indians who operated from a basis of social reform movements which were the precursors of nationalism–and who had also written about their findings in the periodicals published in Bengali (Ganguli 1972). Although they did not belong to the working class, they put themselves forward as defenders of the coolies' rights and acted in the colonial society as pacemakers for public opinion which turned against the planters.

It was to be some considerable time before spokesmen emerged in the Netherlands Indies who could study the life and work of the coolies at close quarters and, more significantly, could identify themselves with their lot to any considerable degree. A few planters distinguished themselves by treating their workers rather more leniently. A director of the Senembah Company, C.W. Janssen, introduced a number of measures that ameliorated the miserable conditions in which the workers lived. An experiment with setting-up schools on some estates, for which the initiative had been taken by Hoetink, was a failure (Senembah Company

1889–1939:25–6; cf. Endt 1917–18:333–4). The Deli Planters Association would have nothing to do with it, but shortly after the First World War Janssen tried it once again, appointing Tan Malaka as one of the teachers. The picture that this revolutionary politician painted of the regime and the conditions of work to which the coolies were subjected in 1920 showed that the situation of the industrial proletariat on the East Coast had changed very little since the beginning of the century.

The class which toils from dawn to dusk; the class which earns a wage just sufficient to fill the belly and to cover its nakedness; the class which lives in a shed like goats in a stable; and is arbitrarily flogged or sworn at and damned to hell; the class which could at any time lose wife or daughter should the white boss lust after her .... that is the class of Indonesians known as contract coolies (Tan Malaka: *Dari penjara ke penjara*, quoted in Poeze 1976:76).

The colonial scandal of plantation labour continued.

GLOSSARY*

adat	: customary law
alang-alang	: tall, plumed grass
anak	: child, *anak* Deli = child born on plantation
anak djawi	: calf
andjing	: dog
atap	: dried leaves used for roof thatching
baba	: derogatory name for Chinese
baksheesh	: tip
bahu	: surface measure (0.7 ha)
boedjang	: bachelor
borongan	: wage payment according to contract
borong hari	: daily task
controleur (D)	: district officer, the lowest rank for Europeans in the colonial civil service
datuk	: native chief
didjemoer	: to dry in the sun
djaloeran	: surface measure (approx. 400 m2)
djankol	: agricultural tool
djoeal djiwa	: to sell one's soul
djoeal kapala	: to sell one's head
djoeroegan	: master
djiwa	: soul
doeit	:.small coin
dokter djawa	: native physician
gambir	: plant used as an ingredient for betelnut chewing
hari besar	: payday, half-holiday
hasil tanah	: land rent
kabaya	: blouse piece
kampong (s)	: locality, village

---

* Chinese or Dutch words are identified by (C) and (D) respectively. The other words are mostly of Malayan origin, i.e. the lingua franca of colonial Indonesia. The spelling reflects a mixture of various styles in colonial literature.

kebon	: estate, garden
kedei (C)	: plantation shop
kheh-thau (C)	: labour intermediary
kijai	: teacher of Islam
kloempang	: kind of tree, often used for the building of houses
koepang	: small coin
kongsi (C)	: gang.
kongsikang (C)	: field hand, unskilled labourer
krakal	: forced labour
krani	: native clerk
ladang	: cultivation on dry and newly cleared field
laukeh (C)	: old hand, trusted worker
mandur	: foreman, gang boss
mataglap	: coolie hunter
menoempang	: casual wage labour
moesimbringin	: 'fire letter' announcing shed burning
nibung	: leaves of palmtree
orang kontrakkan	: contract labourer
orangkaya	: local notables
orang prijman	: free labourer
pangeran	: native chief
perkara	: affair
pikul	: weight measure ($\pm$ 61.75-62.5 kg.)
pondok	: barrack
ringgit	: coin of two-and-a-half Dutch guilders
sarong	: female dress
seperti	: like
shanghai	: (verb) press-ganging
singkeh (C)	: newcomer from China
sinjo (D)	: derogatory name for Eurasians
sjahbandar	: harbour agent in charge of trade
tandil (C)	: foreman, gang-boss
tanggung	: contract based on labour replacement
tengku	: native chief
thai koeng (C)	: foreman, gang-boss
toetoep	: to cover up (liter. lid)
topi	: hat
tuan besar	: liter. big man; owner or manager of plantation

tuan maskapai   : representative of a plantation corporation in charge of various estates

wajang   : Javanese puppet play

BIBLIOGRAPHY

Most of the published material, particularly the books and articles to which I have referred in my study, can be found in the libraries of the Royal Tropical Institute (Koninklijk Instituut voor de Tropen) in Amsterdam or the Royal Institute of Linguistics and Anthropology (Koninklijk Instituut voor Taal-, Land-, en Volkenkunde) in Leiden. The official colonial archives are kept in the General State Archive (Algemeen Rijksarchief) in The Hague. The Central Library of the Royal Tropical Institute also stores the books, pamphlets and other documents which formerly made up the collection of Sumatra's East Coast Institute (Oostkust van Sumatra Instituut). It is interesting to note that I found another copy of the Rhemrev Report, together with many other highly confidential documents, including original memoranda and letters written by the Labour Inspectorate, in the collection of this Institute, which was set up and financed by the plantation corporations operating in the region.

I   PUBLISHED SOURCES: GENERAL
ANONYMOUS
Circular
1899   'Een circulaire van resident Kroesen' (A Circular of
           Resident Croesen'), *De Indische Gids*, 21:845-8.
Commemorative Volume
1941   *Gedenkschrift aangeboden aan den heer Herbert Cremer,*
           directeur N.V. Deli-Maatschappij (Commemorative
           Volume Presented to Mr Herbert Cremer, Director of
           the Deli Company). Amsterdam.
Contribution
1889   'Bijdrage tot de geschiedenis der Sumatra-tabak
           gedurende het tijdvak 1883-1889' (Contribution to the
           History of Sumatra- Tobacco during the Period
           1883-9), *De Indische Mercuur*, 12:24, 26 and 31.
Coolie Emigration
1885   'De Indische Koelie-emigratie in de
           Nederlandsch-Indische pers' (The Indian Coolie
           Emigration in the Netherlands Indies Press), *Tijdschrift*
           voor Nederlandsch-Indië 14-II (n.s.):205-13.

Coolie-Maltreatment
1902   'Koelie mishandeling' (Coolie Maltreatment), *De
            Indische Gids*, 24:1090-1.
Coolie Ordinance
1904   'Een woord over het stelsel der koelie-ordonnantie in
            Deli' (A Word on the System of Coolie Ordinance in
            Deli), *De Indische Gids*, 26:1553-5.
1907   'Een nieuwe koelie-ordonnantie noodig' (A New
            Coolie Ordinance Required), *De Indische Gids*,
            29:1590-4.
Coolie Recruitment
1896   'Koeliewerving op Java voor Nieuw-Caledonië'
            (Coolie Recruitment on Java for New Caledonia),
            Tijdschrift voor het Binnenlandsch Bestuur, 19:295-6.
Deli
1894   'Deli en Java' (Deli and Java), *De Indische Mercuur*,
            17:527.
1903   'De millioenen van Deli' (The Millions from Deli), *De
            Indische Gids*, 25:108-12.
1903   'De positie van Deli' (The position of Deli), *De Indische
            Mercuur*, 12:379-82.
1905   'Delische toestanden' (Conditions in Deli), *De Indische
            Gids*, 27:97-8.
Employers and Workmen
1879   'Werkgevers en werknemers in Britsch-Indië'
            (Employers and Workmen in British India), *De Indische
            Gids*, 1-I:515-16.
Final Report
1921   *Eind-verslag van den voorzitter van de commissie tot het
            houden van een onderzoek naar de arbeidstoestanden op
            Java en Madoera en tot het uitbrengen van een verslag aan
            de regeering vergezeld van de noodige voorstellen* (Final
            Report of the Chairman of the Committee
            Investigating the Labour Conditions on Java and
            Madoera together with Proposals Submitted to the
            Government). Weltevreden.
In Memory
1921a   'In memoriam Johannes Van den Brand' (In Memory
            of Johannes Van den Brand), *De Banier*, Christelijk
            Weekblad voor Nederlandsch- Indië, 13:577-8.

1921b 'In memoriam Mr J. Van den Brand' (In Memory of
Mr J. Van den Brand), *De Taak*, 5:822-3.

Labour Inspection
1904 'Arbeidsinspectie op Sumatra's Oostkust' (Labour
Inspection on Sumatra's East Coast), *Weekblad voor
Indië*, 1:713-16.
1904 'De organisatie der arbeidsinspectie op Sumatra's
Oostkust' (The Organization of the Labour
Inspectorate on Sumatra's East Coast), *De Indische
Mercuur* 27:726.
1905 'Arbeidsenquete, arbeidsinspectie en sociale
wetgeving' (Labour Inquiry, Labour Inspectorate and
Social Legislation), *Tijdschrift voor het Binnenlandsch
Bestuur*, 28:85-91.
1912 'Eerste verslag van den Dienst der Arbeids-Inspectie
en Koelie- werving door een planter' (First Report on
the Labour Inspectorate and the Agency for Coolie
Recruitment by a Planter), *De Indische Gids*, 34:1470-7.

Labour Legislation
1918 'Arbeidswetgeving' (Labour Legislation), *De Indische
Gids*, 40:1005-6.

Labour Question
1887 'Het arbeiders-vraagstuk meer bijzonder met het oog
op de Deli- ondernemingen' (The Labour Question
with particular reference to the Deli Estates), *Tijdschrift
voor Nederlandsch-Indië*, 16-II (n.s.):459-73.

Minutes Federation European Employees
1921 'Notulen van de 2de jaarvergadering der Federatie
gehouden te Soerabaia op 13 en 14 september 1921'
(Minutes of the 2nd. Annual Meeting of the
Federation held in Soerabaia on 13 and 14 September
1921), *De Federatie; Maandblad van de Federatie van
Europeesche Werknemers in Nederlandsch-Indië*,
2:1-2,9-10.

Obstacles to Emigration
1887 'Belemmering der emigratie van Javanen naar Deli'
(Obstacles to the Emigration of Javanese to Deli),
Tijdschrift voor Nederlandsch-Indië, 16-II (n.s.):289-91.

Portrait Cremer
1903   'Karakterschets J.T. Cremer' (Portrait of J.T. Cremer),
              The Hollandsche Revue, 8:555-67.

Relationship Assistant and Coolie
1912   'De verstandhouding van assistent en koelie in Deli'
              (The Relationship Between Assistant and Coolie in
              Deli), *De Indische Gids*, 34:803-4.

Review
1887   'Overzicht betreffende de particuliere
              landbouwondememingen in de rijken Deli, Langkat
              en Serdang (residentie Oostkust van Sumatra) over
              1885' (Review concerning the private agricultural
              estates in the states of Deli, Langkat and Serdang
              (Residency East Coast of Sumatra) in 1885), *De Indsche
              Mercuur* 11:145-6.

Statistics
1914   'Een statistiek van de aanvallen op assistenten ter
              Oostkust van Sumatra' (Statistics of Attacks on
              Assistants at the East Coast of Sumatra), *De Indische
              Gids*, 36:576-9.

Tobacco Cultivation
1883   'Nota omtrent den toestand van den tabaksbouw in
              Deli; de vooruitzigten daarvan en wat verder daartoe
              betrekking heeft' (Memorandum on the Condition of
              Tobacco Cultivation in Deli; Prospects and Further
              Observations Concerning This), *Tijdschrift voor
              Nijverheid en Landbouw in Nederlandsch-Indië*,
              27:193-210.

1887   'Tabakskultur in Sumatra' (Tobacco Cultivation in
              Sumatra), *Deutsche Kolonialzeitung*, 4:206-08.

1888   'De vestiging der tabakskcultuur op Deli' (The
              Introduction of Tobacco Cultivation in Deli), *De
              Indische Mercuur*, 11:223-5.

1900   'Die Tabakkultur in Sumatra' (The Tobacco Crop in
              Sumatra), *Globus*, 77:254-7.

ALLEN, G.C. & A.G. DONNITHORNE
1957   *Western Enterprise in Indonesia and Malaya: A Study in
              Economic Development*, New York.

BALBIAN VERSTER, J.F.L. de (ed.)
1919   *Deli-Maatschappij; Gedenkschrift bij gelegenheid van het vijftigjarig bestaan* (The Deli Company; Commemoration of its Fiftieth Anniversary), Amsterdam.

BALCKE, W.
1899   *Beschouwingen over de toekomst van Deli* (Thoughts on the Future of Deli), Amsterdam.

BARTELDS, H.G.
1894   'Een koelie-ordonnantie voor Java; Een advies van een belangstellende' (A Coolie Ordinance for Java; Advice from an Interested Person); reprinted from the *Soerabaiasch Handelsblad*, October 1894, Surabaya.

BLANKENSTEIN, M. van
1929   *De poenale sanctie in de practijk* (The Penal Sanction in Practice), Rotterdam.

BLINK, H.
1926   *Opkomst en ontwikkeling van Sumatra als economisch-geographisch gebied* (The Emergence and Development of Sumatra as an Economic- Geographic Region), The Hague.

BLOMMESTEIN, F. van
1917   *De nieuwe koelie-ordonnantie voor de Oostkust van Sumatra* (The New Coolie Ordinance for the East Coast of Sumatra), Amsterdam.

BOEKE, J.H.
1953   *Economics and Economic Policy of Dual Societies as Exemplified by Indonesia*, Haarlem.
1955   Economie van Indonesië (The Economy of Indonesia); 5th. revised edition, 1st. printing 1940, Haarlem.

BOOL, H.J.
1903a   *De Chineesche immigratie naar Deli* (Chinese Immigration to Deli), Utrecht.
1903b   *De landbouwconcessies in de residentie Oostkust van Sumatra* (Land Grants in the East Coast of Sumatra Residency), Utrecht.
1904   *De arbeidswetgeving in de residentie Oostkust van Sumatra* (Labour Legislation in the East Coast of Sumatra Residency), Utrecht.

BOSCH, K.H.

1948   *De Nederlandse beleggingen in de Verenigde Staten* (Dutch Investments in the USA; Doctoral thesis, Economic University of Rotterdam), Amsterdam, Brussels.

BRAND, J. Van den

1902   *De millioenen uit Deli* (The Millions from Deli), Amsterdam/Pretoria.

1903   *Slavenordonnantie en koelieordonnantie gevolgd door een ontwerp- arbeidswet* (Slave Ordinance and Coolie Ordinance followed by a Draft Labour Law), Amsterdam/Pretoria.

1904a   *Nog eens: De millioenen uit Deli* (Once Again: The Millions from Deli); 2nd. printing (1st. printing 1903), Amsterdam, Pretoria.

1904b   *De practijk der koelie-ordonnantie* (The Coolie Ordinance in Practice), Amsterdam, Pretoria.

1907   'De arbeidsinspectie in de Residentie Oostkust van Sumatra' (The Labour Inspectorate in the East Coast of Sumatra Residency), *Ons Tijdschrift*, 12:408-18.

1918   'Arbeidswetgeving' (Labour Legislation), *Vrijzinnig Weekblad*, I:590-2, 624-5, 670-2, 687-9, 740-2.

1921a   'Een weerstandskas' (A Strike Fund), *De Planter*, 13:3442-4, 3462-4.

1921b   'De weerstandskas verworpen!' (Rejection of the Strike Fund!), *De Planter*, 13:3554-6.

BREMAN, J.

1983   *Control of Land and Labour in Colonial Java: A Case Study of Agrarian Crisis and Reform in the Region of Cirebon During the First Decades of the 20th Century*, Royal Institute of Linguistics and Anthropology, No. 101, Dordrecht.

1985   *Arbeidscirculatie en rurale transformatie in koloniaal Azië (Labour Circulation and Rural Transformation in Colonial Asia)*, CASP Working Paper, Rotterdam.

1988   'Het beest aan banden? De kolonial geest aan het begin van de twintigste eeuw' (Taming the Wild Beast; The Colonial Mind at the Beginning of the 20th. Century), *Bijdragen tot de Taal-, Land- en Volkenkunde*, 144:19-43.

BROERSMA, R.
1919   Oostkust van Sumatra; I. De ontluiking van Deli (The
             East Coast of Sumatra; I. The Opening-up of Deli),
             Batavia.
1922   *Oostkust van Sumatra; II. De ontwikkeling van het gewest*
             (The East Coast of Sumatra; II. The Development of
             the Region), Deventer.

BROOSHOOFT, P.
1901   De ethische koers in de koloniale politiek (The Ethical
             Course in Colonial Policy), Amsterdam.

BROUWER, B.J.
1958   De houding van Idenburg en Colijn tegenover de
             Indonesische beweging (The Attitude Taken by
             Idenburg and Colijn Towards the Indonesian
             Movement), Doctoral Thesis, Free University of
             Amsterdam, Kampen.

BRUIN, A.G. de
1918˙   *De Chineezen ter Oostkust van Sumatra* (The Chinese on
             the East Coast of Sumatra), East Coast of Sumatra
             Institute, Communication No. 1, Amsterdam.

BRUININK-DARLANG, A.M.C.
1986   *Het penitentiair stelsel in Nederlands-Indië van 1905 tot
             1940* (The Penitentiary System in the Netherlands
             Indies from 1905 to 1940), Doctoral Thesis, University
             of Utrecht, Alblasserdam.

BURG, C.L. van der
1898   'Bespreking van "Dr P. Adriani, Medische
             herinneringen aan Deli en Langkat (Oost-Sumatra)" in
             het Nederl. Militair Geneeskundig Archief 1898, 22ste
             jaargang, blz. 205' (Discussion of Dr P. Adriani:
             Medical Reminiscences of Deli and Langkat [East
             Sumatra], in the Netherlands Military Medical
             Archives 1898, Vol.22, p.205), *Tijdschrift van het
             Koninklijk Nederlandsch Aardrijkskundig Genootschap*, 15
             (2nd. series):740-3.

BIJLERT, A. van
1913   'Tabak' (Tobacco) in: K.W. van Gorkom, *Oost-Indische
             cultures* (East Indian Cultures), re-published under the
             editorship of H.C. Prinsen Geerligs, Part II:503-627,
             Amsterdam.

CATS Van de RAET, J.A.M. Van
1876   'Vergelijking van den vroegeren toestand van Deli,
           Serdang en Langkat met den tegenwoordigen;
           Reisverslag van Februarij 1867' (A Comparison of the
           Former Condition of Deli, Serdang and Langkat with
           the Present Time; Report on a Journey made in
           February 1867), *Tijdschrift voor Indische Taal-, Land- en
           Volkenkunde*, 23:20-39.

CENSUS 1930
1936   *Census 1930.* Part VIII. *A Survey of the Netherlands
           Indies*, Batavia (in Dutch).

CHANDRA, B.
1966   *The Rise and Growth of Economic Nationalism in India;
           Economic Policies of Indian National Leadership,
           1880-1905*, New Delhi.

CHARITE, J (ed.)
1979   *Biografisch woordenboek van Nederland* (Biographical
           Dictionary of the Netherlands), Vol. I. The Hague.

CH'EN, J. & N. TARLING (eds.)
1970   *Studies in the Social History of China and South-East Asia.*
           Essays in Memory of Victor Purcell 26 January 1896-2
           January 1965, Cambridge.

CLERKX, L.
1961   *Mensen in Deli; Een maatschappijbeeld uit de belletrie*
           (People in Deli; A Portrait of Society Obtained from
           Belles-Lettres), Sociological-Historical Centre for
           Southeast Asia, Publication No. 2.

COLIJN, P.A.
1922   *De beteekenis van de poenale sanctie voor de ontwikkeling
           der buitengewesten van Nederlandsch-Indië (The
           Significance of the Penal Sanction for the Development of
           the Outer Provinces of the Netherlands Indies)*, Utrecht.

COLLET, J.A.
1903   *Le tabac; Sa culture et son exploitation dans les régions
           quatoriales* (Tobacco; Its Cultivation and Industry in
           the Equatorial Regions), Brussels.

COUPERUS, L.
1924   *Oostwaarts* (Eastwards), The Hague.

CREMER, J.T.
1876   *Een woord uit Deli tot de Tweede Kamer der*

Staten-Generaal; Art.2 No. 27 van het politie-reglement voor inlanders, met het oog op werkovereenkomsten met vreemde oosterlingen (A Word from Deli to the Lower House of the General Assembly; Art.2, No. 27 of the Police Regulations for Natives, with Respect to Labour Contracts with Alien Orientals), Amsterdam.

1881   *De toekomst van Deli; Eenige opmerkingen* (The Future of Deli; Some Comments), Leiden.

1882   *The Deli Coolie Question,* Singapore.

1885   'Emigratie van Hindu's naar Sumatra's Oostkust' (The Emigration of Hindus to Sumatra's East Coast), *Tijdschrift voor Nederlandsch- Indië* 14-1:301-11.

1888-90   'Delische schetsen' (Sketches from Deli); *Eigen Haard,* 14:534-7, 558-60; 15:56-61, 261-6; 16:564-8, 587-9, 675-80.

DAVIS, A.R. & A.D. STEFANOWSKA (eds.)

1982   Austrina: Essays in Commemoration of the 15th. Anniversary of the Founding of the Oriental Society of Australia.

DELI COMPANY

1894   *Verslag over het vijf-en-twintigjarig tijdvak 1869-1894, uitgebracht in de Buitengewone Algemeene Vergadering der Deli- Maatschappij op 1 November 1894* (Report on the 25-years 1869-1894, Made to the Extraordinary General Meeting of the Deli Company on 1 November 1894).

DINGEMANS, A.J.E.

1921   'In Memoriam Mr J. Van den Brand' (In Memory of Mr. J. Van den Brand) *De Planter,* 13:3822-4.

DIXON, C.J.

1913   *De assistent in Deli; Practische opmerkingen met betrekkingen tot den omgang met koelies* (The Assistant in Deli; Some Practical Remarks Regarding Dealings with Coolies), Amsterdam.

DONGEN, F. van

1966   *Tussen neutraliteit en imperialisme; De Nederlandsch-Chinese betrekkingen van 1863 tot 1901* (Between Neutrality and Imperialism; Netherlands-Chinese Relations Between 1863 and 1901), Doctoral Thesis, University of Groningen, Groningen.

DOOTJES, F.J.J.
1938-39   'The Land of Agricultural Enterprises', *Bulletin of the Colonial Institute of Amsterdam*, 2-I:45-55; 2-II:122-30.

DIJKSTRA, J.F.
1906   *De corruptie in de Nederlandsch-Indische ambtenaarswereld, of: Mr Rhemrev als regeerings-commissaris* (Corruption Amongst Officials of the Netherlands Indies, or: Mr Rhemrev as Government Commissioner), Rotterdam.

ENCYCLOPAEDIE
1918   'Koelie, koeliecontract, koelie ordonnanties', Encyclopaedia van Nederlandsch-Indië (Coolie, Coolie Contract, Coolie Ordinances, Encyclopaedia of the Netherlands Indies), 2nd. ed., II, pp. 360-6, The Hague/Leiden.

ENDT, P.
1917-18   'Vrije arbeid in Nederlandsch-Indië' (Free Labour in the Netherlands Indies), *Koloniale Studiën*, 2:317-39.
1919   *Wanderarbeiterverhältnisse in den farbigen Kolonien (Mit besonderer Berccksichtigung von der Ostküste von Sumatra, Niederl.-Indien)* (Migratory Labour in the Coloured Colonies; With Special Reference to the East Coast of Sumatra, Netherlands Indies), Amsterdam.

ENTHOVEN, E. (ed.)
1929   *N.V. Deli-Maatschappij; Gedenkschrift bij gelegenheid van het zestigjarig bestaan, aansluitende bij het gedenkboek van 1 November 1919* (The Deli Company; A Memoir on the Occasion of its 60th. Anniversary, Further to the Commemorative Volume dated 1 November 1919), Amsterdam.

FABEL, J.
1909   'Werkwijze en arbeidsloonen op de ondernemingen van Sumatra's Oostkust' (Working Methods and Wages on the Plantations of Sumatra's East Coast), *Tijdschrift voor Nijverheid en Landbouw in Nederlandsch-Indië*, 78:207-11.

FASSEUR, C.
1979   'J.T. Cremer', in: Charité **(ed.),** *Biografisch woordenboek van Nederland* (Biographic Dictionary of the Netherlands), pp. 122-5, The Hague.

GANGULI, D.
1972   *Slavery in British Dominion*, revised with introduction
            by K.L. Chattopadhyay, Calcutta.

GORKOM, K.W. van
1888   'De vestiging van tabakscultures op Deli' (The
            Introduction of Tobacco Cultivation in Deli), *De
            Indische Mercuur*, 11:238-9.

GRAMBERG, J.S.G.
1881   'De Oostkust van Sumatra' (The East Coast of
            Sumatra), *De Indische Gids*, 3-1:356-72, 586-93, 788-95,
            1036-46.
1882   'Geographische aanteekeningen betreffende de
            residentie Sumatra's Oostkust' (Geographical Notes
            on the East Coast of Sumatra Residency), *Tijdschrift
            van het Aardrijkskundig Genootschap*, 6:100-13.

GUHA, A.
1977   *Planter-Raj to Swaraj; Freedom Struggle and Electoral
            Politics in Assam 1826-1947*, New Delhi.

GUYOT, G.
1910   *Le problèe de la main-d'oeuvre dans les colonies
            d'exploitation; La cte est de Sumatra* (The Problem of the
            Workforce in the Colonies of Exploitation; The East
            Coast of Sumatra), Paris, Amsterdam.

HAARSMA, G.E.
1889   *De tabakscultuur in Deli* (Tobacco Cultivation in Deli),
            Amsterdam.

HALEWIJN, E.A.
1876   'Geographische en ethnographische gegevens
            betreffende het rijk van Deli (Oostkust van Sumatra)'
            (Geographical and Ethnographical Data on the State
            of Deli [East Coast of Sumatra]), *Tijdschrift voor
            Indische Taal-, Land- en Volkenkunde*, 23:147-58.

HALL, C. van & C. van den KOPPEL (eds.)
1946   *De landbouw in den Indische archipel* (Agriculture in the
            Indian Archipelago), 3 Vols., The Hague.

HAMEL, G.A. van
1881   'De strafbepaling tegen het verbreken van
            werkcontracten' (Penal Provisions against the
            Violation of Labour Contracts), *De Indische Gids*,
            3-II:529-49.

1892   'De ordonnantiën tot regeling van de
            rechtsverhouding tusschen werkgevers en werklieden
            in sommige gewesten van Nederlandsch- Indiën hare
            toepasselijk-verklaring voor Java' (The Decrees that
            Regulate Legal Relations between Employers and
            Workers in Some Regions of the Netherlands Indies
            and their Applicability to Java), *Verslagen der the
            Algemeene Vergaderingen van het Indisch Genootschap:*
            55-94.

HANEGRAAFF, A.

1910   *Hoe het thans staat met den assistent en de veiligheid aan de
            Oostkust van Sumatra* (The Present Situation regarding
            the Assistant and Security on the East Coast of
            Sumatra), The Hague.

HEEKEREN, E.A.A. van

1914   'Het derde verslag van den Dienst der
            Arbeidsinspectie en Koeliewerving in
            Nederlandsch-Indië' (The Third Report of the Labour
            Inspectorate and the Agency for Coolie Recruitment in
            the Netherlands Indies), *De Indische Gids*, 36:978-85.

HEIJTING, H.G.

1925   *De koelie-wetgeving voor de buitengewesten van Neder
            landsch-Indi* (Coolie Legislation for the Outer
            Provinces of the Netherlands Indies), The Hague.

HISSINK, D.J.

1904   'Een en ander over Deli' (Some Information on Deli),
            De Indische Mercuur, 28:807-10.

HOETINK, H.R.

1903   'De brochure van Mr Van den Brand over Deli' (Mr
            Van den Brand's Pamphlet on Deli), *De Indische Gids*,
            25:46-7.

HOGENHUIS, O.W.

1981   *Inventaris van het archief van de Centrale Dienst der
            Arbeidsinspectie, Algemeen Rijksarchief* (Inventory of the
            Central Labour Inspectorate's Files, General State
            Archives), The Hague.

HOYNCK van PAPENDRECHT, A. (ed.)

1927   *Gedenkschrift van de Tabak Maatschappij Arendsburg ter
            gelegenheid van haar vijftigjarig bestaan, 1877-1927*
            (Commemorative Volume of the Arendsburg Tobacco

Company on the Occasion of its 50th. Anniversary, 1877-1927), Rotterdam.

INDONESIAN ECONOMICS
1966   *Indonesian Economics: The Concept of Dualism in Theory and Policy*, The Hague.

IONGH, R.C. de
1982   'The Guardians of Lands—Sultans, Planters, Farmers and Tobacco Land in East Sumatra', in: Davis & Stefanowska, pp. 540-56.

JANSSEN, C.W. & H.J. BOOL (eds.)
1939   Senembah Maatschappij 1889-1939 (Senembah Company 1889-1939), Amsterdam.

KIELSTRA, J.C.
1914   'Derde verslag van den Dienst der Arbeidsinspectie en Koeliewerving in Nederlandsch-Indië' (Third Report of the Labour Inspectorate and the Agency for Coolie Recruitment in the Netherlands Indies), *Tijdschrift voor het Binnenlandsch Bestuur*, 46:455-9.

KOCH, D.M.G.
1960   *Batig slot; Figuren uit het oude Indië* (Net Profits; Figures from the Traditional Indies), Amsterdam.

KOHLBRUGGE, J.H.F.
1907   *Blikken in het zieleleven van den Javaan en zijner overheerschers* (Insight into the psyche of the Javanese and of its Rulers), Leiden.

KOL, H. Van
1901   'Ontwerp-program voor de Nederlandsche koloniale politiek, te behandelen op het congres der Sociaal-demokratische Arbeiderspartij te Utrecht 1901' (A Draft Programme for Dutch Colonial Policy, to be Discussed at the Congress of the Social-Democratic Labour Party at Utrecht 1901), *De Nieuwe Tijd*, 6:197-220.
1903   *Uit onze koloniën; Uitvoerig reisverhaal* (From our Colonies; An Extensive Travel Account), Leiden.
1911   Nederlandsch-Indiïn de Staten-Generaal van 1897 tot 1909; Een bijdrage tot de geschiedenis der koloniale politiek in Nederland (The Netherlands Indies as Discussed in the General Assembly Between 1897 and

1909; A Contribution to the History of Dutch Colonial
Policy), The Hague.

KOOREMAN, P.J.

1903a   *De koelie-ordonnantie tot regeling van de rechtsverhouding
tusschen werkgevers en werklieden in the residentie
Oostkust van Sumatra toegelicht* (An Explanation of the
Coolie Ordinance that Regulates the Legal
Relationship Between Employers and Workers in the
East Coast of Sumatra Residency), A lecture given in
Amsterdam.

1903b   *Nog eens: de koelie-ordonnantie tot regeling van de
rechtsverhouding tusschen werkgevers en werklieden in de
residentie Oostkust van Sumatra* (Once Again: The
Coolie Ordinance that Regulates the Legal
Relationship Between Employers and Workers in the
East Coast of Sumatra Residency), Amsterdam.

1904-5   'Het debat in de Tweede Kamer der Staten-Generaal
over het rapport-Rhemrev' (The Debate in the Lower
House of the General Assembly on the Rhemrev
Report), *Orgaan der Vereeniging 'Moederland en
Koloniën'*, 5-2:1-86.

KRAAIJ, C.

1901   'Koelie-emigratie uit Zuid-China' (Coolie Emigration
from South China), *De Indische Mercuur*, 24:309-10.

LANGENBERG, M. van

1977   'North Sumatra under Dutch Colonial Rule; Aspects
of Structural Change', *Review of Indonesian and Malayan
Affairs*, 11-I:74-110; 11-II:45-86.

LANGEVELD, H.J.

1978   'Arbeidstoestanden op de ondernemingen ter
Oostkust van Sumatra tussen 1920 en 1940 in het licht
van het verdwijnen van de poenale sanctie op de
arbeidscontracten' (Labour Conditions on the
Plantations on the East Coast of Sumatra Between
1920 and 1940 after removing the Penal Sanction from
the Labour Contract), *Economisch- en Sociaal-Historisch
Jaarboek*, 41:294-368.

LASKER, B.

1950   *Human Bondage in Southeast Asia*, Chapel Hill.

LEFEBRE, L.J.
1903   'Causerie over het leven en de tabakscultuur in Deli'
          (Narrative of Life and Tobacco Growing in Deli), *Het
          Koloniaal Weekblad; Orgaan der Vereeniging Oost en West*,
          pp. 2-43.
LIM KIM LIAT
1962   'The Deli Tobacco Industry; Its History and Outlook',
          in: D.S. PAAUW (ed.), pp. 1-19.
MARINUS, J.H. & J.J. van der LAAN
1929   *Veertig jaren ervaring in de Deli-Cultures* (Forty Years'
          Experience on the Deli Estates), Amsterdam.
MARSDEN, W.J.
1811   *The History of Sumatra, Containing an Account of the
          Government, Laws, Customs, and Manners of the Native
          Inhabitants, with a Description of the Natural Production
          and the Relation of the Ancient Political State of that
          Island.* London (3rd. ed.), OUP, Kulala Lumpur 1975.
METAL INDUSTRY REPORT
1926   *Rapport van het hoofd van het Kantoor van arbeid over de
          arbeidstoestanden in de metaalindustrie te Soerabaja*
          (Report by the Head of the Labour Office on Labour
          Conditions in the Metal Industry of Surabaya),
          Publications of the Labour Office No. 1, Weltevreden.
MEYIER, J.E. de
1912   'Het eerste verslag van den Dienst der
          Arbeids-Inspectie en Koeliewerving in
          Nederlandsch-Indië' (The First Report of the Labour
          Inspectorate and the Agency for Coolie Recruitment in
          the Netherlands Indies), *De Indische Gids*, 34:1326-42.
MIDDELBERG-IDENBURG, C.J.
1935   *A.W.F. Idenburg*, The Hague.
MODDERMAN, P.W. (ed.)
1929   *Gedenkboek uitgegeven ter gelegenheid van het vijftigjarig
          bestaan van de Deli Planters Vereeniging*
          (Commemorative Volume Published on the Occasion
          of the 50th. Anniversary of the Deli Planters'
          Association), Weltevreden/Batavia.
MOLHUYSEN, P.C. & P.J. BLOK (eds.)
1911   *Nieuw-Nederlandsch Biografisch Woordenboek* (New
          Netherlands Biographical Dictionary), Vol. I, Leiden.

MORESCO, M. (ed.)

1925   *Deli-Batavia Maatschappij 1875-1925* (The Deli-Batavia Company 1875-1925), Amsterdam.

MULIER, W.J.H.

1903   *Arbeidstoestanden op de Oostkust van Sumatra* (Labour Conditions on the East Coast of Sumatra), Medan; reprinted from the *Deli Courant*.

MULLER, W.C.

1914   'Uit het leven der koelie's op ondernemingen in Deli'(From the Life of the Coolies on Estates in Deli), *Tijdschrift voor Economische Geographie*, 5:438-49.

NAUDIN ten CATE, A.W. (ed.)

1905   *Deli in woord en beeld* (Deli in Words and Pictures), Amsterdam.

NEUMANN, J.B.

1914   *Over en tusschen blank en bruin* (On and Between White and Brown), Amsterdam.

NIENHUYS, J.

1888   'De vestiging der tabakscultures op Deli' (The Establishment of the Tobacco Estates on Deli), *De Indische Mercuur*, 11:223-5.

ONG ENG DIE

1943   *Chineezen in Nederlandsch-Indië; Sociographie van een Indonesische bevolkingsgroep* (Chinese in the Netherlands Indies; The Sociography of an Indonesian Population Group), Assen.

OTTO, E.

1903   *Pflanzer- und Jägerleben auf Sumatra* (A Planter's and Hunter's life on Sumatra), Berlin.

PAAUW, D.S. (ed.)

1962   *Prospects for East Sumatran Plantation Industries; A Symposium*, Yale University, Southeast Asian Studies, Monograph Series No. 3.

PELZER, K.J.

1978   *Planter and Peasant; Colonial Policy and the Agrarian Struggle in East Sumatra, 1863-1947*, Royal Institute of Linguistics and Anthropology, No. 84, Leiden.

1982

Planters Against Peasants; The Agrarian Struggle in East Sumatra 1947-1958, Royal Institute of Linguistics and Anthropology, No. 97, Leiden.

PITHENOS

1889   'Bijdrage tot de geschiedenis der Sumatra-Tabak gedurende het tijdvak 1883-1889' (Contribution to the History of Sumatran Tobacco during the Period 1883-1889), *De Indische Mercuur,* 12:289- 90, 313.

POEZE, H.A.

1976   *Tan Malaka, strijder voor Indonesië's vrijheid; Levensloop van 1897 tot 1945* (Tan Malaka, Fighter for Indonesia's Freedom; His Life from 1897 until 1945), Royal Institute of Linguistics and Anthropology, No. 78, Leiden.

RAFFLES, T.S.

1814   *Substance of a Minute recorded by the Honourable Thomas Stamford Raffles, Lieutenant-Governor of Java and its Dependencies, on 11 February 1814; on the introduction of an improved system of internal management and the establishment of a land rental on the island of Java; to which are added several of the most interesting documents therein referred to,* London.

REDJANG-LEBONG

1901   *Verslag van de directie der mijnbouw-maatschappij Redjang-Lebong over het vierde boekjaar (1900)* (Report of the Directors of the Mining Company Redjang-Lebong on the Fourth Accounting Year [1900]), Batavia.

REID, A.J.

1969   *The Contest for North Sumatra; Atjeh, The Netherlands and Britain 1858-1898,* London.

1970   'Early Chinese Migration into North Sumatra', in: Ch'en and Tarling (eds.), pp. 289-320, Cambridge.

RIDDER, J. de

1935   *De invloed van de westersche cultures op de autochtone bevolking ter Oostkust van Sumatra* (The Influence of Western Estates on the Native Population at the East Coast of Sumatra), Wageningen.

RÖMER, J.

1885   'Tabakskultur und Kulis auf Sumatra' (Tobacco

Cultivation and Coolies on Sumatra), *Deutsche Kolonialzeitung*, 2:417-23.

ROO de la FAILLE, W.de
1905   'Bespreking van "Nog eens: de koelie-ordonnantie tot regeling van de rechtsverhouding tusschen werkgevers en werklieden in de residentie Oostkust van Sumatra"' (Review of 'Once Again: The Coolie Ordinance to Regulate the Legal Relationship between Employers and Workers in the East Coast of Sumatra Residency'), *Themis*, 66:295-302.

ROOKMAKER, H.R.
1903   'Moderne slavernij' (Modern Slavery), *De Nieuwe Tijd*, 8:14-22, 85-93.
1904   'Voordracht gehouden op 18 november voor de Nederlandsche afdeeling van de Nederlandsch-Indische Maatschappij van Nijverheid en Landbouw' (Lecture given on 18 November to the Dutch Branch of the Netherlands Indies Society for Industry and Agriculture), *De Indische Mercuur*, 27:808-16.

ROTHE, C.
1946   'De arbeid in den landbouw' (Labour in Agriculture), Van Hall & Van den Koppel (eds.), Vol. I, pp. 310-47, The Hague.

SAID, M.
1977   *Koeli kontrak tempo doeloe* (Contract Labour in the Past), Medan.

SANDICK, L.H.W. van
1909   *Chineezen buiten China; Hunne beteekenis voor de ontwikkeling van Zuid-Oost-Azië, speciaal van Nederlandsch-Indië* (Chinese outside China; Their Significance for the Development of Southeast Asia, especially the Netherlands Indies), The Hague.

SANDICK, R.A. van
1892   'De crisis der tabaksondernemingen in Deli' (The Crisis of the Tobacco Estates in Deli). *Vragen van den Dag*, 7:81-94.

SAVORNIN LOHMAN, W.M. de
1911   'Keuchenius', in: Molhuyzen & Blok (eds.), *Nieuw-Nederlands biografisch woordenboek* (New

Netherlands Biographical Dictionary), Vol. I, pp.
1246-50, Leiden.

SCHADEE, W.H.M.
1918-19   *Geschiedenis van Sumatra's Oostkust* (The History of
          Sumatra's East Coast), 2 Vols. East Coast of Sumatra
          Institute, Communication No. 2, Amsterdam.

SCHUFFNER, W. & W.A. KUENEN
1910   'De gezondheidstoestand van de arbeiders verbonden
          aan de Senembah-Maatschappij op Sumatra,
          gedurende de jaren 1897 tot 1907. Een bijdrage ter
          oplossing van het vraagstuk, hoe een gunstige
          gezondheidstoestand bereikt kan worden in groote
          cultuurondernemingen gevestigd in tropische
          gewesten'(The Health of Workers Employed by the
          Senembah Company on Sumatra during the years
          1897 to 1907. A Contribution to Solving the Problem
          of how a Favourable State of Health can be Attained
          ·on Large-scale Agricultural Enterprises in the Tropical
          Regions), translated from the *Zeitschrift für Hygiene
          und Infektions Krankheiten*, Amsterdam.

SCHUURMAN, J.A.
1922   'Historische schets van de tinwinning op Banka,
          1816-1900' (Historical Survey of Tin Mining on Banka,
          1816-1900), *Jaarboek van het Mijnwezen in Nederlandsch
          Oost-Indië*, 48 (1919), I-XXIII: 1-388.

SINAR, H. TENGKU LUCKMAN
1978   'The Impact of Dutch Colonialism on the Malay
          Coastal States on the East Coast of Sumatra During
          the Nineteenth Century', *Papers of the Dutch-Indonesian
          Conference Noordwijkerhout 19-22 May 1976*, pp. 178-89.
          Leiden, Jakarta.

STIBBE, D.G.
1913   'Eerste verslag van den Dienst der Arbeidsinspectie en
          Koeliewerving' (First Report of the Labour
          Inspectorate and the Agency for Coolie Recruitment),
          De Indische Gids, 35:8-25.

STOLER, A.L.
1985   *Capitalism and Confrontation in Sumatra's Plantation Belt
          1870- 1979*, New Haven, London

TAUSSIG, M.
1987   *Shamanism, Colonialism and the Wild Man; A Study in Terra and Healing*, Chicago, London.

TAUKEH
1906   'Eenige jaren bij de tabak in Deli' (Some Years in Tobacco in Deli), *De Levende Natuur*, 2:35-7, 56-7, 96-7, 118-19, 125-7.

THEE KIAN-WIE
1977   *Plantation Agriculture and Export Growth: An Economic History of East Sumatra, 1863-1942*, Jakarta.

TICHELMAN, F.
1967   'De S.D.A.P. en Indonesië 1897-1907; Enkele gegevens en problemen' (The SDAP and Indonesia 1897-1907: Some Data and Problems), *De Nieuwe Stem*, 22:683-729.

TIDEMAN, J.
1917-18   'De koelie-ordonnantie en hare toepassing' (The Coolie Ordinance and its Application), *Koloniale Studiën*, 2:31-74.

TRAN TU BINH
1985   The Red Earth; A Vietnamese Memoir of life on a Colonial Rubber Plantation, as told to Ha An. Translated by John Spragens Jr., Center for Southeast Asian Studies. Ohio University Center for International Studies.

TSCHUDNOWSKY, J.A.I.
1899   *Contributions à la géographie médicale de l' archipel malais* (Contributions to the Medical Geography of the Malayan Archipelago), Paris.

VERSLUYS, J.D.N.
1938   *Vormen en soorten van loon in den Indischen landbouw* (Types and Modalities of Wages in Indonesian Agriculture), Leiden.

VETH, P.J.
1877a   Voordracht over Deli en de Deli-Maatschappij opgenomen in het verslag der dertiende algemeene vergadering van het Aardrijkskundig Genootschap' (A lecture on Deli and the Deli Company, included in the Report of the 13th. General Meeting of the Geographical Association), *Tijdschrift van het Aardrijkskundig Genootschap*, 2:146-7.

1877b   'Het landschap Deli op Sumatra' (The Region of Deli
         on Sumatra), *Tijdschrift van het Aardrijkskundig
         Genootschap*, 2:152-70.

VOLKER, T.

1928   *Van oerbosch tot cultuurgebied; Een schets van de
         beteekenis van de tabak, de andere cultures en de industrie
         ter Oostkust van Sumatra* (From Jungle to Cultivated
         Land; A Sketch of the Significance of Tobacco, Other
         Crops and Industry on the East Coast of Sumatra),
         Medan.

WAARD, J. de

1924   'De openlegging der Indische Buitengewesten' (The
         Opening-Up of the Outer Provinces of the
         Netherlands Indies), *De Socialistische Gids*, 9:1035-51.

1934   'De Oostkust van Sumatra' (The East Coast of
         Sumatra), *Tijdschrift voor Economische Géographie*,
         25:213-21, 255-76, 282-301.

WEIGAND, K.L.

1911   'Der Tabakbau in Niederländisch-Indien; seine
         ökonomische und kommerzielle Bedeutung mit
         besonderer Bercksichtigung von Deli-Sumatra'
         (Tobacco-Growing in the Netherlands Indies; Its
         Economic and Commercial Significance with Special
         Reference to Deli-Sumatra), *Probleme der Weltwirtschaft,
         Schriften des Instituts für Seeverkehr und Weltwirtschaft
         an der Universitt Kiel*, No. 4, Jena.

WEISFELT, J.

1972   *De Deli Spoorweg Maatschappij als factor in de
         economische ontwikkeling van de Oostkust van Sumatra*
         (The Deli Railway Company as a Factor in the
         Economic Development of the East Coast of Sumatra),
         Doctoral Thesis at the Netherlands Economic School,
         Rotterdam.

WERTHEIM, W.F.

1956   *Indonesian Society in Transition: A Study of Social
         Change*, The Hague, Bandung.

WESTERMAN, W.

1901   *De tabakscultuur op Sumatra's Oostkust* (Tobacco
         Growing on Sumatra's East Coast), Amsterdam.

WINTER (pseudonym of H.R. ROOKMAKER)

1900 'Naar Eldorado; Een bezoek aan de goudmijnen' (To Eldorado; A Visit to the Goldmines), *De Indische Gids,* 22:1298-1320.

WISELIUS, J.A.B.

1884 'De emigratie van Britsch-Indische koeli's naar Overzeesche gewesten, in verband met eene eventueele emigratie van Hindu's naar Oost-Sumatra' (The Emigration of British-Indian Coolies to Overseas Regions, in Connection with a Possible Emigration of Hindus to East Sumatra), *Tijdschrift voor Nederlandsch-Indië,* 13- II:321-70.

II PUBLISHED SOURCES: PARLIAMENTARY PAPERS (In Dutch)

Colonial Report: Annex to the Report of the Proceedings of the Lower House of the General Assembly: 1874-1905, The Hague.

Report of the Proceedings of the Upper House of the General Assembly, 1904-1905, The Hague.

Report of the Proceedings of the Lower House of the General Assembly 1889-1890, 1898-99, 1899-1900, 1900-1901, 1901-1902, 1902-1903, 1903-1904, 1904-1905, 1905-1906, 1918-1919, The Hague.

Report of the Proceedings of the Volksraad (Popular Council), 1st Ordinary Session 1921, 2nd Ordinary Session 1921.

Review of Reports and Recommendations submitted in the Netherlands Indies with regard to Art. 2, No. 27 of the Police Regulations for Natives (Indisch Staatsblad 1872, No. 111), Annexe (B4.47) to the Report of Proceedings of the Lower House of the General Assembly 1876-7.

III UNPUBLISHED SOURCES (In Dutch)

A. *ALGEMEEN RIJKSARCHIEF* (GENERAL STATE ARCHIVE), THE HAGUE.

Bio-data of civil servants in the Netherlands Indies (2nd. Division, after 1836) - B. Hoetink-W 112; J.C.T. Rhemrev-X 231, 573.

Mail Report No. 546, 1902
A statement of leased taxes in 1901 and 1902, specified according
to Residency.
Vb.14-2-1902, No. 25
Results of the inspection tour by Dr A.G. Vorderman and Mr B.
Hoetink of the mining enterprise Redjang-Lebong. Hoetink also
reported on his second visit to the same mine, 26 August 1901.
Another report, submitted on 23 August 1901, deals with his
visit to the Lebong Soelit mine exploited by the same company
(Erdmann & Sielcken).
Vb.9-12-1902, No. 49
Request made by the Minister for Colonies to the Governor-
General that he should start investigating the accusations made
by Van den Brand in his booklet and also make suggestions as to
how this issue should be handled.
Vb.3-3-1903, No. 7
On the inclusion of a clause in the Coolie Ordinance compelling
labourers to extend their service in the case of inadequate work
performance.
Vb.27-3-1903, No. 13
Vorderman Report on medical inspection of the coalmines of
Sawah Loento on 28, 29 and 30 April 1901; Hoetink Report of a
visit to the Ombilin mines on 4 September 1901. Also various
other reports, including subsequent comments by departmental
heads.
Vb.31-3-1903, No. 34
Report by Hoetink on his visit to the Singkep Tin Company on
24 June 1902.
Vb.31-3-1903, No. 40
Report by Hoetink on his inspection tour of the mining
enterprises Soemalata (3 February 1902) and Kota Boenan (7
February 1902).
Vb.1-4-1903, No. 48
Correspondence over Hoetink's reports on his visits to the mining company Redjang-Lebong, including a reply from that
company's Board of Directors (15 February 1902) and a letter
from the Director of Justice to the Governor-General on the
progress made by Hoetink (2 June 1902, No. 4853).
Vb.29-4-1903, No. 39

Report by Hoetink on his visits to the plantations on the East
Coast of Sumatra on 19 July 1902, pp. 78.
Vb.12-10-1903, No. 26
A file of 'slanderous articles on the Dutch East Indies', published
in the foreign press.
Vb.3-12-1903, No. 15/3353
A letter from the Minister of Colonies to the Governor-General
in which, on the basis of questions raised in the Parliament, the
Minister enquires about the progress made by Rhemrev in his in-
vestigations.
Vb.14-3-1904, No. 8/766
A letter from the Governor-General to the Minister of Colonies
on the new draft of a Coolie Ordinance to be made by Hoetink
(No. 2699/4, 26 December 1903). Departmental memorandum
on the subject.
Vb.26-10-1904, No. 55
On the expansion of the police force on Sumatra's East Coast.
Memoranda submitted by the Resident of the region (20 August
1903, No. 3378/4 with two appendices, and 29 June 1904, No.
2924/1 with one appendix). Comments by the Director of the
Civil Service (20 April 1904, No. 13 with one appendix, and 28
July 1904, No. 1). Recommendations made by the Council of the
Netherlands Indies (13 May 1904, No. XXI and 12 August 1904,
No. XIII). Letter from the Governor-General to the Minister of
Colonies 3 September 1904, No. 1994/38.
Vb.21-11-1904, No. 28
Departmental memoranda in response to a request by a Par-
liamentary Committee that it should be given access to the
Rhemrev Report, including a departmental draft of the reply to
be made by Minister Idenburg (20 & 21 November 1904).
Vb.28-1-1905, No. 6
(a) A letter written by the Governor-General to the Minister for
     Colonies, including correspondence on the establishment of
     a Labour Inspectorate
Rhemrev Report (pp. 183) together with various memoranda
written by departmental heads and the General-Secretary to the
Netherlands Indies Government.
(b) A letter written by the Governor-General to the Minister for
     Colonies (24 July 1904, No. 1664/3), including
     correspondence on the proposal to appoint Hoetink as Head

of the Labour Inspectorate. Hoetink's reaction to this proposal.
(c) Various memoranda and letters written or received by departmental officials, including letters addressed to Minister Idenburg by Van den Brand, Cremer and former Resident Van der Steenstraten.
(d) A letter written by the Minister for Colonies to the Governor-General giving a summary of the parliamentary debate on the Rhemrev Report, and asking the Governor-General to consider whether the penal sanction in the Coolie Ordinance ought to be retained (24 January 1905, No. 6/322);

Departmental memoranda and comments on the Coolie Ordinance (24 & 30 January 1905);

Minister Idenburg's reaction to these documents suggesting a further analysis on how to deal with 'the coolie question'.

Vb.30-5-1905, No. 33

The Minister for Colonies returns to the Governor-General the Historical Review of the Legal Regulations of the Work Contract in the Netherlands Indies, most probably written in 1897 by Ballot, who was then Director of Justice.

Vb.19-9-1905, No. 32

Memoranda on the recruitment of Chinese coolies for the Banka tin-mines, written by J. van der Stadt, an official in charge of Chinese Affairs, and sent to South China on a mission.

Vb.19-9-1905, No. 34

Instruction by Governor-General Van Heutsz to H. Colijn, the later Prime Minister of the Netherlands but at that time Captain of the Military Police, to investigate the urgent need to expand the police force on the East Coast of Sumatra.

Vb.19-10-1905, No. 75

A letter written by the Governor-General to the Minister for Colonies, including the report submitted by Captain Colijn.

Copy of the Circular (8 September 1903, No. 3891/2) which Resident Schaap had published, after consultation with Rhemrev, and which enabled planters to detain until the next morning any coolie whom they accused of having committed a crime or offence.

Vb.27-12-1905, No. 65/3737

Recommendations made by high-ranking colonial officials in the Netherlands Indies (including Governor-General Van Heutsz

and Hoetink in his capacity as Head of the Labour Inspectorate)
not to do away with the penal sanction in the Coolie Ordinance.
Reaction by Minister for Colonies Fock. Report submitted by
Van Blommestein (24 October 1905) and a comparative study by
Bool (Secretary of the Deli Planters Association) of coolie labour
on the plantations of Sumatra's East Coast and in the tin-mines
on Banka. Reactions by Van Blommestein and departmental officials.

Vb.14-2-1906, No. 23
A letter written by the Minister for Colonies to the Governor-
General recommending that a Court of Justice be established in
Medan.

Vb.24-11-1906, No. 62
A secret instruction dated 21 August 1906 at the instruction of
the Office of the General Prosecutor of colonial headquarters in
Batavia to investigate accusations made by Van den Brand about
malicious acts committed against him by officials on Sumatra's
East Coast.

Vb.10-12-1906, No. 57
An official denial of accusations made by Dijkstra, a planter,
about misdemeanour and fraudulent practices by colonial officials in the Lampung District of South Sumatra.

Vb.6-2-1907, No. 56
A letter written by Van den Brand's brother to the Minister for
Colonies (1 February 1904). File on the outcome of the proposal
made earlier to establish a Court of Justice in Medan.

Vb.26-8-1907, No. 6
Report submitted by General Prosecutor Van der Zwaan (6 April
1907) regarding complaints made by Van den Brand against officials on Sumatra's East Coast.

Vb.19-10-1907, No. 19
The decision reached by colonial authorities not to prosecute
magistrates on Sumatra's East Coast whom Rhemrev had found
guilty of malpractices; a letter written by the Resident of the
region to the Director of the Civil Service (25 May 1904, No. 35,
secret); a memorandum submitted by the Director of the Civil
Service to the Governor-General (27 January 1905, 18/A, secret);
and a letter from the Secretary of the Colonial Government to
the Director of the Civil Service (23 February 1905, No. 109,
secret).

B.   *KONINKLIJK INSTITUUT VOOR DE TROPEN* (ROYAL TROPICAL INSTITUTE)

ANONYMOUS

(a)   *Catalogued*

Comments (on articles written by Van Kol), *Soerabaiasch Handelsblad 1902*. [The anonymous author, writing on paper with the letterhead of the Senembah Company, makes detailed reference to the Coolie Ordinance as applicable to the Straits Settlements, Contract into which Chinese coolies in Singapore must enter for employment on the estates of L. Michaelski on Sumatra's East Coast in the 1870s;
Draft of Coolie Ordinance for Sumatra's East Coast; explanation for members of the Deli Planters' Committee on the draft designed by Hoetink on 8 July 1904;
Revised draft of an Ordinance regulating the rights and duties of employers and workmen of Native and other Oriental origin on Sumatra's East Coast, Batavia, 1906.]

Heinoldt, C.
1897   *The Emigration of Chinese to Banka*, 24 September.
Hoetink, B.
1898   *Mission to China in Connection with Emigration to Deli.*
Kuenen, W.A.
            The Examination, Accommodation and Transport of 1906. Migrants (from Java) to Medan, September.
Stecher, J.
1905   *Javanese Emigration to Deli*, Medan, 25 October.
1905   *Report on Recruitment and Labour Conditions of Chinese.* Coolies in Billiton, Singapore, 21 April.
1905   *Chinese Recruitment for Banka.* Various reports addressed to the Management of the Deli Company in Medan.
Sternberg, H.
1929   *Work Organisation on Plantations under European Management on Sumatra's East Coast, with particular reference to industrial relations* (in German), Langensalza.

(b) *Non-Catalogued*

Various files No. 14
Circulars despatched by the Regional Head of the Civil Service
of Sumatra's East Coast.
Coolie Ordinances 1885-1915.
Inspection reports by the Medical Service at Bindjei, Tebing
Tinggi, Petoembukan and Upper Langkat, submitted by the
Labour Inspector on Sumatra's East Coast 1901-1906.
Letter written by J.F. Cremer to C.W. Janssen, The Hague, 17
December 1904.
Medical reports on the inspection of hospitals by F. Maier,
Regional Health Officer, 10 October and 24 November 1901.
Memorandum on the agreement drawn up between members of
the Planters' Association, designed by H.J. Bool, around 1905-
1906.
Memorandum by the Board of the Deli Planters' Association in
Medan concerning the competence of estate managers to deal
with coolies who were caught in the act of a criminal offence or
misdemeanour.
Memorandum by the Planters' Committee to the Governor-
General concerning the conclusions of the Rhemrev Report,
which were made public in the Dutch Parliament, Medan, 27
January 1905.
Minutes of meeting held by officials of the Regional Civil Ser-
vice, 15 April 1902.
Newspaper clippings concerning *The Millions of Deli* by J. Van
den Brand (including letter written by J. Deen to C.W. Janssen,
Director of Senembah Company, 24 April 1904).
Rejection of this Memorandum by the Governor-General, Buiten-
zorg, 23 May 1905
Report of the debate on proposed amendments to the Coolie Ordinances after 1902. Manuscript by anonymous author, around
1916.
Various files, No. 84
Containing reports and correspondence written by, or addressed
to, officials of the Labour Inspectorate on Sumatra's East Coast,
1902-7.

INDEX

1. The first generation of planters of Sumatra's East Coast. Standing second to left is Cremer, who made the Deli Company into the biggest colonial enterprise.

2. A *tandil* and his gang. Women workers were still absent.

I the undersigned (   ) Chinese Coolie acknowledge to have received from Mr. L. MICHAELSKI of Deli, Sumatra, the undermentioned advances in Cash in presence of the undersigned two witnesses, before starting for Deli, and in consideration thereof I hereby agree to work as labourer on the Tobacco, Cocoanut, Coffee, Nutmeg and other Estates and Properties belonging to Mr. L. MICHAELSKI at the monthly salary of dollars six per month for a period of not less than one year and until full acquittal of the advances received before starting or afterwards.

The said Mr. L. MICHAELSKI agreeing in return.

1.—To supply house and medical treatment free of Charges and in case of death to have my body decently and properly buried according to Chinese customs and observances.

2.—To provide food at market prices.

3.—To make the necessary advances for my comfort and well being while in his service.

4.—To keep correct accounts between party and party.

5.—To allow a holiday on the first and fifteenth of every Chinese Moon.

Singapore,_____187 .

3. Work contract made up in Singapore in the early seventies. Note the generosity shown to the coolie after his death.

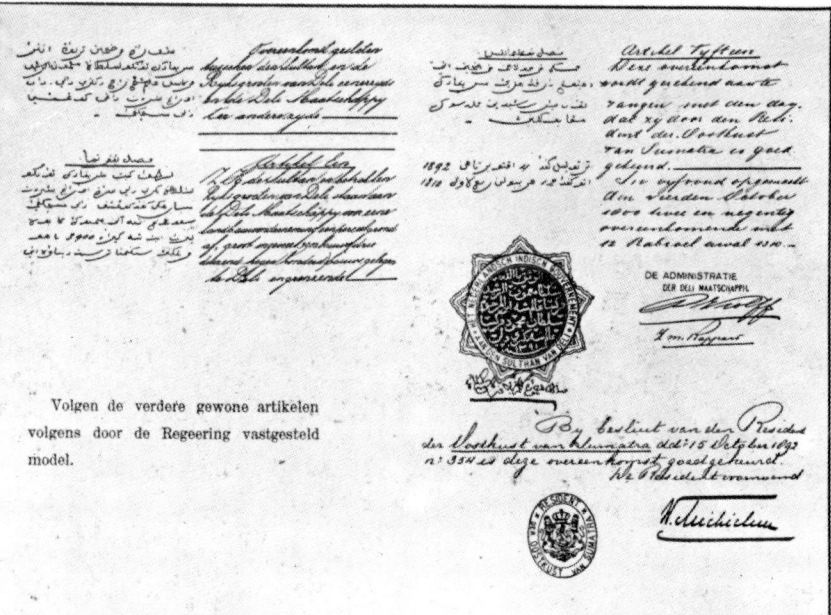

4. Land contract legalized by the signature of the Sultan of Deli. It frequently happened that he gave away rights over land, which did not belong to him.

5. Jungle clearance was highly labour-intensive.

6. Fencing the plantations against attacks by Bataks who did not surrender their land willingly.

7. The building of roads and drainage canals caused injuries and diseases invalidating a high proportion of the workforce.

8. Ethnic diversification reinforced racial stereotypes which in turn were used to control labour.

9. Armed guards, many of them Indian, escorted the transport of coins with which coolies were paid. Raids by gangs of run-away coolies who roamed the region made this protection necessary. The primitive mode of transport was characteristic of the conditions on the East Coast during the first few decades.

10. Installation ceremony of the Sultan of Langkat in 1894 in the presence of the Resident and other civil servants, military officers, Chinese headmen and prominent planters. The dominant position of the European VIPs, occupying the centre of the stage as it were, reduced native rulers to the position of persons in an entourage, very much in the background.

11. The fields were constantly patrolled in order to facilitate the supervision of the work of the coolies.

12. Women at work in the drying shed; they were made to sit in rows in order to allow better control of their work performance and to create a feeling of competition among them.

13. Transport of the tobacco leaves. In the foreground the field bungalow of an assistant; behind it, a drying shed.

14. Coolies in the fermenting shed sorting out tobacco leaves. Note the maintenance of strict discipline in the workplace. The industrial nature of the production process was an outstanding feature of the plantation economy.

15. Work supervision. Note the intimidating posture of the white supervisor.

16. The head-manager's bungalow was in the centre of the estate but no coolie dared to go near. Hierarchy and segregation went together.

17. Living close to the coolie quarters. The young planters complained in their letters home, about the loneliness on the plantations, sometimes not seeing another 'human being' for days on end.

18. The planters sought each other's company at the end of the working day, playing cards and drinking beer.

19. Field barracks of Chinese coolies.

23. 'The Wild East' in the early 1870s. The town became the heart of the plantation business when the Deli Company decided to establish its headquarters there.

24. The same street in Medan after thirty years.

25. The Sultan of Deli who lived in a rather modest wooden house in a *kampong* along the coast, when the first planter arrived, was handsomely paid for his services, as is evident from his palace.

26. The first colonial civil servant who appeared on the East Coast set up house and office in the bungalow of the pioneer-planter.

27. Not to be outdone by the native rulers in their show of splendour, the Dutch Resident thirty years later also opted for a more opulent life-style.

28. The European planters in front of one of their still primitive bungalows in the 1870s. They are surrounded by their *tandils*.

29. At the beginning of the twentieth century, life had become more comfortable. The number of white ladies and children increased while Asian intermediaries receded into the background. Behind the new facade of civilization however, cruelties against the coolies went on as before.

34. The Chinese coolies received their contract on the plantation. This ceremony brought home to them the fact that they had indeed lost their free will. They were measured for length, which together with other marks of identification helped to track them down if they ran away.

35. The irony, of the situation. European employers were dominant but had the strength of numbers!

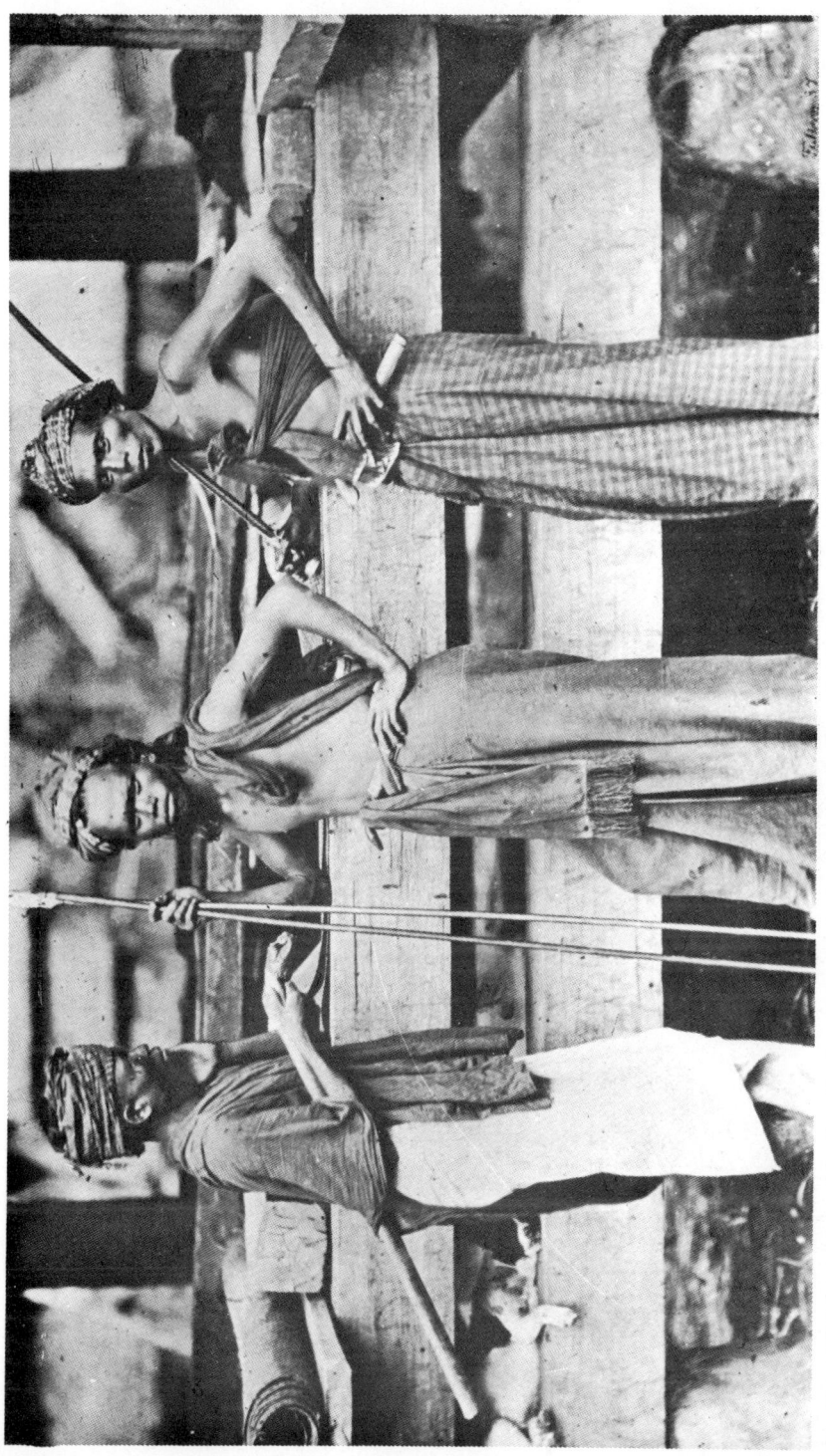

36. Young Bataks were used for 'hunting' coolies, who had escaped to the hinterland. They carried their catch back to the plantation exactly as they carried a hunted pig—tied to a pole.

37. Prison in Medan where many coolies were detained for a breach of contract.

38. Flogging of coolies who did not 'behave'. This form of punishment took place on state-owned plantations as well, where it was even legalized! On privately-owned plantations— terror reigned supreme.

39. The police force was kept ready in order to deal with the constant threat of coolie riots.

40. The leaders of a revolt which broke out among the Chinese workforce in the tin mines of Banka, an island off the East Coast of Sumatra, in 1899. This picture is remarkably representative of the situation on the plantations as well.

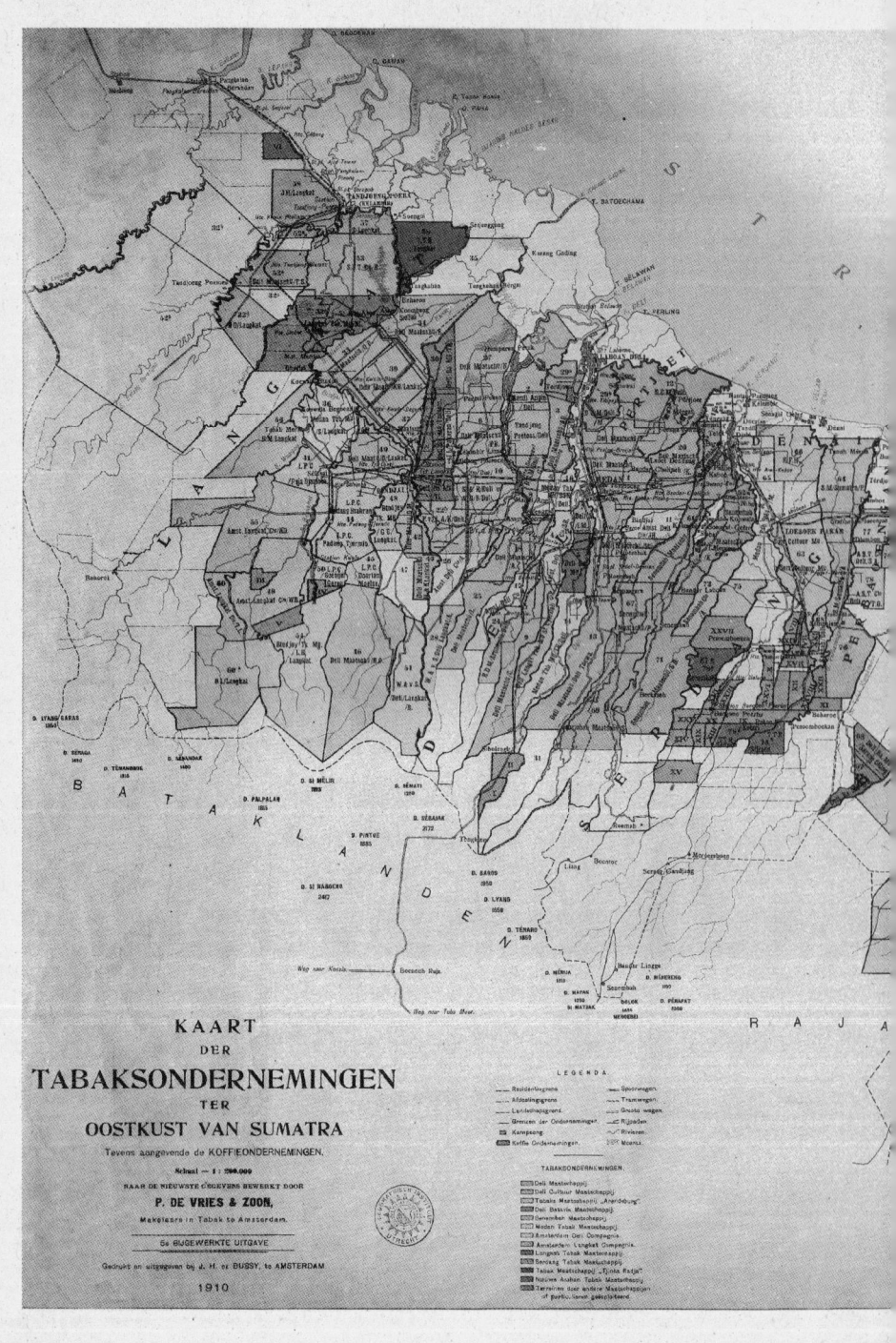

KAART
DER
TABAKSONDERNEMINGEN
TER
OOSTKUST VAN SUMATRA

Tevens aangevende de KOFFIEONDERNEMINGEN.

Schaal — 1 : 750.000

NAAR DE NIEUWSTE GEGEVENS BEWERKT DOOR

P. DE VRIES & ZOON,

Makelaars in Tabak te Amsterdam.

5e BIJGEWERKTE UITGAVE

Gedrukt en uitgegeven bij J. H. DE BUSSY, te AMSTERDAM

1910

LEGENDA.

- Residentiegrens.   — Spoorwegen.
- Afdeelingsgrens.   — Tramwegen.
- Landschapsgrens.   — Groote wegen.
- Grenzen der Ondernemingen. — Rijpaden.
- Kampong.   — Rivieren.
- Koffie-Ondernemingen.   — Moeras.

TABAKSONDERNEMINGEN

- Deli Maatschappij.
- Deli Cultuur Maatschappij.
- Tabaks Maatschappij "Arendsburg".
- Deli Batavia Maatschappij.
- Senembah Maatschappij.
- Medan Tabak Maatschappij.
- Amsterdam Deli Compagnie.
- Amsterdam Langkat Compagnie.
- Langkat Tabak Maatschappij.
- Serdang Tabak Maatschappij.
- Tabak Maatschappij "Tjinta Radja".
- Nieuwe Asahan Tabak Maatschappij.
- Terreinen door andere Maatschappijen of particulieren geëxploiteerd.